Tribal Pastoralists in Transition

The location of Luristan in western Iran, showing the Zagros Mountains and principal cities.

Anthropological Papers
Museum of Anthropology, University of Michigan
Number 100

Tribal Pastoralists in Transition

The Baharvand of Luristan, Iran

by

Frank Hole
and
Sekandar Amanolahi-Baharvand

Ann Arbor, Michigan
2021

Printed in the United States of America
ISBNs: 978-0-915703-99-9 (print), 978-1-951538-74-3 (ebook)

The Museum currently publishes two monograph series: Anthropological Papers and Memoirs. Contact the Museum by email at umma-pubs@umich.edu; by phone at 734-764-0485; or through our website at www.lsa.umich.edu/ummaa/publications.

Library of Congress Cataloging-in-Publication Data

Names: Hole, Frank, author. | Amanolahi-Baharvand, Sekandar, author.
Title: Tribal pastoralists in transition : the Baharvand of Luristan, Iran / by Frank Hole, and Sekandar Amanolahi-Baharvand.
Other titles: Baharvand of Luristan, Iran
Description: Ann Arbor, Michigan : University of Michigan Museum of Anthropology, 2021. | Series: Anthropological papers ; No. 100 | Includes bibliographical references.
Identifiers: LCCN 2021001820 (print) | LCCN 2021001821 (ebook) | ISBN 9780915703999 (paperback) | ISBN 9781951538743 (ebook)
Subjects: LCSH: Bahārvand (Iranian people)--Social life and customs. | Nomads--Iran--Luristān. | Migration, Internal--Iran--Luristān. | Luristān (Iran)--Description and travel.
Classification: LCC DS269.B27 H65 2021 (print) | LCC DS269.B27 (ebook) | DDC 955/.62053--dc23
LC record available at https://lccn.loc.gov/2021001820
LC ebook record available at https://lccn.loc.gov/2021001821

Cover design by John Klausmeyer
All photographs by Frank Hole, except where noted.
Maps by Frank Hole and John Klausmeyer.

Supplementary material: View photographs and five documentary films about the migration at https://doi.org/10.3998/mpub.12031336.

The paper used in this publication meets the requirements of the ANSI Standard Z39.48-1984 (Permanence of Paper).

Dedication

We dedicate this book to the tribal peoples of Luristan, whose lives since 1973 have been transformed beyond all imagination. Their once insular world—of pastoral groups that moved their flocks with the changing seasons in endless rounds of migration—no longer exists. The ways of the older generations, born in tents, whose visions were limited to the ridges and valleys of their territories, are scarcely imaginable today. This book is for the young, who will never experience the limited opportunities and ceaseless apprehension of the weather and dangers from man and predators. It is also for the elders, who adapted to new ways—this book provides a chance to relive their pasts and to convey their essence to the young. This book and the five short supplementary films (available at https://doi.org/10.3998/mpub.12031336) attempt to document, for the young and old alike, some aspects of traditional life nearly 50 years ago.

Table of Contents

List of Illustrations

Five short documentary films by the authors—with scenes of the 1973 migration, agriculture, weaving, nomadic life, and the traditional markets of Luristan, Iran—are available on Fulcrum at https://doi.org/10.3998/mpub.12031336.

Preface

The villagers crowded around as we loaded up. A big strong mule was saddled for me, and I heaved myself onto his back. Suddenly the mule reared up, pawing the air, while I pulled back hard on the halter to control him. The harder I pulled, the higher the mule reared, and it started to bolt away. Only quick thinking by one of the villagers, who grabbed the mule's head, prevented him from throwing me. Laughing at my narrow escape, they told me that I should not pull so hard on the halter; it would make the mule rear up. Accordingly, I left the halter slack and the mule stood there calmly. Of course, this left me with no visible means of control, but I knew very little about mule psychology and was willing to follow advice.

When the mule and I had calmed down we set off. Sekandar led the way through the village on his mule, down a path that led to a small wooden bridge over a canal. Sekandar's mule turned smartly and trotted across the bridge. Mine did not. Instead it started to run along the bank of the canal. Following instructions to the letter, I continued to leave the halter slack, and the mule quickened its pace, much to the horror of all who were watching, and to my own. Suddenly the mule made an abrupt left turn down one of the narrow lanes, while I hung on desperately. Clearly the mule had its own ideas about where it was going, and I was only going to be a spectator—as long as I stayed on the animal. It ran down the lanes like a rat in a maze between the mud-brick walls that enclosed small courtyards and one-room, flat-roofed houses.

Suddenly, and without warning, a small boy stepped out of a doorway and the mule slid to a quivering stop inches from the lad. I held on, grabbing the mule's neck as I slid forward.

The boy sized up the situation immediately and seized the halter. Behind me I heard the shouts of a troop of people running toward us. Half the village, with Sekandar in their midst on his mule, were galloping up to see the carnage. When they saw that I was unharmed, smiles and laughter began to replace their distraught expressions. The whole thing became a huge joke.

Sekandar was visibly shaken by the experience and told me that when mules run away with their riders, they sometimes run through low gates to knock them off. He said some of the Lurs have been killed in this way, and I should count myself very lucky.

"Why didn't you pull up on the halter?" he asked.

"But," I protested, "you just told me not to."

"Oh," he replied, "that was different."

By the time we returned from this trip, my mulesmanship had improved considerably, but I still mistrust them.

This book tells the story of transition: first and most literally, the transition (or rather, migration) of a Lur family from their winter home in Chin-i Zal at the foot of the Zagros Mountains to their summer pastures in a high mountain valley. Their story takes place in the context of another transition: that of a tribal society from strength and prosperity to impotence and poverty under the inexorable political and economic changes of the modern world. Finally, the authors themselves undergo transition—not just as part of the migration that is the focus of the book, but in their personal lives: one of them, an outsider, comes to a deeper understanding of the nomadic culture; the other, raised in Luristan and connected by tribal affiliation, writes of his journey into the larger world and his life as a scholar in the United States, England, and back home in Iran.

The focus of the book is on the Baharvand, a Luri-speaking people who inhabit the mountains and valleys of central western Iran (see the frontispiece for a map showing Luristan). Until recently, the Baharvand lived year-round under the cover of black goat-hair tents. They migrated each spring and fall with their families and animals to freshly greened pastures within their remote tribal territory, following a way of life that had existed for as long as anyone in their tent camps could remember.

In the spring of 1973, we were allowed to travel with the Baharvand as they migrated from their winter home to their summer home. (See Chapter 1 for the story of how I came to be on the migration and Chapter 2 for the story of my co-author, Sekandar Amanolahi-Baharvand.)

On one of my first evenings in the region, before the migration had begun, I stood atop a steeply inclined sheet of deeply eroded limestone overlooking five black tents clustered on the vast Chin-i Zal plain. I felt as if I were standing on the edge of time (Figure 0.1). Below me, dots barely discernible as sheep and goats moved slowly in search of the few remaining morsels of sparse, browning forage. Raucous braying arose from the throat of a distant donkey, strangely muted and detached. Lazy plumes of dust devils mingled

Figure 0.1. Looking down over the Chin-i Zal Valley, with Morad Khan's five black tents in the foreground. The Zal River flows through the gorge in the mountain ridge.

with gray ribbons of smoke from tiny campfires and ascended into the hazy orange heavens. As the sun dipped beyond Mesopotamia to the west, the ridge beneath my feet cast its shadow longer on the plain, until one by one, the living things faded from view, leaving only sounds and flickering fires to remind me of their presence.

I sat quietly, enveloped by darkness, weakly illuminated by the moon and stars. Without daylight, time itself had retreated. The sounds from the valley might have come from around campfires lit 8000 years ago. I imagined myself peering into a prehistoric past, where families sitting on the earth around similar fires talked quietly as they shared a simple meal at day's end.

Even then there were hints that this way of life was facing unprecedented changes. I wondered whether this scene, which had been repeated day after day, season after season, for over untold generations, would continue far into the future. I wondered how long it would be before the daily campfires would finally be extinguished.

The book is dedicated to the cultural heritage of these tribal people. Because they lacked a written language, their history has been mainly written by outsiders, and it focuses on leaders rather than common people. In the narrative that follows, we focus instead on the lives of individuals and families. We see how pervasive and invasive development affects people and their futures. Without such a view, even a generation later, the rich heritage of life under tents could not be recreated and would inevitably fade from memory. We hope that this book will help succeeding generations remember the strength of their tribal heritage.

This is the story of a tribal people and how they live. It is also the story of an elder tribal leader whose failing fortunes mirror the careers of other tribal leaders, just as his tribe mirrors the fates of similar tribes. These are real people, and their story touches our emotions just as what happened to their way of life affects our minds. Indeed, in the episodes that follow, we can see humankind in a way that belies the relative insignificance of one small herding camp. It is a human story, and in that sense, it is a story about us.

Although the events we describe took place in one camp of Luri nomads, the general features of this life were the same for a million or more other tribal nomads in Iran, and indeed for the many millions more throughout Southwest Asia who migrated seasonally with their flocks. This was a way of life that was deeply steeped in tradition, forged out of millennia of experience—and under threat. The official policies of the Iranian government, beginning with the rise of Reza Shah in the 1920s, aimed to eliminate the nomadic way of life as unbefitting a modern civilization. Those efforts succeeded in many ways, and yet in 1973 the Lurs and other tribal people still retained some traditional migratory lifeways.

As co-authors, Sekandar and I are responsible for different parts of this book. I (Frank Hole) wrote the diary of the migration. Sekandar, who taught for 29 years at Shiraz University and has devoted his life to studies of the tribal people of western Iran, contributed his impressions of the migratory experience, but also—importantly for the heritage of the tribe—pieced together the last 150 years of Luristan history. In the years since the migration, Sekandar has continued to research the history of Iranian tribes through archives, extensive travel, and interviews with tribal elders.

As participant observers of one camp of tribal nomads during their annual migration, we describe their daily lives and their personal prospects. We see how change has decimated traditional ways. The photographs and five short films (available on Fulcrum at https://doi.org/10.3998/mpub.12031336) provide visual documentation that helps to capture what remained of their heritage. The essential narrative of this book was written in 1974; at that time, out of a total population of about 30 million in Iran, nearly 60% were "rural." In 2020, with a population of 84 million, 25% were "rural." Of these, Lurs comprise about 6%. In 1975, Iranian nomads and semi-nomads comprised fewer than 2 million (DaBell 2013; Jacqz 1976; www.macrotrends.net).

The narrative that follows is an attempt to convey something of the quality of nomadic life, as I was able to understand and appreciate it. I am, and will always remain, a foreigner to these people. My interpretations may sometimes miss the mark, although Sekandar's intimate knowledge of the people has helped me avoid most pitfalls. Inevitably, like all foreigners, I see Luri life through my own structure of thought, which has been developed through professional training in anthropology and archaeology. I see some things and not others. What I think is important was not always appreciated as such by the nomads. Some of what they think is important, I have probably missed.

In the beginning my concern was to obtain details on domestic life that I could use for archaeological interpretation. After recording features of the environment, herding, the nature of campsites, routes of travel, and so on, I became more aware of social factors. Rather than focus exclusively on archaeological interests, I spent a great deal of time observing what people were doing and their attitudes concerning the relations of men to women, the rearing of children, the uses of leisure, the nature of cooperation among camps, and the way nomads perceive themselves, as well as how outsiders perceive nomads.

By the time I had gotten to know them as people, I realized that there was much more to tell than just my archaeological results. Beyond their value as the source of information on matters of archaeological interest, I saw them as human beings, important in their own right. I realized that the story of their lives was as important as any information I could discover about the past. What follows in these pages is a story of tribal nomadic life in Iran in 1973.

Structure of the book

Chapter 1 explains how the project began: why I decided to study a nomadic tribe during its migration. In Chapter 2, Sekandar Amanolahi-Baharvand writes about his life and the extraordinary journey he made, from his birth in a black tent to universities in the United States and back again to Iran, this time as a professor. Chapter 3 discusses Luristan, a relatively isolated, rugged mountain terrain, and its natural resources. In Chapter 4 we explore what is known about the pastoral nomads of Luristan, based on sources ranging from archaeological research to nineteenth-century travelers' records to twentieth-century documentary films. Books on the tribes of Luristan and surrounding provinces are briefly reviewed.

Chapters 5 to 13, the central part of the book, describe the migration and daily lives of the nomads. These chapters follow the sequence of the migration, from its inception to its terminus. Chapter 5 takes us from the city of Dezful to Chin-i Zal, where we joined the tribe. Chapter 6 describes Morad Khan's winter camp. The principal characters that we follow through the journey are introduced here. In Chapter 7, before the migration starts, I reflect on nomadic life, the relation between the nomads and farmers, and how life in the camps in the tribe's territory has changed. Chapter 8 describes the tension building toward the start of migration. We describe the breakdown of the winter camp and packing for the migration. Chapter 9 discusses the anxiety engendered by the presence of dozens of tribes and thousands of livestock pressing toward the bottleneck, the imposing mountain, Kialon Kuh. Chapter 10 describes a disastrous river crossing and the routine in overnight camps. Chapter 11 focuses on settlers practicing agriculture in tribal territory, and our exploration of a mysterious cliffside villa. Chapter 12 is an interview with Atawak, a man well into his 80s and the oldest known Lur, who reminisced with Sekandar about tribal history. Chapter 13 sees the tribe achieve its objective, the summer pastures high in the mountain, overlooking the Khorramabad Valley.

Chapter 14 moves the scene of investigation to Khuzistan, where we briefly excavated a nomad camp some 8000 years old, providing proof-of-concept that our observations during migration could be applied to the past. Incidentally, it also shows the plight of other Luri former nomads in Khuzistan, now relegated to day labor. In Chapter 15 we briefly return to the summer pastures to search for archaeological sites. In Chapter 16, I reflect on the migratory experience and on the nature of nomads and nomadic life in Luristan in the twentieth century. Chapter 17, written by Sekandar, is a concise history of his tribe, the Baharvand, based on his personal research.

Chapter 18 is a postscript that tells of changes in tribal life and that of both of the authors subsequent to the migration. The main narrative focused on Morad Khan's camp; we explain what happened to its members since 1973 through photographs and brief biographies. During the migration we were aided and educated by Mohammad Ali, one of Morad Khan's *homsa*. The story of his transformation and that of his family is as remarkable as that of Sekandar's.

Frank Hole
New Haven, CT

Acknowledgments

My special thanks must go to the Baharvand Lurs of Morad Khan's camp, who accepted me as extra baggage without ever really understanding what I was trying to do, and who were generous in patiently answering the innumerable questions that I asked. Sekandar Amanolahi-Baharvand, my graduate student, assistant, and companion, facilitated entry into the group and did his best to help me understand Luri life; he must get a large share of the credit for this work.

The trip was supported by the National Science Foundation as part of a larger research project designed to investigate the origins of nomadic pastoralism. The NSF grant to Rice University allowed me to take a leave of absence during the spring semester of 1973 to carry out the work.

In Iran, my project was greatly aided by Dr. Jerome Clinton, director of the American Institute of Iranian Studies. He helped to steer my proposal through the proper government channels toward its ultimate approval. Dr. Firuz Bagherzadeh, director of the National Center for Research in Art History and Archaeology, provided official government sanction to the research.

As always, there were numerous individuals, private citizens, foreign scholars, and technical personnel associated with many different enterprises who in one way or another lent assistance, knowledge, advice, and hospitality when we needed it most. Among these I should mention Jane Clinton, in whose house we lived during our trips to Tehran; Professor Henry Wright, who allowed us to board at his house in Dezful and provided lively discussion about our work, and his students Rob Wenke, Nanette Pyne, Melinda Zeder, and Richard Redding; M. Jean Perrot, director of the French Archaeological Mission at Susa, and his staff; Professor Ezat Neghaban and his staff at his excavations at Haft Tepe; and personnel at the Safiabad agricultural research center—Drs. Dabiri and Niknajad, and agricultural scientists Vaughn, Fine, and Wilson—all of whom gave valuable information on animal husbandry and forage crops.

Special appreciation must be owed to Iskandar Amanolahi-Baharvand and members of his family, who shared their house with us when we stayed in Darayi, and to Rustam Pourmand, who provided the same hospitality when we stayed in Deh Luran.

While none are to be held accountable for the substance of this book, I am grateful for comments on an early draft of the manuscript from Edward Norbeck, Patty Jo Watson, Carol Kramer, John Pfeiffer, and Harold Conklin. Over the years I have discussed the project with students at Rice, Yale, and Mazaryk universities, and their questions and insights have helped clarify some points. My wife Bonnie's thoughtful and critical reading of the penultimate version led to important amplification of a number of issues. For editorial assistance and help finding maps and photos I am indebted to Yukiko Tonoike and Dawn Brown. Finally, I am grateful for the patient and astute editing by Elizabeth Noll, who alerted me to inconsistencies, asked pointed questions, and helped sharpen the focus. The appearance of the book has been greatly enhanced by John Klausmeyer's creative and skillful rendering of maps and photos. I am grateful to Joyce Marcus, who suggested that I publish in the Memoir series and provided timely encouragement and advice. My thanks to all these and others who supported me in one way or another over the decades that it took to finally bring this story to its conclusion.

Frank Hole
New Haven, CT

Chapter 1

Genesis of the Migration Project

My interest in the nomads of Iran grew directly out of my interest in the archaeological history of domestication, an interest that was developed at the University of Chicago, where I studied anthropology in the late 1950s. During those years, I studied under Dr. Robert Braidwood, who had done pioneering archaeology in several countries of Southwest Asia. In 1958, I joined an expedition led by Braidwood near the town of Kermanshah in western Iran. That was my first field experience in the archaeology of domestication and my first encounter with pastoral peoples who moved seasonally with their herds of sheep and goats.

I took many photographs of the nomads and their camps; they left a lasting impression on me as a way of life I would like to understand.

I returned to Iran in 1961 to begin a series of archaeological surveys and excavations; my purpose was to find archaeological sites related to the early stages of agriculture. At each site, we attempted to estimate the age of the tells (small hills made by successive occupations) by the pottery or flints on the surface. Our field notes described the sites, but in the absence of detailed maps, we could only roughly plot their locations against the chance that we might return to excavate them (Hole 1962). At that time, Iran was poorly explored archaeologically, and a modern road system had yet to be built. My journeys into the remoter parts of the Zagros Mountains took me to people who had never seen outsiders before.

My companions were Kent Flannery, a fellow graduate student who had also worked on Braidwood's team (now at the University of Michigan), and Mohammad Moushirpour, an Iranian assigned by the government to accompany us. Traveling by Jeep and on foot for four months, the three of us made a rather superficial journey through the western mountainous part of the Iran, following primitive roads and trails. This was a hard trip, but fascinating. Because of the rugged topography, this part of Iran is sparsely settled, and much of it had no roads suitable for vehicular traffic. During those days we had a chance to observe local people as they farmed, herded animals, and shopped in the markets. Without being totally aware of the process, I was assimilating information that I would one day use in my interpretations of archaeological sites. This experience stoked my desire to travel with a nomadic tribe.

In technological terms, we were essentially living in the nineteenth century: no electronics, no cell phones, mail that traveled by sea, absence of hotels, shortage of food, and continual breakdown of the Jeep. We carried a kerosene Primus stove to heat water and food, and we slept on floors and benches. Our guidance was maps produced by the British military, drafted by plane table in the early twentieth century. GPS had yet to be invented, so our locations were often a matter of guesswork. Without Moushirpour, we could not have traveled through military checkpoints and changes in dialect: he was fluent in Kurdi. We learned later that he traveled in the Elburz Mountains with the legendary explorer Wilfred Thesiger, whom he said started his day's hike with only raisins for a meal.

In subsequent years, Flannery and I excavated a series of caves and rockshelters in the western part of the country, dating back in time nearly 50,000 years (Hole 1966; Hole and Flannery 1967). People who hunted game before the invention of agriculture had occupied the caves. We also excavated Neolithic villages of 6000 to 9000 years ago, where we documented some of the first efforts at farming and stock raising. The earliest village, Ali Kosh, lies on the Deh Luran Plain near the border of Iran and Iraq (Hole et al. 1969). People who practiced only rudimentary agriculture and whose domesticated livestock showed only slight morphological changes from wild animals founded Ali Kosh some 9000 years ago. At first, neither the barley and wheat nor the sheep and goats were very far removed from their wild states.

In the successive layers of Ali Kosh and in the nearby sites of Chagha Sefid and Tepe Sabz, we were able to document the gradual development of stock raising and farming (Hole 1977). We could see how the first villagers at Ali Kosh harvested mostly wild foods, planting only to supplement the natural resources. Gradually, as they became more skillful at farming and began to deplete the wild resources, the people planted larger fields and kept more livestock. After many generations, probably people who split from the growing Ali Kosh founded Chagha Sefid, another village of the same type several miles away. For more than a thousand years, people continued to live at Ali Kosh. After that it was abandoned, and the land was never reoccupied, probably because their sources of water had dried up.

At about the time Ali Kosh was abandoned, new people—bringing with them dogs and cattle, hybrid races of grains, and the techniques of irrigation agriculture—arrived on the Deh Luran Plain. Some of them settled at Chagha Sefid; others built new villages. The population began to grow more quickly than before, although it was still sparse: only a few hundred people occupied tens of thousands of square miles at the base of the towering Kabir Kuh, the first range of the Zagros Mountains that leads to the lands of the migratory pastoralists. From around 6000 BC onward, village houses and agriculture existed in recognizably modern form, with only the plow yet to be harnessed.

When excavating at Chagha Sefid, I had expected to find a situation very similar to that of Ali Kosh: people who gathered a lot of wild plant foods, did small-scale agriculture, hunted the game on the plain, and kept a few livestock. Although the two villages were occupied at the same time and were just beyond eyesight of one another, the people at Chagha Sefid apparently obtained all of their meat from their herds, without any reliance on the hunting of wild game. In other words, they were far more specialized in herding than the people of Ali Kosh. Because of the extremely hot temperature in the summer, I expected that these people—possibly the entire settlement—would have travelled into the mountains to find summer pasture and comfortable temperature. Because of the often suffocating summer heat on the plain (122°F or 50°C), and with the cooler mountains in plain sight, it is only reasonable that these early villagers already practiced a kind of seasonal transhumance that was only a short step removed from living in tents year-round. As sheep and goats are not native and were not adapted to Deh Luran, they must have been imported from older settlements at higher elevations (Zeder and Hesse 2000). The rationale for transhumance, if not its practice, must have been evident from the first.

Sekandar Amanolahi-Baharvand

My graduate student and companion on the migration was a member of the Baharvand Luri tribe. Only a fortunate and unpredictable circumstance brought us together. (Please see Chapter 2 for a more complete version of Sekandar's story, told in his own words.)

We met in 1969, while Kent Flannery and I were excavating at one of the rockshelters near the town of Khorramabad in southwestern Iran. This turned out to have been the camp of people who lived about 20,000 years ago, who migrated in the mountains and hunted onagers (*Equus hemionis*, a kind of wild ass) and gazelle. The excavation was painstaking work: we recovered minute projectile barbs, cutting tools, and hide scrapers, all made of flint. Pottery would not come into use for another 10,000 to 12,000 years, and permanent settlements did not exist (Hole and Flannery 1967).

For several scorching, dusty weeks we had labored on this isolated, rocky island, which rose abruptly from the golden waves of wheat that covered the otherwise flat agricultural valley (Figure 1.1). Day after day we peeled back the many layers of the rockshelter, employing men and boys from nearby villages. These workers were Lurs, speakers of one of the major tribal languages in western Iran. A thin dirt road meandered by the site, leading from Khorramabad to the scattered rural villages. Along this road, one cloudless, hot day, came a bicycle trailing dust. As the bicycle drew abreast of Gar Arjeneh, our rocky hill, it turned and headed directly toward us, along a narrow footpath that snaked across the wheat fields. Dusty green in color, the bicycle was identical to thousands of others, made in India and sold throughout Iran to workers who were only then gaining their independence from walking. At the base of the hill, the rider laid his bike down and began to pick his way up the rocky slope to where we were digging.

When he got to the top, he was not even breathing hard after his ride and rapid climb up the hill, nor was he sweating, although the temperature was well over a hundred degrees.

Figure 1.1. We were excavating at this rockshelter, Gar Arjeneh, in the Khorramabad Valley when we first met Sekandar.

He was obviously Iranian, yet his clothes were not like those of our workers. They had the look of the city about them. He was dressed in dusty, Western-style trousers and shirt of somber earth tones. As he approached, the rider spoke with our workers in the native dialect, which we did not understand. Clearly he knew some of the men and they knew him. I looked curiously at the clean-cut bareheaded man of about twenty who stood before me.

Walking up to me, he said, speaking in heavily accented English, "Hello meester, how are you?"

"Hello," I replied.

He went on, "My name is Sekandar. I wish to practice English. I have learn English from school. I teach in secondary school."

It was not unusual for young men to accost us this way in town. Some had a genuine interest in speaking English, and others were merely curious about us. But such a meeting at the site, some ten miles outside Khorramabad, was astonishing.

We struck up a short conversation, in which he revealed that he was from one of the nearby villages and was largely self-taught in English. In fact, he had received some rudimentary English instruction in high school from a Persian who himself was not fluent. But Sekandar had pursued the language on his own after he left high school and had become a country schoolteacher. His chances to practice the language were rare, as there were few English-speaking persons around. Construction companies, which were building roads and industrial facilities in Luristan at the time, employed most of these. Only a keen ear would be able to learn English from the mixed accents of the international construction workers who lived in field camps. Much as I sympathized with the young man's desire to learn English, his visit came in the midst of the digging, and I was not eager to prolong the conversation. I told him he was welcome to visit us in town or come back to the site another day. We saw Sekandar at the site several times in the next few weeks. Always he came for conversation rather than to observe the archaeology.

Then a most fortuitous event occurred. A team of Americans representing the Fulbright commission was touring Iran, visiting schools to recruit students for an English language workshop. Sekandar was invited and gladly accepted. After the workshop, one of the commissioners told me that Sekandar was one of the brightest, most dedicated students he had met. He offered Sekandar a chance to study in the United States.

Two years passed before he was permitted to leave the country and begin his American education. Sekandar enrolled in general education at the University of Baltimore, and then at Morgan State University, majoring in sociology. During this time, Sekandar and I corresponded intermittently. After graduation, he decided to study anthropology and was admitted to the University of Maryland, where he worked toward a master's degree. By then I was formulating plans for my research on nomads, and I asked him if he would be interested in helping me. He was eager to participate, as my plans involved research in Iran.

Initially I was unable to secure funds for this ethnographic research. But we both agreed it would be a good idea if, in the meantime, Sekandar enrolled at Rice University, where I was teaching and could supervise his work toward a PhD. After transferring to Rice, Sekandar took two years of courses in anthropology. Finally, the National Science Foundation funded my project.

Sekandar was an integral part of my plan from the beginning. He knew intimately the people and the country I wished to study. Moreover, he spoke the Luri dialect, which I was unable to understand. We thus worked out a deal: he would work with me on my project while I would supply him with travel funds and the financial support he needed for simultaneously carrying out research for his doctoral dissertation. In fact, our two projects were complementary, because he was interested in studying changes in his own tribe from an anthropological perspective. I also was interested in changes in the tribal people, which would shed additional light on the relationship between modern pastoralists and those of the distant past. Fortuitously, Sekandar's tribe was one of many that migrated seasonally from their winter pastures in the lowlands (like Deh Luran) to their summer territory in the mountains above Khorramabad.

Our collaboration was one of those rare circumstances when all of the necessary pieces fall neatly into place. Alone neither of us would have accomplished nearly as much. For my part, his participation was essential. For his part, the chance to travel enlarged his understanding of the tribes and resulted in some rare encounters.

Sekandar completed his dissertation (The Baharvand: Former Pastoralists of Iran) in 1975 and returned to Iran to teach at the University of Shiraz. He continued his research among tribal people of Iran and has written a number of books and articles on Iranian tribes. Among these are the following: "The Luti, an outcast group of Iran" (1975); *Tales from Luristan* (1986); *The Tribes of Iran* (1988); "Reza Shah and the Lurs" (2002); and "The Lurs of Iran" (2016).

Preparations for studying nomadic pastoralism

After I had secured funding from the National Science Foundation for an ethnoarchaeological project, Sekandar and I traveled to Iran for an overview of nomadic pastoralism from the lowlands (like Deh Luran) to the mountainous highlands, where the pastoralists migrate for the summer. Toward the end of February 1973 until early April, we visited campsites and interviewed pastoralists about all aspects of herding livestock. We learned how diseases and natural disasters such as drought and blizzards affect the herds and the reproductive cycles of the animals. We also recorded routes of migration and the physical remains left in places where pastoralists camped, and we inquired about where and why the people camped where they did. Collectively, these interviews and observations provided the basis for making generalizations about how and where we might find ancient sites and what we might expect to find at them. They also provided some insight into intertribal relations and economic conditions in tribal areas. With these experiences and knowledge, we set out in April to study one camp of nomadic pastoralists while they migrated from their winter to their summer pastures.

As an archaeologist, my primary interest was to study migratory ways to gain insight into how they may have developed in remote antiquity. Archaeologists had long been concerned with how agriculture emerged from a background of hunter-gatherers, but the complementary investigation of the development of animal husbandry—the domestication of livestock—had been little explored archaeologically. It was generally assumed that farming and herding arose together as an agro-pastoral system, rooted in sedentary villages. As an alternative hypothesis, I proposed that nomadic pastoralism may have arisen independently of farming, but there was little or no evidence to support it. This project began as an attempt to learn about the origins of animal husbandry and of nomadic pastoralism through studying modern ways. What equipment is essential to carry on migration and sustain life on the move? Was nomadism possible before agriculture? Did migrations emerge as a way to avoid agricultural fields? Did migrants require support from agricultural settlements? Did migration always require the use of pack animals? Importantly for archaeological purposes, what evidence might remain from transitory campsites for archaeologists to find? I hoped to gain some insight into such questions by living with a tribe on migration.

Chapter 2

Sekandar's Story

by

Sekandar Amanolahi-Baharvand

As a member of the Baharvand tribe, I have experienced the transition from pastoral nomadism to small villages and towns in Iran, and then to metropolitan cities such as Washington, D.C., Houston, Boston, London, and Tokyo. Now, as a retired professor, I live in Shiraz, the legendary city of south Iran.

When I was nine years old, a wandering fortune-teller, who claimed to be a Sayid (a descendant of the Prophet), visited my family and told my fortune. He looked at me and said to my parents, "He will get out of the country and go to a faraway land, where he will study for many years, then return to Iran and have an important job; he will eventually become a rich man. Furthermore, he will marry twice; one of his wives will be from a reputed family." After that, he looked at my older brother, who incidentally was the first child and was very dear to my parents. He said, "Do not count on this one, he is going to be nobody!"

Darayi Village

The mismanagement of the Qajar princes, who ruled over Luristan from 1794 to 1924, led to anarchy and tribal revolt. The Baharvand conquered the entire Koragah (Khorramabad) Valley, including the Darayi village, around 1897. This is the best part of Luristan, with good agricultural land and rivers. They divided the territory between the lineages of the tribe, and Darayi became my grandfather's property. The Baharvand continued their traditional migration, but also continued farming in their winter and summer territory, including in Darayi.

Darayi is located around 8 km south of Khorramabad. The village is named after the Darayi lineage, which owned it and resided there until the end of the nineteenth century. Residents deserted the village because of anarchy that reigned in Luristan during the nineteenth century. Then a Qajar prince, who was the governor of Luristan, expropriated their land. Unfortunately, there is no historical record about the village. As part of the program to settle nomads, the modern village was built on top of an ancient graveyard by the government in 1929.

The downfall of the Qajar dynasty and the establishment of the Pahlavi regime (1925–1978) changed the traditional relationships between the state and the pastoral nomads. After years of fighting, Reza Shah (1925–1941), the founder of the Pahlavi dynasty, subdued the pastoral nomads of Luristan and settled them forcibly. In 1921, members of the Baharvand tribe were forcibly settled in the Koragah Valley, near Khorramabad. The Baharvand, including my grandfather and his followers, were settled in Darayi. The government built a fort for my grandfather, who was the most influential leader (*khan*) of the Baharvand tribe, and his followers settled around the fort (*ghala*). The same year that the village was founded, my grandfather was imprisoned in Qasr-i Qajar jail in Tehran for six years.

After the forced settlement, the army disarmed the pastoral nomads, and they lost their traditional power. In the meantime, the urban residents gained power, because they were in close contact with the governmental officials and became acquainted with the new laws and regulations. In 1933, a businessman from Khorramabad, who was cooperating with the army and was in close contact with the governmental offices, bought the village from the Qajar prince in Tehran for 160,000 *rials*. As a result, the Baharvand lost ownership of our land. However, the landlord pledged not to demand any share of farm products from my father's and my two uncles' farms.

The government permitted my younger uncle, along with several families, to continue pastoral nomadism in order to utilize the natural pastures in winter territory in Chin-i Zal. In 1938, the year I was born, my mother and my two-year-old brother joined my uncle's family migrating to the winter territory in Chin-i Zal. The next spring, as they were returning from Chin-i Zal to the summer territory in Darayi, I was born at the foot of the Kialon Mountain, in mid-April 1938. My uncle continued pastoral nomadism, but my father, along with his second wife and children, remained in Darayi.

The exact date of my birth is not known. According to my birth certificate, I was born on January 10, 1938, in the Darayi village, near Khorramabad, the capital of Luristan. However, in reality, I was born in the first half of April 1938 in a place known as Beringe Kar, at the foot of Kialon Mountain, in the tribe's winter territory, around 90 km south of Khorramabad.

Unexpected events in 1941

Three events took place in 1941 that had a great impact on Luristan. First, the occupation of Iran by the allied forces resulted in the abdication of Reza Shah and the weakening of the central government. Second, the weakening of the central government allowed the resumption of pastoral nomadism by the settled tribes. Third, this was a year of famine, caused by drought and the interference of the allied forces in Iran.

In 1942, the American army started building a military camp near Badrabad village west of the Darayi, bringing the people of Luristan in close contact with the Americans for the first time. Some people from Darayi, including my cousin (my father's sister's son), whose name is Abozarg (now ninety years old), were working with the American armed forces in that military camp. Abozarg's memories helped me decide to go to America. He learned to speak English while working in that camp, and he always praised Americans and said that they were friendly, humble, and generous. Unlike the Russians, who were harsh and mistreated the natives, the American armed forces were friendly and treated people fairly well. They left a pleasant impression. As I grew up, my cousin continued telling stories about American friendliness and generosity. As a result, I dreamed of going to America and I decided to learn English.

Life in Darayi village

In 1949, when I was nearly twelve years old, the entire village consisted of seventy-seven families. Of these, forty-five families were from the Baharvand, and thirty-three families belonged to the Mir tribe. I remember the location and the names of the heads of each household, along with the names of their wives. All the heads of the household, except two, and all of the wives, except four, had passed away by 2019. My two uncles, along with several families attached to them, continued traditional pastoral nomadism.

The main occupation of all families was a mixture of farming and, to a lesser degree, animal husbandry. However, prior to their settlement, they were engaged in herding and did only a little farming in their summer and winter territories. Since most of the land of the Darayi village was unirrigated, people depended on dry farming to cultivate wheat and barley, which were used mostly for their daily bread. To a lesser extent they cultivated other crops, such as lentils, peas, and opium poppies, to sell in the market. The small patches of land that were irrigated by the river were used to grow corn, watermelon, cucumber, onion, and tomato. Only two orchard gardens were irrigated by the water from the *qanat* (subterranean canal): one belonged to the landlord and the other was owned by my father.

The Baharvand also cultivated wheat in the highland of their traditional summer territory, which was known as Baveh, located some 20 km south of Darayi. Although the Baharvand were officially settled from 1950 until 1977, they pursued a semisedentary way of life. They migrated to Baveh in early April and stayed there until early July. During this period, they grazed their goats, sheep, horses, donkeys, mules, and cows in the mountains. At the beginning of summer, they returned to Darayi to harvest their wheat and barley and cultivate their land for the next planting. They remained in Darayi until April, when the men returned to Baveh.

They obtained their necessities by selling their farm surplus in Khorramabad, where they bought commodities such as tea, sugar, rice, salt, cloth, and shoes. Their diet consisted mainly of bread, milk products, and occasionally meat and rice, along with other traditional dishes. At this time the Baharvand lacked tractors, bicycles, electricity, telephones, refrigerators, and the like. Rather, they depended on animals and humans to do various tasks.

Sociopolitical relationships

The social relationship among the Baharvand was based on kinship and nonkinship alliances. The kinship system among the Baharvand was based on consanguinity (blood), affinity (marriage), and milk (an infant having breast milk from someone for two or three days or more). The consanguinity consisted of patrilineality and patrilocality, while affinity was based on marriage. The Baharvand basically practiced monogamy, but there were cases of polygamy, particularly among the leaders. In 1949, there were two cases of polygamy in Darayi. In 1949, there were four extended, three joint, and one incomplete family, while thirty-six families were nuclear.

Politically speaking, the entire village was divided into two separate groups: the Baharvand, who occupied the eastern section of the village, and the Mir, who resided in the western section. The Baharvand were under my father's supervision, while the Mir were supervised by their own leader, who had married my aunt's daughter (my father's sister's daughter). These two men were responsible for maintaining law and order. Furthermore, they negotiated between the landlord and the people of the village, and they represented the government in negotiations between their followers and the governmental agencies. The two men maintained a cordial relationship.

Socialization and education

In 1949, both the Baharvand and the Mir continued their traditional preindustrial way of life, including their pattern of socialization and training. There was no modern school. With the exception of four men, who could barely read and write, the entire population was illiterate. Socialization took place gradually and practically through participation in daily activities and parental advice. In this way, the children gradually learned the norms and values of their society and also learned farming and animal husbandry. Furthermore, they learned how to utilize their environment and protect themselves by cooperating with their kinsmen. They also learned patterns of proper behavior and the social ethical code.

Elementary education

When I was eleven years old, a Baharvand who had completed two years of high school decided to open a private school in Dinarvand village, 5 km east of Darayi. His name was Mohammad Taghi (Luri=Matayi), and he was one of the children who were forcibly sent by the government to Darol Tarbiya (boarding school), which was built in Khorramabad in 1924 by Reza Shah. Mohammad Taghi had completed six years of elementary school. However, since there was no high school in Luristan, the government sent him, along with others, to Darol Tarbiya in Tehran. He completed two years of high school, but unfortunately the school was closed by the government. As a result, Mohammad Taghi and the other students from different tribal groups had to leave Tehran and return to their homeland. I can imagine the disappointment and the frustration of those who had experienced the city of Tehran and had to return to the villages. In 1948, he decided to establish a four-grade elementary school in Dinarvand. He sent a message to my father asking him to allow me and my older brother to attend his school that spring. Thus, we started going to school when I was eleven years old and my brother was thirteen years old. Until that time we were both completely illiterate.

The school consisted of one mud brick room, and there were no chairs. We sat on the ground. We paid a small tuition monthly. Dinarvand village was 5 km from our village, so we had to walk 10 km daily, regardless of rain and snow. But things became even more difficult. The Baharvand of Darayi migrated to Baveh in early April and remained there until the beginning of August. Our campsite in Baveh was about 20 km from Darayi. Since school continued while we were in Baveh, we had to walk some 20 km in the morning from Baveh to Dinarvand to attend school and then climb 20 km up the mountain to reach our camp in Baveh in the afternoon.

At Baveh, we lived in a traditional tent. Life in the tent was not ideal for studying, particularly during the evening, when we had to sit near a hearth full of smoking firewood. It was hard to do homework under such circumstances, yet we managed to complete the first and second grades within just one year because of our devoted teacher and our great interest in pursuing an education.

In 1949, the government of Luristan province formally recognized the school as a nonprivate government school and named it Khaghani School. After that, our teacher was formally hired by the government and received his monthly salary from the Department of Education. A representative from the Department of Education came to Dinarvand to test our knowledge. We passed the first and second grades formally and thus entered the third grade of elementary school, which we completed in 1949.

In 1950, a four-grade elementary school was established in Darayi, and we were able to complete the fourth grade in our village. In the spring, we had to make the long trek from our camp in the mountain to school on the plain every day.

After we completed the fourth grade in Darayi, we had to go to Massoor, a village located 10 km west of Darayi, to complete the last two years (fifth and sixth grades) of elementary school. Again we had to walk 20 km daily. During this period, we remained in Darayi and did not go to our camp in Baveh during spring migration because of the long distance.

High school education

I completed my elementary education in 1952. Since there was no high school in any of the neighboring villages, we had to go to Khorramabad, the capital of Luristan, which at the time was a small town. My brother and I began studying at the Pahlavi High School in 1953 (Figure 2.1). We rented a room in Khorramabad and thus we began a new stage of our lives: an urban way of life. While we attended school in Khorramabad, we had to wear a suit (coat and pants) instead of our traditional Luri costume. We were not allowed to wear our Luri hat while attending classes, or to speak in Luri; we had to speak Farsi, as we also had to do during elementary school.

I was extremely excited when entering high school, because I could start taking English courses. Learning English was an important factor in paving the way for my trip to America. I worked hard and devoted a lot of time to learning English. By the time I completed the third year of high school, I had some speaking proficiency. In the spring of 1956, I met an American military official who was training the Iranian army in Luristan. As I talked to him, he asked me where I learned English. I told him, "I am a high school student and I am learning English in school." He was surprised and said, "Let me tell you honestly, this town, this province and this country is too small for you. You must get out of here." I told him that I hoped to go to America some day.

I managed to find pen pals in America and several other countries, and I tried to get information about studying in these countries.

After completing four years of high school, I decided to switch to the Training Teaching School (Daneshara) in 1957. I passed the entrance exam and started to study to become a teacher. I switched to the Training Teaching School for two reasons: First, I would start teaching automatically after

Figure 2.1. Sekandar as a high school student in 1954.

graduation and would be hired formally as a teacher by the Department of Education of Luristan while continuing my studying. This was a great success, because I became financially independent and had the opportunity to further my plan of going to America.

Employment and further studies

In summer 1957, I managed to find a temporary job working as an interpreter in an American company, which was constructing an oil refinery in Chenar, a place near Khorramabad. It was an exciting experience. First, I was provided with a separate bedroom, which was equipped with a modern bed, shower, restroom, and small refrigerator, something which I never had before. Second,

I was served free food, including breakfast, lunch, and dinner. Third, I was provided with a car and a driver. Fourth, I had an office, which was close to the office of the company manager and his assistants, including Americans and Iranians. Fifth, my salary was beyond my expectation. I received twice the monthly salary of a high schoolteacher. This was the first time in my life that I had so much cash. The greatest advantage of my job, however, was that I had close contact with the Americans. This contributed to advancing my English and also gave me the opportunity to learn about American society: their values, their system of education, and particularly their political system. The more I learned about life in America, the more I wanted to go there.

My job entailed various responsibilities, including: 1) participation in meetings of various kinds; 2) translating in English, Luri, and Farsi (Persian); 3) reporting the daily activities in English to the main office in Tehran via telegram; and 4) playing an active role in settling disputes of various kinds between the company and the laborers. As a native of Luristan, speaking Luri, Farsi and English, and also knowing the culture of the people of Luristan, I played an important role in settling disputes and also in hiring laborers. The oil refinery was located in the Chagani tribe's territory. When Sayad Abbas Hatemi, the chief of the Chagani tribe, met me for the first time, he told me he had learned that I was from the Baharvand tribe, but did not know from which lineage. When I told him that I was the grandson of Husain Khan, he grabbed me and kissed my forehead three times. Then he looked toward the sky, thanking God three times for blessing Husain Khan with such a wonderful grandson, who would carry on his name. Then he told me that his father maintained a cordial relationship and a close alliance with my grandfather. I thanked him and promised to introduce him to the managing director of the company. I talked to the managing director and explained why we need to maintain a good relationship with him. Eventually we invited him for lunch and maintained a friendly relationship with him as long as I was there.

Becoming a teacher

I graduated from the Training Teaching School in June 1960 and started teaching in Jami Elementary School in Koohdasht in September 1960. Koohdasht was located about 60 km west of Khorramabad. There were six teachers, all from Khorramabad. All were single, except for one. We rented a house consisting of three rooms, a hall, and a kitchen. I lived alone in one of the rooms, while the others occupied the other two rooms. I lived alone because I wanted to study English and other subjects, and I used to study until midnight. My colleagues ate together and gathered in the hall in the evenings, chatting, playing, and enjoying themselves, whereas I lived alone, seldom joining them. They were surprised at the way I lived, and they often asked me how I could continue such a way of life. Overall, life in Koohdasht was not pleasant. I felt I was in exile. When I had lived in Khorramabad, I had been close to my parents and would spend the weekend with them. I taught only one academic year in Koohdasht and requested to come back to Khorramabad. However, I was transferred to Pala Baba Husain village, located about 15 km east of Khorramabad.

Teaching at Pala Baba Husain (1961)

The school consisted of three rooms without a surrounding wall. It had been completed just before my arrival, so I was confronted with three empty rooms without benches, tables, chairs, or even a blackboard. Life in this village, like other villages in the region, represented a preindustrial way of life. There was no electricity or any element of a modern industrial society.

At registration, there were twelve boys and three girls. All of them were first-grade students. I decided to use one of the rooms for the class, another for a kitchen, dining room, and office, and the third for resting and sleeping. I cooked my food, but the head of the village, who was an affinal kinsmen, provided fresh bread daily. He insisted that I live with his family instead of sleeping alone in the school, because he was concerned about my safety.

When the class began, the students had to sit on the ground. Each student brought something to sit on, and I had my chair. It took four months before we received the necessary equipment, including benches, tables, and chairs. They arrived just a day before the school inauguration by the governor general and the head of the Department of Education of Luristan Province!

My teaching schedule consisted of three shifts: morning and afternoon for daily students, late afternoon till evening for the adults.

While in Pala Baba Husain, I bought a bicycle and rented a room in Khorramabad. I went there on Thursday afternoons and returned to school on Saturday morning. While in town, I bought whatever I needed for the whole week. I also checked to see if I had letters from my foreign pen pals.

The outcome of the Fulbright seminar (1961)

I continued teaching in Pala Baba Hussain until the end of winter 1962. Fortunately, the Fulbright Cultural Exchange Commission held a seminar for high school English teachers in Khorramabad in fall 1961. I participated in that seminar, despite the fact that I was not an English teacher. Fortunately, it led to my transfer to Khorramabad. Mr. Regal, the director of the seminar, noticed that I spoke English. He asked me which high school I was teaching in and from which university I had graduated. I told him I had never attended a university and was teaching in an elementary school in a village. He was surprised and said, "You deserve to teach English in a high school." He met with Mr. Purparviz, the director of the Department of Education of Luristan, and told him that I should be teaching English in a high school. He told him that I spoke English well and my teaching would be a great advantage to the students. In short, he managed to convince Mr. Purparviz to meet me immediately. When I met Mr. Purparviz, he congratulated me and told me that I would be transferred to Mohammadi High School in Khorramabad within a week.

Thanks to Mr. Regal, I was transferred to Khorramabad and started teaching at Mohammadi High School in late winter 1962. This was a significant event, because it made it possible for me to participate in the next Fulbright seminar, which was held in Hamadan City, the capital of the Hamadan Province, in summer 1962.

Meeting Frank (1963)

In summer 1963, Frank Hole and Kent Flannery were excavating in Gar Arjeneh (the Hill of Jinn) near Khorramabad. I decided to visit them. At that time, I had no idea about archaeology and anthropology, nor did I understand the purpose of their excavation. But I had heard that these foreigners were actually treasure hunters and they were merely searching for *ganj* (treasure). I decided to meet them just to speak English and to make new friends. I rode my bicycle to the site, where I met Frank and Kent. I was surprised to see them working hard that hot summer, in the middle of the dusty ground along with the laborers.

As Frank has pointed out, I introduced myself and started talking to Frank without knowing that I was talking to a professor of archaeology from Rice University. I never imagined that he would be my PhD dissertation adviser at the Department of Anthropology at Rice University twelve years later! Nor could I imagine that I would be honored to be the coauthor of this book some fifty-seven years later. Frank was a blessing and he has made a great contribution to my life. I will always cherish his friendship and his kind support.

Second Fulbright seminar (1963)

The second Fulbright seminar was held in July 1963 in Hamadan City, the capital of Hamadan province, which is adjacent to Luristan. Several English teachers from Khorramabad, including myself, were sent by the Department of Education to participate in that seminar. My participation in that seminar was a fabulous achievement, since it facilitated my trip to America. Mr. Donald Wilson and three other Americans, including Mr. Davis and Miss Smith, headed the seminar. Fortunately, I did well in that seminar. Mr. Wilson was impressed by my gregariousness, my friendly relations with many of the participants, and also the fact that I spoke English better than most of the participants. One day there was a quarrel between several participants from Hamadan and Luristan provinces, and I managed to end the quarrel before it got out of control. Mr. Wilson told me he wanted to talk to me. When we were sitting together, he asked me about the cause of the quarrel, which I explained for him. He told me that I was qualified for leadership and then he asked me which university I had graduated from. I told him I had never attended a university, but that I would like to go to America and continue my education. He promised he would see how he could help me.

At the end of the seminar, when he was returning to Tehran, he asked me to go with him. When we got to Tehran, he arranged an appointment with the Minister of Education. He took me to the office of the minister. After we had a cup of tea, he introduced me to the minister and told him, "This young man is an English teacher from Luristan, who speaks English fluently without attending any university. He desires to go to America to study English and then return to Iran. I would like to ask you to agree with his leave of absence from teaching even without any payment."

Fortunately, the minister agreed. Mr. Wilson, who resided in Baltimore, told me that when I came to Baltimore, I was welcome to stay with him. He said that he would enroll me in the University of Baltimore.

I took the letter from the Ministry of Education and submitted it to the Department of Education of Luristan. They provided me with a letter indicating that I was formally on leave of absence. Then it was time to apply for a passport and a visa.

Passport and visa (1963 to 1964)

It took a year to get my passport and a visa from the American embassy in Tehran. At that time, they did not issue passports in Khorramabad, so I had to travel to Tehran. When I applied for an Iranian passport, I was told that since I had not served in the army, I could not leave the country. I had to get a letter from the Department of Education to the army officials. When I arrived, there were three officials, to whom I handed the letter. I told them that the letter proved that I was going abroad to continue my education. They told me that the letter didn't prove anything, and that I would be drafted shortly. It was a terrible situation.

After a few minutes, one of them took my hand and guided me out of the room. He told me that if I wanted to solve the problem, I must provide a gift to one of the officers. Of course he meant giving a bribe. Since I did not have any experience with bribes, I asked him how I could do that. He told me he would show me the way.

We returned to the officers. They looked at him and he winked at them. Both of them left the office. When they went out of the room, the officer told me to put the money under a paper at the corner of the table and come back one hour later. I did as he said. When I returned to the office an hour later, the officers were all there. The one who had told me I would be drafted looked at me and asked what the difficulty was. I repeated what I had told him before. Then he looked at the letter from the Department of Education of Luristan, and he said, "I do not see any problem."

He then issued a letter to the passport office indicating that I could leave the country. It was a relief after so much tension!

I took the letter, along with other documents and photos, to the passport office. They told me it would take some time before my passport was ready. I finally got my passport in March 1964.

United States visa

To apply for a student visa, I took my passport, along with formal letters of support from Mr. Wilson and one of my pen pal friends from New York and a letter of acceptance from the University of Baltimore, to the American

Consulate in Tehran. After an interview, I obtained my long-sought visa. When I got my passport and glanced at my visa, I could hardly believe that I was finally going to go to the United States of America.

Study in America

As soon as I obtained my visa, I returned to Khorramabad to make preparations for my departure. It was an exciting moment for me, but it was a cause for great sadness and mourning for my family, relatives, and friends, who did not know what would happen to me in that distant land.

While working on my passport and visa, I got information on the least expensive way to get to America. I would travel by bus, train, and ship as far as possible, and then fly on Icelandic Airlines, which offered the lowest air ticket from Iceland to New York. Accordingly, I took the TBT bus from Khorramabad to Tehran and from there to Munich, Germany. I had to stay in Munich for ten days, but I do not remember why.

Unexpected offer

While in Munich, I found a room in a pension, which was owned by an old couple who were very friendly towards me. Surprisingly, one day, their secretary—who was a beautiful, young, English-speaking girl—told me that the owners had invited me for dinner. I gladly accepted the invitation and joined them that evening. After dinner, they told me they would like to talk to me about the possibility of staying there and becoming a member of their family. I was not sure what they meant. I asked the young lady who translated our conversation to explain what they meant. They said they had been impressed by my friendly behavior and they would like me to stay here. They said they had no children and they would treat me like their own son. In addition, they mentioned that they owned two pensions, which I could manage when I learned to speak German. Furthermore, they indicated that eventually I would inherit their properties!

I was surprised and thanked them. However, no offer in this world could have changed my mind about going to my dreamland. I thanked them for their kind offer but told them I intended to go to America to continue my education. They told me that I could attend a university in Germany, and they would take care of me. When I told them my friends were waiting for me in America, they said they would pay my expenses to go visit my friends and stay for three months. Again, I politely turned down their offer. Then they said something else, but the young lady just smiled pleasantly without translating what they said. I asked her what they had said. Again, she smiled without telling me anything. Finally, they talked to her again. This time she turned to me and told me that they had said if I stayed there, she would be my girlfriend and we could enjoy our life together. This was an unusually tempting offer, and I thanked them again for being so kind to me, but I told them I must go to America. I did not accept those wonderful offers for two main reasons. First, I thought if I accepted those offers and stayed with them, I would lose my independence. The second reason was my extreme desire to go to America—I could not accept any offer that would prevent or delay my visit.

As I was ready to leave Munich, I talked to those lovely people and sincerely thanked them from my heart for being so nice to me. I could see from their faces that they were very sad. They were already missing me. As I was ready to leave, they hugged and kissed me. They gave me their telephone number and the address of their pension. All of us started weeping as I walked out of the pension. I will never forget that mournful sad moment.

Arrival in New York

In order to reach Reykjavik, the capital of Iceland, I had to travel by train first and then by ship. I spent the night in Reykjavik and flew to America, arriving on March 9, 1964. The view of New York City from the air was magnificent, and the drive from the airport to downtown and eventually to a bus station presented a different reality of life in America than I had imagined.

I went to Baltimore by Greyhound Bus. When I arrived there, Mr. Wilson took me to his house. He gave me a large bedroom to stay in, along with a studying desk, and breakfast, lunch, and dinner every day. In short, I was well treated and comfortable, thanks to the late Mr. Wilson.

University of Baltimore (1964–1966)

I started to study at the University of Baltimore in September 1964. I registered for the associate of arts degree, which consisted of two years of general education, including biology, psychology, economics, history, sociology, French language, political science, American history, English literature, music, and more. That first semester I took five courses of three credits each. Taking into consideration that English was not my native language, I had to work extremely hard. After dinner I studied until three o'clock in the morning and woke by seven o'clock in the morning. In other words, I slept only four hours each night. Once, while we were eating breakfast, Mr. Wilson told me he was worried about my health because I was not resting enough. Nevertheless, I completed the first semester successfully.

When I had become acquainted with the city, I decided to find a place where I could live independently. I found a one-bedroom apartment near John Hopkins University for $20 per month. I continued my education at the University of Baltimore, and I graduated in June 1966.

After graduation, I got my driver's license and bought a secondhand car for $100, and I got a job at the Sun Cab Company. I started driving a taxi during the summer and continued to work part time when school started.

Morgan State University (1966–1968)

While taking various courses at the University of Baltimore, I decided to study sociology. I went to Morgan State University and registered for a bachelor's degree in sociology in September 1966.

University of Maryland (1968–1971)

While I was studying at Morgan State University, I took a course in cultural anthropology, which was interesting and impressed me greatly. Furthermore, while in a secondhand bookstore in Washington, D.C., I came across a copy of E. Adamson Hoebel's *Anthropology: The Study of Man* (1966), which I bought. As a result of reading that book, I chose anthropology as my field of study. I received my bachelor's degree in sociology from Morgan State University in June 1968 and was accepted into the University of Maryland's master's program in anthropology.

Luckily, the University of Maryland provided me with a tuition-free scholarship and also a teaching aid position, for which I received $300 per month. I rented a small apartment in College Park, near the university, and I kept my part time job at Sun Cab in Baltimore and worked during the weekends.

Frank Hole and Justice William Douglas

While I was studying at the University of Maryland, the annual meeting of American Anthropological Association took place in Washington, D.C. While

I was at that meeting, I unexpectedly met Frank Hole. He was surprised to see me and asked me what I was going to do after graduation. I told him I was going to continue working toward a PhD degree. He mentioned the possibility of going to Rice University, where they offered a PhD program in anthropology. I told him I would be glad to join them. That was the opening of a new chapter in my life, because it provided the opportunity to work with Frank for the next few decades.

I also had the honor of meeting the late Supreme Court Justice William O. Douglas in Washington, D.C. Justice Douglas had visited Luristan in 1949, when I was eleven years old. He was the guest of Ahmad Khan, the chief of the Papi Tribe, an affinal relative of Sekandar's family. We waited on the road to welcome him while he was going to Ahmad Khan's summer residence in Taf Mountain, southeast of Khorramabad. He was escorted by a number of American and Iranian officers and high-ranking government officials. Fortunately, he enjoyed his trip, and in 1951 he published a book, *Strange Lands and Friendly Peopl*e, which I have in my library.

While at the University of Maryland, I called him and introduced myself. I told him that I was a graduate student from Luristan and a relative of Ahmad Khan Papi. Amazingly, Justice Douglas remembered him and told me that he would like to see me the next day at ten o'clock in the morning. I took a beautiful small prayer rug and went to his office. He greeted me cordially. While I had a cup of coffee with him, he asked about my life circumstances and my academic activities. He then asked about Ahmad Khan and the political situation of Iran in general. He pointed out that he and others supported Prime Minister Mosadeq, but unfortunately, CIA interference led to the overthrow of the prime minister and the return of the Shah to power. Finally, he told me as long as I was in the U.S., if there was anything he could do for me, I should call him immediately. I told him I was grateful for his kind treatment and felt happy for the opportunity of meeting such a distinguished person. When I stood to leave, he walked me out. I will never forget that meeting. He sent me a letter a few days later, thanking me for the gift I had given him. "Thank you very, very much indeed for the lovely prayer rug which you sent to my office. It is beautiful and something which I shall always cherish. It was exceedingly kind and thoughtful of you to remember me in such a handsome fashion." It was signed, "Yours faithfully, W. O. Douglas, January 11, 1969."

I completed my master's program in anthropology in June 1971. Thanks to Frank, I had already been accepted for the PhD program in anthropology at Rice University in Houston. However, I decided to stay in College Park during the summer vacation and work full time driving a taxi in Baltimore.

I do not remember why I waited until the last minute to go to Houston. When I contacted the anthropology department on Friday and asked about registration, they said it would take place on Monday morning!

Unfortunately, I could not fly to Texas, because I had to take my car and belongings. I packed up my belongings, including a small tent, and left College Park at 11 a.m. on Saturday. I was young and energetic, and I covered the distance between Washington and Houston in 35 hours. When I reached Houston, I went to a city park and pitched my tent. Early Monday morning, I packed my tent and drove to Rice University to take care of my registration. After that, I found an apartment near campus.

Rice University (1971–1974)

Rice University is a private institution and one of the top universities in America; it is very expensive. Fortunately, I received a free tuition scholarship. Also, I was paid $400 for being a teaching assistant, which enabled me to work full time on my PhD degree.

I completed the coursework from September 1971 to 1972. In the meantime, I collaborated with the late Professor Edward Norbeck, the head of the Anthropology Department at Rice, on my first published article, which was entitled "The Luti: an outcast group in Iran" (1975).

Fieldwork (end of 1972 to September 1973)

I chose to write my doctoral thesis about the changes among my tribe, the Baharvand. In the meantime, Frank managed to get a grant for my fieldwork by having me on his project, which was entitled, "The Ethnoarchaeology of Nomadic Pastoralism." I had two tasks on this project. First, I had to make arrangements for Frank's visit to Luristan, which would include migrating with a group of Baharvand from their winter territory to their summer location. This also entailed making arrangements for his visit to various nomadic camps in Luristan and Ilam provinces. In addition, I made arrangements for his excavation at the Tula'i site in Khuzistan (Xuzistan) Province. Second, I had to carry out fieldwork concerning cultural changes among the Baharvand in order to write my PhD dissertation.

Accordingly, I left Houston and went to Darayi at the end of 1972 to conduct research. Frank arrived in February 1973, after which we started traveling to Ilam and Khuzistan, visiting nomadic pastoralist camps as well as archaeological sites.

Migration with nomadic pastoralists

Frank's participation in the spring migration of the Baharvand, while focused on archaeological matters, gave me an opportunity to see the annual migratory route of my ancestors and the activities of the contemporary Baharvand during their migration.

As a student of Frank's, a native of Luristan, and a member of the Baharvand, I was considered Frank's host, and I was concerned about his health and his security. There were all sorts of questions that worried me, such as: Would the foods endanger Frank's health? What would happen if members of a hostile tribe attacked us at midnight in a remote locality? Would Frank survive the long hours of riding a horse in such a steep and mountainous region? Would he be able to sleep well on the ground in a cold tent with the constant barking of dogs and other noises throughout the night?

Frank proved that he was an able horseman, and, as a matter of fact, he tolerated the hardships of nomadic pastoralism better than I. I admit that I consider the nomadic pastoralists' way of life undesirable and full of hardships and difficulties. Traditional nomadic pastoralists who had not experienced the advantages of a modern life probably viewed their way of life as desirable and perhaps superior. However, I have often heard contemporary nomadic pastoralists complain that "God has created them for just suffering from living." The connotation is that they daily suffer a miserable life.

Preparing the PhD dissertation

I returned to Houston in the beginning of September 1973 to write my dissertation. The title of my dissertation was "The Baharvand, Former Pastoralists of Iran." Frank was my thesis adviser. One of the things I remember most clearly about that time was that I worked so hard to complete my thesis that I became severely ill.

When I took a course on anthropological theories with the late Professor Norbeck, he invited me to his office and told me that the competition at Rice University was high, and for that reason some people get ulcers. He pointed out that he already had lost part of his stomach because of an ulcer. He advised me to rest sufficiently and to take care of my health. It was good advice, but I did not follow it carefully enough.

It was 2:30 a.m. on Saturday, October 13, 1973, that I became severely sick. The note in my calendar reads: "This event is the saddest event in all of my life." I could hardly stand up, and I felt dizzy. I could not eat or drink for nearly three days. I had become extremely weak and tired. I went to the hospital and it became clear that I had a severe stomach ulcer. The physician told me I had lost nearly forty percent of my blood. He advised me to rest fully and to eat half-cooked liver, and he prescribed some medicine for me. I followed his instructions fully, and I recovered within several weeks. When he checked me, he was surprised that I had recovered my blood and was getting well. In the meantime, he advised me to rest enough and to avoid eating certain foods.

Life as a professor

Pahlavi University

Two years prior to my graduation at Rice University, Pahlavi University (now Shiraz University) invited me to teach there after getting my PhD. I accepted the invitation and was therefore granted a one-year scholarship (1974) of $300 per month. Accordingly, I returned to Iran after my graduation.

I started teaching as an assistant professor in the Department of Regional Planning and Sociology (currently the Department of Sociology) in the summer of 1974 and continued teaching and research until my untimely retirement in 2005.

Harvard University

In 1985, I had the opportunity of going to the Divinity School at Harvard University as a visiting professor. While there, I prepared a book in collaboration with Professor Wheeler Thackston, who was teaching Farsi (Persian) and Arabic at the Center for Near Eastern Languages and

Civilizations of Harvard University. I helped Wheeler learn the Luri dialect of Luristan, which he did in only four months. We translated material from Luri folklore, which I had collected over the years into a manuscript entitled *Tales from Luristan*. The text is both in Luri and English. It was published by the Harvard Iranian Series in 1986, with an introduction from the late Professor Richard Frye, editor of the Iranian Series (Amanolahi-Baharvand and Thackston 1986).

My affiliation with Harvard has continued over the years. I spent my sabbatical there, as well as two years' leave of absence from Shiraz University. In all, I have been there seven years. I must express my deep gratitude to the late Professor Frye and to Professors William Graham, John Carmen, Byron and Mary-Jo Good, Wheeler Thackston, and C.C. Lamberg-Karlovsky.

I met Professor Frye for the first time in 1975, when he was teaching at the Asian Institute of the Pahlavi University. That meeting was the beginning of a long friendship, which lasted for nearly thirty years. He was very kind to us, and he loved Iran. He wanted to be buried in Isfahan, and he asked me to make the arrangements for his burial. In one of his last trips to Iran, he asked Ahmadinejad, the president of Iran, to let him be buried in Isfahan. Ahmadinejad promised to make the arrangements for his burial there. However, when Professor Frye passed away in 2014 at the age of ninety-four, Ahmadinejad's term had expired, and Professor Frye was accused of spying for the United States against Iran. Under those circumstances, I was unable to do anything.

I must point out that I never noticed anything that led me to think Professor Frye spied against Iran. Unfortunately, I was not in a position to defend him, nor could I do anything about his burial in Iran. I was outside of the influential political circle of the Islamic Republic of Iran, and I had to limit my activities to teaching and research.

Predicting the downfall of the Pahlavi regime (1976)

In the fall semester of 1976, I was teaching a course entitled "The Peoples and Cultures of the Middle East" at Pahlavi University. This was a year prior to the downfall of the Pahlavi regime. One of the students raised his hand and asked about the future of the political condition of Iran. Considering the fact that there were members of the secret police (SAVAK) in classes, this question was not easy to handle. Yet I decided to tell the student what I thought. I said that I was not equipped with supernatural powers that would allow me to predict the future, but that I would share what I thought was going to happen. I also asked those unknown secret agents in the classroom to kindly not add anything to what I was going to say: I hoped they would just report my actual words.

I pointed out that the Shah (King) had made a great mistake in dissolving all political parties and establishing his own party, the Rastakhiz (Resurrection) party. In doing so, he disregarded the Constitutional Law of 1906. I pointed out that political parties are essential for democracy, because the parties unite people and they become politically active and informed through lectures and periodical publications. Further, people get to know about their political leaders through the political parties.

I mentioned that the second mistake of the regime was the censorship of mass media, which deprived people of the truth. Because of this, I said, corruption would expand. I also mentioned that the regime interfered in the elections for the National Assembly and other institutions. Such procedures deprived people from choosing their representatives in various governmental institutions and agencies.

I indicated that under such circumstances, some of the opposition groups had already started guerrilla warfare. However, it was my opinion that the clergy would overthrow the regime and demolish the opposition groups. The student then asked why I thought the clergy would take power, rather than other opposition groups such as Jebhay-i Melli (National Front), Mojahedin-Khalq, or Hezbe Tudeh. I indicated that religion was deeply rooted in every aspect of our culture and it played a great role in our lives. The clergy were in charge of religion and religious activities, which in turn influenced every aspect of our lives. Furthermore, the clergy were spread all over the country, in the villages, towns, and cities. Not only were they present everywhere, they understood the masses psychologically and they talked to them accordingly. In addition, the clergy, unlike the political parties, were informally organized. Modern transportation and modern technology, such as telephones and tape recorders, made it easy to contact each other. In addition, while the government could easily execute or imprison political leaders or simply forbid their political activities, it was not easy for the Pahlavi regime to confront the clergy and their followers in the same manner. The regime did forbid the activities of some of the clergy, including Ayatollah Khomeini and few others, but it was practically impossible to disband the political activities of the clergy totally, because that meant a confrontation with religion. Furthermore, the clergy, unlike the political parties, had informal organizations and were not under a single political leader—rather, there were many leaders.

The clergy had great influence upon the masses through religion and religious activities. Only the clergy were able to organize the masses and bring millions of protestors into the street.

I also pointed out that the clergy claimed that a religious government was the most perfect one, since it was the domain of God. The clergy promised a unique socio-political system—one that was based on divine justice and equality and had no injustice or corruption: in other words, something that did not exist among the world's political systems.

In 2016, the student who had questioned me (by that time a professor himself) wrote down his recollection of the episode.

"In one session in November, when the professor was explaining the structures of government in the Middle East, I asked him if the government of Iran were to change, what group would gain power. 'The clergy,' he answered without hesitation, 'because they are organized.' The professor's reasoning was unsatisfactory for me, because this exchange took place shortly after the 'ten nights of poetry' of the Union of Writers of Iran, and the atmosphere among the enlightened at the university could not tolerate the thought of such a choice. After class I consulted with the professor for him to elaborate further. This time he said in Persian, 'They (the clerics) are organized. They are not an official party or group that can be neutralized.' Now when I remember all that has passed and that discussion, I praise the perspicacity of that dear professor and remember him fondly. Wherever he is, may God protect him." Signed, Dr. Said Kia Kojuri, April 24, 2016.

The university retired me in 2004, three years sooner than expected, as a result of university and department politics. Full professors are retired at the age of seventy, so my early retirement was against policy. Unfortunately, the year after my forced retirement, after many years without faculty raises, the university gave a fifty percent increase to those still on the faculty. I protested to the chancellor and deputy of education of Shiraz University and then to the minister of higher education in Tehran. After that the deputy fired me. I then took the case to the Court of Administrative Justice in 2006. The court issued a verdict that my retirement was illegal, but the verdict was not enforced. In 2012 the court reversed the verdict, finally ending my case. Despite this protracted fight for justice over politics, I have remained dedicated and active in my research.

About ten years ago I decided to establish a charity foundation to support poor students, with the proceeds from the sale of my farm in Luristan. Unfortunately I became the victim of a former friend, who convinced me to invest the money from the sale of my land in his company. When I asked for my money I was put off and then given a check on an account that he had closed. The court in Shiraz ordered him to pay, but he was able to escape to Canada, where he now resides. In spite of this setback, my dream of establishing the charity foundation has not died.

Over the years I have been a visiting professor, scholar, or researcher at many universities, most prominently Harvard, where I visited seven times between 1985 and 2020. I was at the following universities for shorter stays: Aarhus University, London University, Bergen University, Yerevan State University, and Daito Bunka University.

I attribute my successful career to a number of factors. First, I have maintained good health and vigor. Secondly, my innate curiosity, which led me as a child to want to travel to America, has kept me interested and focused on my research. I have always been driven by goals: to learn English, to finish high school, get a university education, create a program in anthropology at Shiraz University, and finally to carry out research among tribal people in Iran. These goals required planning, decisive action, and dedication. I have always been optimistic and have accepted life's ups and downs as "part of life," and I have not let misfortune deter me. My strengths are captured in the Farsi expression: *Tawan ma nehan ast, Nehan a bicran ast.* (Our strength is not visible to us, but it is tremendous and beyond imagination.)

Chapter 3

Luristan: Homeland of the Baharvand

Luristan is an administrative province of western Iran, in the heart of the Zagros Mountain chain, which runs a thousand miles (1,600 km) from Lake Van in the northwest to the Persian Gulf in the southeast. This mountainous region is the traditional homeland of many tribes of former pastoral nomads. "Traditional ethno-geographic divisions of the Zagros Highland have real significance, for the lands of the various tribal groups are different. Each has a character of its own. Accordingly, Kurdistan, Luristan, the Bakhtiari, Kuhgalu, and Fars are distinctive geographic entities in a physical sense as well as an ethnic sense" (Oberlander 1965:9). Ethnically, the inhabitants of Bakhtiari, Kuhgilyu and Boyer-Ahmad, and Mamasani are Lurs, whose territories are defined by natural boundaries and tradition (Figure 3.1). Each group has a locally distinct dialect, yet all speak Luri, which is based on New Persian, an Indo-European language stock with roots that go back several thousand years. The dialects are not intelligible to speakers of Farsi, the

Figure 3.1. Locations of the prominent subdivisions of the Lurs.

official language of Iran. Historically, the Lurs' territory was divided into Luristan Kuchek and Luristan Buzorg (little and greater Luristan). The tribe that concerns this book is in the easternmost territory of Little Luristan, known as Bala Griveh. "The land south of Khorramabad, the principal city of Luristan, is enclosed on three sides by the Kashgan, the Karkheh (that is, the southern reaches of the Saimarreh) and the Dez, up to and including the southern tail of the Garin range" (Black-Michaud 1986:12). This is the territory of several tribes, including the Baharvand, the tribe with which we migrated (Figure 3.2).

The landscape and climate

Most of Luristan is mountainous, but it also stretches across the northern part of Khuzistan, which has been winter pasture to numerous Luri tribes. The successive folded ridges and narrow valleys of the Zagros Mountains rise abruptly from the Khuzistan plain, advancing like a series of stair steps with increasing elevation to the 3,000-meter heights of the Zardeh Kuh in the interior of Iran (Figure 3.3) (Oberlander 1965). The unusual series of northwest-southeast trending ridges are a consequence of the enormous pressure that resulted from the Arabian plate sliding under the Eurasian plate, which folded the latter like an accordion (Haynes and McQuillan 1974) (Figure 3.4). The amount of deformation along the Zagros chain gives rise to the unique qualities of each segment. The extent of folding determines the size of the valleys between ridges, and the rivers that drain and water them. The rivers in the Zagros seemingly defy the natural lay of the land, abruptly cutting through the ridges via a series of narrow, steep-sided gorges (tangs) rather than following the valleys. This effect arose when the folding occurred under preexisting rivers, whose erosive power offset the pace of uplift. Luristan is in the heart of this chain of mountain ridges. In Bala Griveh, the ridge tops are from 5000 to 7000 feet above sea level, and they are often covered with snow for several months in mid-winter. While rivers are often absent in the valleys, ultimately all the waters of Luristan drain through gorges to the major rivers—the Kashgan/Saimarreh/Karkheh, the Dez, and the Karun—which debauch on the plains of Khuzistan.

Throughout recorded history, Luristan has been a separate geographic and cultural unit, distinct from other parts of Iran in its topography and people. It is a difficult country. Much of the territory is naturally wooded, though

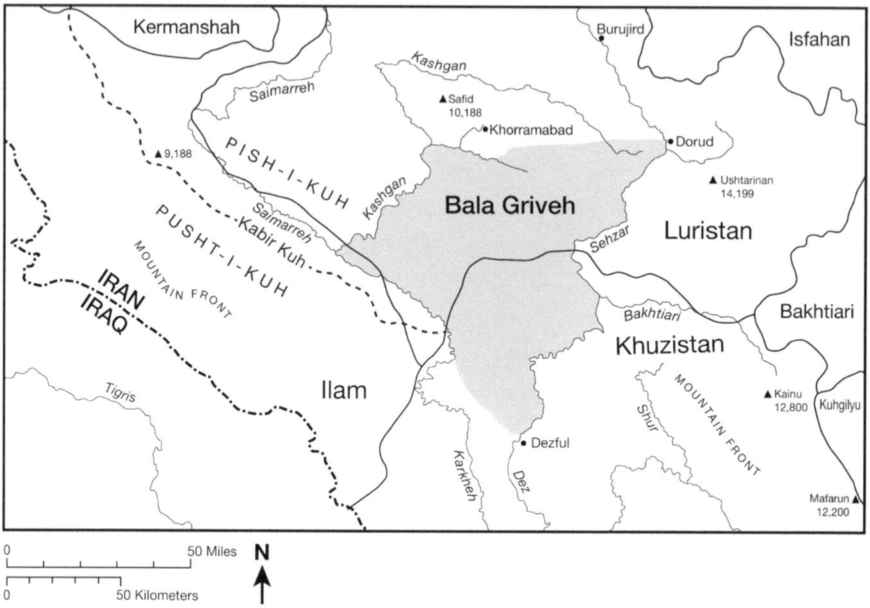

Figure 3.2. The territory of Bala Griveh, homeland of the Baharvand Lur tribe.

only stunted trees grow today. The land suffers from a sharp seasonal cycle of winter snow and rainfall and summer drought, with extremes of summer heat and winter cold. In some years, the parched autumn grasses scarcely regenerate in the spring before the searing winds and relentless sun dry them once again. In other years, the grass grows deep enough to impede travel on horseback, and entire valley floors become shallow lakes. After heavy rains, the shallow-rooted, overgrazed vegetation on the rocky hill slopes does little to forestall the rush of mud into swollen streams, where its fertility is eventually spread onto the sterile salt marshes of Khuzistan, far short of the sea.

Luristan has a continental version of the Mediterranean climate, in which summers are hot and dry (110°F or 45°C) and winters are cold and wet. Depending on the year, winter may bring blizzards, heavy snow, and flooding; dry years may result in widespread drought and loss of crops and forage. With either extreme, considerable loss of livestock can occur, and

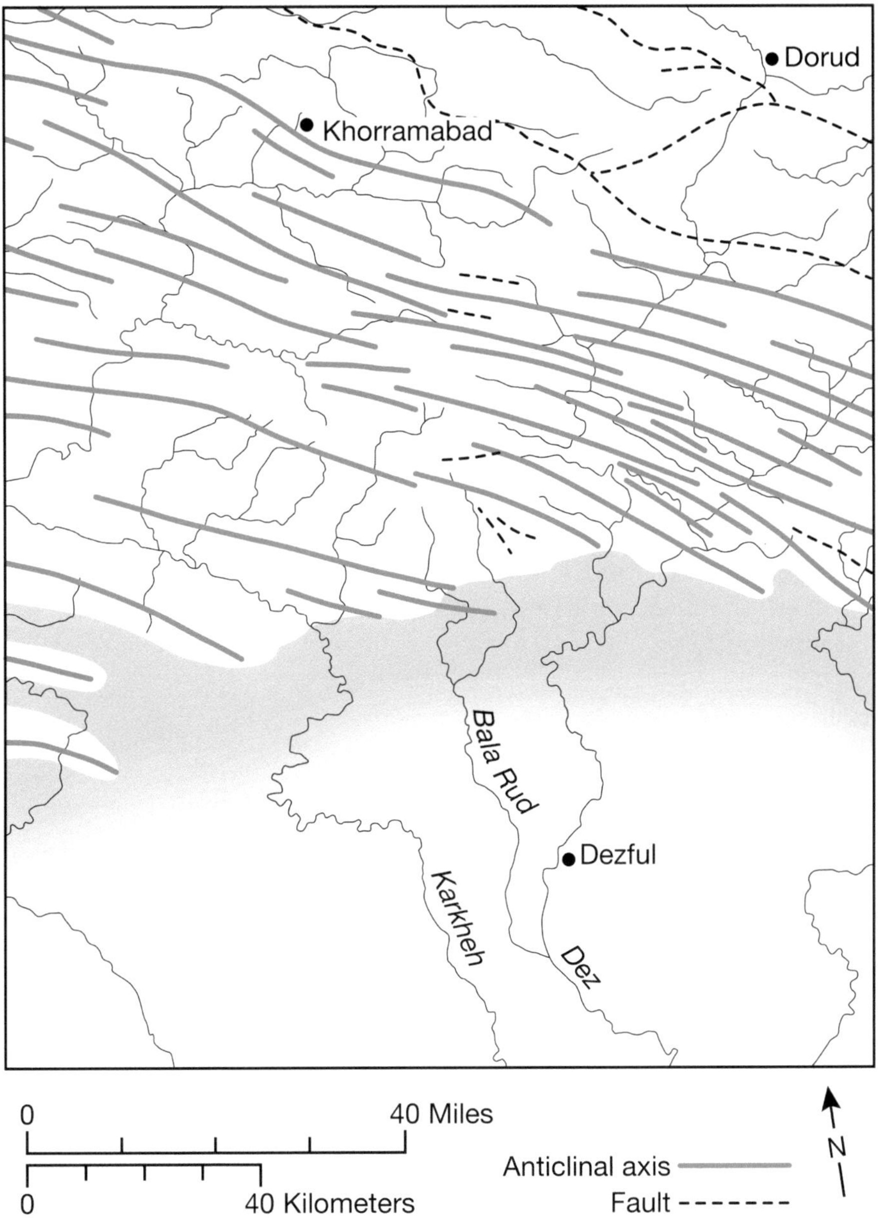

Figure 3.3. Luristan is composed of a series of anticlinal ridges, squeezed accordion-like by the Arabian continental plate sliding under the Eurasian plate. From Khuzistan to Khorramabad, the ridges and valleys ascend in height.

humans suffer accordingly. These difficulties appear in historical records. "In the *yailaqs* [summer pasture] this year there is no spring rain for the grass. It will be a hard year, God protect us" (Garthwaite [1983] 2009:161).

Weather is also tied to the incursion of locusts, which can ravage crops. In 1878, a drought year, "Countless locusts came to 'Arabistan. In all 'Arabistan and Bakhtiari mountains they bred...10 days before Aid Nau Ruz, [March 21] there is not grass enough in all 'Arabistan and the Bakhtiari for the sheep to eat their fill...God have mercy on us" (Garthwaite [1983] 2009:160). The locusts came again the following year (1879; 1296 AH): "This was the year of sheep dying, and many sheep in all the Bakhtiari and other places have perished" ...This year [too] many locusts came to 'Arabistan, and have hatched many young. God knows how it will end" (Garthwaite [1983] 2009:160).

While uncertainty about the weather is a constant for people living on self-made subsistence, there is also predictability. The lowlands will always be hot in summer and the highlands cold; hence the need to move seasonally. When the grass dies in Khuzistan, it thrives in the mountains. When snow envelopes the mountain pastures, Khuzistan's warmth fosters the renewed growth of pastures.

Bala Griveh

> The extreme insularity for which the Zagros people are famed is traceable to this characteristic of the terrain. Communications in these mountains are unusually difficult, for riverine routes are disrupted by bottlenecks whose rock walls rise vertically out of boiling torrents that are frequently impossible to negotiate. Impassable gorges together with steep mountain walls and serrate crestlines so compartmentalize the country that trunk streams occasionally have different names above and below a single defile. (Oberlander 1965:9)

The fragmented landscape of Bala Griveh requires that pastoral nomads cross over rather than go around most of the ridges as they migrate. Outside Khorramabad and a few agricultural valleys, there were no permanent

Figure 3.4 (opposite page). Seen by satellite, Bala Griveh is mostly mountainous, with only narrow valleys between the ridges.

Khorramabad
Darayi
Kialon Kuh
Chin-i Zal
0
10 mi
0
10 kilometers
N

settlements in Bala Griveh in 1973. In fact, were there no nomads, whose peregrinations take them across the most barren and remote sectors of this inhospitable landscape, humans would scarcely visit much of the Zagros. For settled populations, the welling up of springs and the flowing of rivers through tillable lands provide the spark of life that sustains each generation in turn. For the nomad, it is the stream of animals who timelessly migrate from pasture to pasture, from barren plain to craggy mountainside, that provide the needs for today and the hope for tomorrow. The contrast between the desert and the sown, between the nomad and the farmer, between the mountains and the valleys, stands in sharp relief, yet these are complementary ways of life that made higher civilization possible. Between them exists a mutual interdependence born of necessity, and a latent hostility born of the different rhythms, demands, and customs that these different lives engender.

> None of the three other main territories in Luristan is as sparsely populated as Bala Giriveh [sic], where gypsum outcrops and associated brackishness of the water make for a difficult environment. Although extremes of cold, the rockiness of the terrain, and the shortness of the growing season obviously limit the feasibility of planting crops much above the 2000-metre contour, it may not be so readily appreciated that high summer temperatures can constitute a deterrent to permanent settlement in the lowlands which is almost as compelling. Thus a lack of shade and good fresh water, combined with temperatures which frequently exceed 45°C, make goodly tracts of southern Bala Giriveh rather less than tolerable from after harvest in late May to early September (Black-Michaud 1986:14)

Much of the quality and beauty of Luristan lies in contrasts and change. It is a stark, rugged landscape that changes with the light and passing seasons. Luristan's bold mountain ridges march in ranks under broad, bright skies, testimony to the awesome squeezing pressures that created these accordion folds a million years ago. During the day, light plays on the ridges. Day by day, the ridges change their form and mood, as the sun's angle follows its annual cycle. As green growth turns to brown and the mountains are covered with snow, the character of Luristan changes.

There is a certain splendor in the searing sun that has lost its form in the haze of summer's dust, and in the full moon that is coldly, crisply luminescent amidst the glitter of countless stars. In summer, rivers move sluggishly through their baking rocky beds. Suffocating streams of dust-laden air drawn up from Khuzistan's infernally hot plains hang heavy in the atmosphere. Toward summer's end, a brief rain shower may introduce a blessed freshness and flash of cool to the choking air. In winter, the icy blasts of howling winter winds bring blankets of snow one day that may disappear the next under the sun's warm radiation and give rise to a myriad of sparkling rivulets that eventually cause fields to burst forth green. With spring, melting mountain snows bring raging floods that fill canyons with an awesome roar as the majestic, tumultuous rush of water sprays high above the boulders and cliffs that line the river channels. In time, the rivers calm, and the shimmering water splashes among the rocks while fragile pink almond blossoms whisper in the wind against the ancient and rocky slopes above.

Viewed from the high spots, the emptiness of this land can be overwhelming. One sees no asphalt highways or road signs; no steel spans the rivers that meander through the countryside. The only indicators of direction are the signs of nature. There are no skyscrapers, no houses, and no buildings. Not even a farm dots the landscape. No power lines or fences trespass into this vast territory. But soon the practiced eye detects the faint line of a dirt trail winding up the side of a rocky hill, and then another—paths through the mountains trodden for millennia by sheep and goats and the people who herd them. By and by one detects a person, carrying water or driving his flocks. This person will lead the eye to a small cluster of black tents, barely visible.

Historical accounts of Luristan's landscape and wildlife

Under modern conditions, Luristan is poorly endowed with natural resources. This is particularly true of Bala Griveh. In the 1970s, when we joined the migration, only vestiges of the forests remained, and the once-abundant wild game had largely been extirpated. To gain an appreciation for what once existed there, we consider the writings of early travelers, who tell how different the conditions were a hundred or more years ago. Some of the plants and animals they encountered no longer exist in the mountains of Luristan.

In 1840, Baron Clement Augustus De Bode, first secretary of the Russian Legation in Tehran, traveled through parts of Luristan. Regarding natural resources, Baron De Bode was the most observant of any of the travelers. Below are his notes on some of the plants he noticed.

Near Behbehan: "The meadows are covered with narcissuses, and another bulbous plant, with a root as large as a strong muscular fist, and called by the natives *piyaz*, (onion)" (De Bode 1845b:377).

De Bode sent one of these roots to the botanical gardens in St. Petersburg and it bloomed with blue and white flowers.

The *konar*, a tree in Kuhgilyu territory: "On quitting Basht…a valley full of oaks, wild almond trees in blossom, and the Kuhnar, a tree peculiar to the south of Persia…The fruit of this tree, something like that of the servis (Sorbus domestica), is yellow when ripe, slightly acid, and pleasant to the taste. When unripe, it is green and red" (De Bode 1845b:253:fn1). These, along with Spina Christi (see below) grew near our camp on the Deh Luran Plain in the 1960s.

Spina Christi, near Shapur's cave and Kazerun: "cluster of trees, among which the Gercheck (Rhicinus Palma Christi, from which castor-oil is extracted), grows wild, and instead of being a plant, resembles a moderate-sized tree, from twelve to fourteen feet in height" (De Bode 1845b:207).

Flowers and grass in Sha'b-bevan: "My sense of smell was agreeably affected by the perfume of the narcissus, spread like a white carpet over the field, for the space of many miles. All our party pushed into this rich parterre up to their horses' girths, to enjoy the fragrance as much as possible" (De Bode 1845b:233).

The Plain of Lishtar: "It was in these meadows that a part of the stud of the former Ferman-Ferma (Governor) of Fars, was kept, on account of the abundance of grass, with which these are covered in the spring" (De Bode 1845b:260).

Acorns among the tribes of Kuhgilyu: "Their usual food is the acorn, which is first bruised between two stones, and made into flour, by being dried in the sun. The women bake cakes of this flour. The paste is likewise eaten raw, and is considered very nourishing" (De Bode 1845b:283–284). Commenting on a Bakhtiari man who went as his guide, De Bode wrote:

> His only provision for the journey was a bag filled with the moist flour, or raw paste of the acorn, which he obligingly offered me to taste, and was surprised at my not relishing it. In the Bakhtiari mountains it forms the principal food of the wandering tribes. I think I have noticed elsewhere, that their women gather the acorns as they drop ripe from the trees, and bruise them between two stones, in order to extract the bitter juice: they then wash the flour, and dry it

> in the sun, and this is the whole process. They either bake cakes of it, or eat the paste raw, and find it excellent (De Bode 1845b:395).

Another European, Lieutenant A. T. Wilson, scouted Luristan Bozorg in 1911 for military and political reasons, after the discovery of oil in Bakhtiari country. He too wrote about eating acorn bread.

> I have noticed whenever we were riding that the Khan and his sons always looked to see how the acorns were ripening, for acorn bread is here a staple food in bad seasons for everyone – in good seasons for the poorer tribesmen. I have eaten little else here. The acorns are ground with a boulder on a great slab of rock and the flour or rather fibre left to soak in running water for two days or so to get the poison out of it. Then it is used like barley flour, or mixed with it. The product is harder than barley bread and needs a lot of chewing: it is also liable to constipate even a horse which is not used to it – but I have stomached it successfully! (Wilson 1941:65)

Captain C. J. Edmonds kept a diary of his travels in 1917, with notes on the people and landscape, although the places he named are often hard to find on maps. Edmonds scouted routes that might be used for commercial traffic. He identified one: the Zal bridge–Dalich road that ran from Dezful to Khorramabad (Edmonds 1922). This was essentially the route we traveled on migration—almost sixty years after Edmonds's visit. The details he gives are some of the best evidence we have of the quality of the countryside and its resources at that time. Edmonds also talks about the food he ate, including acorn bread.

> To-day I sampled acorn bread for the first time. In colour it is blackish tinged with green; the taste is musty and unpleasant, but in justice to the Lur it must be added that it is usual to mix a small proportion of wheat flour with it. Acorn bread is very indigestible, and too much causes acute constipation (Edmonds 1917:30)

> The valley was green with maize cultivation of the Judeki…I had a meal of savoury kebab of kidneys with roasted corn cobs, but these last were not rendered more appetizing by being rubbed in the grimy hands and blown with the doubtful breath of the Lurs to remove the blacks (Edmonds 1917:31)

Of the Kialon Pass, Edmonds said that a hajji (a man who has made the pilgrimage to Mecca) from the Mir tribe told him how difficult it was and that "he had given ten tumans to everyone who helped to carry the loads" (Edmonds 1917:25). Edmonds's troop stopped for the night at Beringe Kar, where dwarf oak and myrtle began to appear (with the increase in elevation). On the first of September, he "left Birinjaar [Beringe Kar] at 4 a.m. The Kiyalun pass is steep, the path narrow and winding. I had taken the precaution of mounting a mule, so accomplished the ascent in comfort. Reached the top of the pass at 4:40" (Edmonds 1917:29). Proceeding farther into the mountains, he said, "The Dalich pass is for the most part easy going over stones of blinding white. A small spring flows down it and near the top, just above the spring, are the remains of an old watch tower, several pomegranate trees belonging thereto, and signs of road-making, dating back beyond the time of Nazim-i-Khalavat" (Edmonds 1917:29).

This is probably the pomegranate grove that we saw (see Chapter 6).

As these travelers navigated the land, they often commented on the trees, which were once much more abundant—even just a few decades before our visit. One of these explorers, J. V. Harrison, was a field geologist employed by the Ango-Persian Oil Company. In 1934–1935, shortly after the pacification of the Luri tribes, he undertook to survey, with plane table, the entirety of Pish-i Kuh. His maps formed the basis for many of our surveys.

"In 1934 the motor road along the Kashgan had just opened up virgin woods to the rape of the charcoal burners, who felled and burnt the trees and loaded the product on to the lorries running empty to the railhead at Andimeshk" (J. V. Harrison 1946:66).

"On the east side the plateau overlooks Sehzar; on the north-east it fades into the outskirts of the Khurramabad plain. The whole lies between 5000 and 6000 feet, and is unusually thickly wooded (Plate 5) … How much fauna lives in the region is best discovered after a fresh fall (of snow), when the trails of many animals cross it. The rock partridge, which is the most common of all game, is at a real disadvantage in soft snow. Normally the birds are great runners and rise reluctantly. They can do neither in soft snow, and are relatively easily captured" (J. V. Harrison 1946:67).

"In the larger valleys, dense thickets of rushes shelter pigs by day and innumerable birds by night" (J. V. Harrison 1946:68).

Wild game

Game once consisted of wild goats and sheep, both edible, and animals to be feared, such as lions, bears, and leopards, all of which were reported to be abundant in the past. For example, Baron De Bode, whose travels in 1840 skirted the heart of Luristan, but did cross the *garmsir* (winter pasture in Khuzistan), reported, "There are lions and leopards in the plain of Kazerun." He mentions wild game on several other occasions: "A desert tract called Mohur, extending towards the Persian Gulf, inhabited only by lions, wild boars and antelopes..." and "Lions are seldom known to attack men in these parts; they generally fall on cattle. This is near Imamzadeh Baba-Ahmad. A little further on at a river crossing choked up with reeds, 'lions hide themselves during the day.' " De Bode also mentioned the famous "lion tombs" of the Bakhtiar, as well as birds. "The thickness of box on the plain afford shelter to wild boars, pheasants, and the turaj. This bird is smaller than the pheasant, and is black, with white spots. Its meat is tender as that of the pheasant, and of a superior flavour." He had seen the same bird in the Caucasus and Central Asia (De Bode 1845b:200–401).

Gene Garthwaite, author of *Khans and Shahs: A History of the Bakhtiyari Tribe in Iran* (2009), compiled the history through documents and extensive interviews with members of the leading families. Garthwaite, like Hole, had his first experience in Iran with Braidwood's archaeological team in 1958–1959.

In a diary written in 1873 (AH 1290), Husain Quli Khan Ilkhan, head of the Bakhtiari, wrote, "I went to Malamir for several days hunting wild boar. We killed 250 head of wild boar. The group that went against the Bahmanh'i killed 460 boar in two days at Gulgir on Kuh Asmari."

The following year, he wrote of other hunting excursions. "At Asmari we killed 200 head of game." "I went to the mountains for five days' hunting and we killed 20 head of game." "I was in Dizful hunting gazelles, and we killed many." "I left Malamir for hunting at Kuh Asmari, where we killed 200 head of game."

In 1877 (AH 1294), he was at Ab Bid. "Every day we hunted gazelles, and of course every time we rode out we killed 50 head of gazelle" (Garthwaite [1983] 2009:149–153).

One may expect some exaggeration in Quli Khan's accounts, but considering that he always hunted with a large entourage of riflemen, it is likely that they did engage in mass killings.

More than once Edmonds refers to large herds of gazelles and pigs. (Edmonds 1917:32).

During one of my earlier stays in Iran, I was told that some of the military had shot 50 boars from a helicopter. (I have seen the damage that even a small herd of boars can do in rooting out edible vegetation.) When we had our archaeological camp in Deh Luran, there were still herds of gazelle. They were hunted by Arabs who brought falcons to aid them. In 1959–1960, I saw small herds of wild sheep on the Kermanshah plain, and I watched one of the Laki hunters shoot a wild goat with his muzzleloader rifle. Bears were still found and feared in the mountains and occasionally mauled a person, and I watched a wolf hamstring a donkey outside a village. Hyenas howled at night and lurked near refuse dumps and around our camp in Deh Luran.

Products of Luristan

Luristan has relatively few resources of more than local commercial value today, other than pastures and patches of arable land. In the past, however, a modest commerce was sustained, as noted by the European travelers.

According to Wilson, most valuable were mules: "which this province produces in greater numbers and of finer quality perhaps, than any other part of Persia," but he noted that the supply among different tribes was uneven (Wilson 1911:54). Wool, *ghi* (clarified butter) and skins were next in importance. Gum tragacanth and *gaz* (tamarisk sap, used in sweets) were collected and sold, and oak bark, galls, and oak leaves for tanning were exported, as well as charcoal and firewood (Wilson 1911:54).

De Bode also wrote about the use of natural resources in commerce. "Khorramabad carried on a trade in chubuks [cherry wood] for pipes; in otter-skins, as this animal is found in all the rivers of Luristan and Kurdistan; in the juice of the pomegranate, the produce of its gardens, where fine grapes likewise grow" (De Bode 1845a:256–257).

"The forests of Luristan, as well as those of the Bakhtiari, produce wild cherry-trees, which are cut for chubuks, or pipe-tubes, and exported to Baghdad...Otter-skins, and the bladder of the animal, form likewise an article of trade" (De Bode 1845a:293).

"The country furnishes the bazaars of Burujird, Nehevand, Hamadan, and Kermanshah, with mutton, cheese, and butter, from their numerous flocks, and with a large quantity of charcoal, which is prepared in the woody part of Luristan, and transported on the backs of oxen and donkeys." Also mules, and "carpets from the wool of their flocks, and of felt coverings for horses" (De Bode 1845a:292).

Before sugar could be purchased in the bazaars, honey provided sweets. Wilson came across a donkey load of honey, near Khorramabad.

> The honeycombs, broken from the straw bee-keps or skeps of the type seen in England in my boyhood, were cylindrical in form, some 6 inches in diameter and 8 or 4 inches high, made completely airtight by layer after lay of mud made with finely powdered straw and a little plaster of Paris so hard and firm that it turned the edge of a knife. It was as effective as any tin and more resistant to rough usage than most. I bought several of them and carried them with me loose in a saddle-bag for weeks (Wilson 1941:253).

It is likely that bee hives were kept in village houses as they are today (Watson 1979:115–116), and made available to nomads for trade or sale. Needless to say, any large-scale keeping of bees requires adequate flowering plants.

"The Bakhtiari traded local produce consisting of charcoal, gallnuts, tobacco, cherry wood for pipestems, gum tragacanth, and wild animal skins —including fox, bear, and marten—for wheat and barley" (Garthwaite [1983] 2009:23). They also collected wild celery for personal use and trade.

In the next chapter we consider the people of Luristan and the lifeways of pastoral nomads, and we examine what little is known about their prehistory and history.

Chapter 4

The Pastoral Nomads of Luristan

In this chapter we explore what is known about Luristan's pastoral nomads: their lifestyle and their history. What we know of the prehistory of the region comes from archaeologists; what we know of written history comes from a range of sources, including the work of historians and ethnographers, the records of European travelers, and a handful of documentary films.

Pastoral nomadism

In essence, pastoral nomadism means taking livestock from pasture to pasture, normally in response to the seasonal weather and growth of forage. This is a common practice worldwide and is known as transhumance. In some cases, mobility may cover short distances—as little as a day's trek—if topography juxtaposes suitably different environments. While such situations exist in western Iran, more typically herders in Luristan take days or weeks to move in the spring from the lowland pastures to those in the high mountains and reverse the migration in the fall. When conditions are suitable, transhumant herders may also plant crops in both the winter and summer territories. Far from having a life of unfettered freedom, pastoralists follow a rigid cycle that ensures pastures for their herds and security from farmers as well as pastoralists of other tribes.

The nomads' way of life is marked by the use of moveable shelters, heavy dependence on animal products for subsistence, the use of only minimal technology and equipment, the grouping of several families together in camps, and the movement of these camps across territory held in common by the tribes of which they are a part. In pastoral societies, people generally trace their descent from a single ancestor. Some branches of the family are more highly ranked because of primacy of birth. There is an emphasis on warfare and raiding, and an ethic that disparages the farmer and distrusts all outsiders.

The tent camps of herders may contain 20–30 people and are often a kilometer or more from each other. To Westerners, the isolation in this life is hard to imagine. The geographic isolation arises of necessity, for this is poor land, lacking sufficient water and arable soil and suffering from extremes of weather. But for all the apparent solitude of small camps scattered over vast plains or nestled in remote mountain niches, the life of the nomad is preeminently social. Nomads may perfectly well pass all their days without ever having spent a single one of them alone.

Most nomadic peoples place a high value on hospitality, less out of a sense of morality than out of a thirst for news in their sparsely populated land, and in the hope that when the roles of visitor and host are reversed, similar respect will be accorded. There is a sense of honor in the display of hospitality. Tribal leaders are generous even if they are impoverished as a result of entertaining, for to refuse hospitality to a stranger would be to cast dishonor upon the host and his entire tribe as well as upon the guest. Thus it is said, "The true nomad is a poor nomad" (Lattimore [1940] 1962).

The tribes are distinguished from each other by dialect, dress, and customs. An experienced observer can readily recognize members of different tribes by their headgear, clothing, and footwear even without hearing them speak. Physical appearance also varies; the shape of the eyes, nose, stature, and even gait serve to distinguish members of different tribes and to testify to their isolation from one another.

In the early history of Persia, the political base of the Achaemenid Empire 550–330 BC) was composed of tribes whose representatives can still be seen carved in sharp detail upon the grand staircase of Darius's capital at Persepolis, bearing tribute to their king of kings, the supreme leader of their tribes. The Persepolitan reliefs capture the power and the glory of tribal life and its pivotal role in the history of Southwest Asia. The tribe lies at the core of the traditional monarchies, some of which still claim descent from the time of Mohammad, the founder of Islam. In few places today, however, do the tribes remain either independent or very influential. With the advent of modern arms and communication, they have been forced to yield to centralized governments whose traditions derive less from tribal patterns than from European and Asiatic models. The tribes of Iran no longer retain economic or political leverage because oil and the commodities its wealth can buy have relegated their animal products to secondary importance.

Today the great tribes are little more than memories. But in the tents of the pastoral nomads, a vestige of tribal life prevails, in spite of the political and economic circumstances of the surrounding world. The irreducible, and perhaps irreplaceable, unit necessary to sustain the production of livestock over much of Southwest Asia has always been the pastoral camp. Under its leader, each camp is a microcosm of tribal life in the large. The concerns of individual camps are the concerns of tribal nomads everywhere, and the methods of dealing with social and political circumstances in the small camps are no different from those used in the great audience halls of ancient palaces. Only the scale varies, for the ways of coping are political, and the means are force or its threat.

Forces over which the nomads have no control threaten the continued existence of tribal pastoralism. Tribal territories are appropriated for highways, communication networks, power transmission, forest and soil conservation, and massive agricultural development, thereby dislodging the herders from their traditional grazing land. The rising cost of supplies and the disappearance of local handicraft industries in favor of manufactured goods have left many nomads barely able to survive economically. Moreover, incessant increases in population have brought new settlers to occupy tribal lands, with a consequent acceleration of erosion, deforestation, and fouling of the environment. Policies of universal education, coupled with expanding opportunities for jobs in towns and cities, have undermined the value of traditional life. The rugged flexibility of the nomads to adapt to changing circumstances is undergoing its greatest test, and the outcome is in doubt.

Better than some areas of Iran, and worse than others, Luristan occupies a middle ground between the cities of the Iranian plateau and those of Khuzistan—a middle ground that can be circumvented only by laborious detours. The area has served as a buffer, a no-man's-land between political enclaves that are frequently at odds. Far more important than its ability to support productive populations is the role of Luristan in the political aspirations of rulers from outside, who have sought to control both the wild native peoples and the crucial mountain passes and routes that cross their countryside.

Luristan occupies critical land between lowland Mesopotamia, the Persian Gulf, and the commercial and political capitals of the Iranian plateau. Its difficult terrain has, until recent times, precluded effective control by outsiders, with only brief exceptions. The Medes and Persians and even Alexander the Great were frustrated by the tribes of Elam, as were the Mongols later. Outsiders have seldom been a match for the tribes of Luristan, and this painful realization has caused the armies of empires to fight with slander and deception when their swords proved ineffective, impugning the morals and intellect of peoples they could not subdue, and turning one tribe against another.

For as long as we have any written records or traces of legend, Luristan has been contested, seldom left in peace long enough to develop its own base of political power or higher culture. Throughout this time, Luristan has supported mostly nomadic peoples. Only during rare periods of political calm has farming spread outside the limits of small villages in the most fertile of the valleys. For the nomads of Luristan, the vicissitudes of political fortune are no more remarkable than the predictable violence of nature's own periodic rages. To the outsider, Luristan has been an unavoidable evil, a hostile land fit for only these wild, shadowy people.

Although the Lurs have fared badly in fact and in legend, they remain a strong and proud people whose way of life has been forged in the crucible of necessity and cast in the mold of tradition. It is a society based on cooperative families of herders who pass their nights under black tents woven of goat hair and who spend their days under the open skies guiding their sheep and goats from pasture to pasture. In the process they enjoy both the spirit of freedom and sustenance for their bodies.

As expressed by Professor Firoozi, as late as 1970, "There are about 3,000,000 tribal members living a nomadic or semi-nomadic life in various regions of Iran. They are reluctant to change and to adopt ways of life more in line with the political, economic and social goals of Iran. Their tribal system is an impediment to rapid growth and modernization of the country. One may disagree with an authoritarian policy of sedentarization, but Iran could not afford to be indifferent to tribal insurrection and adopted a way to deal with the problem" (Firoozi 1970:226).

A thoughtful rebuttal to this by Philip Salzman emphasizes the value of pastoralism to the economy of Iran and its ability to utilize resources that are not suited to agriculture. "Nomadism allows use of areas when they are usable and the avoidance of areas when they are not usable. Given technological limits, areas can be thus exploited, which would otherwise provide no sustenance for human populations. In this perspective, nomadic movement can be understood as a tool that groups of people use in making their living" (Salzman 1971). He goes on, "tribesmen have not maintained their adaptation to be stubborn, but because with the available technology and the conditions of the environment, nomadic pastoralism is a viable adaptation" (Salzman 1971:330).

Prehistory

Archaeological remains show that Luristan was first occupied by people who left traces of their presence in caves and rockshelters as long ago as 50,000 years (Hole and Flannery 1967). For the next 40,000 years, small camps of hunters continued to live in the mountains and valleys. But around 12,000 years ago, we find traces of the first domestic livestock, chiefly goats. From this beginning, the pastoral way of life in modern Luristan grew. At about the same time, people began to plant wheat and barley and live in small villages on fertile bottomlands, where there was enough rainfall to grow their crops. In these remote periods, Luristan appears to have been thinly populated and peaceful (Hole 1987). The essential unity of the region and its difference from surrounding areas are evident in the pottery and other artifacts found on the surfaces of archaeological sites (Hole 2017).

Around 5,000 years ago, the archaeological remains begin to show influences from more rapidly advancing areas like Mesopotamia. New kinds of pottery and larger structures, sometimes small villas or palaces, appeared in Luristan for the first time (Haerinck 1986). There are hints that even at this early period, northern Luristan had become an important crossroads for trade. But the crucial change came with the intrusion into Iran of Indo-European-speaking peoples, who brought with them the horses that provided the mobility required by nomadic life as we know it today (Potts 2014). Although this is conventional wisdom, we should not forget that donkeys, still the prime beasts of burden, were bearing loads in Mesopotamia 5000 years ago, well before the introduction of horses from Central Asia.

By 1000 BC, parts of Luristan were occupied by groups of mounted warriors. Their tombs, which contained bronze horse trappings and weapons, became the archaeological hallmark of the era. Despite the large numbers of so-called "Luristan Bronzes" that have been looted from tombs, and in the absence of settlements, there is no agreement on who the horsemen were and exactly when in the first millennium BC they died. The best guess is the bronzes were made and used in the first half of the millennium, having disappeared by Achaemenid times (Haerinck 2012; Muscarella 1989). At this time, the tribes of Luristan were nominally within the political sphere of Elam, a powerful civilization whose capital was located at Susa, sixty-five miles from the mountains of Luristan on the flat Khuzistan plain. That the Elamites had much control over the people of Luristan is doubtful. More likely, only trade routes circumventing Bala Griveh were secured, leaving most of the country effectively outside of immediate influence, a situation that prevailed until recently.

In fact, because no convenient route crosses the region, most commerce, immigrations of outside peoples, and wars of conquest took place on the periphery of Luristan, especially along the Khorasan Road, which led from Baghdad past Kermanshah to Hamadan. This route passes through large fertile valleys and major cities of Pish-i Kuh, northern Luristan. To the south, a route passed through Bakhtiari country, through Behbehan to Shiraz. Other routes lay still farther to the north, ending in the Lake Urumiya basin. Most of this mountainous territory is considered part of Kurdistan today. The main commercial artery from Baghdad to Tehran today follows the Khorasan Road through northern Luristan. This route was followed as early as Achaemenian times (555–330 BC) and was suited to the king's use of wheeled carriages. By contrast, the routes to the south were difficult and were only intermittently accessible until the late nineteenth century. Thus the heartland of Luristan remained largely undisturbed by external interests.

The Sasanian period is represented particularly well in Khuzistan. In AD 244, the Sasanians defeated Valerian's Roman army and put the captured soldiers to work. Their greatest achievement was the hydraulic system: a dam/roadway, irrigation canals, and water-driven mills, which still stand as a UNESCO World Heritage Site. The bridge crossing the Dez River is attributed to Shapur I, as is the building of Jundi Shapur, the world's first "university" and center of medieval medicine. It was also Shapur's military garrison and capital. Until recently, the inauspicious mud-brick ruins of Jundi Shapur occupied land used as summer pasture by migratory Luri tribes. In Luristan itself, there are numerous stone foundations of towns and agricultural terraces that can be found wherever irrigation agriculture is possible, even in narrow and secluded valleys. These have been well studied in the Deh Luran Valley, just to the north of Khuzistan (Neely 1974; Neely and Wright 1994). Apparently the powerful, highly organized Sasanian administration, based in Khuzistan, sent colonists and engineers into underdeveloped parts of their empire to reshape the land. Although it is known that the Sasanians appointed a governor of Luristan and Khuzistan, no records of his administration have been recovered.

Sasanian hegemony over Luristan was broken in AD 641 by the Arab conquest, but we do not know to what extent the Arabs actually occupied Luristan at that early date. What is clear is that Luristan was made part of the Kufa province, which was roughly the same as the old Sasanian units of Luristan and Khuzistan.

Language

Over the centuries, if not millennia, the area we know as Luristan has seen a complex intermingling of people from widely diverse ethnic and linguistic groups. Owing to the absence of specific historic sources, it is possible only to piece together a loosely woven narrative. Of necessity, this is based on accounts of military campaigns, dislocations of populations, political intrigue, the decimation of towns and cities, forced relocations, and massacres of populations. Mongols, Turks, Arabs, Greeks, Romans, and Persians comprise this mix. The people who are known as Lurs today have emerged from a stew of historical circumstances and have preserved a sense of ethnic identity for hundreds of years.

Some authors have claimed that the Lur are an original Iranian stock and have occupied Luristan since the dawn of time (see Mortensen 1993:43).

However, "it should not be forgotten…that when the Islamic conquest was completed in AD 651, several Arabic tribes settled in the central Zagros as well as in other parts of Iran. In the 11th century came the invasions of Turks from Central Asia, and the Seljuks crossed Iran to overrun the whole of Mesopotamia, Armenia and Asia Minor" (Mortensen 1993:44). Then came the Mongols, who sacked Khorramabad in 1386 and returned in revenge to destroy what was left in Luristan (Mortensen 1993:44).

The Arab conquest of Iran in AD 651 ushered in an era of governments and some semblance of history. Despite what appear to have been recurring and devastating incursions, it is notable that from Kurdistan through Luristan, the languages are based on a branch of Indo-European known as Old Persian, suggesting that a core of native life persisted and resisted potential linguistic contamination.

Because of Bala Griveh's relative isolation and difficult access, it is likely that local tribes were able to evade much of the turmoil. Indeed, there would have been little spoil for the conquerors except the herds and any grain stores.

Today in western Iran, four major linguistic groups encompass most of the tribal people. In the northern and central Zagros Mountains live Kurdish-speaking peoples, whose traditional range includes parts of Iraq, Turkey, and Syria. Just to the south of the Kurds are the Lurs, and to their south is a closely related group called the Bakhtiari. All of these people speak languages that are derived from the same roots as English and closely related to Farsi, the official language of Iran. Still farther south are the Qashqa'i, a large tribe of Turkish-speaking people who were forcibly settled in a region that is predominantly of Indo-European stock.

Some evidence points to a local language, which began to pick up Indo-European nouns as early as 1700 BC. Many of the place names in Luristan may derive from this earlier language. But the complete adoption of an Indo-European tongue, a form of Old Persian, may not have taken place until the formation of the Achaemenid Empire (550–330 BC) and its successors, the Parthian (331 BC–AD 226) and the Sasanian (AD 226–641) periods.

Written history

We turn now to what is known of the Lurs in historic times. Much of the following account is based on the following publications: *Nomads of Luristan* (Mortensen 1993); "Lur" (Minorsky 1936); *Persia and the Persian Question*

(Curzon [1892] 1966); The Baharvand: Former pastoralists of Iran (Amanolahi-Baharvand 1975); "The Lurs of Iran" (Amanolahi 2016); "Reza Shah and the Lurs" (Amanolahi-Baharvand 2002); and *Luristan* (Wilson 1912).

The written history of Luristan begins with the dynasty of the Atabegs (AD 1184–1596) after they succeeded in supplanting Arab control. Their capital was Khorramabad, but the rules maintained at least a summer presence in Bala Griveh and a winter presence in Deh Luran. At this time, Luristan was divided, as it had been since the early tenth century AD, into two parts: Greater (Luri Buzorg) and Lesser (Luri Kucheck) Luristan. The former now encompasses the territory of the Bakhtiari, whereas the latter comprises today's province of Luristan. Closely related in language and custom, the peoples in these two areas have nevertheless remained distinct, divided geographically from one another along the drainages of the Dez River. These areas were ruled by two dynasties of Atabegs, whose history, according to the Russian scholar Vladimir Minorsky (Minorsky 1936:45), "is filled with feuds, murders and executions but in domestic affairs the state of the country was fairly prosperous."

Around the end of the fourteenth century, Lesser Luristan was ravaged by the Mongol forces of Timur, who were able to gain control for a short time. This so weakened the Atabegs that they eventually succumbed to domination by the Mongol Safavid dynasty. In 1596, Shah Abbas, the founder of the Safavid Dynasty, appointed Husain Khan the *wali*, or governor, of Lesser Luristan. Husain Khan's father had married the aunt of the last Atabeg, and it was on the basis of this kinship that he received the position of *wali*, ruler of Luri-Kuchek. Thus began a tradition of local governorship of Luristan by Lurs that endured until 1929. The role of the *wali* was to protect the western flanks of Iran from Ottoman incursions. Successive *walis* governed through the Afshar, Zand, Qajar, and early Pahlavi dynasties. During these centuries, the *wali* and his forces alternated between aiding and fighting against the government of the time.

The Safavid period was marked by continual hostilities between Iranian forces and those of the Turks, who controlled what we now call Iraq. In 1736, the Safavids were replaced by another Turkic dynasty, known as Afshar, which lasted only 14 years. The Zands (1750–1794), a Lur dynasty from Luri-Kuchek, replaced the Afsharids. In turn, the Zand dynasty was overthrown, after bitter fighting, by the Qajars (1794–1924), Turkic pastoralists from northern Iran. Among other things, the Qajars exiled several Luri tribes to central Iran. This was a period of increasing instability, which culminated with the overthrow of the Qajar monarch in 1906 by an armed force of Bakhtiaris.

Concerning the Qajars, it is worth quoting some passages from George Nathaniel Curzon's book, *Persia and the Persian Question*, published in 1892.

> From the Shah downwards, there is scarcely an official who is not open to gifts, scarcely a post which is not conferred in return for gifts, scarcely an income which has not been amassed by the receipt of gifts…Hereby is instituted an arithmetical progression of plunder from the sovereign to the subject, each unit in the descending scale remunerating himself from the unit next in rank below him, and the hapless peasant being the ultimate victim (Curzon [1892] 1966: 438, 443).

Despite having only irregular fighting forces at their disposal, the Qajar governors maintained control by fomenting tribal feuds. A. T. Wilson noted this as well.

> The policy of every governor is to pit tribe against tribe, utilizing the services of one to coerce the other, such a policy is only temporarily successful, it ends by impoverishing the district and embittering tribal relations…Salar-ud-Dauleh, Governor-General in 1904 and 1906, is responsible to a large extent for the prevailing anarchy. His ideas of government were limited to inciting one tribe to plunder another: he aimed openly at becoming Shah, and sought to enlist the support of Lur tribes, but without success (Wilson 1912:10).

During the nineteenth century, Agha Mohammad, one of the Qajar kings, divided Lesser Luristan into two parts, now known as Pish-i Kuh and Pusht-i Kuh. The latter refers to the land south and west of the Kabir Kuh. Pusht-i Kuh remained under control of the *wali*. From the view of the government of Iran and foreigners who wanted to establish trade routes through Luristan, the area was in a constant state of anarchy.

Around 1900, treaties arranged by the British with the *wali* and other tribal leaders granted safe passage through Luristan. For the next five years, caravans plied the route from the Persian Gulf through Luristan to

Khorramabad and thence to Tehran, but by 1905, the routes were closed again. After 1917, this time with foreign help, caravans once more moved through Pish-i Kuh. This period of peace was made possible partly because the government of Iran conferred the title of *wali* upon Nazar Ali Khan, the last officially sanctioned holder of the office and a lineal descendent of the first *wali*. In his official capacity, the *wali* dealt directly with the British in establishing and maintaining caravan routes and in signing concessions for oil exploration. The latter interests were centered in Deh Luran and put under the direction of Yadolah Khan, the *wali*'s son.

Within his domain, the authority of the *wali* was absolute, or as nearly so as his force of mounted, well-armed militia, the Kaka Siah, could enforce. Reportedly, 2,000 tents of followers surrounded his fort on the Deh Luran Plain. Punitive raids were the *wali*'s stock in trade. The relocation of recalcitrant tribes was one of his chief means of achieving stability. Decisive leadership backed by swift action had enabled the *walis* to control Pusht-i Kuh for three hundred years.

The power of the last *wali* was broken eventually in 1929 through the time-honored ploy of turning members of the family against one another and attacking the divided forces individually with modern armaments and the full weight of the resources of the centralized government. The *wali* and his supporters fought back briefly, fled, and ultimately merged into the new political reality.

The Qajar dynasty was overthrown by Reza Khan, the founder of the Pahlavi dynasty (1925–1979). "While the Qajar dynasty was responsible for the spread of anarchy among the Lurs, the Pahlavi dynasty was responsible for their political disorganization, social disruption and the loss of political freedom and semi-independent status" (Amanolahi 2016).

Reza Shah began with an exhortation to the tribes to yield to his authority. In 1925, he had messages to the tribal leaders dropped from an airplane (quoted in Nobakht, *Shahanshah-i-Pahlavi*, Vol. 1:227):

> Oh, my zealous children! In the present epoch there remain on the historical scene no traces of the signs of savagery and other barbarity, and today, when even the blacks and beasts of Africa have elected the paths of progress and advancement, it is neither permitted nor appropriate that the sons of the ancient land of Iran, with its resplendent historical tradition and civilization, should still roam

> and wander like savage beasts across the deserts and mountains. All of you must abandon this wandering and nomadic existence and resume once more that mode of life of your illustrious forebears who caused cities to flourish and prosper.

The period beginning in 1922 and ending in 1941—when the Reza Shah, who had sided with the Nazis, was forced to abdicate after the Allied invasion—was particularly difficult for the people of Luristan. From 1922, when the national army entered Luristan, until 1933, sporadic fighting occurred between the tribes and the army. During the winter of 1923, when the tribes were in their winter pastures, the army captured Khorramabad. In response, the tribes besieged Khorramabad the following spring. Discord among the tribes eventually caused several of them to withdraw, leaving the army firmly in control of the city. At this time, General Ahmedi sent the following letter to leaders of the tribes (Amanolahi-Baharvand 1975:facing p. 52):

> June 3, 1924
>
> To Kadkhoda Husain Khan, the leader of the Moradalivand... By this order we guarantee security for you and the Moradalivand tribe. Henceforth you are under the protection of the Army. You must convey this message to every member of your tribe and encourage them to serve His Excellency the Prime Minister and Commander in Chief of the Army so that they will receive allegiance from other tribes in return for their favors. Security is extended to all those who seek allegiance with you and who are willing to receive the favor of the government. You must introduce these persons to me so that they may be granted security and instructed to take up farming.
>
> Commander of the Western Division
> General Ahmedi

The Baharvand, also known as the Moradalivand, withdrew from further fighting against the army.

In 1925 the Reza Shah appointed a governor, General Ahmadi. He instituted a series of measures that resulted in the forced settling of the majority of nomads, sometimes outside Luristan, and the execution or imprisonment of the more fractious tribal leaders, among them Sekandar's grandfather.

General Khazai, an Army commander sent to Khorramabad in 1925, invited a number of influential tribal leaders to negotiate a peace. When the leaders arrived in Khorramabad, he captured and hanged thirteen of them, including some who had been sympathetic to the army's cause.

In 1929, General Ahmadi, known by the Lurs as "The Butcher of Luristan," invited Husain Khan and his brother to Khorramabad. They were arrested and sent to Tehran and Mashad, where they remained imprisoned until their release by British and Russian forces in 1941.

By 1929, the army was strong enough to force settlement on the tribes. The army decreed that henceforth there was to be no migration. The black tents were confiscated and replaced with white tents. Only small detachments of tribesmen were allowed to take the herds to winter pastures. The tribes were disarmed. The people were required to wear the "Pahlavi" hat, a Western-style headpiece with a bill that was favored by the Reza Shah. The government began to register land, where previously territories had been somewhat imprecisely defined and fluctuated according to the relative strengths of the tribes. To enforce these policies, the army maintained a strong presence in Khorramabad. Fighting ceased entirely by 1933.

After the abdication of the Reza Shah early in the Second World War, many tribal people resumed their nomadic ways. But after the end of the war, official government policy was to continue to push for the settlement of nomads and expand the agricultural production of the region. The policy was greatly aided by the construction of a modern highway through Luristan and by the introduction of electric power lines, industrialized agriculture, compulsory formal schooling for the children, and military service for the men. None of these changes was easy for the Luri people. In Chapter 17, we address the specific history of the people of the Baharvand.

European portrayals of the Lurs

The fate of the Lurs in modern times is a product of both their history and their portrayals in the books and films of nineteenth- and twentieth-century Europeans. Luristan has been invaded and fought over by kings, shahs, princes, and khans, not to mention Greek and Ottoman troops, Arabs, and the British. The Luri people have been renowned for their treachery, lawlessness, and incessant feuding: a reputation based in part on decades of intertribal conflicts encouraged by local leaders. Governors of Luristan have exacted onerous taxes through force and fomented feuding that pitted one tribe against another, and Luristan's national rulers, local governors, and tribal khans shared a common strategy of governing, expressed as early as the nineteenth century by De Bode.

> The Shah-Zadeh and his Vizier hope to uphold their own authority by keeping alive the animosity between the two rival parties, and in this respect they only follow the policy pursued all over the empire, and which appears from time immemorial to have been the system of government in Persia. It happens still oftener that the Prince, who is named governor of a province, embraces the cause of one party, while his minister sides with the adherents of the other. One can easily imagine what sort of order and harmony may exist, when such elements compose the administration" (De Bode 1845b:181–182).

Another reason that the character of the Lurs has suffered in written history is that they have not commanded the narrative; outsiders have written it. The impressions that follow are a sample of what was written about the Lurs before anthropologists and ethnographers entered the scene. Most Europeans who visited Luristan were motivated by military/commercial purposes or the urge to explore exotic places that could be described in lectures at the Royal Geographical Society in London. These encounters were sporadic, and for the most part, the observations were superficial. The actual migrations of Zagros nomadic pastoralists have seldom been observed or described: in the last part of this chapter, we describe the few documentary films and scholarly books focused on portraying and understanding this way of life.

Travelers and government officials

The more remote regions of Persia attracted adventurous travelers, including Baron De Bode, who described his time there with attention to the details of daily living.

After a day of being soaked during a long ride by horseback, De Bode found refuge in a Bairekvand camp (Boerekevend). "In order to preserve my riding-horse from getting wet, I was obliged to take him inside my tent and close to my couch, there being no other place for his accommodation, as the remaining part of the tent, separated only from my bed-room by a low partition of plaited reed, was filled with the numerous members of the family and my servants, and a whole lot of young lambkins and kids, in separate cages or pens of plaited reed. The latter kept sneezing and bleating the greater part of the night" (De Bode 1845a:220–221).

On another occasion he wrote, "the fuel allotted for my consumption consisted of dried manure, fashioned into cylindrical cakes, such as are used in many parts of Irak, where wood is scarce. In burning it emits a thick smoke, but the cakes have the advantage of retaining the heat for a long time" (De Bode 1845a). Observing the baking of bread, he noted that the woman "took a piece of the kneaded paste, and, spreading it into a thin leaf in the palm of her hand, in the form of a pancake, applied the paste against the inner walls of the oven, first baking one side then the other" (De Bode 1845a:263).

De Bode characterized the tribes of the area thus:

> The Lurs…like their Bakhtiari neighbors, are greatly addicted to plunder, but in a less open manner than the latter; nor do they go out in such strong bodies. They likewise differ in the mode of attack, as they generally perform their assaults on foot; whilst the Bakhtiari proceed on their forays on horseback ... I must do the Luristani the justice to say, that I have no reason to complain of them, for although I never had more than three or four men with me, I never was molested by any of the tribes; on the contrary, wherever I went I met with hospitality (De Bode 1845a:293).

He also wrote, "I could not help admiring the agility with which my guides jumped from rock to rock, like mountain goats with the assurance and nonchalance as if they were walking over level ground" (De Bode 1845a:213).

> The women are seen with their spinning-wheels on their shoulders, some twisting woolen yard, others bent forward, and advancing slowly with their children astride on their backs, clasping their little arms around their mother's neck, and twisting their little legs around the waist: the smaller ones are usually tied up in a bag behind her back, while infant babies, together with clumsy cradles, are hoisted on the heads or shoulders of their fond mothers, sinking under the weight…The bodily fatigues a poor Iliat (tribal) mother has to undergo, are, perhaps greater than those felt by women in any other condition (De Bode 1845a:255–256).

The British lieutenant Arnold T. Wilson, who spent seven years in southwest Persia as a surveyor and political officer, shared the same sentiment:

> I have come to regard the wives and daughters of the tribesmen with whom I have been living with real admiration. Their powers of endurance are a perpetual source of wonder to me. They bear, quite literally, the burden of the day, and also heat and bitter cold, though less well clad than their men. They bear, too, many children, unaided by any but their own kind, suckle them long, and carry them often for great distances. They and they alone milk the sheep and goats, prepare food, weave carpets and tent cloth, saddle-bags and much else. They help to load and unload the pack animals, but go afoot oftener than men. Without a wife a man is as helpless and useless as half a pair of anything else—and she knows it. (Wilson 1941:156–157)

While Wilson carried out many topographic mapping surveys himself, he had other sources of information about the land and its people, apparently confidential reports (not available). In his memoir, *SW Persia: A Political Officer's Diary* (1941) he describes his difficulties with the Baharvand. "Next day at Walmiyan, near Jaidar, news came that the Baharvand Mirs (who attacked Lorimer) had seized the next pass and barred the way against us: they demanded rahdari—road toll—to the amount I had promised my friends for the whole trip from Dizful to Khorramabad" (Wilson 1941:151–153).

Despite threats, the stealing of flocks from his companions, the wounding of a boy, and the killing of a man, Wilson resisted paying the toll. Fighting ensued.

> The tribesmen ran to their tents, where they cast down any superfluous garments they might have, and emerged, a moment later, lithe, barefooted, half-naked figures and, with extraordinary skill and speed, ran up the rocky slopes that lay between them and the enemy.

Thus began an armed conflict, which lasted into the following day.

> An hour later the fight was over: on balance we had won, for our dead were three to their four; our captured sheep and goats three hundred head to their one hundred.

Wilson did admire the fitness of the Lurs. "One of them had a home-made sling and killed a partridge with a stone at 80 yards to show his skill. They were thin, tough, wiry, barefoot, with spare homespun clothes and leapt from rock to rock like goats. They would make good infantry if not put into boots and drilled too much" (Wilson 1941:61).

> The tribe are notorious for their predatory habits, but this is because they are on the main caravan road between Dizful and Burujird, and have had greater opportunities than other tribes of exercising their talent in this direction, at the expense of the general public. So far as the writer has observed, their ingrained love of theft is characteristic of all Lurs without distinction. They rob and pillage not only outsiders, but members of their own tribe; the blood feuds, which are one of the chief pre-occupations of their chiefs, arise almost entirely from the killing of a member of the tribe, when in the act of robbing some other family or clan, and vice versa. Blood is only extracted for blood when there is no chance of obtaining its pecuniary equivalent (Wilson 1911 #16163:27).

De Bode addressed this aspect of the tribes as well. During one encounter, women and boys, who were collecting acorns, fled upon seeing De Bode's party. He concluded, "This trifling incident was the best criterion by which I could judge the unsettled state of the country" (De Bode 1845b:224).

The forts of khans (tribal leaders) that he encountered repeatedly—usually not occupied or in ruins—attested to states of unrest, as did a great many ruined settlements of no great antiquity. "Basht resembles the castles of the old feudal barons in Europe. It consists of the Chief's fort, enclosed by high walls, and flanked with turrets. All around are groups of habitations of his vassals, who live under the shadow of his protection, and furnish him with the means of resisting his enemies" (De Bode 1845b:251).

Many foreigners regretted their decisions to travel through Luristan during those periods, when the only law was tribal law, a set of customs created to cope with internal tribal affairs, but hardly likely to afford much succor to the wealthy, pompous outsiders whose principal concerns were commerce and international politics, in which the only profit for the tribes was that which they themselves could exact on the spot.

The British officers and travelers found Luristan nearly unbearable. They traveled through the country only when they had to, and in fear. To help insure their safety, they commonly held hostages from the tribes whose territory they intended to pass through. C. J. Edmonds recounts the elaborate precautions taken by a survey party traveling through the territory of the Mir tribe in 1914 (Edmonds 1922:343). “Hostages were taken, Qur’ans sealed, and wages to the tribes fixed.” In spite of these preparations, the caravan was looted the first day out from Dezful and the mission was abandoned.

Edmonds’s fears were not misplaced. In 1917, he was detained for seventeen days in Khorramabad on a trip into Luristan and was held there for a further three months upon his return. Although troops had accompanied him, he held no hostages himself that time. He had been more successful earlier, when he visited tribal territory occupied by four branches of the Mir tribe. “It was therefore arranged that each branch should give one hostage, to be retained in the Agency at Dizful until my safe return, while the elder Mirs were to accompany me to Mungarreh, entertain me there, and escort me back” (Edmonds 1922:349).

We should note, however, that in 1934–1935, when Wilson surveyed Pish-i Kuh, he was apparently not molested despite not traveling with a military escort.

Not everyone was entirely dismissive of the Lurs. While dining with an army colonel, the American reporter Marguerite Harrison asked him whether the Lurs were brave. The colonel replied, “Once I commanded four field guns against them. All morning we fired at the enemy. They returned the fire and killed many of my men. At noon they rose up among the rocks and mocked us. And we saw that just five Lurs had held all our artillery at bay.” He further remarked, “A Lur wants only a little sour milk, a fistful of chestnuts and his gun and cartridges. Then he is ready for war” (M. Harrison 1935:97).

Luristan in documentary films

In the twentieth century, a new medium emerged: the documentary film. Two remarkable documentary films about the Bakhtiari—both about dramatic, difficult migrations—helped shape outsiders’ understanding of transhumant pastoralists in Iran. The films are *Grass* and *People of the Wind*. A third film, *Taraz*, was released in 1988.

The commercial video of a Bakhtiari migration, *Grass*, has had a lasting impression on generations of viewers and is regarded as one of the classic depictions of an extinct way of life. In 1924, a team of three—filmmaker

Merian Cooper, photographer Ernest Schoedsack, and reporter Marguerite Harrison—made the film. With funding from Harrison, the trio set forth on camelback from Anatolia.

The trio eventually reached Luristan at the time of the spring migration and they found the ideal tribe to film. The video has some of the most dramatic and remarkable scenes ever filmed, of migration over nearly impassable rocky trails, fording a raging river on goat skin rafts, and struggling barefoot up and over snow-covered mountains. The movie's subtitle, *A Nation's Battle For Life*, refers to the Bakhtiari's relentless search for green pastures that could sustain the herds until late summer, when they had to reverse the trek. In no sense can the film be regarded as an ethnographic study, yet it documented in raw detail the perilous journey of Bakhtiari tribes to summer pastures, high in the Zagros Mountains. While the film was not a great commercial success, Harrison lectured with it for decades later.

There is no doubt that *Grass*, with its short subtitles, depicts the reality of a traditional way of life. At the time of the filming, the Lurs, just to the north of the Bakhtiari, occupying similar country, were under siege from the Iranian army and in the process of being conquered. The Bakhtiari anxiously watched these events and kept their rifles at the ready. The vast majority of their tribe was intact and constituted a formidable force in their remote mountain valleys, but modernization, in the form of a road through their territory, presaged an opening for the penetration of the army and other outside influences.

Grass focuses on the dangers and severity of conditions of life on the move, but ignores normal daily camp life, so viewers might falsely conclude that the nomads, apart from their leaders, lived a life of savage brutality and endless movement. What the film omits are the prolonged stops along the route where the tribe and their herds were refreshed before the next physical obstacle. Moreover, as Cooper makes clear, he and his companions elected to take the most difficult route (Cooper 1925:211), while other tribes of the Bakhtiari followed easier routes. The intention and emphasis of the filmmakers was to show the harshest aspects of nomadic life, with the implication that our forebears eons ago had traveled this same route to civilization. "We had been able to record a phase in the evolution of civilization, or rather, we had come into a backwater where civilization had stood still for two thousand years" (M. Harrison 1935:635).

The value of *Grass* is much enhanced by reading Harrison's account of the event, written ten years after the migration. Cooper also wrote a diary, and it was published, with Schoedsack's photographs, just a year after the film was made. The making of the film was a heroic effort similar to that endured by their Bakhtiari hosts.

However, one does not simply arrive at a pastoral camp and decide to travel with the tribe. "They were advised by British politician Sir Arnold Wilson, chairman of the board of the Anglo-Persian Oil Company, and by the chief of British intelligence for Iraq, Gertrude Bell" (Nafici 2006:123). Wilson contacted the British Consul, Peel, who introduced the trio to the Shushtar governor general and to the Bakhtiari leader, Rahim Khan. Khan arranged for their safe travel and accommodations with the tribe. One would like to have a diary by the hosting tribal leader, the Il Khan, with his commentary on the migration and his accommodations for the Americans. No doubt there was culture shock and strong opinions on both sides.

At the time *Grass* was filmed, the great tribe of the Bakhtiari was strong and in possession of hundreds of villages and great oil revenues, and could stand up to the Persian government (Garthwaite [1983] 2009). Indeed, it was through the powerful influence of the Anglo-Persian Oil Company that the Americans were allowed to travel with the tribe.

In 1936, Cooper attempted another version of the migration, this time in technicolor. "He assembled a large fifteen-person, Hollywood-style crew consisting of technical personnel, guards, and actors along with half a dozen muleteers and some forty-three mules, who carried their gear, tents, cameras, vodka, orange juice (imported from the United States), canned food (corned beef and hash), and sleeping bags. Most would not eat the tribe's food" (Nafici 2006:136). Under government supervision and with a script, they filmed scenes of Bakhtiari life, but they ran out of time, money, and steam to carry out their plans. The film was never finished.

Fifty years later, a second film, *People of the Wind*, showed the migration of the Baba Abadi tribe of the Bakhtiari, over roughly the same route shown in *Grass* (Howarth 1976). The quality of the photography was much better than that in *Grass*, and there was voice-over narration rather than subtitles, but the film essentially duplicated the older one, albeit with considerably more attention to individuals and a story line beyond merely the quest for grass. The film shows many good scenes of domestic activities, including the killing and skinning of a sheep, spinning woolen thread, baking bread, collecting water from a spring, and the marriage of a reluctant girl. While the film uses narrated comments on the scenes, the viewer can hear unique and authentic sounds of the herds and the cries of people urging them over rocky trails. These sounds help make real the anxiety of the people and the urgency of forceful, immediate action.

The circumstances that allowed the filmmakers of *People of the Wind* to travel with the Bakhtiari tribe have not been fully revealed, but it is likely that the migration was "staged" for their benefit. The Bakhtiari men were outfitted with traditional clothing and the women with colorful dresses and scarves. Both men and women wore molded rubber shoes, and the men smoked cigarettes, used matches, and were not armed. None of these was seen in *Grass*. Their presence in the later movie attests to wider contacts and access to cash to spend in the markets. According to the books by Cooper and Harrison, the men in *Grass* prized two things: a horse and a rifle. The Baba Abadi tribe was well outfitted, probably because they had substantial income from oil revenues that allowed the market purchase of their traditional clothes. Nevertheless, their rifles had been confiscated, and the tribe was no longer a political or fighting force.

People of the Wind was filmed without directing the actors, but a narrative was constructed for the film with careful editing. Both *Grass* and *People of the Wind* provide quite a bit of purely documentary information, and one would be hard pressed to construct such films today or find people with the will or the knowledge to make the migration.

The most recent commercial film of the Bakhtiari migration, *Taraz*, is apparently of the same tribe as seen in the previous films. It is the work of an Iranian filmmaker, Farhad Varahram.

The narration is in Farsi, and the cinematography is excellent. The film has extensive footage of an arduous migration, especially of moving herds over rivers and mountains. The film begins in the winter pasture, with the tribe in well-secured, stone-walled "houses" in rockshelters, and moves on migration, with the tribe using tents. It is interesting to see the use of canvas rather than traditional black tents, but tent life is the same. There is good footage of milking and making bread, loading animals, collecting water, and other domestic chores. Much of the film depends on visual scenes, often without narration, to convey the story and the stark beauty of the landscape.

In terms of archaeology, none of the films contributed much to our understanding of how this way of life emerged. The need for transhumance to keep the sheep and goats alive is well recognized, but there is nothing in the films to enlighten us on how it may have developed and been carried out in ancient times. We must strip away the horses, mules, donkeys, and cows to begin to imagine transhumance without them. We should also remove the heavy overlay of the Bakhtiari tribal confederation, with its strongly feudal hold over enormous territory and its people, enforced by men with firearms.

During our 1973 migration we also made a film in color, but without sound. (See the film and four other short documentary films on aspects of nomadic pastoralist life in Luristan on Fulcrum at https://doi.org/10.3998/mpub.12031336.) We wanted to record the daily routine, with special attention to domestic activities and the handling of the herds. The filming was entirely opportunistic, taking advantage of scenes as they occurred. Often filmed from the back of a moving horse, using 3 minute super 8 reels, the film lacks the professional quality of *People of the Wind* or *Taraz*, but it does provide an accurate view of the pace of daily activities. It also shows the Lurs in a much-reduced economic state. There was a lack of manpower to manage the gear and herds, and the men by this time were wearing Western-style clothes rather than the native costumes of the other films. The contrast in the economic fortunes of the Baharvand and Baba Abadi is apparent, as will be discussed later.

Books with a geographic and topical focus on tribes of Iran

There are several books that are relevant to our subject: scholarly works on nomads in this part of the world. These include Jacob Black-Michaud's detailed ethnography of traveling with a tribe of Hasanwand Lurs, called *Sheep and Land: The Economics of Power in a Tribal Society* (1986). By focusing on the interplay between tribal politics, the government, and the economic and social realities of life as mobile pastoralists, Black-Michaud successfully records "the last successful efforts at adaptation of a society soon to be overwhelmed by radical political and economic change" (Black-Michaud 1986:5). *Techniques des Nomades Baxtyari d'Iran*, by Jean-Pierre Digard, is a purely descriptive account of the material culture of Bakhtiari nomads (Digard 1981). For those interested in tools and techniques, this book provides both descriptions and illustrations. *Nomads in Archaeology*, by Roger Cribb, examines the relevance of studies of contemporary nomads to archaeology (Cribb 2004).

Traversing the route that would be taken by a railroad line through Luristan, Danish ethnographer Carl Gunnar Feilberg joined a tribe of Papi Lurs in 1935. His books *La Tente Noire* and *Les Papi*, both published in the Nationalmuseets Skrifter series, describe geography, tribal life, and material culture (Feilberg 1944, 1952).

Inge Mortensen, working alongside archaeological investigations, collected inscriptions on tombstones in northern Luristan. The resulting study, *Luristani Pictorial Tombstones: Studies in Nomadic Cemeteries from Northern Luristan, Iran* (Mortensen 2010), was published in the ACTA Iranica series. She also published an excellent book, *Nomads of Luristan: History, Material Culture, and Pastoralism in Western Iran* (1993), in which she discusses Luristan history and culture. Included in this work are photos, drawings, and commentary on Feilberg's collection of 1935.

Other works on nomadic and semi-nomadic people of the Zagros Mountains of Iran are largely historical, including *Khans and Shahs: A History of the Bakhtiyari Tribe in Iran* (Garthwaite 2009) and *Nomadism in Iran: From Antiquity to the Modern Era* (Potts 2014), a comprehensive work on what is known about the history of nomadism. *Frontier Nomads of Iran: A Political and Social History of the Shahsevan* is a historical study of the Shahsevan nomads of northwestern Iran (Tapper 1997).

A long-term study of the Boir Ahmad, a linguistically related Luri tribe, by von Reinhold Loeffler and Erika Friedl, has resulted in several publications.. Among these are "Eine Ethnographische sammlung von der Boir Ahmad, Sudiran" (Loeffler and Friedl 1967) and "Die Materielle Kultur von Boir Ahmad, Sud Iran" (Loeffler et al. 1974). Friedl has written several other acclaimed books, including *Women of Deh Koh* (1989) and *Folktales and Storytellers of Iran* (2014). These are highly detailed studies of Luri material culture, similar to Digard's book, cited above.

Lois Beck, an anthropologist, has carried out multi-decade studies of the Qashgai pastoralists of southern Iran (Beck 1980, 1986, 1991, 2015).

In the next chapter, the heart of our story begins: in the town of Dezful, Iran, we prepare to join a camp of pastoral nomads for their summer migration into the mountains.

Chapter 5

From Dezful to Chin-i Zal

The nomads winter in the *garmsir*, on the flat Khuzistan Plain or in the lower foothills of the Zagros Mountains (see Figure 3.2). Khuzistan is a flat alluvial plain that stretches from the mountains to the Persian Gulf. It is home to the cities of Dezful, Shushtar, and Ahwaz. Khuzistan is hot. From the end of May to early October the daily temperatures average 110°F (40°C) and often exceed 120°F (50°C). Winters are relatively mild, with intermittent rain, but most agriculture depends on irrigation from the Dez and Karun rivers. These extreme seasonal contrasts give rise to the need for transhumance: grass that sprouts in late winter is desiccated by June, and sheep fare badly in extreme heat.

Dezful

The name Dezful means "the bridge across the river Dez." I first saw this big, bustling city from the ancient bridge, its new asphalt surface layered atop the older, arched stone foundations, which were built by Roman prisoners around 300 AD. Stretching to both sides of the broad, shimmering waters of the river, Dezful, though large—it is home to about 250,000 people—possesses the ambience of the ancient city it is (Figures 5.1, 5.2).

Ever teeming with people, insistent trucks, and recalcitrant herds, the bridge links the old and new sections of the city. During the day men and boys tread its narrow sidewalks in either direction. Small herds of sheep and goats are driven to market to the constant urgings of their herders. Taxis, pushcarts, and horses, competing for the narrow space, contribute to the cacophony. On Thursday evenings, the artery is jammed with women, black chadors clutched between their teeth to hold them tightly across their faces, moving en masse to the cemetery just across the river for their graveside vigils.

Below, the shallow Dez River once flowed brown. Now its sparkling blue testifies to a modern dam in a narrow gorge upstream, where the Dez River emerges from the mountains. The dam traps the sediments that formerly enriched the fields downstream. The broad gravel banks of the river lie barren and dusty, awaiting the next surge of floodwaters that will scour them clean. Wading into the waters on the west bank, men wash trucks, cars, and herds of sheep.

On the east bank is the old city. Jutting out from the bank, the foundations of abandoned water-powered mills, as old as the bridge itself, now serve only as diving platforms for young boys out for a cooling swim. The bank gives rise to buildings that seem to grow out of the irregular contours of gravel and silt. Away from the river rises a solid mass of two- and three-story houses. An infrequent tree shows above the courtyard walls. From a distance, the view suggests an unbroken façade, until figures emerge into the light to disclose the presence of narrow lanes opening onto the riverbank.

Old Dezful is a warren of crooked lanes that change their character with each corner. At times they are scarcely more than tiny footpaths on either side of a channel that drains water and catches debris. These twisting canyons are flanked with bare, slanting walls of horizontal row upon row of mud bricks that disappear from sight above (Figure 5.3). Here, the unpracticed eye has difficulty picking out individual houses from the anonymous walls set at odd angles, except where houses of white baked brick stand bare and alone. The

Figure 5.1. The old city of Dezful is built alongside the Dez River. The Sasanian bridge and foundations of ancient mills jut into the river. People swim and wash their trucks and sheep and goats in the river.

white brick houses have regularly spaced rectangular windows and severe perpendicular lines, which are jarring against the chaotic irregularity of the roughly textured, weathered mud-brick houses with fluid, arched openings. In the white houses live traditional families, whose wealth stems largely from landholdings and merchant activities. Families with untraditional wealth, recently accumulated in connection with the agricultural development and military projects in Khuzistan, live some distance away, in sprawling suburban districts that have little in common with the heart of this ancient city.

The Dezful bazaar, in the heart of the old town, is a bustling street with numerous tiny shops shaded by awnings of white muslin. Fresh-picked greens are mounded in clusters on the ground. Burlap bags of nuts, peas, and lentils await buyers. In the sweet shops, large round trays of halva cut into bite-sized chunks are stacked inside glass cases enveloped by flies, and honey oozes from between layers of flaky pastry. Pink carcasses of fat-tailed sheep

Figure 5.2. Traditional houses with arches and interior courtyards have been cut to make way for new thoroughfares into the heart of the city.

hang from iron hooks in the doors of booth-size butcher shops, where women watch anxiously as the butcher slices pieces into their parcels. A mélange of odors—from fabric, fresh fruits and vegetables, and meat and livestock—permeates the bazaar.

By midmorning the lane is awash with the cries of vendors, the cajoling of donkey drivers, and the quiet, patient haggling of housewives. Merchants sit cross-legged on small carpets surrounded by bolts of their wares. These elderly hajjis (men who have completed the pilgrimage to Mecca) with green turbans drink tea and converse with their cronies from nearby shops. In small, open cubicles, boys work expertly, shaving wooden combs or adze handles. Next door a carpenter drives his lathe with a bow while he directs his cutting tools as skillfully with his feet as we might with our hands. Down a side alley, toward the edge of the bazaar, the handlooms are humming as weavers sit in pits fabricating the traditional coarse white and black Luri coats. A resonant thumping down another street comes from the wool fluffer, who sits in a pile of wool playing his one-stringed "harp"

Figure 5.3. A typical lane in old Dezful with arches, crooked streets, and a wastewater stream in the center. Photo by Bonnie Hole.

with a wooden mallet; this causes the string to vibrate through the wool preparatory to folding it into felted rugs. Still farther away is the rhythmic hammering of the iron and copper smithies.

The bazaar is the nomad's department store. Each shopkeeper has families of townspeople and pastoralists with whom he regularly deals. These are business relationships of tradition, convenience, and limited trust. The new stores on paved streets displaying plastics, canned goods, and machine-made clothes are not frequented by the nomads in their baggy black pants, white shirts buttoned at the neck, and felt caps.

Traditionally the nomads shop in town twice a year, just before or after the seasonal migrations. They pay cash when they have sold their livestock, and they buy on credit when necessary. Although they haggle for prices like everyone else, they pay more than city folk for the same goods. The pastoralists, as foreigners in the city, can expect no favors from shopkeepers who, like good businessmen, charge what the market will bear. The nomads bear more than the locals.

Our trip begins

In 1973, the year of our migration project, a new bridge crossing the Dez had been completed. The service roads that led to the new bridge pierced straight through the oldest part of the city, stripping walls from houses and leaving roofless rooms victim to the glare of the desert sun (Figure 5.4). The new avenues of Dezful were lined with remnants of majestic old houses, their arched windows looking out at irregular heights, while their massive arches protected interior courtyards. Their mud-brick façades had been shoved out of the way, and the houses stood shamefully unveiled, jagged reminders of a way of life stopped short. Pastel interiors of rooms, ornate, delicately domed ceilings, and graceful columns silently spoke of times past, when these skeletons housed wealthy families.

That spring the scars were being covered. New shops were beginning to appear, along with new walls for old houses. Aligned with the new streets, rigidly geometric white baked brick houses and shops with steel girders, metal sheeting, and plastic panels were attached to the old earthen structures. The new buildings began to cover the open wounds like crisp white bandages over wrinkled brown flesh.

The day Sekandar and I left Dezful, our Jeep driver, Reza, drove us along one of the new roads. I ached to have an architectural plan of the old city before it was totally destroyed: the endless lanes and the fine old houses with their underground caverns ultimately leading to the river, where people retreated during the hottest days. These were the product of a fascinating history of architectural fads and changes over centuries, of princely splendor and abject pauperism intimately juxtaposed. Their memory was worth preserving, for they were uniquely the product of Dezful and its people.

The wide new avenues symbolized progress and were efficient in moving goods through the city, but they also allowed howling dust storms to sweep their length, scouring the walls of the abandoned structures. There was nothing native about the modern avenues. They defied both tradition and reason: if you preferred less wind, less sun, less noise, and fewer diesel trucks, you would stick to the old city center.

Across the river, we followed the asphalt road as it narrowed and headed toward the town of Andimeshk, known by the tribespeople as Salihabad. Andimeshk grew up around a railway station and now stretches along the highway that carries freight from the Gulf to Tehran. A stream of cooperative

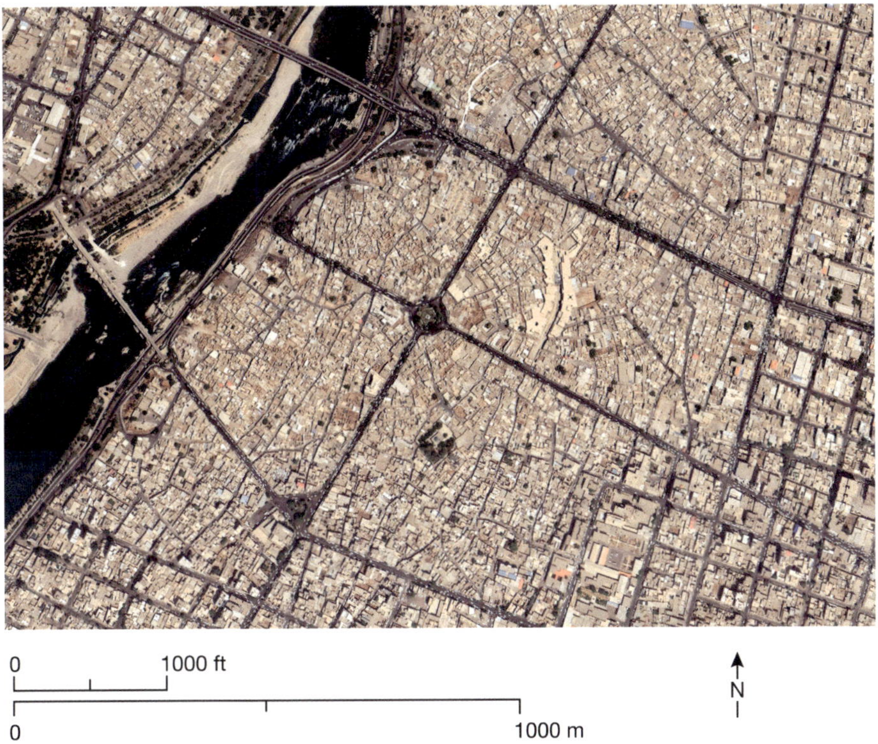

Figure 5.4. In modern Dezful, the riverside houses have given way to new roads, and the old city center is surrounded by gridded housing developments. (Google Earth Pro)

taxis and minibuses carry passengers at all times of the day and night between Dezful and Andimeshk, a distance of some 10 miles (16 km). About halfway to Andimeshk along this road the air force base lies behind a tall chain-link fence. Driving past it, we first discerned the barracks and houses of the enlisted men shimmering without relief on the baking tan plain and then the villas of the generals, situated on the tops of tells (archaeological sites), surrounded by trees and green irrigated gardens. Farther down the road was a community built along the lines of an American suburb. Brick, ranch-style houses sat on small lots along tree-lined streets. This community, built for workers on the American-designed agro-business irrigation project of the Khuzistan Water and Power Authority, was entirely self-contained, with a swimming pool, clubhouse, golf course, and offices. By 1973, most of the

Americans living in the enclave had been replaced by Iranians, who quickly adapted to the American style of suburban life.

To Chin-i Zal

Past Andimeshk, Reza turned the Jeep toward the mountains. At intervals of about sixty seconds, heavy diesel trucks carrying steel girders, pipe, electrical equipment, and crates of goods from around the world hurtled past us on their dusty way to Tehran or to the new factories and military bases being built in the interior.

After a while, the slight incline in the road became more noticeable, and we entered low, gravelly foothills. In time, the walls of the mountain ridges rose above the road to either side. We ascended for an hour or more to a small agricultural plain and then turned onto a rough dirt road leading eastward toward Chin-i Zal, where the nomad camp was preparing for migration. Reza was a very deliberate driver, easing his Jeep around obstructions, carefully crossing ditches, and sliding expertly into four-wheel drive when grades were steep. In spite of his care, the Jeep rode hard. Its stiff frame amplified and transmitted every topographic nuance in the road to our bodies, which were braced against changes in pace and the constant side-to-side tipping.

After bumping along on the dirt road for a quarter of an hour, we came to the ruins of a vast and curious site: the remains of a large community, whose walls were built entirely of boulders, situated on the edge of a small, clear stream. We stopped to have a look. Rectangular foundations stretched as far as I could see. I climbed up onto the remnant of a wall to get a better look, but I was still unable to make out the limits of the site. Streets were laid out along a rectangular grid. The road we were driving on had been a main street of the extinct community. Sekandar said the road was now used by the tribes during migration.

The buildings of the abandoned town were rectangular and many had an open but walled yard adjacent to them. Sometimes these open areas fronted on a street. The whole layout of the town—its rectangular grid structure, the construction of the buildings, their association with streets—made it appear to be a planned community, perhaps for construction workers on an ancient road-building or irrigation project or for traders along a caravan route. Or perhaps it was a garrison from which tribes could be controlled.

At first I thought that the town might have been abandoned during the Second World War, when the new road was built. As I looked around trying to find pieces of pottery that might tell me the age of the site, I realized that no agricultural land was situated nearby. In fact, the whole region was strewn with boulders from an ancient landslide, and the town had been built of these boulders. I could not definitively identify the few pieces of pottery I found on the ground, but they resembled sherds I have found many times before at other remote boulder-built villages. I suspected that the site dated to Sasanian times, some 2000 years ago, but without proper investigation I could not be sure. If the site was from the Sasanian period, it would correspond with a time of unprecedented prosperity in Khuzistan and adjacent highlands; a period about which, unfortunately, we know little.

Further investigation would have to wait for another time, as we were anxious to reach the camp of our hosts. Without removing anything from the site, we climbed back into the Jeep and drove out of the ghost town toward Chin-i Zal.

Chin-i Zal

Sekandar had visited the camp only two days before to check on preparations for migration and to make sure that we would be welcome. He had not said much about his visit and I had not pressed him, but there was no question that he was apprehensive. I would not know why until later.

Chin-i Zal is a small plain set into the lower ranges of the Zagros Mountains (see Figure 3.4). The Ab-i-Zal, or Zal River, is a vigorous but slightly brackish river. It enters the plain through a deep cleft in the steeply tilted limestone ridge that forms the north edge of the plain and departs through a rugged gorge to merge with the Saimarreh River, which eventually flows into a desolate salt marsh in Mesopotamian Iraq.

As we drove across this plain, following only a donkey trail, I was surprised to see scattered cultivated fields with wheat nearly knee-deep, and equally surprised to see no people. I did not know at the time that Luristan had suffered a severe drought and the crops were stunted. The quiet emptiness, soft green grass, and pastel spring flowers contrasted strangely with the jarring, bumpy, creaking Jeep as it strained slowly across the rough terrain. When we had entered the plain—from a slightly higher elevation—it had appeared flat, but as we drove along its bottom, I saw deep gulleys, isolated hills, and ledges of rock. As we rounded one of these, the camp came into view.

We arrive at camp

The camp selected by Sekandar was headed by Morad Khan, a widely respected, elderly leader of the Baharvand and a cousin of Sekandar's father. In the weeks preceding this visit, Sekandar had conferred with his father and brothers about the trip. He had visited Morad Khan's camp in Chin-i Zal only a few days earlier. Because of Sekandar's influential position in the tribe, we expected to be treated very well in this camp. Still, Sekandar did not seem eager to dismount from the Jeep and enter into camp life.

The first thing I noticed was two white canvas tents—one about a hundred yards from the main group and the other alongside the black tents.

"That's the one we're going to use," Sekandar said, "That's where the schoolteacher has been living." He went on to explain that, since migration was about to begin, the school, which was held in the other white tent, would be moved along with the nomads to the summer campground. During migration and the summer months, school would not be in session.

I had expected Morad Khan to greet us, but he was nowhere in sight. Except for the women and small children, the camp seemed deserted. We had started to unload our baggage near the white tent when a man hurried into camp to give us a hand. Sekandar introduced him to me as Mohammad Ali.

Like the other nomads, Mohammad Ali was slight of build (about 5' 6"), with a slight moustache and without a trace of fat. Bright-eyed and quick to smile and joke, Mohammad Ali's senses were closely attuned to nuances of gesture, facial expression, and tone of voice, searching for clues in attitude to which his own behavior was quick to respond. His dress was typical for the Lurs (Figure 5.5). He wore the traditional baggy pants that tie at the waist, a light-colored shirt open at the neck, and a dark-collared suit coat. On his feet he wore the plastic molded shoes that had replaced the crocheted *givas* of the past. Mohammad Ali moved over rock and plain alike with the unhurried grace of a man who has seldom felt pavement beneath his lightly shod feet. It was clear from the first that he was as interested in us as we were in him. Bright, alert, and without pretensions to tribal power or influence, he would prove to be a good companion and informant.

Figure 5.5. Mohammad Ali, our constant companion, wore typical men's dress: a Western-style suit jacket, shirt unbuttoned at the neck, baggy Luri pants, a felted skullcap, and molded plastic shoes.

Mohammad Ali spoke quietly but with animation as he explained that Morad Khan was away searching for a mule that had strayed or been stolen. He had been gone for several days and was expected back at any time. Mohammad Ali defended Morad Khan's absence by emphasizing the obvious: A strong mule is a nomad's most valuable possession, especially with migration nearing, when the mule would be needed as a pack animal.

As we soon learned, searching for missing animals was a recurring activity; the loose management of herds allowed ample opportunity for an animal to disappear of its own volition or to be stolen. The thought of theft was uppermost in the minds of the nomads, who attributed most losses to thieves. They worried incessantly, especially during migration, about raiding. It was generally acknowledged that Morad Khan's mule had been stolen. But by whom? The venerable leader had mounted his horse and gone in search. He would visit scattered camps to inquire if they had seen his animal, and he would engage in talk of politics, weather, and the impending migration. As elder statesman of the tribe, Morad Khan was called upon to participate in decisions, to arbitrate disputes, to discuss the merits of possible marriages, and to lend his expert knowledge to whomever needed it.

While we were unpacking, one of Morad Khan's wives began heating water for our tea and soon invited us to sit on a carpet in the guest area of his tent. Tribal leaders often screen off the right-hand third of their tent to serve as a guest room. The remainder of the tent is used for domestic activities and serves as the women's area when guests are present. When the water had been heated, she handed the pot to Mohammad Ali, whose family had been with the Baharvand for generations. He served us in Morad Khan's stead, pouring the tea into little glasses. While we drank the tea, the old woman prepared a tray of food. When we had finished the tea, she laid before us a large, round aluminum tray with a lunch of newly baked flat bread, yoghurt, *dugh* (buttermilk), and fried eggs, which we consumed voraciously and perhaps a bit self-consciously while we engaged in desultory conversation.

Although the members of the camp knew who Sekandar was and knew that he was affiliated by family ties, I was clearly an outsider. Together we represented a remarkable combination of the familiar and the exotic. Under normal circumstances, Morad Khan would have hosted the breakfast and led the conversation. The other members of the camp would have sat nearby watching and listening. But without Morad Khan's direction, no one knew quite how to act. The people were both curious and apprehensive. It was the same with us. By reputation, Sekandar knew the people, but he had never lived among them. I was an unabashed tourist, taking in all that my eyes and ears could sense of my new surroundings. Under the circumstances, conversation did not come easily. We all wondered how we would get on with each other. As I sat sipping tea, I began to wonder about Mohammad Ali, the young man who served us and was kneeling attentively in the front of the tent, facing us while we ate.

Like other pastoral peoples in Iran, the Lurs are divided into tribes headed by males of named lineages. The people we were camped with are descended from Bahar, hence the tribal name, Baharvand (see their genealogy in Chapter 17). In turn, the Baharvand comprise one of the Dirkavand tribes, who descended (perhaps only in myth) from Dirak. According to tradition, Bahar lived in the late sixteenth century, eleven generations ago. Naturally there are relatively few persons who can claim direct descent through the male line, and thus the title Baharvand. The land, won through generations of fighting other Luri tribes, belongs, according to tribal custom, to the descendants of Bahar.

The other people in the tribal territory are *homsa*, Sayids, and Lutis. The Sayids are people who claim to be descendants of the Prophet Mohammad. By virtue of their birth, they are entitled to support from all the people. The Lutis are an outcast group who play music at celebrations, perform circumcisions, and provide other services for the tribal people. These people have neither land nor respect, but they occupy an important niche in the tribal system. Neither Sayids nor Lutis traveled with the Baharvand tents.

The *homsa* have no genealogical claims to either leadership or respect. In its various connotations the word *homsa* means neighbor, member of the camp, and persons of lower rank (in the sense of persons who are subject to another or do not enjoy all the privileges of the society). The *homsa* are a mixed group, many having become attached to the Baharvand after their own tribes were defeated in battle. Traditionally, the *homsa* occupy the land in return for their services. In return, the Baharvand provide leadership and security through binding together a strong following among the *homsa*. The relationship is like that of patron and clients bound together in mutual service and obligation. Thus it is through traditional rights and obligations that Morad Khan leads the nomads and Mohammad Ali serves him.

Chapter 6

Morad Khan's Camp

After lunch, Mohammad Ali needed to return to his herds, and it was time for me to stay out of the way. I wandered around, investigating the traditional winter camp. Morad Khan's camp was one of about fifty of the tribe's camps that were scattered throughout the region. It consisted of five rectangular tents, each roughly 12 by 18 feet (4 x 6 m), with screens on three sides made of reeds closely woven together with goat hair string in geometric patterns. The screens were supported by stakes. The tent covers were of loosely woven black goat hair, supported by posts and a ridgepole along the midline (Figure 6.1). The front side of the tent was open so that the tent cover, supported by thin poles, created a shelter from sun and rain. The tent was tied down by guy ropes and its base was surrounded by a low, protective shield of thorn bushes to keep prying animals outside. Domestic activities were carried out in the front part of the tent. In the evening, the valuable horses and mules were tethered a few yards beyond—close enough to be watched but far enough to keep them from being entangled in the guy ropes.

Figure 6.1. Morad Khan's tent. He is at right, removing brush from the base of the walls, preparatory to taking down the tent and closing camp.

Figure 6.2. Morad Khan's winter camp is sheltered by a small ridge on the north side. There are five black tents. The canvas tent, used by the schoolteacher and later by us, is on the left.

The five tents were arranged roughly into two rows, with the open sides facing south. Morad Khan's tent occupied the front center. As befitted the head of a camp and the respected leader of the tribe, Morad Khan's tent was somewhat larger than the others, but otherwise was no different from the tents of the *homsa* who shared his camp. Mohammad Ali's tent was always to the left rear, and the tent of an elder *homsa*, Safarali, was to the right rear (Figure 6.2). The teacher's tent was to the right of Morad Khan's, a position that we, as its new occupants, were to maintain throughout the trip. We discovered later that the tents maintained the same spatial relationship wherever the camp was pitched.

Figure 6.3. Winter camps are sheltered with stone walls that enclose the tents.

The people in Morad Khan's camp were bound together by traditional rights and obligations as well as by convenience and requirements that changed with the seasons. The same people were not always in the camp, although the overall structure remained the same from year to year. During the winter, the nomads occupied tent sites bounded on three and sometimes four sides by walls made of dry-laid stones, which shielded the tents from chilly winds (Figure 6.3). These camps were located in well-sheltered areas to provide further natural insulation. As the weather warmed, the nomads abandoned the stone foundations and moved to less sheltered grounds, where there was fresh grass, a change of scenery, and fewer vermin. During the remainder of the year, tents were set up in open areas with the protection of only the surrounding reed screens.

Exploring the surroundings

Our camp was pitched just at the base of a steep ridge that formed the southern boundary of the flat plain. Inasmuch as there was little activity in camp, I decided to have a look around the valley. Cameras in hand, I climbed to the top of this ridge for an overview of my surroundings. I could see how the Ab-i-Zal had cut directly through the northern ridge and then wound across the plain to erode its way through the ridge on which I was standing. This was typical of rivers in Luristan: they cut through mountain ridges rather than flowing along them, because the rivers were in place before the land pushed up to form the mountains.

By midday, bright sun and heat close to 100°F (38°C) caused the flat land below me to shimmer, making the outlines of rocks and ridges indistinct. I could make out parallel horizontal lines at the bases of the crags. Some of them lay within planted fields, but others were on apparently barren hillsides. I recognized these linear features as terraces. Someone had gone to great effort to create these ribbons of flat land like steps up the sides of the slopes. Who had done it, I wondered? It was evident that whoever had built them had depended solely on rain to water the fields, for there was no possibility of primitive irrigation: water does not flow uphill, and above the terraces were only rough mountainsides of soilless dry rock.

Back in camp, I rejoined Sekandar. Morad Khan's wife Taji was sitting in front of her tent making a basket. Using withies that she had cut early in the spring and buried in the river to soften, Taji was completing the base of a coarse basket that would eventually be used as a chicken coop. As I watched, her gnarled fingers swiftly wove the over and under pattern that radiated out from the center.

Looking for something to do, Sekandar asked her if there were fish in the river. She replied, "Why not?"

We asked her for some dough to use as bait. When we told her we would catch some fish for her, she advised that the largest fish are in the deep pools. I asked whether the people in camp fished. She shrugged, implying that they did not bother. Taji went into the women's side of the tent, where she removed a basketry tray from the top of a copper pot and scooped out a small handful of dough that was sitting in preparation for the evening meal.

Taking the dough and some of my own hooks, Sekandar and I walked down to the river, which was only a few hundred yards from camp. At that point, the river flowed through a steep, narrow canyon that prevented us from reaching the water, although we could see large fish swimming lazily in the deep green pools. Following a narrow footpath, we worked our way downstream along the bank until we found a spot where we could clamber out onto a large, smooth rock. At that time of the year, and lacking recent heavy rains, the river was clear, allowing us to see the fish against the rocky bottom.

Taking a glob of dough from the little plastic bag where I had stored it, I pressed a small bit on the hook and expectantly dropped the line into the water, letting it drift slowly toward the fish. As soon as the hook came into their view, the fish darted after it, fighting for the chance to snap up the morsel. As the first fish hit, I jerked the line and pulled a small squirming carp out of the water. Quickly Sekandar slipped a line through its gills and dropped the fish back into the water. Strike followed strike and soon we had a nice string of little catfish and carp.

I was so thoroughly engrossed in harvesting the fish that I did not immediately notice the small crowd of spectators that was growing behind us. When I looked up, half a dozen women and small girls were peering at us from behind some tall boulders, giggling and whispering among themselves. A few of the young boys from camp hunkered quietly close by, attentively studying our angling technique. It turned out that we were fishing only a few yards from the spring where the women fetched water. The spectators tittered nervously, but were too shy to talk to us. Nevertheless, when I released the smaller fish back into the river, I could hear the clucking sound that Persians customarily make with their tongues to indicate disapproval. Later this waste was reported to Taji, who informed us that, in the future, all fish, large or small, should be brought in.

By the time we arrived back in camp, the white school tent had been dismantled and was being tightly folded so that it would fit onto the back of a donkey. Because of its shape and single-piece construction, it could not be rolled into two equal parts to hang on either side of the pack animal, as black tent covers were. Ill-adapted to these circumstances, the tent had to be folded and piled on top of a donkey (Figure 6.4). Two men heaved it aboard and then

Figure 6.4. Sekandar (left) and Safarali finish packing a donkey for its trip to the highway, where its baggage will be loaded onto a truck. Kialon Kuh is in the background.

cinched it down for its short trip to the highway, where it would be loaded on a truck for shipment to Deh Mohsan, a small settlement near Khorramabad, where sedentary members of the tribe lived.

Mohammad Ali later told us that because of the lack of sufficient pack animals and manpower, many nomads who winter close to a road ship some of their belongings by truck to their summer territory. In fact, some of the members of our camp and some of the black tents would also travel by truck.

As we returned to our tent, the women who had been to the spring were already making late afternoon tea and beginning preparations for dinner. Mohammad Ali, who had remained most of the day close to camp in his capacity as host, served our meal. After tea, he took Sekandar out to try his luck at hunting partridge. This gave me the opportunity to explore the terraces I had glimpsed after lunch and to look for archaeological ruins that had been reported to lie along one bank of the river.

It was good for me to have an excuse to leave camp alone, for this gave me some time to begin sifting through my first impressions. Up to this point, I had had no real contact with the nomads, because my relations with them were still formal. We were just getting accustomed to one another. It would take some time to get acquainted with the surroundings and the daily routine and to learn the names of the people. For their part, the nomads displayed what I took to be subdued curiosity about me: my age, my family, my clothes, my baggage, and the reasons why I was with them. They did not ask at first; they just observed intently. It was time to step back away from camp and take a longer look.

I headed away from the tents toward the spring along a trail worn by the feet of women carrying water, and then I diverged from this track to continue upstream along the bank of the river. I followed a footpath across stretches of dirt and picked my way through the rocky sections, keeping close to the river so that I could look for caves or other features that might have archaeological implications. The late afternoon sun at my back cast long shadows, accentuating the irregular terrain and reflecting vivid orange off the waters of the river. The site I was looking for was called Chin-i Zal, after the name of the valley. An archaeologist by the name of Sir Aurel Stein had visited the site in 1935. He reported that it contained stone buildings with barrel vaults still standing and that it was probably of Sasanian age (Stein 1940). The site had never been thoroughly studied, but it sounded similar to Dareh-Shahr, a Sasanian city in the Saimarreh Valley to the west, which had been conquered by the Arabs in the seventh century AD. Some weeks before, we had visited this site, which was still remarkably intact (Figure 6.5). It seemed that the Sasanians had made concrete to withstand two millennia of exposure.

As I walked along, I was struck by the lack of any obvious sites of ancient habitation. In most of the flat plains of western Iran, there are mounds that contain the ruins of mud buildings built upon ruins of older mud buildings, sometimes spanning hundreds of years. Here nothing broke above flat land except glaring white, eroded gypsum hills, and there was no sign whatsoever of the site I was looking for: only fields of wheat, dust, and thorny shrubs.

Figure 6.5. The remains of Dareh-Shahr, a Sasanian city that was conquered and destroyed during the Arab invasion of AD 641. Similar vaulted buildings are in Chin-i Zal and other valleys of Luristan.

I wondered why there were no mounds. Had the plain, except for a brief time, been occupied seasonally only by nomadic people? If my conjecture was accurate, I might be able to find the traces of ancient pastoralism that I had come to Iran to find. Was the site reported by Stein built on top of an earlier prehistoric site, as so many historic towns and villages are? With this at stake, I quickened my pace across the boulder-strewn plain, searching the landscape ahead for telltale signs.

A mile or so beyond, I came to a bluff overlooking the river, isolated from the plain by a deep gully. Just at the edge of the little bluff, the random scatter of stones that covers most of the plain suddenly began to show a pattern. A line of rocks here, and another there, joined at a corner. This had to be the edge of an old site. Rapidly striding ahead, I caught sight of a vault nearly hidden under a camouflage of turf. Its front was open enough for me to crawl inside, but peering in, I saw that the room, about fifteen feet long and tenwide (five by three meters), was nearly filled with straw that nomads had stored for their animals. In 2000 years, the vault had scarcely cracked at all. The interior stones were firmly cemented together with a hard concrete. The building itself was partly dug into the ground, so that the tops of the walls were just above the surface. This explained why I could not see them from a distance. In the millennia that had passed since the last people lived here, dirt had formed a thin layer on the roof. Grass had taken hold in the dirt and now the vaulted buildings were merely grassy hummocks hardly distinguishable from the surrounding land.

Quickly I climbed to the top of the bluff for an overview of the site. In the lengthening rays of the setting sun, I was able to see across the plain to the ridge that walled in the north side of Chin-i Zal. There I could see the agricultural terraces on the flanks of the ridge (Figure 6.6). Below me, around the site, I could see stones that had been piled up by modern farmers to clear fields for plowing. From my vantage point, I could make out many vaulted buildings, most of which were broken, some with half a vault, others with no roof at all. It was a ruin without majesty. Half suffocated by earth, it looked like a wretched hamlet of troglodytes.

My initial disappointment was dispelled soon by the realization that, in all of Luristan's history, people had succeeded in constructing permanent residences in only one short period. Nearly 1500 years ago, someone had invested in the labor of channeling rainwater, building agricultural terraces, and constructing nearly imperishable houses. Who were they? What happened to them? Today the site lies nearly unnoticed, except for playful herders who dislodge rocks to throw them into the river or to build little walls to screen themselves from the sun or wind, and by nomads who store straw or wheat in the abandoned old buildings. At the time of the Roman Empire, there may have been hundreds of people living here. What is there left to tell us of them?

I searched the ground for pieces of pottery or other artifacts. Previously on archaeological survey, at sites of this age, I had found large quantities of sherds, stone tools, and even coins. But there were only a handful of nondescript sherds made in a style I was not familiar with. The site was disappointing in a way, but a larger mystery because of it.

Figure 6.6. Despite low rainfall, which makes rain-fed agriculture problematic, people in the ancient past—perhaps Sasanian times—cultivated crops on terraces, the remains of which are seen here as parallel horizontal lines on the talus of the distant mountain.

Evening was rapidly approaching as I kicked around the rubble, trying to gain an impression of the layout of the community. The task seemed futile without mapping instruments, so I turned and headed back toward camp. On the walk back I wondered why the nomads did not build houses like the ancients had. Tents are singularly drafty in the cold, they leak when it rains, and they cannot be secured against marauders. At the very least, why didn't the nomads rebuild some of the vaults to provide more secure bins for their straw and grain? Nothing at the ancient site suggested that any recent improvements had been made. With the evidence right before their eyes, lack of knowledge that such things were possible could not be the explanation.

Winding my way back to camp, my gaze stuck close to the ground in the hope of spotting some evidence of an ancient nomad camp, a piece of characteristic painted pottery, some stone tools, or the remains of a tent site no longer in use. The search yielded nothing. I returned to camp, puzzled by the past but in anticipation of what might happen next among the living.

Just before I reached camp, Sekandar joined me and we walked the last hundred yards together. Sunset was nearing. The herders were returning to a bustling camp. The soft evening light filtered through the clouds of dust enveloping the herds as they milled aimlessly around. Their owners checked to make sure every animal was accounted for. The lambs and baby goats bleated excitedly as they nuzzled up against their mothers. Smoke scented the air where women were building fires to bake their evening bread. Safarali, returning to his tent after securing the horses and mule, was greeted by his snarling dogs. They kept a discrete distance when he raised his arm as if to throw a rock.

The return of Morad Khan

Across the plain, a lone rider mounted on a large brown mare slowly plodded toward camp. From a distance we could see only a darkly clad man wearing a fedora, wearily slumped forward in his saddle. As he drew close, he exchanged a few words with the herders but did not interrupt his progress until he arrived in front of his tent. There, Safarali rushed up to hold the reins of the horse, as the fatigued old man dismounted. Morad Khan had returned alone: the mule was still gone.

Sekandar and I returned to our tent to watch and wait. Morad Khan greeted Taji and then began to unsaddle his horse. He worked slowly, with deliberate movements, laying the saddle down just outside the guest end of his tent. He covered the saddle with the pad and then removed the halter and added it to the pile. Safarali led the horse a short distance away to graze, while Morad Khan stooped to enter his tent and wearily settled down on his carpet.

Sekandar obviously expected some sort of greeting, but the old man took no notice of us. In a low voice, Sekandar began to tell me some things about Morad Khan. He said the leader was regarded as the most knowledgeable of any of his generation about the internal politics of the tribe. Some men are known for their fighting abilities; others for their political skills. Morad Khan was not a fighter. He was a talker, a man widely sought for counsel and arbitration. For Sekandar's purposes—learning the history of the tribe—Morad Khan was the best possible informant. However, Sekandar believed Morad Khan had used his position to his own advantage rather than the tribe's general benefit by making deals in which tribal lands were given to other people in consideration of monetary or other favors.

"If that is the case," I queried, "won't Morad Khan object to your presence?" Sekandar acknowledged that this was likely, but a situation he nonetheless savored. In a society where trust does not run deep, one tends to suspect the worst, even among members of the same lineage.

Sekandar had spent the afternoon hunting with some of the *homsa*. According to them, in the last several years, Morad Khan had begun to display the erratic behavior of senility. His arbitrary and often unpredictable demands had caused a number of the *homsa* to leave his camp to live elsewhere. Moreover, they told Sekandar, Morad Khan wanted to take another, very young wife to comfort him in his declining years.

As we were speaking, our venerable leader sat on a carpet before his tent, alone and quiet. Bareheaded, revealing his closely cropped graying hair, he pulled gold-rimmed spectacles from a pocket in his jacket. From another pocket he fished out a green flowered cloth and unwrapped a worn copy of the Koran, which he fingered with mechanical deliberation. The old man then began to read in serious contemplation, moving his lips in silent words. As the sun set, he stood up, and, pouring from a copper pitcher, splashed water over his calloused hands and feet. Then he stood facing Mecca and began his evening prayers. The other members of the camp paid no attention.

Following prayers, the old man stood in front of his tent and surveyed the camp, counting the animals and checking equipment. Safarali helped him tether the mules and horses in front of his tent. In time we learned that this routine was invariable. While Safarali rounded up the animals, Morad Khan searched among the baggage for chains and stakes, which he drove deep into the ground to secure the animals. When the horses and mules were led to the front of the tent, Morad Khan clamped iron cuffs around their forelegs and locked them with crude keys. After the animals were secured, Safarali returned to his own tent and Morad Khan made a tour of inspection, visiting briefly with the men at each tent. When he was satisfied that everything was in proper order, he returned to his tent and sat quietly at his fire. Then he was ready to receive guests for dinner.

Both Sekandar and I were puzzled by Morad Khan's apparent disinterest in us. Throughout these proceedings, he had not so much as glanced our way. I was ready to dismiss this as a case of first things first, but Sekandar felt slighted and wondered if we had inadvertently done something to offend the old man. There was no graceful way to find out. We just sat and watched and waited.

To me, Morad Khan looked like any other Lur. Certainly there were no remarkable signs of status about him, except in Safarali's deference. In his seventh decade, he was the traditional leader of some 150 tents of nomads and still physically vigorous, although he suffered some forgetfulness and lapses of graciousness. The *homsa* attributed this to his advancing age. He carried his six feet with the erect posture that characterizes all nomads, and he walked with the same measured, gliding steps whether he was on flat ground or on steep, rocky slopes. But he had developed a paunch that was not typical of nomads, even those of his age.

Morad Khan wore the traditional baggy black trousers of the Lurs. His trousers were worn through at the knees and ragged at the bottoms. At various times, his shoes, like Mohammad Ali's, were made of molded rubber, but he also wore traditional Luri crocheted *givas*. Like most Lurs, he wore a suit jacket of Western cut rather than the traditional cotton cloak (*kordin*). And like most of the nomads, he had only one suit to his name. In camp he wore the traditional Luri *kola* (a felted, bowl-shaped cap), but for important occasions he put on a battered fedora. He was a man of status who displayed none of the tangible symbols of power and respect.

I observed that he participated fully in the chores of handling animals, loading baggage, and even working with the animals in the fields. Later he told me that in times past he would never have done those chores, because then his claims to the services of the *homsa* were absolute. As the traditions of his way of life were eroding, Morad Khan was becoming isolated and abandoned. While he tried to maintain a façade that nothing had changed, his situation—in tattered clothes, without adequate labor—and the gossip of the *homsa* belied this.

In fact, Morad Khan retained little power. Through a long series of governmental interventions into tribal politics and land tenure, through his own political machinations, and through his irascible nature, he had lost both legal and moral sanctions of control over most of his people. But as one of the genealogical heads of his tribe, as a man of age and literacy, and as one whose ascetic life was an example for others, he still commanded respect.

He was far from the richest of his tribe. In the relatively egalitarian Luri tribes, the leaders are the first to become impoverished during hard times. Customs of hospitality require them to welcome all guests, whether strangers, friends, or relatives. The worst insult to a man's reputation is to accuse him of being inhospitable. Leaders are bound by tradition to share what they acquire and to pursue only traditional lines of endeavor. Only the *homsa*, with no social standing to lose, can accumulate property and grow rich at the expense of their higher born brethren. Thus, like many of the formerly powerful and even wealthy traditional leaders whom we visited in our travels, Morad Khan was a poor man. Unlike some of them, he was never really wealthy, even by nomad standards, but he said that once he was surrounded by twenty-five tents. By local standards that was well off, but a far cry from the leader of the Papi tribe, with 2000 tents, or the *wali* of Pusht-i-Kuh, who had 2500 families of retainers at his camps.

At his age, Morad Khan should have had no more cares about running his household. He should have had strong and able sons with families of their own to make his remaining years comfortable and easy. Instead, his oldest son Mukhtar was a sore disappointment to Morad Khan, who saw him as an effete and ineffectual youth. And Mukhtar's open denigration of his father's way of life brought deep sorrow to the old man.

Morad Khan's comfort was in his wives. Taji, some fifty years old, shared her husband's acid tongue and sometimes-surly disposition while she ran his tent with a firm hand. Worn beyond her years, as most Luri women were, she was a voluble talker and one of the most skillful persons in camp. Her knowledge of traditional Luri life was unexcelled, and we learned as much from her about Luri life as we had questions to put to her. Taji shared Morad Khan's encyclopedic knowledge of people, places, and events. When his memory failed, Taji had the answer. If Morad Khan was the premier tribal politician, Taji was the power behind the throne and the overseer of women. She traveled from camp to camp as incessantly as he and for the same reasons: to keep the political fences mended, to give advice and counsel, and of course to spread gossip, pick up rumors, and help arrange marriages. When Taji was away on business, Ghamartaj, Morad Khan's younger wife, assumed responsibility as hostess and manager of the household, a job she performed with tact and grace.

The camp consisted of twenty-five people comprising five families; there were fifteen males and ten females. Twelve were immature and unmarried, three were older than fifty years, and ten were under thirty.

One evening Morad Khan told us that the ideal family has six males, two to three females, six cows, five mule/donkeys, and one hundred fifty to two hundred sheep/goats. In his prime he had twenty-five tents under his control. His situation in 1973 was quite different. The mature animals for the entire camp totaled only fifty-five sheep and one hundred and seventeen goats, an average of only thirty animals per tent.

Morad Khan moved slowly and with dignity. He seemed to be a man quietly resigned to his fate, and he was the only person in camp that I observed carrying out any religious activity.

Morad Khan's household included himself, two wives, and five children, who ranged in age from about twenty years to ten months. As accurate ages are not recorded systematically in Luristan, they are only approximate. At the time of our visit, Morad Khan was about seventy-two years old. His birth, around 1900, could be established in reference to events in Luristan that Sekandar could date on a calendar. He had two wives: Taji, about fifty, and Ghamartaj, who was in her mid-thirties. His household included two teenage sons, a daughter aged twelve, a baby girl, and an unrelated shepherd. In addition, he had two adult daughters living elsewhere.

Mohammad Ali was about thirty years of age and had a wife, Khawar, who was about twenty-five. An unrelated shepherd lived with them. Mohammad Ali's family had served the Baharvand for some generations.

Originally from the Malzeri lineage of the Papi tribe, Safarali had been attached to Morad Khan's camp for about twenty years. He was said to be around sixty years old, while his wife was around fifty. One of Safarali's sons, about thirty, lived in his father's tent with his wife of about the same age, and a daughter. Another adult daughter was married and living in another camp.

Safarali, a grizzled old *homsa*, was in charge of the mules, donkeys, and cows (see Figure 6.4). He had been attached to Morad Khan's camp for many years and provided many necessary services. He was particular adept at catching mules and other animals, and he sometimes carried calves on his back. We saw him catch a mule by offering it a plate of salt. When the mule sniffed the salt, Safarali grabbed its front leg and engaged in a short dance with the animal until he could secure a halter on it.

Panjali, Mohammad Ali's brother, had been with Morad Khan all his life. He was about twenty-three years of age and had a wife, Golafruz, and two teenage brothers.

Hirdali, another brother of Mohammad Ali, was about twenty-three and was married to Sadigha, who was about twenty-five. They had a son, Iraj.

Paina, cousin of Mohammad Ali, was a young man not yet eighteen. He and his wife, about twenty, occupied the remaining tent. They had been with Morad Khan for about ten years. Paina's mother and a teenage cousin also lived with him. Paina and his wife were married at the age of twelve, a decade or more earlier than normal. This came about because Paina's father had passed away when he was just a few years old. Since he was the only child, his mother arranged for an early marriage so that he would have children soon—preferably a son, to carry on the name of the family.

Mohammad Ali, Hirdali, and Paina were all originally from the Qalavand tribe. We saw in this mixture a typical camp composition, but not an inevitable one, for members may switch allegiances. Morad Khan told us that if a member of his camp left, he would chase him down and bring him back.

Morad Khan's son Mukhtar was a strapping young man and the teacher of the tent school. He had a seventh-grade education (Figure 6.7). As an army conscript, he was assigned to the school: he taught there, but at a third of a teacher's salary. He had no interest in the pastoral life and did not participate in the migration. This deprived Morad Khan of an able-bodied man and ensured that his pastoral legacy would not endure. Mukhtar talked with disdain of nomadism, but on our return visit to the summer pasture a month later, it was Mukhtar in charge of the camp in his father's absence.

Figure 6.7. Mukhtar (left), son of Morad Khan, taught boys from nearby nomad camps. School was held in the white tent or in the open, depending on weather.

Mukhtar dressed in Western-style clothes: a short-sleeved white shirt unbuttoned at the neck, Western-style trousers with a belt, and white and black sneakers. Some fifteen to twenty male children from surrounding camps attended the school he taught, learning elementary skills in basic subjects. Since the school year would not be completed by the time migration took place, the tent would be re-erected in the summer pasture, where it would remain to begin the fall term. At the time of the return migration, the tent would be packed back to Chin-i Zal.

Taller than the average nomad, Mukhtar was an outgoing and outspoken young man with no intention of following in his father's footsteps. His intense dislike of tent life was shared by many of the youths who attended the school. The promise of education, even on a very elementary level, was a life free of manual toil. It was doubtful whether many of the children seduced by the prospect of such a life would remain in the mountains.

Throughout the trip, we repeatedly heard that Morad Khan regarded Mukhtar's disinterest in the traditional ways as a disgrace. That opinion was shared by most of the elder nomads, who normally would begin to turn to Mukhtar for advice and counsel as the logical inheritor of his father's role. As it was, with no suitable successor in the offing, the men were anxious about a future without a tribal leader. Morad Khan's remaining few years were their only buffer between the life they understood and a future for which they were not prepared by training or disposition.

Taji, Morad Khan's older wife, was a voluble source of information and advice. She participated in discussions, voiced her opinions, and interacted with Sekandar and me. She also called Morad Khan by his first name: Sekandar said that this was the first household he had seen where a woman did so. Taji participated, as did others in the camp, in preparations for the migration. On the trail, she took advantage of proximity to drop in on other camps where she had relatives, and she sat where she could hear the men discuss their businss. She did a man's work in loading pack animals, and she ran the household with a firm hand. Some said, however, that she was the one who kept other tents away and contributed to Morad Khan's troubles.

Most of the tents in any camp were occupied by *homsa*: people attached to the Baharvand but not through genealogical affiliation. Many, including Mohammad Ali and his brother Hirdali, had been attached to the Baharvand for several generations. In the past they served at the order and pleasure of the leader.

Mohammad Ali, one of the *homsa*, was the most able man in the camp. In his late twenties or early thirties, he managed his own household and provided assistance for Sekandar and me. Seemingly always cheerful, he was slender, agile, and indefatigable. It was he who worked incessantly to keep the pack animals moving and on the trail, retying their loads when needed. He normally dressed in a Western-style suit jacket and Luri baggy pants, although toward the end of the migration he donned a checkered tunic, wore a bandolier, and carried his rifle. Away from government authorities, the tribesmen seemed more at ease.

Khawar, Mohammad Ali's wife, had yet to bear a child—a source of concern among the pastoralists. Like other women, her face was uncovered, although she had a headscarf and headband. Her long hair hung on either side of her face down below her shoulders. She wore a long, loose, flowered dress over loose pantaloons, and on her feet were molded rubber shoes. Unlike women in some tribes, the women in this camp wore little or no jewelry.

The camp had two babies: Hava (Morad Khan's daughter) and Iraj (Hirdali's son). The babies occupied each other when they were not riding on their mothers' backs or being nursed. As there were no toys, the babies crawled on the ground, handling whatever caught their attention. They were chubby, dressed in sweaters and scarves, and appeared to be quite happy. They seldom cried (Figure 6.8).

Two herd boys, both teenagers, took the sheep to pasture by dawn and often returned after dark, as it was the practice to stay out until the sheep stopped eating. At noon they returned to camp with the herds and held each animal as it was milked; then they relaxed with sugar-laced tea (Figure 6.9). In the evening they sat by the campfire warming their bare feet and singing Luri songs to the sound of milk sloshing in the goatskin churn.

Sekandar spent his time interviewing members of our camp and others about Luri and Baharvand history. In the evening he played Luri music for the herders and others. I observed as much as possible of the daily routines, took extensive notes, and took photographs and video to document the trip and the people. We lived entirely on the schedule and diet of the camp, staying observant but not intrusive.

This group shared customary responsibilities. To be sure, the *homsa* served, but in the absence of Morad Khan, Mohammad Ali led the camp, and during the summer he had his own separate camp. The women worked constantly, milking the sheep and goats (Figure 6.10), tending the chickens, cooking, making tea, gathering firewood, churning milk, and much more. If the migration ended late, the women had to churn the day's milk at night (Figure 6.11). The women managed the tents: their service to husbands and guests gained prestige for their families. Their most important role was to bear and rear children, especially males.

Figure 6.8. Little Iraj, nephew of Mohammad Ali and son of Hirdali and Sadigha, is watching his mother work.

Morad Khan's teenage daughter, Ozra, was a flurry of activity—packing, chasing animals, and doing other chores. Typically, girls were in charge of collecting water in goatskin bags. They attached these bags to their backs with straps and then, bent from the load (which probably weighed close to 40 pounds or 18 kg), carried them to the camp. Ozra often looked after the lambs and kids that had been left loose while their mothers were being milked. This involved running after them, trying to "herd" them in the right direction, and, when that failed, grabbing one under each arm and depositing them into a screened pen

Figure 6.9. The boys spent most of the day with their herds in pasture, but when they returned the flocks for milking they could rest and have a cup of tea. It is customary to take a lump of sugar in the mouth and drink the tea through it.

for the night. On the trail she chased down kids, scrambling with ease over rocks, and took the switch to horses and cows that needed encouragement.

Although modern conditions had reduced the circumstances of many nomads, in this particular region, the family herds had seldom exceeded one hundred animals. The sparsely vegetated, rugged terrain, and the necessity for cooperative camping units to provide mutual security, limited the size of the herds. A single family with large herds could not protect them against marauding, nor would they have the womanpower for milking and other

Figure 6.10. At noontime each woman milked her own flock (center right), while the kids and lambs were kept out of the way.

necessary tasks. Among nomads, meat on the hoof is the most prized booty, for it can be driven off under its own power and later eaten or converted directly into money or other tangible goods.

Most scholars of pastoral nomads would consider the livestock in Morad Khan's camp to be too few to maintain the viability of the camp. It has been estimated that, in Iran, sixty head are required for each family—which was twice the average found in Morad Khan's camp. However, it should be pointed out that the sizes of herds fluctuated from year to year. Also, by the time of our visit, the Baharvand depended on the animals less for sustenance than for the cash they got when they sold them. Clearly people who depend on meat need many more animals just to maintain the viability of the herd. But the Baharvand ate little meat. They milked the animals, made dairy products for their own consumption, and sold the wool. Young males were sold early in the summer. With the cash, the Baharvand bought a few things

Figure 6.11. During migration it was often necessary for the women to churn butter in the evening, after the camp had settled in a new location.

in the markets, but they had relatively simple needs. They grew wheat and barley for bread and animal feed, and when the crops failed, they ate acorns. Thus, unlike some other tribes, the Baharvand managed with herds that were inadequate by some standards.

This had important consequences for cooperation within the camp. As Mohammad Ali explained, when families did not have enough milk to make butter and cheese, all the milk was pooled and given in rotation on successive days to the separate tents. This pooling of resources was one way the solidarity of the camp was maintained. In earlier times it was chiefly the need for security against raiding that held people together. Formerly the bonds between families were stronger, and they were maintained with the rigid discipline necessary for military organization.

It may seem surprising that nomads planted crops, because conventional wisdom holds that nomads disdain farming and trade with villagers for the wheat they require. Although farming was a relatively new practice among these people, it was certainly not disdained in the past. Throughout Luristan, Sekandar and I were repeatedly told that several factors had discouraged farming. Long ago, we were told, there were fewer people, larger herds, and adequate meat. Moreover, hunting of wild game supplemented the diet, and the abundant acorns of Luristan served as a kind of substitute grain. Finally, when tribes were constantly fighting, planted fields and stored crops were in constant jeopardy. It was thus unnecessary and unprofitable to farm.

The cessation of all but sporadic fighting enabled the nomads to plant crops successfully, usually in both the summer and winter territories. Unfortunately, this practice led to a decrease in grazing land and encouraged denser settlement in what had formerly been pastures. As a consequence, rather small herds were typical in much of the area we traversed. Under good conditions, farming has considerably greater economic potential than herding. However, in Luristan, the nomads remained more interested in animals than in farming, and they were somewhat cavalier about methods of planting. The fact that they planted in marginal farmland, which required either above average rainfall or irrigation to produce high yields, dictated that farming might contribute relatively little to their overall standard of living. Most nomads told us that their standard of living had declined in the last generation or two.

Dinner

As I sat watching and reflecting on the camp, the chores were gradually completed and the people began to cluster around their fires to have dinner. Morad Khan called from his tent to inquire if we were ready to eat. We stood up, walked the few steps to his tent and greeted him with the customary *salaam aleikum*. We took off our shoes and sat down on the carpets, which had been spread for us around the small guest fire in the men's section of the tent.

By this time it was dark outside, but Morad Khan had lit a small kerosene lantern, and its feeble flame softly illuminated the central part of the tent. Morad Khan motioned for us to sit toward the rear of the guest area, where Taji had put pillows for us to lean on. The round pillows were about the size of a loosely rolled sleeping bag, covered with a brightly printed fabric purchased in the bazaar. Morad Khan, Mohammad Ali, and Safarali sat cross-legged, facing us, with their backs to the open entryway of the tent. Behind them, at a respectful distance, some boys stood outside, watching and listening. Taji and Ghamartaj worked behind a reed screen that separated the women's and men's parts of the tent.

As soon as we were comfortable, Taji set a large round aluminum tray on the carpet in front of Sekandar and me. On the tray were large round flaps of flat unleavened bread. Pieces of chicken, roasted over the open fire, lay on one piece of bread. A stew made of potatoes, lentils, and sour lemons was served in an aluminum bowl with a heaping tray of rice. Taji had prepared a feast.

The right hand is the primary utensil. It is customary to use the bread to grasp the chicken and stew, thus keeping one's hands clean, and also to use it as an aid in gathering up the rice that one compacts into a ball with the right hand before inserting it directly into the mouth. I watched and tried my hand at balling rice, but I wasn't as deft as the natives, and I spilled some onto the carpet. Men eat quickly, keeping their mouths full, often with bulging cheeks. In some camps, tablespoons are used to ladle the gravy over the rice and to aid in eating it, but this is hardly a universal practice. Most nomads do without any tableware at all.

This mode of eating is not second nature to most Americans, but it can be learned fairly quickly. I never became really confident handling the rice, probably because rice was rarely served. As we ate, the nomads watched us intently, keeping their observations to themselves.

One eats quickly in a nomad camp, for the members of the family and assorted other guests are waiting to share the food. The meat was served on a tray shared by Sekandar and me; Morad Khan, Mohammad Ali, and Safarali shared another. Each in turn ate quickly, speaking little. When the men had finished, Taji returned to take the trays to the family side of the tent, where the women and children would finish off the remaining food. In the meantime, Morad Khan prepared tea over the small fire next to the rug.

The preparation and serving of tea that evening was a duplication of a pattern that we had observed repeatedly: a host serving his guests. As guests, Sekandar and I were seated back from the front of the tent on the best carpets. Just inside the tent, hollowed out of the bare dirt, was a small fireplace lined with stones. Morad Khan sat to the side of the fireplace. Using a large perforated iron spoon, Taji brought glowing embers from the women's cooking fire to the fireplace and set an *aftabe* (a large brass pitcher) full of water into the coals to heat. Then she brought in two small, straight-sided glasses and two small china saucers. She put the glasses and saucers into a small aluminum bowl, which she handed to Morad Khan. Pouring hot water from the aftabe into the bowl, he swished the small glasses and the saucers round and round. Two or three little glasses and saucers could easily be accommodated in the bowl, as the glasses held no more than three ounces each. After each washing, Morad Khan removed a glass and saucer from the bowl. The glass was then filled with hot water, which was poured over the saucer into the bowl. When all of the glasses had been processed, they were placed on a small round tray, ready to be used.

While this was being done, Taji brought the sugar bowl, a round wooden vessel on a short pedestal, along with a cone of sugar and a small adze. Sugar, purchased in town, is sold in hard cones rather than in granulated form. With the adze, the host breaks the sugar cone into smaller lumps in the wooden vessel, which looks like a bowl with a chopping block in the center. By this time, Taji had also brought Morad Khan the china teapot and a handful of tea. He added tea and hot water to the pot, which he placed upon the coals to steep. When the tea was ready, glasses were poured for the guests only. Rarely did we see more than two glasses in a tent, as drinking was generally done sequentially rather than together. Honored guests often had their glasses filled with lumps of sugar before the tea was added—a custom most Westerners find distasteful, because it yields a sweet syrupy drink. Often the nomads poured the tea into the saucer and drank from it rather than the glass. The sugar invariably left a residue, a sugary sludge, in the glass after the tea was consumed.

When the glass is returned to the tray, the host rewashes it by pouring boiling water into it and then pouring the water over the saucer and into the aluminum bowl. The glass is refilled repeatedly until the guest signals he is finished. The signal may be a verbal "I don't want any more," or the guest can return the glass to the tray on its side.

Hosts normally attempt to press additional glasses on their guests, but after three glasses have been consumed, the tea is usually presented to the next in rank, who drinks from the same glass, rinsed in the same procedure. When the guests, hosts, and all the miscellaneous male onlookers have had their tea, the pot is returned to the women, who finish what remains.

Serving tea is a formal, standardized ceremony varying only in the style of equipment used, not in the general procedure. Nevertheless, formality may break down among familiar members of the same camp, even amid considerable differences in rank. For example, Morad Khan drank tea along with Mohammad Ali and Safarali and even with his wives when they were relaxing together *en famille*.

Guests are to be shared by all, and that evening was no exception. Whenever we visited nomad camps and seated ourselves for tea, all males who were not engaged in something more important would arrive and arrange themselves cross-legged along the front of the tent to share the society. In their turn, they would be served tea, but whether they entered into discussion would depend on circumstances. At these times, especially in the evenings when the herders were in camp, boys of all ages came together with the adults. The boys never spoke, unless spoken to.

The women were not entirely excluded, for they remained no more than ten feet away, screened from the men by a reed partition. It was not uncommon for them to enter into discussions, unless the event was very formal. The women had to be attentive so that they knew what was needed in service. Also, as complementary members of the society, they wanted and needed to know as much as the men about what was going on. The women of other tents eavesdropped from a short distance or waited until their men returned to learn the details of the conversation.

One might expect nomads to retire early, with the waning of daylight, but that was not the case. The Baharvand had only a few hours of undisturbed sleep under the best circumstances. They usually waited until near midnight to lay out their bedrolls and lie down. Their endurance astounded me, as I often sat with head nodding, wishing to conclude the activities of the evening in order to get some sleep. More often than not, it was Sekandar and I who first felt the need for sleep. When we excused ourselves and returned to our tent, Mohammad Ali often followed us for some lingering conversation. He would tag along, assuming, I suppose, that we, like the nomads, did not like to be alone. Certainly he was also interested in our belongings, although he showed this only by intent observation. Only when we pulled the covers over our weary bodies would he leave.

Chapter 7

Tribal Customs

Our first night in camp passed uneventfully. We slept soundly on the floor of the canvas tent until almost six o'clock the next morning, when we woke to the sounds of animals heading to pasture and domestic activities around us. Emerging from the tent, we found Taji ready to serve us breakfast, which she brought to our tent on a tray. This morning, like every morning to come, she laid on the tray two or three round pieces of newly baked, unleavened bread, a bowl of yoghurt, two tablespoons, and a pot of tea. One eats yoghurt (*mast*) either by dipping bits of bread in it or with a tablespoon. It is customary for several people to share the same bowl of yoghurt and, not infrequently, the same spoon. This morning Sekandar and I ate alone. For us breakfast was leisurely, an uninterrupted chance to reflect on the previous day and anticipate what would come next. In our tent, we conversed in English.

Since Sekandar and I had no specific duties, and there was no urgency to getting started with anything, we asked for some hot water for shaving. Taji brought the water in a small aluminum bowl, the same one used the night before for washing the tea glasses. These bowls are an essential household item. They are used to scoop water out of springs before pouring it into skin bags, for serving food, and as ladles for dipping the heating milk for making yoghurt. The bowls fit neatly on the top of the head, where women carry them when they are returning from the springs with their goatskin bags full of water.

While waiting for Sekandar to shave, I worked on my notes and thought about our first day with the camp. Sekandar was uneasy and dissatisfied with the way things were going. His brother had warned him against traveling with Morad Khan because he thought the old man would not treat us well. Sekandar's brother had had some dealings with Morad Khan and did not like or trust him. But that was not my preoccupation. As far as I was concerned we were living well, and I had nothing personal at stake in my relations with Morad Khan.

Sekandar went out to empty the bowl and bring fresh water, leaving me to ruminate. After months of visiting pastoral camps and observing the daily routine, I was beginning to understand what it was like to be a nomad. The light from the campfire flickered softly as I contemplated the hardship of nomad life. From early youth, the nomads become inured to adversity: to the weather, to long hours or days of arduous activity, and—on balmy days when the camp was settled—to the oppressive inactivity of watching the monotonous munching of sheep and goats in the pastures. In the spring, the shepherds are in the pasture by dawn. They return to camp at midday and may not crawl into their beds, side by side with their family, until long after midnight. After a few hours of fitful sleep, they are out again to repeat this endless cycle. The needs of the animals and the whims of nature regulate their activities. All else is secondary. From childhood the nomad learns that the future depends on the flocks he tends.

Children are customarily the focal point of group activity around the tent and campfire (Figure 7.1). Because children are thought to be incapable of understanding adult matters, few things are not discussed in their presence. Children grow up with knowledge of virtually everything in their universe. Daily they observe the management of the flocks, the milking, the cooking, and all of the domestic tasks. They are never out of the sight of several persons at once until they begin to go out with the animals. The lives of children are preeminently social and will remain so until they die. Whether seated beside their fathers or behind the reed screen, children hear everything, from the most serious political deliberations to the most scandalous gossip. They learn by heart the legends and songs of the tribe. Nothing is private in a tent camp. Conversations are often carried on between tents, and one can scarcely whisper without being overheard. Domestic squalls, moody silences, and conversations of political import are thus widely shared. Children have ample opportunity to witness sex acts at night in the crowded tents. They are fully familiar with birth and death, which ordinarily take place, sometimes before their eyes, several times a year.

Nomad women

The women in nomad camps are understandably shy at confronting a strange foreigner, but on closer acquaintance they become openly friendly. In their camps, among close friends, they are attentive and dutiful to their husbands, but appear to be anything but meekly submissive. They are resourceful and capable in their own right and interact incessantly with other female members of the camp through conversation, borrowing utensils or food, sharing fire, and babysitting. They are, however, illiterate and isolated from the outside world. They said that they might visit Khorramabad once every two years, but they never visited Dezful, where tea, sugar, and rice were purchased for the migration. The buying of supplies, including cloth and clothing, was strictly men's work.

Ghamartaj, Morad Khan's younger wife, had recently given him a daughter; Taji had not borne children. Ghamartaj and Taji shared the household duties, taking turns carrying water, bringing in firewood, making butter and yoghurt, and baking bread. Both shared in taking care of the young daughter, and they ordinarily got along well, despite their difference in age and the fact that they served the same man under the same tent.

It was a rare man in Luristan who had two wives, for they represented an expense that most could not afford. On the other hand, multiple wives greatly eased the burden of preparing food and tea for the innumerable guests that a leader—such as Morad Khan—expected to entertain. A man was especially fortunate if his wife served her husband and his friends efficiently and without complaining. Nevertheless, multiple wives do pose problems. Even though marriages are arranged, and girls often have little choice in the matter, wives vie for their husband's attentions. One of the wives is usually

Figure 7.1. Khawar, Mohammad Ali's wife, with her nephew Iraj. She is dressed in baggy pants under a loose-fitting dress. Her hair hangs down either side of her face, and her head scarf hangs in back. She wears molded shoes.

dominant, controlling the internal affairs of the household. She controls the food and decides what to cook for guests. She might have become dominant through the social position of her family, or because she had borne more sons, or because she was more attractive than the other wife. Normally each wife expects to share equally in the chores and to receive sexual favors in equal measure. It often happens that the younger wife is subservient to the older and bears the brunt of the onerous chores. But the tables may well be turned at night, especially if the younger wife is more attractive. In these cases, the older woman may find that her husband stops visiting her bed, which may only exacerbate the daytime tyranny she exercises.

Some of the older men we met on our travels expressed a desire to take a girl of about twelve for their remaining years. Morad Khan was no exception, although his prospects for doing so were not good. Morad Khan already had a tent full of women and a rather outspoken companion in Taji, who might expectedly make strong objections to additional matrimony. Men were not totally exempt from these pressures. And, of course, there were financial implications.

One does not find women's liberation in tribal society. Women serve their husbands and, as in Iran generally, are at the beck and call of their masters. Little love appears to be lost in the relations between husbands and wives in much of Iranian society. Yet in Morad Khan's tents, his wives called him by his first name and he called them by theirs. Usually a Luri man simply calls to his wife "*va tonam*" (literally, "to you I am calling"). If she has borne him a son, the man may call her "mother of so and so." Similarly, a woman calls her husband "father of so and so," or "*boway bacho*" (father of children). Generally speaking, the women in Morad Khan's camp displayed an openness of behavior that we did not see among their counterparts in the villages and towns of western Iran.

In the tent camps, tribal women go about unveiled, exposing their faces in a way that would be considered immodest in the towns. They readily engage a man in conversation, on occasion even sitting with men while serving tea to them. Of course, this is done with decorum and reserve, but these acts are measurably different from the custom in the settled areas. The women in the nomad camps are far less restricted in behavior, perhaps because they participate in a way of life that requires intimate cooperation and a performance of required duties by both sexes. In nomad societies, the two sexes are often together. In camp, they are never more than a few feet apart. It is one social world for a husband and wife, who complement one another and embrace the entire camp as an extended version of the family.

Here there is no ambiguity in the roles that are expected of each sex. The women expect to marry at an early age, to bear children, and to serve their husbands. In the restricted world of nomadism, all women do these things. The marriage partners are the focal points of the family, the most important social unit in tribal life. What they do together determines the future of the family and children.

Nomad men

Tribal society emphasizes males. To become an influential and successful Lur there are ten qualities, besides breeding, a man should achieve. A young man should display bravery, fighting and riding ability, and be a good marksman. As he matures and his more vigorous days slip behind him, he must develop his oratorical abilities and be generous and hospitable. As an older man, his most important qualities should be patience, tolerance, and dignity. In Luri, the graybeards (*rish aspeh*) are called *kardida*, or experienced men. They provide advice, leadership, and counsel.

Birth is not celebrated as such. Close friends of the family greet the newborn with a simple "happy welcome" (*va khair o shadi oumoyi*). The mother must not cook or work for a week following the birth. For forty days following the birth, the mother is considered impure and should not have sexual contact. The infant is also considered to be impure for the first two weeks, although people are permitted to touch it. After this, the baby is assured of surviving, and it is given a name from the tribal repertoire. The name cannot be the name of someone living, for this would be an insult.

Infants are at the center of domestic activities, crawling around or being carried in a sling on the mothers' backs. They are seldom disciplined and are indulged when they cry. As children grow older, they gradually assume adult duties. The boys begin to take out herds and the girls carry water and firewood and help with the cooking and with the tending of younger children. One learns by example and participation to become a pastoral nomad. Most skills are mastered long before children are actually able to take charge of their own lives. The transition to adulthood is a gradual one through which children pass almost imperceptibly.

At about thirteen years old, the boys are circumcised in a ceremony performed by Lutis, an "outcast" group that provides services to the tribes, most prominently by playing music for celebrations such as marriage (Amanolahi and Norbeck 1975). Both circumcisions and marriages often take place in the summer pastures, when the camps are in close proximity and the weather is fine.

Young men marry when they have the capital to afford the bride price. Often a man must delay marriage until he is in his late twenties or early thirties, but girls are usually married while still in their mid-teens. After marriage, a man usually lives in the camp of his parents—sometimes in their tent—until he has amassed sufficient capital (usually herds) to strike out on his own.

The death ceremony is the most costly and prolonged ceremony of a nomad's life. It consists of three parts: the burial, the ceremony after the burial, and the afterlife. Immediately after death, relatives begin the obsequies, consisting of demonstrative crying—the women wail "*waywayway*" and the men cry out "*aboway*" or "*abraray*." The women often jump up and down and scratch their faces and cut their hair. In keeping with Islamic custom, burial takes place within twenty-four hours of death. If death occurs during the day, burial takes place as soon as the body has been washed and a Sayid has read from the Koran. Otherwise burial is delayed until the following day, and the people take extra precaution lest the body be stolen by a supernatural being during the night. When possible, a sheep is killed in honor of the deceased for a last supper among the family and close relatives.

Burial consists of wrapping the body in a white cotton shroud, tying the big toes together with string, reading a prayer from the Koran, and placing the body in a grave, head toward Mecca. Graves are usually close by, often along a trail. Few nomads use cemeteries.

After burial, relatives who were not already present are informed by messengers of the date for *pors*, the rite of mourning, an event which might last as long as twenty days in the case of an important person. Guests at this rite, who sometimes arrive in large parties, are expected to bring a gift of cash, animals, rice, tea, or sugar. The ceremony itself consists of a Sayid reading from the Koran and chanting dirges. At the end of forty days, another dinner is given for close relatives, thus ending the death ceremony. The Baharvand have a saying that at death you lose twice: one of your loved ones dies, and you must pay for all the burial rites. Funerals may release the departed to a better world, but they often leave the bereaved families impoverished from the expense of entertaining members of the tribe who come to pay their last respects.

Each year in March, just before the spring equinox, a celebration is held for the dead. For the Feast of the Dead, the women prepare sweets, mentioning the names of the deceased while they are making the food. The act of mentioning the names conveys some of the food to the dead. In a society without writing, this custom preserves memories of relatives and friends long after death.

In Luri terms, the smallest social unit is called the *tazga*, or hearth, rather than the family. Around the hearth, one eats, sleeps, relaxes, and entertains guests. Almost all domestic activities take place in the front center of the tents. Ordinarily, the only time women are absent is when they go, usually in groups, to collect water, fuel, or local plants. At these times they may socialize and bathe. Bathing in the tent area is one of the few activities precluded for women, because men might be present.

In contrast, men may be gone from camp most of the day as they follow the herds through the pastures. A herder enjoys a good deal of solitude, but he is seldom out of sight of another herder. Conversations between herders are carried on over prodigious distances, well over a mile. Their characteristic cries to one another can be heard wherever one travels in tribal areas. When pastures are thin, shepherds allow their flocks to graze well into the night. In Chin-i Zal, animals were commonly brought back to camp near midnight. The herd boys exhibited an agility over rough ground and slippery scree that is learned only with difficulty, if at all, by one who has been accustomed to walking in hard-soled shoes on concrete sidewalks. Even in the black of night, I never saw or heard a man slip or fall over rough terrain.

The livestock are demanding creatures. At night the mature sheep and goats are brought close to camp, and the lambs and kids are penned up inside the tents. Mules and horses are tethered close to the front of the tents, with the donkeys and cattle close by. At night the animals bleat, whinny, and bray; they stamp aimlessly about, and their breathing and cries are punctuated by the barking of dogs and irritable calls of people who have bedded down for the night. For some two hours each night, barring unusual circumstances, the camp is relatively quiet. But let there be rain, thunder and lightning, or the howls of wolves and calls of jackals and hyenas, and the herds never quiet for a moment. On these nights, the nomads are continually up. The dogs bark to what seems the point of exhaustion—if not for themselves, then for the people who have to hear them. Rain drives the animals against the tents, where they become entangled in the guy ropes or crash through the screens.

The fronts of tents are an open invitation for soaking sheep and goats to share some of the humid interior with the miserable people inside. One passes such nights alternating between readjusting bedding to avoid the ubiquitous drips and shooing away animals to avoid their constant trampling. There is no sleep on a rainy night for human or beast.

For the herder, *showma*, or moonlight, is especially prized because one can see on moonlit nights. One Baharvand commented to Sekandar, "How wonderful it would be if we could have moonlight, youth, and spring forever." If there is no moon, and the stars are masked by clouds, the fear of wolves and thieves causes men and dogs to sleep with ears strained against the slightest sounds in the dark. At any suspicious sound, the dogs raise the alarm and the men begin to shout from tent to tent.

Long before the first rays of dawn warm the eastern sky, the camp begins to stir. Women are up lighting fires and making bread. By sunrise, braced with hot tea and bread, the herders are out of camp with their flocks. By the time the sheep and goats have left camp, the cattle, horses, and mules have been untethered and put out to pasture. Within an hour after dawn there are no men in camp.

In the spring, around eleven o'clock, when the sun is near its zenith, the herds of sheep and goats are brought back to camp for milking, a process that takes nearly an hour. Once milked, the animals are allowed to join their lambs and kids for nursing. After helping with the milking, the herders have their tea and bread and a short rest. Around one o'clock in the afternoon they leave for the pastures, not to be seen again until the animals have grazed their fill. When the flocks stop eating, they are herded back into camp. If the forage is lush, this may occur late in the afternoon, but in thin pasture, it may be closer to midnight.

Back in camp, the animals are sorted by owner and counted. If any are missing, the herders return to the hills to search for them. On occasion, the men are gone for several days trying to round up their animals. In the meantime, others in camp—another herder or older children—take care of the remaining animals. The cycle of activities determined by the animals is repeated habitually day after day, and gives way only to the seasonal cycle, which has been repeated year after year for untold generations. It is a cycle to which man has acquiesced his will. Such is the nature of herding.

Farming in Chin-i Zal

I knew the nomads would be leaving on migration shortly, so it was essential for me to gather detailed information on how they used their winter pasture. Around the camp, I could see fields that had been planted the previous winter and others that had only been plowed. The grain looked anemic. It was green but with short, sparse stalks that supported yellowing heads with poorly developed seeds. I was surprised at the number of fields, because I thought that pastoralists did very little planting.

To answer my questions about agriculture, I sought out Mohammad Ali. He said all the nomads plant wheat and barley, using most of the flat land in the valley for this purpose. In spite of this, I observed, the land was not irrigated as it was during Sasanian times. The nomads planted crops on some of the old terraces, but they had not rebuilt those that had fallen into disrepair. Mohammad Ali acknowledged this, but said he did not know who had built the terraces; it must have been "the ancient ones." He offered no explanation for why his people had not rebuilt the irrigation systems. For him, it was enough to say that they belonged to other people and other times.

He explained that in the thin, dry soil, only about one-third of the arable land is cultivated each year, because the soil requires two years to regenerate enough for good crops to grow again. However, more is planted in the fall, when the nomads return from their summer pastures, if it looks as if there will be plentiful rains. When sufficient rains fall, the seeds germinate and the plants lie dormant through the winter months, waiting for the spring growing season. Harvest occurs in the late spring, shortly after migration back to the summer pastures. The tribe had followed this pattern for all of Mohammad Ali's thirty years.

Like all the pastoralists we talked to, Mohammad Ali stressed that formerly the tribe did little planting. Rather than farm, the nomads relied heavily on acorns for making bread, and sometimes they harvested the wild wheat and barley which grew naturally in their territory. They attributed the fact that farming was practiced on a much greater scale than formerly to peace among the tribes and the greater number of people in the territory. When the tribes were constantly fighting, they were not always able to protect their crops. In those days, the nomads were more prepared to move quickly to escape attack. Mohammad Ali lamented the increased number of people competing for the same marginal resources, a problem brought about by pacification and the settling of most nomads in villages. With more people competing for the same grazing and farm land, the herds of each family had to be reduced. Thus the people came to depend more on cereals for their food.

Mohammad Ali clearly recognized the problems faced by the pastoralists, but from his vantage in the mountains he could barely grasp how the modernization of his country was affecting him. He could not link the rising demand for meat in the towns and cities, and the availability of trucks to transport the animals, with the fact that meat had become so costly that nomads could no longer afford to eat their own livestock. Instead they sold it to pay for equipment and supplies that they could not produce for themselves. In effect, the nomads had become hybrids: subsistence farmers who followed herds in a typical nomadic pattern.

Each year the average family needs about 250 *man* (about 1650 pounds) of wheat for bread, and another 250 *man* of barley to feed the chickens and supplement the diet of the livestock in early winter, when little natural forage can be found. Among some tribes, barley is made into bread, although it is considered a poor substitute for wheat. Nevertheless, barley grows better when rains are deficient and, in many years, nomads eat barley bread. The Baharvand said this was not their custom and that they made every effort to buy wheat in the market if their crops failed.

In Chin-i Zal, as in all Baharvand territory, the land was owned by the genealogical Baharvands. The *homsa* planted with permission of the tribal leaders in amounts they specified. Morad Khan, who still controlled the land in Chin-i Zal, planted the largest fields using *homsa* labor. In return for labor, the *homsa* had the right to plant fields for themselves.

Among tribal people, it is customary to measure the amount a person plants by the amount of seed the fields require. On relatively poor land, seed is scattered more thinly than on irrigated plots, so that if a person says he plants 250 *man* of wheat, it is hard to translate this into the acreage involved. Very roughly, 50 *man* will seed two to three acres.

Under ideal conditions, the yield is a tenfold increase, but such conditions seldom obtain. In bad years, there is no grain whatsoever. In most years, the yields are far below the maximum. What hurts villager and nomad farmers alike is that there are often two or three bad years consecutively. One year drought may strike; the next insects; and the third, flooding and erosion. Nomads mitigate these effects by having fields in two places and by irrigating some of them, but because they occupy poor farm land at best, tribal people generally fare poorly in agriculture.

Most of the families of Morad Khan's camp planted about 50 *man* in Chin-i Zal, all of it wheat. Morad Khan planted 250 *man*. To my eye, the crop that year did not look well developed. Early rains had stimulated its growth in the autumn and produced vigorous, tall stalks that gave promise of abundance. But the spring rains did not come when they were needed to bring the heads to fullness. Just before harvest, the stalks stood withered. There had been no rain for almost three months. The grain would be usable only as animal fodder. In most of the fields, it would scarcely be worth harvesting.

It is advantageous to have large separated areas under cultivation. Rains will often fall on one part of the valley and not on others. Crops planted in natural depressions where the water collects after rains, or along banks of ephemeral streams, stand a better chance of success in dry years than do those on rocky slopes or on uniformly flat land. Morad Khan, with his 250 *man*, could ordinarily gain back more than his investment in seed if he planted a number of fields in different locations. The *homsa*, with only one-fifth as much seed in the ground and much less opportunity to spread the risk among the different fields, might well find themselves entirely without wheat.

Apart from his claims to ownership of the land, there was rationale in Morad Khan's having larger fields: as camp leader, he had to serve bread when he entertained guests. He would expect heavy demands to be placed on his supply of food. Moreover, his family was larger than the others in camp. Thus there was some measure of justice in the apparent inequality of the allotment of plots of land. Morad Khan did not prosper at the expense of the *homsa*: what he had, he gave away, as one must with a perishable commodity like grain or livestock.

While the fields ripen, the camp departs for the summer pastures, where the sheep are sheared. A few weeks later, the men return to Chin-i Zal to harvest the grain, leaving the women and children and some of the men to look after the summer camp. Mohammad Ali told us he would be one of those returning after the migration to cut and thresh the grain and store it in bins, where it would remain until the nomads returned in autumn. This supply would be used throughout the winter, until the next migration, when the pastoralists would draw on the supplies left in the summer pasture. In the past, grain would have been ground at one of the water-powered gristmills in tribal territory, but by the 1970s the grain was taken to millers in the city.

Ancient grain bins

As an archaeologist, I focused on the storage bins. I reasoned that if people had stored grain in prehistoric times, I might be able to find evidence of bins in the vicinity of ancient nomad camps. For my study of the history of nomadism, this was very important. With this in mind, I lingered around camp for only a couple of hours, watching the women packing their baggage, and then set out to examine some of the bins.

When I had visited the ruins of Chin-i Zal the day before, I had noticed straw stored in some of the abandoned houses. Mohammad Ali said grain bins were nearby, so I headed back to the site with cameras, notepad, ruler, and compass to record the structures. From the vantage of a low hill I saw them, built into the top of the bank overlooking the river, right in the midst of the ancient site. I could see the modern bins inside some of the old houses, making sensible reuse of the old walls (Figure 7.2). The bins consisted of a roughly rectangular block of small rooms some three to five feet deep, each holding approximately seventy-five bushels of grain. Since the bins had mud walls and plastered interiors—the usual building material in western Iran—they could be constructed quickly in any size necessary. Thus, if there was a large harvest, new bins could be built, and if the harvest was small, some of the previously built rooms would not be needed. When filled with grain, the bins were covered over with a thick layer of mud tempered with chaff to keep the grain safe from rain and rodents alike.

Harvest is one of the busiest times of the year. After the wheat has been cut by hand with sickles, it is loaded onto donkeys and carried to a threshing floor, where animals are driven round and round on it until the grain has been freed from the heads. The threshed wheat is then thrown into the air with a wooden pitchfork to winnow the grain from the chaff. The wheat falls directly back to the ground, while the chaff falls into a pile a short distance away. When it has been separated, the grain is scooped off the ground and put into bins, usually with no further cleaning until it is used in the preparation of food.

The chaff is also a valuable commodity. It is used for tempering bricks and mud walls for houses and storage bins, for beds in stables, and—most important for the nomads—as animal fodder during the winter. The men collect the chaff and straw carefully and store them either in some of the vaulted semi-subterranean houses of the ruined town, or in natural shallow

Figure 7.2. Grain bins built into the remains of an ancient site hold the spring harvest.

caves along the cliffs overlooking the river (Figure 7.3). When both grain and straw have been stored, the nomads return to join the others at the summer pastures.

After recording the grain bins with photographs and drawings, I sat down on a boulder overlooking the river. I wondered why the nomads had built their bins in the ancient site and not near the camp. After some thought, the answer seemed obvious. For one thing, the ancient site provided convenient walls that were already standing and that could be easily modified into bins. Moreover, the nomads moved their camps from place to place in the valley and did not always camp at sites centrally located on the valley floor at a convenient distance from most locations. Probably most important was the

Figure 7.3. After harvest, the nomads store straw in caves along the river bank.

fact that bedrock lay close to the surface across most of the plain, making excavation with simple tools difficult. I later found out that pastoralists frequently used natural holes in the ground or little caves for storage, in preference to digging new bins. Thus, saving labor might have been the major reason for using the old houses. Moreover, because the bins were amid the old houses, their tops were flush with the ground and less visible than if they had been built above ground surface.

Still, the problem of security bothered me. I would have thought that the nomads would hide the stored crops, considering the importance of the grain. The bins in Chin-i Zal could have been fairly well hidden when they were covered over with mud and flush with the ground, but this seemed insufficient to thwart a determined thief. In days before the pacification of the tribes, it was not. But at that time, no other tribes were likely to be in Chin-i Zal, and in fact, there were few people there at all except during the winter season. Security from other people was apparently not much of a problem.

Before Sekandar and I joined Morad Khan's camp, we had traveled through other nomad territories and had seen places where grain bins had been built above the ground. Situated next to trails that nomads followed during migration, those bins seemed vulnerable to raiding. But in all cases, they were located deep in tribal territory, where strangers would be recognized immediately and where it would be nearly impossible to pack out looted grain without being discovered. Without a strong force of armed men, it would have been hard to make off with stored crops, although a few persons might be able to destroy them by breaking open the seals on the bins. But sabotage was not a problem, so grain was relatively secure even in obvious bins, as long as full-scale raiding was kept under control.

The sun was nearing its zenith when I stood up and strolled back toward camp. I arrived around 11:30 a.m. to find Sekandar and Mohammad Ali at our tent making tea over a primus. Ordinarily pastoralists have tea before a meal and then again afterwards. Today was no exception.

A relaxed afternoon

We had arrived back at camp just before noon, shortly after the herders had returned the flocks to be milked. This was a busy time of day for the women, who did the milking, and for the men or boys, who held the animals and selected fresh ones to keep the process moving. In the meantime, the children kept the lambs and kids some distance away until the milking was finished. When the mothers and the young were within sight and sound of one another, it was often difficult to keep them separated. When at last the milking was finished, the baby animals, bleating plaintively, dashed pell-mell to their mothers, who gave them suck to all the milk that remained. Then the animals bedded down around the tents for a noontime nap, while the women returned to the tents to prepare lunch. The herders ate and napped. This was not a very social time of day, as each family tended to its own business.

While Ghamartaj milked Morad Khan's flock, Taji looked after our needs and began hunting up the ingredients for lunch. She decided we should have eggs. Chickens are the property of women, each of whom usually has one or more laying hens and frequently a quantity of chicks. A single woman seldom has enough eggs to serve much of a meal, so when she has guests, a collection is made and the women pool their resources. For lunch this day we had six small eggs fried in a shallow aluminum pan. When nomads fry eggs, sheep fat is poured into the pan to a depth of about two inches and brought to near boiling temperature over coals before the eggs are broken and dropped into the fat. While still sizzling and popping, the soft eggs are served in the cooking vessel. Pastoralists consider sheep fat a real delicacy and eagerly sop it up on pieces of bread. The women had been advised that I had strange tastes and preferred rather less of the valuable oils, so they managed to fry the eggs in a relative skim of sheep fat.

Using the bread as our primary utensil, Sekandar and I ate some of the eggs and yoghurt and then passed what was left to Mohammad Ali. He ate his portion and eventually returned the tray to the women, who consumed what little food remained. Following our repast, it was time once again for tea and then a nap. It was early April, but the temperature was already warm enough at midday to be oppressive, and in the absence of urgent business, everyone slept for a couple of hours.

Household utensils and implements

All the families in the camp had about the same inventory of utensils and implements, most of which men bought in the bazaar or from other Lurs. Each household had an assortment of copper and aluminum bowls for milking, making yoghurt, mixing dough, and cooking. Their lids were usually flat trays woven by the women from reeds. Bags made of goatskin—still bearing legs, for only the head and feet had been severed—were used for carrying and storing water and milk products. The women hung the goatskin bags (called *mashk*) from a wooden tripod to churn milk.

All households had *aftabes*, or jugs with a handle and long spout, usually manufactured of copper or brass. Women stood these jugs in the coals to heat water. They served equally well for pouring water for washing, mixing dough, and the like. Jugs that were used solely for toilet washing, when the water need not be heated, were sometimes made of cheap plastic.

Each family had a tea set, comprising a teapot, usually of china. The pots were often repaired with strips of wire soldered around them like a loosely woven basket. The lids were often tied on with a string. These pots, along with small tea glasses (similar to small jelly glasses), were kept in wooden boxes specially fitted to keep them from breaking during migration. Made in local bazaars, the boxes were sometimes brightly painted or encased in sheets of scrap metal. Such a box might read Maxwell House or Pabst Beer if it was manufactured of damaged surplus tin exported to Iran by American companies. The insides of boxes were usually lined in fabric such as red velvet.

Each woman had a bread pan (*saj*), a concave iron disk about two feet (fifty centimeters) in diameter with an iron handle on the edge. To bake bread, the woman first coated the pan with ash on the concave side to distribute the heat more evenly and then placed the pan over the fire with the ash side down. While the pan was heating, the woman mixed dough in a shallow copper pan and then formed the bread by slapping the disc of dough between her hands until it reached a diameter of about eighteen inches. She draped the circle of dough over the hot bread pan and let it cook for about a minute before she flipped it over to brown on the other side.

Each family also had a flat iron ladle for scooping ashes and for carrying live coals from one fire to another. Metal tongs were sometimes used to move wood around in the fire, but just as often people used their bare hands. (Hands grow remarkably resistant to heat as a result of continual exposure to hard work, the weather, and infrequent washing.) Some wooden spoons, a knife, some tablespoons, and possibly teaspoons constituted most of the remaining equipment necessary for preparing and serving food.

More exploration

Our white tent with its tight canvas weave was like an oven unless the flap was wide open, and then the flies poured in. As I lay on the ground I looked up with dismay at the stubble of flies clinging to the roof of the tent. I blocked them out of my mind by closing my eyes, but I could not ignore them when they descended to perambulate across my face, treading on my eyelashes and poking insistently into my nose. Even my hands were crawling with flies. I flailed at them and turned face downward but they resolutely sought me out. I pulled a sheet over my head and immediately began to sweat from the stifling humidity. What could I do? Suddenly I had an inspiration. I fished around in my baggage for my cummerbund, the yards of finely woven blue material that are wrapped around the waist on the traditional Luri costume. Stretching out full length, I spread the cloth over my entire body and lay down. The material was thin enough to allow ventilation yet tightly woven enough to keep the flies away. I soon drifted off into undisturbed sleep.

After my nap, I decided to do some more fishing. Sekandar and I had just about fished out yesterday's pool, so we tried several others, but without success. Since our subsistence did not depend upon our catching fish, I stashed my hooks and line on a rock and walked downstream alone to see if I could find a place to bathe. Nomads feel little need to immerse themselves in water, ordinarily getting along by washing only the hands and face daily. Few adults ever bathe, although children sometimes go swimming if there is suitable water, and adults may get totally immersed when they are crossing rivers. In my own case, I was less concerned with dirt than I was with cooling off.

After scrambling around Chin-i Zal and sitting alongside fireplaces, I had gotten my khaki pants pretty well smudged with dirt, so it seemed a good idea to wash them while I had the chance. Presently I found one of the rare strips of beach deep inside the walls of the canyon, where I could wade out into the water (Figure 7.4). After stripping, I gave the sweaty clothes a quick wash with a bar of soap and let the flow of the current rinse them. Bushes and rocks provided convenient drying racks in the hot sun.

Then I waded into the river, gingerly, bruising my tender feet on each and every pebble. Without shoes I would have been a cripple in no time, since I was not used to walking barefoot like the nomads. As I waded out into the water, each step seemed more painful. I hoped in vain that the cold water would eventually numb my feet. Finally I found a pool where I could submerge my body and let the water lave away the sweat, while I relaxed without many conscious thoughts.

On either side, the sheer cliffs of the canyon rose directly out of the river bottom. The rushing water muffled any other sounds, and I felt a thousand miles away from another human being. How unlike a nomad I was, deliberately seeking and relishing my solitude. A nomad's life is intensely social; for Westerners it can be offensively intrusive. Lying in the water was so relaxing that I felt no guilt at not being busy climbing up and down hillsides in search of archaeological remains.

On the opposite shore, some fifty feet away, a group of four gray donkeys had worked their way down a torturous trail from the plateau above, to have a drink and stand in the shade. In time the animals picked their way slowly back up the side of the canyon and disappeared over its rim.

Thoroughly cooled and refreshed, I finally stood up and waded on tender feet back to shore, where my clothes were dry and warm. Soon after I finished

Figure 7.4. The river Zal cuts through the Chin-i Zal Valley. In summer it is placid, but it sometimes brings destructive floods to nomads camped in Chin-i Zal.

dressing, Sekandar arrived to tell me that he had no luck fishing either. While we stood on the banks of the river talking, a man arrived, dressed in typical Luri clothes and a felted brown skullcap. Sekandar had met him before and introduced him to me as Khodarahm, who headed another camp in Chin-i Zal. Sekandar invited him to have tea with us, explaining to me that he was a Baharvand from the Amanolahi lineage.

Together the three of us walked back to our tent. Khodarahm asked how we were getting along and when we expected to leave on migration. He said most of the people in the tribe were as anxious to leave as Sekandar and I, but he was perplexed by Morad Khan's reluctance to depart. A respected man in the tribe, Khodarahm was inclined to leave without Morad Khan. He invited us to join his camp and leave immediately.

The prospect was appealing in many ways. Morad Khan appeared to us to be vacillating unnecessarily in his decision. It was a fact that we were more of a burden in his camp than we would have been in Khodarahm's, where, we were assured, adequate manpower was available to handle our baggage. For my purposes, it did not make a difference which camp we traveled with, but for Sekandar it did. After much discussion, Sekandar told Khodarahm that we would stay with Morad Khan. In the end his decision hinged on the fact that Morad Khan was far and away the best informant in the tribe on its earlier history and in particular on the political events that had shaped the present form of the tribe, matters that were especially important to Sekandar's dissertation. Moreover, we were doing the proper thing in staying with the tribal leader. To go against the custom would have alienated Morad Khan and his camp. Khodarahm understood these reasons and accepted our decision without insult, as pragmatic.

In truth, to this point Morad Khan had not been the most gracious of hosts, a fact that upset Sekandar. As a Baharvand, he had expected better. His father and Morad Khan had fought together and prospered together in their youths. In a very real sense they represented the traditional leadership of the tribe. Apart from this, a tribal leader should go out of his way to provide the best he has for distinguished visitors. But Morad Khan was interminably busy with his own affairs and less than forthright in conversation. Sekandar and I failed to appreciate at first that Morad Khan was in such reduced circumstances that he was unable to provide in the customary way. Still, he had made promises to Sekandar before we joined his camp; he had failed to live up to them. The old man had grown insensitive, casual, and even deceitful in his relations with other members of the tribe, a fact that lay at the heart of his present plight and of Khodarahm's suggestion that we travel with him.

Naturally, Khodarahm had more in mind than our comfort and wellbeing. Like any aspiring tribesperson, he was also testing the political waters, probing for a weakness he could exploit. If Morad Khan had been unable to retain us, and the prestige we conferred, his reputation would have suffered. It would have portended a transfer of power from his leadership to a somewhat younger, more vigorous man with many sons. This was a typical ploy, a traditional way of defining the order of importance. In the end, a leader is only as important as the number of men he leads. Morad Khan was nearing the end of his illustrious career. Khodarahm and the others knew it was only a matter of time before he would be replaced.

Khodarahm walked with us back to our tent. He left to return to his own camp without stopping to visit with either Morad Khan or other members of the camp. As we sat on our bedrolls, Sekandar told me that Khodarahm had once been a renowned fighting man. His demeanor had given no hint of this during our quiet conversation.

Mukhtar

Khodarahm's visit had not gone unnoticed. Immediately after his departure, Morad Khan's son Mukhtar entered our tent. Sekandar and I had both begun to write in our notebooks things we had heard or observed. We did this whenever we had some free time, and I made a practice of doing it at least twice a day. But Mukhtar did not hesitate to break in on this activity. He seated himself cross-legged in the doorway between Sekandar and me and began to complain of pastoral life and his father's resolute insistence upon remaining migratory. His thin face was tightly earnest as he spoke, gesturing softly with his hands.

I was annoyed at his intrusion, both because I wanted to write and because I was tired of his constant carping. Once in the tent I knew he would stay longer than he was welcome, for he could be oppressively gregarious. He believed that as outsiders we would be sympathetic to his plight. But although he was in our tent ostensibly to complain, I knew that he was also trying to find out what Sekandar and Khodarahm had been talking about. Seemingly oblivious to any underlying motive, Sekandar skillfully directed the conversation toward Mukhtar's personal life.

Mukhtar had finished the seventh grade and was working on his exams for the eighth, which was the second year of high school. After finishing seventh grade, he had taken a job as teacher of the tent school at a salary of 8000 *rials* a month, or about $106. Shortly after he began teaching, he was drafted into the army, where he was able to retain his teaching position as one of the "Army of Knowledge" (*Sepahi Danesh*), also known as the Literacy Corps.

Although all Iranian youth are subject to military service, some serve most of their two-year term as teachers, health workers, or agricultural agents rather than as soldiers. This was an important part of the White Revolution initiated by the Shah in 1962. The principles that immediately affected the pastoralists were: "Emancipation of the peasantry through a program of land reform and the abolition of the feudal landlord-peasant relationship; Creation of an Education Corps to wipe out illiteracy; and Nationalization of the country's forests" (Ganji and Milani 1976:39). At a minimum, a fourth-grade education is made available to most people, although it has come relatively slowly to pastoral territories. Although the literacy program was a great success in transforming a nation that was largely illiterate, it ignored the interests of native cultures. Students learned the geography of Russia or the United States, but not of Luristan. Sekandar said he could not recall ever having read a school text in which the names of any of the tribes of Luristan were mentioned. (It is also true of most books on Iran published outside the country.) Nor was Luri written or spoken in the schools. Sekandar was particularly irritated that all names of places on maps of Luristan were given in the Farsi rather than the Luri spelling.

Mukhtar expressed no concerns about the curriculum himself. He complained that while he was in the military, his wages were only half what they were when he was a teacher. He was furnished with military uniforms to wear while teaching, but during the summers, instead of taking a holiday, he was required to do three months of active military duty. All through Iran there were young men and women who served in the *Sepahi Danesh*. When they were from towns and cities and were assigned to remote villages or tent camps, their lives could be very hard, for they often did not speak the local dialects and they had no one of equivalent education to talk to. Moreover, their monthly allotments barely sufficed when they had to buy all their food in the market. In town, bread cost three *rials* a piece, and meat was about a hundred *rials* (seventy-five cents) a kilo. It goes without saying that most teachers ate little meat, for in addition to bread, they also had to buy tea and sugar, as well as any personal necessities. Their wages left them little extra for luxuries, but in truth there was not much to buy in most rural villages. At best, the teachers could expect to catch a ride into town on a pickup truck or Jeep for an occasional spree. Mukhtar did not have these problems, but he suffered all the same.

Although the life of a teacher was not luxurious—and for many it was oppressive—teachers were respected for their education and because they represented the government. The villagers often gave them goods and services, which eased the financial restrictions. In fact, insofar as their personalities allowed and local circumstances provided the occasion, teachers became influential members of a community. They were, in effect, teaching the adults to deal with the political world outside the village. In the absence of strong village leaders, some got drawn into mediating local problems as well. For some teachers, there may have been a measure of satisfaction in this, but for most, the isolation and difficult living conditions made their tours in tribal villages a generally unpleasant and unsatisfying experience. (See Chapter 2 for Sekandar's experiences as a teacher.) Some villagers regarded the teachers with suspicion, particularly as they represented a government whose policies were not universally accepted. They were, at the very least, viewed as potentially inimical to the interests of villagers and nomads.

Eventually Mukhtar turned the conversation back to his father's resistance to settling down. In his mind, there was no reason for the stubborn old man not to do so, just as Sekandar's father had done many years before. I was not able to decide whether Mukhtar had a genuine compassion for his father or whether the settling would simply make his own life easier. The root of the problem may have been that Mukhtar was still dependent on his father. Until he was married and received his share of his father's property, Mukhtar was stuck with nomadic life. After that, as a full-fledged adult, he could do what he liked. When the conversation finally trailed off as evening approached, Mukhtar got up and went back to the tent of his father, and I turned back to writing my daily notes. The sun, which had dropped below the ridge in front of our tent, cast a reddish glow through the sky as the shadows advanced silently toward us. Outside, women chattered, exchanging remarks as they prepared dinners in separate tents. The individual noises of livestock and the sharp barking of dogs punctuated the air.

Thinking about dinner, I asked Sekandar what had happened to the food we brought with us. He simply shrugged, seemingly indifferent. When we were preparing for our trip, we had brought food and utensils so we could be independent. We were not sure how well stocked the camp would be and we expected to make side trips by ourselves to look at archaeological remains. Thus we arrived essentially self-sufficient. As it turned out, Morad Khan's wives were fully prepared and expected to cook for us, so we gave them the food we had brought: ten kilos of green beans, a similar quantity of onions, fifteen kilos of rice, a couple of kilos of tea, and about five kilos of sugar. Obviously, we had not expected to consume all of this between the two of us. Taji had not betrayed any emotion when she received it. The nomads seldom have much rice, since they do not grow it, yet rice is an important staple, especially when there are guests to serve. Neither do they grow onions, and without ours, there would have been none of these highly prized delicacies in camp. Similarly, we knew the beans and bundles of other greens would not ordinarily have found their way into Morad Khan's camp. What perplexed me was that after handling our staples over to Taji, we had seen no sign of them again. Nor would we, except for rice.

Dinner was delayed that evening again until well past dark, after all the animals had been tethered and routine camp chores completed. Sekandar and I sat with Morad Khan in his tent for an hour or so before the dinner was served. It consisted of bread, yoghurt, and rice. We ate the rice as pastoralists like it, with clarified butter dripping over the grains.

Morad Khan, the Baharvand, and religion

Morad Khan appeared friendly and in a relaxed mood that evening, so we asked him about traditional nomad life, especially about the relations between leaders and the *homsa*. In a short but revealing discourse, he described the essence of the relationship. In earlier days, he said, he and others of the Baharvand owned the tribal territory and had it in their power to allocate the land to the *homsa* in return for the latter's allegiance. The harvest from the fields of the *homsa* was divided into four parts, one of which went to Morad Khan. The old leader was emphatic that the *homsa* were absolutely bound to him, obligated to provide any services he needed and to supply him with one-fourth of the products of the fields. The only escape from this system was to flee at night and, in that event, he would track the *homsa* down.

The tribal system was one of highly personal leadership, in which men of unusual political ability attracted other men to them. Traditionally, more men meant more fighters, and tribes expanded by taking from those weaker than themselves. People who were displaced in the process were taken into the tribe as *homsa*, and they owed their continued security to their pledge of allegiance and service. Unless leaders enforced their wills strictly and swiftly, the tribe they had built would soon dissolve to follow another man. In such a system, unquestioning obedience was the best strategy for most *homsa*.

During the glory days, there were twenty-five tents in Morad Khan's camp, but neither he nor the other Baharvand reaped huge riches through this system. This fact was evident in our travels, when we saw the palaces and castles of tribal leaders who had reaped riches through exacting heavy taxes on their followers and subjects. The Baharvand, on the other hand, had always been relatively egalitarian, and leaders such as Morad Khan dispensed what they taxed. Tax assessments consisted of food: a commodity not easily hoarded or converted by remote pastoralists into more lasting and valuable goods. It was surprising to learn from leader after leader that none had put his wealth into money, let alone into foreign banks. Even those who once had enjoyed luxuries had used the consumable "taxes" to entertain, feed their households, and to buy labor to build their fortresses. On the assumption that the system would continue into perpetuity, they had never considered saving for a rainy day. Traditionally, their real worth was in the number of families who served them.

After reminiscing in this way, Morad Khan continued with a discussion of another matter that we were to delve into several times: religion. He volunteered that people had much less faith in religion than formerly; this was partly, he said, because the youths went to school. Along with others who were versed in the traditional ways, he believed that some of the teachings were contrary to the Koran. Although formal Islam had hardly penetrated to the tribes, inasmuch as there were no trained religious teachers among them, the older generation had a strong faith in the words of the Koran. Schooling had given the youth new ideas through a deliberate policy of the government to limit competition from the clergy, Morad Khan said, but the faith of the elders also had been shaken.

He explained how this had come about. He and the other elders all affirmed that in former days they believed in divine retribution as an absolute fact. One man told how, as a boy, he had cast stones at a tree that stood next to a holy shrine; he had been so severely chastised that he was in dire fear for his life. But times had changed, and people had realized that if a person made a false oath on the Koran, he would not lose his crops or be struck by lightning or lose a close relative by death. They knew this by experience and observation.

The elders also believed the Koran was less effective than formerly because there were so many infidels and nonbelievers. According to Morad Khan, it was generally accepted among the nomads that the word of the Koran was efficacious in proportion to the number of believers. Just then they were outnumbered. The old leader asserted that Mohammad had predicted this turn of events. He said that when conditions reached their worst, there would be a second coming of the Teacher to lead the people once again into salvation. In the meantime, he shrugged, the believers could only wait.

Whenever the topic of religion was raised, someone inevitably inquired about mine. The question was more than idle curiosity because, according to Islamic law, nonbelievers are *haram*, or ritually unclean. This stems largely from the fact that non-Muslims eat foods like pork, which are not clean and consequently defile the people who eat them. If an infidel should eat from or even touch the utensils of a Muslim, they must be purified ritually through seven washings. In some instances, the utensils are even broken and discarded.

Even without asking, the people knew that I was not Muslim. In their experience, foreigners were ordinarily Christians. Christianity and Judaism were considered legitimate religions because they also were religions of the book and their traditions are part of the foundation from which Islam was developed. Thus Morad Khan could respect my religion while professing his own.

There are many religions in Iran, although the official state religion is the Shi'ite sect of Islam. From the time this sect was founded, as a minority in the world of Islam, it had been customary for its adherents to conceal their beliefs when it seemed expedient to do so. The practice of concealing one's true beliefs has permeated Iran to the extent that a word *taqiyah* (dissimulation) is used to describe it. This practice, formerly confined to religious matters, has become so pervasive that Iranians assume one is concealing the truth. Foreigners, faced with what appear to be patent falsehoods, sometimes assume that Iranians have no regard for veracity. Given these attitudes and customs, it is difficult for anyone, let alone an outsider, to penetrate the façade that people present. I could only assume that the nomads, well practiced in dissimulation themselves, believed that I also was concealing my true purposes and beliefs from them.

In any event, we never discussed religion in any depth. The matter that concerned the nomads most—my eating habits—was handled artfully by

Sekandar, whose reputation was at stake, since he had lived among the Americans and presumably had eaten with them. Yes, he would say, "in America, some people eat pork, but for the most part they eat beef." This would always cause the conversation to turn, for beef was not considered especially desirable meat.

"But you don't eat lamb?" they asked. We said that not many people eat lamb, and in any event, there are no fat-tailed sheep in America.

"How can this be?" they exclaimed. "In America, the land of riches, people have to eat beef!" The people clucked their tongues in disbelief and disapproval. Moreover, they realized that, since we have no fat-tailed sheep, we must have to use the despised vegetable oils for cooking instead of pure sheep fat.

"Yes," I replied, with downcast eyes and disconsolate expression, to the murmurs of commiseration.

Chapter 8

Waiting for the Word

The next morning, Dust Ali, a member of Khodarahm's camp, came to our tent. Sekandar and I boiled some tea on our primus. While we were drinking, Khodarahm invited us to his camp for lunch. We readily agreed to this, both to see another part of Chin-i Zal and to examine another camp. As Sekandar explained to me later, Dust Ali is not a member of the tribe. He is originally of the Zainehvand, a tribe that was under control of the *wali* of Pusht-i-Kuh, the most powerful leader in Luristan two generations ago. At that time, some members of the Baharvand raided the Zainehvand and captured the camp of Dust Ali's grandfather. Following custom, the Baharvand men divided up the booty: the families, the tents and equipment, the animals. Thus Dust Ali's grandfather and ultimately Dust Ali himself became *homsa* to the Baharvand, where they remain even today, although they are increasingly restive and demand their own share of the land.

A visit to Khodarahm's camp

Dust Ali, a strong-looking man in his early thirties, led the way as we headed south out of Morad Khan's camp. After we had hiked for half an hour or so over a low range of gypsum hills, we found the camp nestled in a conveniently sheltered, small flat area. Like our camp, this one was composed of five tents—or rather, tent places surrounded by reed screens, since the tents had already been packed for migration. Khodarahm's people had moved to this location only the day before from a site where they had spent some weeks, after moving with the advent of fine weather from their secure, stone-walled winter camp.

Snarling, vicious guard dogs greeted us, and our hosts rushed out to drive the dogs back. When the dogs were under control, our hosts invited us to Khodarahm's tent. There some carpets—gathered from several families—had been laid out in the shelter of the reed screens. As is customary when guests arrive, an animated discussion ensued about killing a lamb in our honor. As is also customary, we insisted on something less grand and suggested a chicken. While tea was being prepared, a woman appeared, holding a squawking bird upside down by its legs. Dust Ali took the chicken, gave it a drink, turned its head toward Mecca and then cut its throat. He passed the still jerking bird to Khodarahm's wife who, squatting some fifteen feet away, deftly plucked the feathers. This done, she plunged the bird into a cauldron of boiling water and, along with one of the younger women, completed the cleaning by picking off the pin feathers. We turned our attention to conversation while a tub of rice was put over the fire.

As relayed to me by Sekandar, the men in Khodarahm's camp began a profuse outpouring of grievances against Morad Khan. The complaints centered on land and who should use it. According to the men in camp, Morad Khan felt that Khodarahm's people were no longer loyal, even though they had served the Baharvand for two generations. As a consequence, Morad Khan had been talking with people from other areas about moving them in and Khodarahm out. Khodarahm heatedly maintained that he would not leave under any circumstances.

As these and other men told us, Morad Khan had given permission to camps of other tribes to use part of the traditional Baharvand territory. They said he took money in return for these privileges, and squeezed his own people off the land without recourse. But even though the complaints may have been legitimate, and even with the new legal procedures under the Shah's government, an aggrieved individual sought redress outside the traditional tribal structure only with great reluctance. Thus an unscrupulous leader could systematically bilk his own people out of their rightful holdings. His only punishment, if he was punished at all, would be verbal abuse and the withholding of services.

From Morad Khan's point of view, he was simply trying to maintain a system that he inherited from generations of forebears. Ultimately tribes were only as strong as the people who were willing to follow the leaders. If Khodarahm's people were recalcitrant *homsa*, Morad Khan would replace them. He ensured loyalty by using the time-tested practices of creating uncertainty and competition among factions within the tribe and by granting or withholding favors.

The crux of the problem was this: For the most part, the men in any tribe were reared *homsa*, trained strictly to follow and obey. Reprisals by tribal leaders against fractious *homsa* were swift and often terrible. For example, elder tribal leaders told us that *homsa* who did not obey were stood in chains without food or water, and they were beaten or killed if their spirits could not be broken in other ways. In his heart, every man knew that his own security depended on the security of the group. To be isolated from the group was to be an outcast from the only world he knew.

Tribal society is one of unrelenting suspicion. It is hard, if not impossible, to find a man who will claim that he gives his implicit trust to any other man. In the absence of trust, customary roles and obligations that have stood the test of time provide a predictable structure within which people operate.

After I had listened to the grievances at length, we learned that one of the older men of the camp was in jail. While smuggling tea, he and several others were surprised by some gendarmes. The men tried to escape, and in the ensuing fight, two of the nomads' mules were shot. The Lurs retaliated by surrounding the gendarmes and shooting one of them. Eventually the Lurs released the other gendarmes, who reported the incident to their officers. Shortly thereafter, the Lurs were charged with murder and the case came to court. In matters of this kind, settlements are often made out of court, particularly if money can be exchanged. They were told that they could avoid being executed if they would pay a sizeable "fine." The men then appealed to the tribe, whose members contributed money to the colonel of the gendarmes.

As a result of having paid the "fine," in the ensuing court judgment the five men were each sentenced to only five years in jail. No one considered this to be an unusual or isolated case of this particular form of crime and punishment.

Just below Khodarahm's tent, along a dry gully, were the foundations of a winter camp, where all the tent sites had been surrounded by stone walls. Dust Ali said it was so wet last year in Chin-i Zal that the grass grew knee high, the tents were all flooded, and the streams were impassable. In fact, a boy from the tribe had been swept away when he injudiciously ventured out into a raging stream. At this time last year, he said, the grass was so good that people were reluctant to leave on migration. But this year was dry, he pointed out—the rain we experienced that morning was the first in more than two months, and everyone was understandably anxious to move on to fresh pastures.

The men in Khodarahm's camp were angry because Morad Khan did not want to leave, even though the grass was dangerously depleted. But at the same time they conceded that there was more to deciding when to migrate than the state of the grazing or the phase of the moon. The problem was that the major migration route, running alongside Chin-i Zal, was used by many Luri-speaking tribes who winter to the south and west of the valley. As these tribes passed on their way to summer pasture, their herds trampled and grazed nearby fields unless someone was there to put up a show of force. During migration it was every tribe for itself, so the Baharvand waited until other tribes had passed so they could protect their crops. For some weeks, the tribes had been on the move, beginning with those that wintered at the lowest elevations. Finally, when the end to this seemingly ceaseless procession was in sight, it would be time for us to move.

On that note of agreement, the women served an excellent stewed chicken over rice. After eating our share and passing the tray back to the women to finish, we took a short hike to see a natural cave—really a sinkhole in the gypsum bedrock—in which these people stored their grain. The opening of the hole was just large enough for a man to enter, but a man could stand and move around in the chamber below. The hole may have been somewhat enlarged by previous nomads, but it was generally accepted to be a natural feature. The men felt safe with grain stored there because the hole was obscure and there were rarely any strangers in the area while the tribes were in their summer pastures.

While we walked, we discussed the kinds of campsites used by the nomads. I asked how the sites were chosen. Khodarahm (and others of whom we asked the same question) agreed that there were four criteria: level land, shelter from the wind, proximity to water, and pasturage. The seasons of the year have something to do with the values placed on each criterion, but above all, the pastoralists like flat land for their tents. In the winter they also need shelter from the wind. But as women fetch the water, it need not be very close, and animals can be driven, even over a considerable distance, to pastures. Yes, they said, "a flat place to sleep is important."

During the winter in Chin-i Zal, when the blustery winds drive the rain, the weather is cold. Since prevailing winds blow east/west, the tents are aligned with their long axes in the same direction. The ends of the tents thus receive the typically dry westerlies and the wet, stormy easterlies.

Just below Khodarahm's camp was a U-shaped roofless structure made of stone. Although it looked like the foundation of a winter camp, it was set some seventy-five feet from the tent sites where we had lunch, and it was out of sight of the nearest other campsites. When I asked what it was used for, Khodarahm replied that it was a shelter in which men sit during cool weather. It opened to the south, allowing the sun to warm the stone walls and providing shelter against the wind. Leaders used these structures (*diva kho*) for entertaining guests and for relaxing during the day.

This explanation reminded me that often in Iran I had seen villages where it seemed as if all of the men were hunkered against the sunny side of a house, and of others in which there was just a mud wall standing in an open area. As I reflected on it, it became clear that these solitary walls were aligned so that the sun hit one side in the morning and the other in the afternoon. Depending on the season, the men could sit in the sun or in the shade. In the villages, as in the nomad camps, most activities are done outside, where there is room to work or to gather for conversation. In the summer, the only relief from temperatures that usually rise well over 100°F is sitting in the shade, where dry breezes keep the air moving and sometimes blow the flies away. In Luristan, temperatures depend on season and altitude. The winter temperature may fall to below 0°F in the high mountains, while in Chin-i Zal it would be no lower than 40°F. Even at that temperature, relaxing outdoors out of the wind, sitting in the reflected heat of the sun, is not unpleasant.

While we walked back to our camp, with Dust Ali leading the way, I learned about different kinds of pasture. The best was the kind found there among the gypsum hills, where there was a profusion of species of plants: weeds, legumes, flowers, and grass. Dust Ali said this was much better pasture than when only one species of grass predominates. Among the wildflowers, I spotted a number of small red poppies, and asked if the tribes ever grew opium. Sekandar replied that it had been the main cash crop of the Luri villagers, and business had been brisk. As a boy he had tended it. But by the 1970s, its cultivation was illegal, except in government-sponsored fields. The year before, some fields had been planted near Khorramabad under government supervision.

The domestic opium poppy grows waist-high and has a large red flower with a bulbous pod. After the flower has dried and fallen, the farmer goes out in the evening and makes a set of vertical scratches in the pod with a toothed knife. In the morning he returns to the field and collects the milk that has oozed out of the cuts. It first comes out white, but the fluid turns brown as it dries and can be readily scraped off the pod. This process is repeated on each of several days, until the pod is completely scratched and will produce no more fluid. That this procedure has not entirely disappeared was evident during one of our trips to the bazaar in Shustar, where the dried pods were being sold for use in folk remedies. When the gummy fluid was collected, it was usable, but generally it was rolled and kneaded into cigar-shaped lengths to squeeze out the remaining juices. In this form, it was said to have a better taste than when used raw.

One suspects that there were a large number of addicts in Iran, although the number is said to have declined as the older generation has passed on. In contrast with the past government policy, when extremely severe penalties were given to those caught smoking opium, in the 1970s it was possible for addicts to purchase a ration in the market. According to official government statistics, 170,000 registered addicts in 1975 were issued 180 tons of opium. Although they grew it and profited from its sale, we were told that none of the Baharvand had ever smoked opium, and we heard the practice denounced many times as unbefitting human beings. Nevertheless, when it was available, mothers sometimes smeared opium on cranky infants' gums as a palliative.

Beginning to break camp

The following morning, when we looked out at the approaching dawn, we were surprised to see that two tents had already been taken down. Although it was semi-dark, I ventured out in the twilight to try to take movies. At first I thought the migration was beginning, but Safarali told me that some of the tents were going to be shipped by truck. I watched with some amusement because, just like novice packers, the people spent most of their time standing around indecisively, arguing over what should and should not be sent. However, by 8:30 a.m., several donkeys were loaded and sent toward the road (Figure 8.1). In the meantime, the women whose tents had been dismantled set up reed screens around their household belongings, just as they would do during the migration. Since clouds had been building for several days and rain had threatened early in the morning, it struck me as an inauspicious time to remove the covers from one's belongings. I was somewhat reassured that Morad Khan's and Safarali's tents—and, of course, our own white canvas tent—were still standing.

Sekandar had grown increasingly irritated with Morad Khan's casual attention to our needs and interests. After breakfast, he decided to talk with him about hiring some men to help with our baggage, as well as to lend aid to the camp generally during the migration. Looking back on it, I realize that even to have broached such a subject must have been painful for Sekandar because, in effect, he was admitting that what he said we could expect during migration was not exactly accurate. Nevertheless, at the time it seemed to me to be a good idea, because the camp was woefully undermanned.

When the subject was put to Morad Khan, he simply shrugged and replied, "No one obeys me anymore." Worse, he claimed, "Even the men in my own camp avoid me and sometimes I have to call on other camps for aid." Although his demeanor did not disclose it, this admission must have caused him great sorrow and shame. Nevertheless, he made his comments loudly enough that others in the camp could hear him, a technique he often used with good results. Continuing, he maintained, "I have enough pack animals, but not enough men. If it were not for Mukhtar, my ungrateful son who has just departed along with the baggage to take the truck..." After some silence, Sekandar again raised the possibility of hiring some labor, but Morad Khan said it would be impossible because any spare men among the Baharvand would have gone already to one of the cities—Isfahan, Shiraz, or Tehran—to find wage labor.

Figure 8.1. The donkey carries strips of black tent cover that hang on either side, along with tent poles and reed mats on top. Tied on top is a kid that is too young to make the migration on foot.

Although I was not totally prepared at that time to accept his alleged impotence in raising labor, it was becoming apparent to me that Morad Khan was resigned to life without service. I think he compensated by avoiding issues and working himself doubly hard. As we sat contemplating what to do next, he reminisced, as he was given to doing, about the old times, when there were twenty-five tents alongside his, and all of the men and women were subject to his absolute control and authority. Then he had labor! Nostalgically he recalled one of the leaders of the Papi, another Luri-speaking tribe, who once had 2000 tents around him but now had none. We had visited this Papi leader and others like him some weeks earlier, during our surveys before migration. It was the same all over Luristan, and Morad Khan saw himself as no different from the rest.

In effect he was saying, "This is the way it is. No matter where you go, it will be the same." Sekandar was unconvinced, as well he should have been, having been reared with stories of tribal glory. But he also knew Morad Khan's reputation as a cheapskate and a conniving old man. And then there was me, his professor. How could he put up with the slights and not feel as if he was also slighting me? It was a problem that he would have to live with, however much he doubted its inevitability.

One of the ironies of nomadism at that time was that, while labor was relatively scarce and could not be commanded at will, there was more baggage than ever. People had many items purchased in stores that they did not have even a decade ago. The thirst for acquiring material things had also broken down the traditional feelings of mutual support and cooperation, a theme we were to hear from the lips of more than one old man and woman.

We sat in Morad Khan's tent on the tribal carpet woven by Taji and continued the conversation, taking advantage of the opportunity to get some recollections from him while he was not busy with his seemingly endless chores. Once upon a time, he said, a person could get a nice lamb for fifteen *rials*, and the people ate lots of meat. When he was young, he would go out and shoot wild sheep or goats; at that time the tribesmen killed enough game to have meat every day. He lamented the introduction of the shotgun, to which he attributed the demise of the game. When he was a boy, most of the men were armed with only single shot, muzzle-loading rifles, which were ineffective over long distances. Great skill was required to hunt successfully with them.

I said this reminded me of an incident some years before in the mountains near Kermanshah, when we hired a Kurdi nomad to hunt goats for us. Armed with only an ancient muzzle-loader, he climbed the mountain and waited along a trail until a goat passed close enough to be shot. Skill and patience were required to bag game with these primitive arms, but with improving technology—first the breech-loading rifle and then the shotgun—everyone could be a hunter, and soon there was no more game.

Morad Khan stated with conviction that in those days, herds had been much larger. He attributed this to the fact that people had more territory and there was very little farming to compete for space. This was a story we heard often from the Baharvand and others, and it appears to be more than just the dim recollections of old men. When the price of livestock was low, partly because animals could not be taken to market easily, the nomads ate their flocks, a practice that is scarcely enjoyed today.

"Who is the man who can kill a goat?" Morad Khan asked rhetorically.

Making baskets, tent covers, and carpets

By the time we had finished our conversation with Morad Khan, the sheep and goats had returned to camp and the daily cycle of milking began. After lunch, Taji sat down in front of the tent. There she could follow the activities of the camp while she began weaving a tray out of thin reeds. Such a scene was repeated nearly every day when the camp was not migrating. In the afternoons, the women got out their spinning or basketry and passed the hours gossiping while doing necessary tasks. The Luri women are expert at weaving baskets, tent covers, carpets, and the reed screens that surround the tents. Each of these types of weaving is carried out during its own season. Baskets are made in the early spring, when the reeds are young and supple. To make baskets, the women cut the reeds, selecting those of uniform size, and then lay them to soak in a stream to make them pliable for weaving.

Tent covers are also made entirely by the women. They are made of goat hair, which is spun and then strung on long looms staked close to the ground. Simple over-and-under weaving with homemade instruments is all that is required to make the cloth strips, which are about two feet wide and twenty-five feet long. Eight to twelve of these are pegged together to make a tent cover. Repair work for tents and other gear is usually done shortly before migration.

The women make carpets during the summer. After the sheep have been sheared, the wool is spun and dyed (usually in town) and then strung on either horizontal or vertical looms. The Luri women seem to prefer the vertical looms and they make their flat-weave rugs on them with the same tools used to make tent covers. The carpets made by the nomads are woven rather than tied. (In the villages, using vertical looms, the women tie the threads.)

All of the things in a nomad tent must be durable: the things that the nomads make, like baskets, carpets, and bedding, and the things they buy, such as heavy copper pots, tent poles, and bread pans. The nomads are proficient at tying baggage on pack animals, but nonetheless, the migrations are hard on luggage because of the constant movement. As the animals make their way over uneven ground, the baggage shifts and rubs against the tight cords that bind it onto their backs.

The tribal people manufacture much of the equipment they carry, including tents, trays, reed screens, and ropes. Still, a great many things are bought in the market, because nomads do no metalsmithing, carpentry, leatherworking, or weaving of fine cloth. They buy all their pans and jugs, bedding, cradles, clothing, metal tools, tethers, saddles, bread trays, charcoal spatulas, tea glasses and pots, and any tableware. Although there is not a great deal of such equipment, it is vital and must be bought with the little cash the nomads can acquire. The sale of surplus grain, pack animals, wool, and sheep and goats, supplemented with some wage labor when it is available, provides the pastoralists with a small annual cash income.

When we were there, the nomads had not yet discovered the many uses of plastics. They did not use matches to make fires, nor did they smoke cigarettes—they used water pipes instead. Strike-a-lights, using flint and steel, were still pervasive, but firebrands exchanged among tents kept the fires burning. It would be a few years before Chinese-made goods flooded the markets and extinguished much of the local handicraft workshops.

As discussed above, the women did all of the weaving. The men made frames for the women's looms out of trees and branches; they also made stakes and repaired worn equipment. Otherwise, the men generally did not work on handicrafts. Even relatively simple devices like spindles were bought in town from woodworkers or from Lutis. The men were concerned almost exclusively with tending the animals and fields and with talking, for gossip and politics were central concerns. As described above, women did the weaving, churning, and cooking, although the men could prepare their own food, as they sometimes had to when they were away from camp.

Watching the camp

The afternoon was overcast and pleasant, and we relaxed in camp, watching the daily routine. My attention focused on the cattle, a rather sorry bunch of miniature animals compared with the dairy cows of more agreeable climates. That day the largest cow in the herd was in season and being pursued by several small bulls. To the amusement of everyone, in a scene of bovine seduction, the cow would trot through camp, across the fields, into the hills and then back again with two to six of the young bulls following directly behind her.

When she slowed momentarily, one of the bulls would try unsuccessfully to mount her, then off she trotted again to continue the procession. The parade lasted nearly the entire day until the poor cow collapsed in exhaustion against the back wall of Morad Khan's tent, threatening the stability of the structure itself. According to Morad Khan, they let this go on for one day and then tie the cow so that she can be serviced by one of the bulls. When copulation is completed, they wash the cow and plaster her vagina over with mud to prevent further chasing and intercourse, which would only weaken the animals just before the rigors of migration.

Mohammad Ali had been absent from camp all morning, but early in the afternoon he rode into camp on a fine-looking high-spirited gray stallion. Like most nomads, Mohammad Ali was equally at home riding or on foot. Nomads often ride the animals with only a blanket or a pad over their backs. As he staked the horse, everyone turned to watch. The horse had been brought for me to ride during migration, but Mohammad Ali reported that it had thrown him twice. He suggested discretely that it might be best for Sekandar to ride it. I readily acquiesced, being deficient in horsemanship and knowing no Luri horse commands.

The Lurs place a high value on a man's ability to ride, and they believe a real leader should be a good horseman. This fact caused Sekandar some concern. He confided that he was not sure he could control the horse. After all, it had been a number of years since he had ridden. If he was thrown, he would be the butt of jokes around the camp. After the horse had a chance to rest and graze, Sekandar approached it. The sleek strong horse was nervous and tried to break from its tether. Without being obvious about it, all the people in camp were watching. Sekandar knew this well.

The horse was too wild to be saddled, so Sekandar simply untied him and leapt onto his back, hoping to steer him using the halter alone into the plowed fields, where he would risk less in falling than he would on the rocky terrain. With a mind of its own and the strength to match, the animal galloped off across the fields and disappeared behind a low range of hills. I said a silent prayer as the clouds of dust, the only sign of Sekandar's direction, dissipated. An hour passed without a sign of either horse or rider, and I grew increasingly concerned. Finally I spotted them trotting smartly back to camp. Sekandar's white jeans had remained white throughout the ordeal. He had mastered the animal, but he never told me how.

With the arrival of the horse, our anticipation of the impending migration heightened. Sekandar was still concerned about the shortage of manpower. While we took a late afternoon walk, he asked Mohammad Ali and Safarali whether they could lend us a hand with our baggage and animals. They agreed, but it was clear to all of us that such an arrangement served only to delineate responsibility rather than to solve the pressing problem of lack of manpower in Morad Khan's camp.

Having cast our lot with the elder leader, we dispensed with the cooking equipment we had brought. The untidy piles of spare baggage heaped around the tents continued to grow throughout the day. Some members of the camp continued to tie bundles on the backs of donkeys and mules, so that they could be sent by truck to Dehmohsan, a tribal village in the Khorramabad Valley, thus alleviating some of the burden. All of the packing was tedious and slow, as everything had to be carefully secured.

Near sunset, I climbed one of the ridges overlooking the plain for an hour of solitude away from the bustling camp. Made of sharply folded beds of limestone, the ridge shuts off the southern edge of Chin-i Zal like a wall. Toward the top, it becomes only a cracked, eroded, stark sheet of rock, almost devoid of vegetation and still hot from the intermittent sun. From this vantage, I could survey the majesty of the Zagros ridges, standing one behind the other in splendid silhouette against the late afternoon sun. In Figure 8.2, the nine-mile-wide landslip, which left a notch a thousand feet deep in the ridge of Kabir Kuh, is seen in the distance (and see Oberlander 1965:Fig. 32). The Zal River below, a scarlet thread, reflected the sun where its light penetrated deep between canyon walls. Our camp was a dot on the otherwise uninhabited brown plain. Only muffled sounds rose from the camp, where puffs of smoke from the fires played momentarily with the breeze before vanishing into the deepening haze.

The sun was to my back, and the shadows advanced gradually across the valley floor, leaving only the far ridge with its deep gorge brightly lit. As the huge fiery disk dipped beneath the jagged horizon, it continued to send rays of red through the cloudy skies. The afterglow reflected off the clouds and warmed the valley with a fading blanket of oranges and violets; those surrendered in turn to purples and indigos and darkness. To the east, the nearly full moon began to rise with an aura of haze. With a jolt, I realized it was time to return to camp for tea and dinner.

Figure 8.2. The Chin-i Zal Valley lies between limestone ridges that are sparsely vegetated. The Kabir Kuh, with its massive landslide, is visible to the south.

Morad Khan was very quiet that evening. Sekandar and I sensed that something was wrong. In place of the customary friendly banter among the men in camp, accompanied by sharp remarks from the women, everyone was silent. The cause of the silence was a mystery. Sekandar thought it may have been the result of a family quarrel, for Morad Khan's dour behavior revealed that he was unhappy with someone or something.

Taji called us to dinner, so Sekandar and I joined the leader in his tent. He exchanged only the most perfunctory greetings and then fell into a sullen silence. Presently we attempted to draw Morad Khan into conversation. Staying clear of controversy, I inquired how the nomads break horses. With more resignation than enthusiasm, he told me that when a horse is two and a half years old, the nomads put a halter on it and lead it around. When the horse has grown accustomed to this, a saddle is placed on its back and it is led around again. Eventually a rider climbs aboard and rides the horse, just as Sekandar had done with the gray stallion.

Morad Khan then turned with a wry smile and asked me, "How do you break horses in the United States?" He was not so much interested in turning the tables on me by making his own queries, as he was incredulous that a grown man would ask such silly questions.

I said that I grew up in a city without much contact with livestock, and we do not have nomads like the Lurs in the United States. I explained how cowboys break horses by riding them. The clucking sounds of disapproval indicated immediately that none of the men in camp would consider breaking a horse in such a way. During my stay in the camp the people endured my interminable questioning with admirable patience and sometimes with considerable amusement. But that night conversation was not to prove productive.

It was obvious that Morad Khan was going through the motions of being hospitable. Sensing that it was about time to leave, we asked once again when we would leave on migration. Sekandar and I were both anxious to get on with the trip. It appeared to us that Morad Khan was almost perversely reluctant to leave. This was hard to understand, since all the nomads we had talked to were also anxious to leave. The grass in Chin-i Zal was short, and dust devils danced across the plain. Day by day the weather grew hotter. Everyone was looking forward to Dareh Nasab, the summer pasture. Morad Khan put us off by simply remarking that we ought to stay a while longer. He talked vaguely of putting a roof on a small mud building he had built for storing grain, but he admitted this was not really important. It finally developed that tomorrow was an unfavorable day for travel; it was the eleventh of the lunar month and no trips are made on such a day.

Morad Khan's part in the conversation grew increasingly perfunctory. As he talked, the old man gradually eased himself into a horizontal position. His tattered brown fedora slipped down over his face, his breathing became more relaxed and regular. He soon began to snore. Sekandar suspected he was feigning sleep, but we politely excused ourselves. No sooner had we entered our tent than we heard the old man in agitated conversation with his wives. We knew then that it was a domestic squabble that had caused the silence in the camp.

On the fifth day in camp, we awoke at five o'clock in the morning to another great commotion outside. This time it was the animals. The herds were leaving for the pasture. The gray stallion tied beside our tent was whinnying and pulling at his tether. When we looked out, Morad Khan was taking down his tent under dark, threatening, overcast skies. As soon as the tent fell to the ground, the skies opened and the rains that had been foretold by the hazy moon the evening before poured forth. The women scurried to protect bedding and baggage, which was exposed, and Sekandar and I retreated to our tent. There was no panic at this turn of events, just brisk activity. The rain fell gently and without much wind from solidly gray skies. The people seemed more resigned than surprised at this turn of events, an attitude which is helpful in a society where the unexpected always seems to occur, since foresight is little exercised and the future is unknown.

In fact, the rain disrupted the routine very little, for in the middle of the commotion, Taji brought us some bread, a bowl of yoghurt, and tea. By 7:30 a.m., a new tent had been raised over Morad Khan's site. His tent lay on the ground in its component parts, but Safarali's tent had been taken down and set up over the leader's belongings. The relative roles of leader and *homsa* were evident in this transaction, but there was more to it than that. Since Morad Khan's tent was the largest in camp, requiring an extra pack animal, it was to be sent by truck. In an emergency, Morad Khan would use Safarali's tent. Although this was a reasonable solution to the packing of baggage for migration, it did leave faithful Safarali out in the rain for a time. By the time his tent was up, the sun was out and there was no problem drying the wet baggage. The shower turned out to be a welcome refresher. As soon as the rain dampened the ground, a cool breeze carried the fresh scent of wet earth through the air.

Exploration and recreation

With the packing well underway, Morad Khan went with the baggage to arrange for a truck to carry it to a village near Khorramabad, where Sekandar's family lived and the pastoralists had relatives. Ghamartaj (Morad Khan's wife) made a point of telling Sekandar that Morad Khan was angry with him for being impatient and for hinting that the old man might just as well take the truck himself, leaving us in charge of the *homsa*. The intimation that we could do just as well without him was a grave insult to Morad Khan.

Since Sekandar is himself a Baharvand with a wide range of acquaintances and an intimate knowledge of tribal politics, the venerable leader would not let him operate on his own among Morad Khan's camps. As an archaeologist, I could learn just as much from one camp as any other, but as an ethnologist, Sekandar was vitally interested in tribal politics. He could not afford to alienate Morad Khan, but he was not above applying a little pressure.

Little of interest for me was going on in camp while people continued with their packing. With the overcast skies moderating the temperature, I decided to try my luck at fishing again.

When I asked Taji for a dough ball, she quickly complied, but she was emphatic in her instructions.

"This time bring all the fish back," she said.

"But aren't some of them too small?"

"No, they are all good medicine."

That was when I realized why she had not served us any of the previous catch. She had kept them all for her own purposes.

The Zal River was clear and low, but with a strong current. Because it was confined between steep cliffs, there were few places to walk along its narrow banks. I picked my way from patches of sand to boulders, a couple of miles upstream. There, in a deep pool, some large fish were hugging the sides of a boulder in the river some distance from the bank. Leaping unsteadily from rock to rock, I managed to gain a boulder near the center of the river and dropped my line in. I was rewarded almost instantly with a heavy tug. With a jerk I set the hook and pulled a catfish some fifteen inches long onto the rock. Before I could secure it, flapping in protest, the fish snapped the line and wriggled back into the water with a splash. Lying on my belly, I peered into the water, catching only fleeting glimpses of the big fish. I continued to dangle the baited hook and landed a string of smaller fish for my efforts. It was nearly an hour before I hooked the big one again. With care I pulled him out of the water onto the boulder, but this time I clamped him securely against the rock with my foot.

Sekandar had joined me just before the catch, and he suggested that we kabob the fish for ourselves. The idea appealed to me, so I turned the fish over to him. He jumped back to shore, where he built a fire while I continued to fish. In about fifteen minutes he yelled that he was ready. By the time I had made my way back to shore, he was standing by a fire, grinning in anticipation. Our steaming snack was skewered on a branch that Sekandar had ripped from a bush. We tore eagerly at the fish with our fingers, sucking the juicy white meat from the tiny bones. When we were finished, only the head, skin, and piles of bones remained. We placed these on top of a boulder for whatever creature might pass that way.

Refreshed, I leapt back out to the rock and almost immediately hooked a fish equal in size to the one we had just devoured. I heaved it quickly onto the rock but as I grabbed at it, the fish jerked suddenly, snapped my thin line and plunged back into the water. That finished my hooks for the day, so Sekandar and I returned to camp with eight good-sized fish for Taji and the smug satisfaction of having already consumed the prize. Although Taji was excited at the string of fish, we were apprehensive over the reception we would receive from Morad Khan.

When we arrived in camp, Morad Khan was occupied shoeing a horse in front of his tent and took no notice of us. We sat by our tent, waiting and watching to see what would happen next. Finished with the horse, and paying no attention to us, Morad Khan began to repair the straw-stuffed pads that are placed over the back of donkeys before the loads are tied on. The old man was totally preoccupied as he sat outside his tent, stuffing new straw through the tears in the fabric and mending the holes with a sail maker's needle. There was no conversation. Finally he looked our way and invited us into his tent. He said he was lonely.

Dinner was relaxed and friendly that evening, and Morad Khan was a gracious and convivial host. He responded cheerfully, albeit evasively, to a long series of questions about politics and politicians. Everyone agreed that Morad Khan was preeminently a politician, although he did not fit my stereotype of one. In Luri society, the successful politician or leader knows his people and treats them well. The politician continually works on their behalf, attempting to strengthen the tribe through arranging alliances and settling disputes. A politician manipulates people for what he considers to be the good of the tribe. Leaders do what is necessary to retain control and, if possible, to expand at the expense of someone else.

Sensing that Morad Khan wanted to talk, Sekandar began to ask about some of the maneuverings that had left the tribe's lands depleted, but all he got for his trouble were some airy generalities. Morad Khan did admit what was obvious to everyone—that one must go about things in a devious manner—

and he explained how this could be done. In his own case, since he knew the people very well, and had his own means of gathering intelligence, he could guess in advance what the response would be to one of his ideas. Thus he might propose something that was quite aside from what he really wanted. He knew his adversary would know he was doing this, and Morad Khan had already anticipated several moves ahead, much as a chess player sets up his opponent. Morad Khan's success lay in his status as a traditional leader and in his ability to plan his strategy farther ahead than most. When it came down to final decisions, he knew full well he could enforce his will, because any protests would consist of verbal abuse rather than physical action. It seemed a simple game to play, but most men had neither the temperament nor the skill to carry it out.

We lingered in conversation until the flocks were brought in, near midnight, and then went to bed, taking a last look at the moon with its ominous ring of haze.

In the middle of the night we awoke to a terrific thunderstorm. Brilliant flashes of lightning sheared across unusually black skies with deafening claps of thunder. High winds tore at the tent. About three o'clock in the morning, with the tent flapping dangerously, we went out and tied down some of the guy ropes that had pulled free. Then it rained. The rain, driven by gusty winds, continued until around eight that morning, preventing the pastoralists from any serious attempts to protect their gear. The herds went out at dawn as usual.

When the rain stopped, Mohammad Ali told us that no one in camp had had any sleep. Since the tents had been taken down, most were caught outside in the rain and had to scramble for the protection of the two tents that remained. More serious than the drenching, which was usually accepted with cheerful resignation, was fear of thieves. It was generally thought that thieves were out in the foulest weather, when camps were in disarray and there was no light from moon or stars. Of course, no animals were taken from our camp. It seemed improbable to me that a thief would want to be out in such weather, if for no other reason than he too would have been guarding his flocks against other thieves.

In spite of the soaking, the people were cheerful. The rain would help the crops, which were suffering severely from drought, and the animals would give more milk. Rain meant prosperity. In truth, it was not all that unpleasant to get wet as long as the weather was warm. As Mohammad Ali put it stoically, "We are used to getting wet."

Since the tents leaked, some things got soaked in the heavy rain. In the morning, the women carried their damp belongings out into the sun to let them dry, as if this task were as routine as the daily baking of bread.

Since my arrival in Morad Khan's camp, I had spent most of my time just watching the people as they carried out their daily tasks. As time passed, both the men and women grew accustomed to seeing me, and gradually our shyness broke down. I was able to more closely observe activities which at first I had watched only from a distance. Nevertheless, there was a limited variety in the daily goings on, so I was able to spend considerable time away from camp exploring and getting to know the country. This was important for my archaeological research, and it gave me a welcome relief from the slow pace of camp life.

Sekandar too got away for some recreation. He had been particularly anxious to carry a shotgun while we were on migration so that he could hunt partridges and supplement our diet. He was also mindful that carrying a weapon was a mark of status in pastoral society, even though the law prohibited guns. In Sekandar's case, he had applied through official channels for permission to carry a hunting gun, but his application was still tied up in the inevitable red tape of bureaucracy. Nevertheless, someone had loaned him an antique shotgun and he went off in search of a bird (Figure 8.3). In wet years the birds were abundant and not too hard to shoot, but that year they were very sparse. However, after nearly a full morning of chasing up and down rocky hillsides, he managed to bag a nice partridge, which Taji cooked for our lunch. Mohammad Ali, who had accompanied Sekandar on the hunt, joined us in devouring pheasant on rice.

After lunch we went out to watch the milking. At that time of year, the sheep and goats were milked only at noon because the lambs and kids still required nursing. In another month or so, the animals would be milked twice a day, morning and evening. At milking time, the women, each with a wide-mouth copper pot, stationed themselves on the edge of the herd, a few feet from the tents. The herders brought each family's animals to the woman doing the milking. The woman squatted with her pot between her legs, held the animal's hind legs in a firm grasp, then backed the animal into position. If the animal was restless, the herder straddled it, facing the milker. When

Figure 8.3. With a borrowed shotgun, Sekandar sets out to hunt partridges.

the ewe was in position, the woman squirted the milk into the pot. When she was finished, she sent the animal on its way with a shove while the herder brought another.

Each family recognized its own animals, however large the herd was. In Morad Khan's camp, the five families' 115 sheep and goats were herded together. The herders and women recognized the animals by their ears (Figure 8.4). In the local terminology, the basic distinction was between animals with round ears and those with flat ears. It should be understood that all the ears were long and hung down alongside the head, but some curled whereas others lay flat. This was the difference between "round" and "flat." Secondly, the ears were distinguished by color. There was great variety in color among the local sheep and goats, especially around the ears and face. Thus a ewe whose brown ears were rounded and had white tips was easily distinguished by a

Figure 8.4. The boys know each animal individually by the characteristics and color of its ears.

Lur from one with flat brown ears with white tips. Had any difficulty arisen, it could have been resolved by the animal's age and color of fleece. Neither the herders nor the women had any doubts whose animals they were milking, nor did the men when they counted the animals at night. When an animal was lost, news of its coloring spread quickly from one camp to another, and any herder would readily recognize the lost animal. To me, all the animals looked pretty much alike.

After taking pictures and getting names of the varieties of animal colorations, I went back to the fishing hole to try to catch the big one that got away. This time I was equipped with some strong line and some hooks that Sekandar had hammered out of wire. I was determined not to let the tackle stand in the way of catching the fish. After procuring a dough ball from Taji, I headed for the river, while Sekandar went off to visit another camp. Weighted down with rocks, my hook stayed below the surface and tempted the big cat to take the bait. No sooner had he started to run than he broke the cord, and ruefully I had to consider still heavier tackle. Working with what I had available, I doubled the line, weighted it properly, and let it down next to the rock to wait for a second strike. About half an hour later, as I was despairing of catching the fish, it struck. This time I flopped it up on the rock and lunged at it with my foot, only to have it slip free of the barbless hook and plunge back into the water. In disgust, I freed the two small fish on my string and trudged back to camp empty-handed.

On the way I explored the old site of Chin-i Zal some more. In the 1930s, Sir Aurel Stein reported seeing a rock-cut canal emanating from a spring and leading to the cliffs above the river. After a bit of searching I found the spot, but I discovered that the spring had dried up or was choked with rocky debris and no longer flowed. Later I learned that some fifty years ago the channel had led to a grain mill, driven by water—a type that was in use in Sasanian times. It looked to me as if it might be possible to clean out the spring and get the water flowing again, but since water was no longer needed for a mill, there was no local interest in such a move. The pastoral people did not operate the mill; instead, millers made trips seasonally to the tribal territory to grind the grain. By the 1970s, the tribal people were taking their grain to mills in town, which were run by gasoline or diesel engines. For this service the millers took a percentage of the flour.

Thinking about the spring, I was impressed by the casual way pastoral nomads seemed to live. They allowed a spring to fall into disrepair. They failed to repair or improve ancient agricultural terraces. They avoided making use of the durable, secure houses that had stood on the plain for two thousand years. I thought about the great amount of time it took to manage herds. Much of the effort seemed needless to me, but then, I saw time as a commodity and extra work as a liability. Luri nomadism seemed hopelessly inefficient. It had not really occurred to me before I joined Morad Khan's camp that it would be so. What I had read about nomads always emphasized their ability to move quickly, and the very nature of pastoral life suggested that it would center around basic tasks that could be carried out efficiently. But there I was, in the midst of people who seemed to muddle through everything they did.

For example, almost every evening a herder reported that some animals had strayed from the flock. That meant the people had to go out and hunt for them over rough terrain in the dark. When the sheep and goats were all back in camp, they were continually running in and out of the tents keeping their owners up all night long. It seemed to me that simple corrals could be set up for the sheep and goats and that a hitching post would be preferable to the stakes that were driven into the ground to hold the pack animals. As it was, almost every night at least one mule or horse broke away and had to be chased down.

Apparently in the winter these problems were lessened, because many of the animals were penned in caves or natural shelters to protect them from the cold winds, and there were no newborn sheep and goats to keep in the tents. Using similar pens during the summer was apparently not deemed either necessary or feasible, even though there were piles of rocks all over Chin-i Zal that had been picked out of agricultural fields, which would have served very well for the construction of pens.

It seemed to me that if land were fenced in Luristan, herds could be kept separated and the labor to manage them could be considerably reduced. Of course the reason why land was not fenced was that it was free for all to use. To close off portions would prevent migration and completely disrupt one of the strongest adaptive features of nomadism: the ability to move where the grass was best and thus ensure the survival of the greatest number of animals. As it was (without fences), each herd had to be closely watched to prevent it from straying and protect it from raiding. This was one way to take care of livestock, but there were other ways. Livestock companies could use the land more efficiently: They could employ fewer herders if the ranges were fenced and if there were no concerns about rustling or attacks by wolves. However, that would destroy the essence of the tribal system, which was based on common use of territory. It would also require a large capital investment in fences, herding camps, storage facilities for feed, and the like. After thinking about it, I was not sure that was really what Luristan needed.

The last evening at Chin-i Zal

With one last look at the river, which was rising rapidly in response to rains higher in the mountains, I returned to camp with the waning rays of the sun. Mohammad Ali was in our tent having tea with Sekandar. With animation he told us, as had Dust Ali, how last year after a heavy rain, one of the boys had been swept away in the flooding river. The water was so high—some thirty feet above normal—that tent camps on the cliffs over the river had actually been flooded.

Although the flood was an unusual occurrence, hazards in general were not uncommon in pastoral life. Most of the men in camp had had experiences with bears, and more than a few bore scars from such encounters. There were stories of wolves carrying off children. Occasionally at night someone would fall off a cliff. Considering the fact that people got kicked by mules, fell while herding or migrating, and sometimes were attacked by dogs, they showed relatively few disabling injuries. In fact, the incidence of crippling injuries among the nomads was far less than among laborers in a city.

Nomads use the lunar calendar to calculate their travels and the passage of time, and that evening was the twelfth day of the lunar month. We had been told that it was not good to travel on the thirteenth, although we were all anxious to leave. The full moon would be on the fourteenth. Mohammad Ali recited the things that should not be done on certain days, very much as a Yankee farmer might do with his almanac in hand. Faced with the prospect of more rain (which made the tents impossibly heavy to handle), the need of the flocks for grass, and the growing restlessness of the people, Morad Khan had to make a decision about moving. Practical considerations might have to outweigh tradition.

When asked about leaving on the thirteenth, he said, with a shrug of resignation, "What can you do?" But he made no commitment.

He entertained us at dinner by telling more about the lunar calendar and tradition relating to propitious days for moving.

When I asked him how people know what the date is, he replied, "Those who know share with those who don't."

That was another clue to his control over the tribal people. Among the adults, he was the only one who could read and apparently the only one who had more than a rudimentary knowledge of the contents of the Koran. Thus he freely dispensed moral advice and gave information on other esoteric matters, all of which his followers accepted without question. With respect to those matters, the nomads turned to him for advice and decisions.

That was the traditional way. It was true that nomad children were going to school, but there they learned mostly about things that had little relation to traditional Luri life. Furthermore, the children were too young to be asked for advice. It was still the elders, with their weight of experience, who commanded respect in matters that affected nomadic life. The children who went to school and then chafed under the tribal system would most likely leave the camps and seek work outside tribal society.

A spectacular display of lightning and thunder emanating from Kabir Kuh, the highest range in sight, evoked from Morad Khan the observation that he understood the relation between thunder and lightning. He did not reveal this information to us, but the onlookers seemed to agree that if anyone were privy to this esoteric knowledge it would be Morad Khan.

We went to bed uncertain whether we would leave in the morning.

Chapter 9

Crossing Kialon Kuh

Pragmatism prevailed over superstition. Taji called us at dawn to prepare for the migration. The migration was to take an irregular route from Chin-i Zal across a series of mountains and valleys eventually reaching Dareh Nasab, above the tribal villages (Figure 9.1). Although it had rained during the previous night and the date was not propitious for traveling, Morad Khan had finally decided to leave. When I emerged from the white tent, everyone was busy with last-minute packing. Safarali, who was anxious to move out with the cattle, watched as we packed. He helped Sekandar and me stuff articles into a pair of gunny sacks that had been sewn together so that they would hang over the back of a donkey, one sack on each side. As soon as we had moved our bedding out of the tent and stuffed it into cloth bags that we had brought to Chin-i Zal for the purpose, we took the tent down, leaving Mohammad Ali and Safarali to pack it onto a donkey.

Figure 9.1 (opposite). The migration route: from Chin-i Zal to the pastures beyond Hashtad Pahlu above Khorramabad. We followed traditional trails and crossed one mountain after another. Campsites and valleys along the way are indicated.

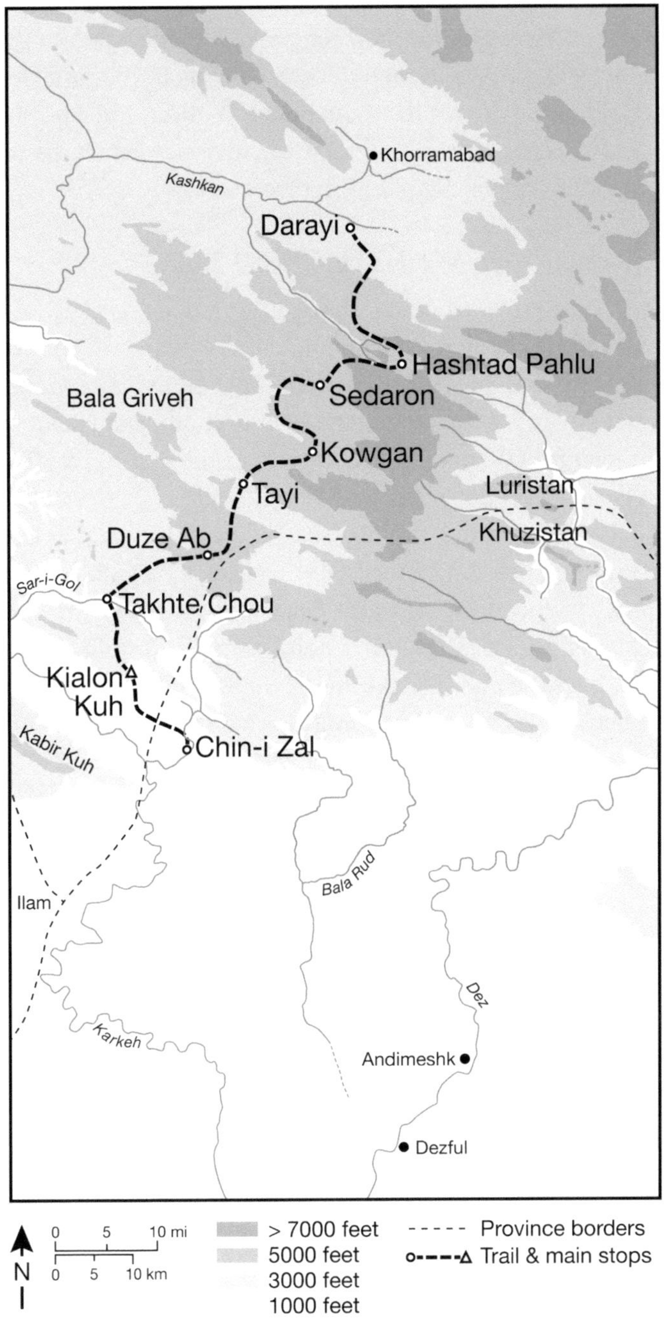
Khorramabad
Kashkan
Darayi
Hashtad Pahlu
Sedaron
Bala Griveh
Kowgan
Tayi
Luristan
Khuzistan
Duze Ab
Sar-i-Gol
Takhte Chou
Kialon Kuh
Kabir Kuh
Chin-i Zal
Bala Rud
Ilam
Dez
Karkeh
Andimeshk
Dezful
N
0 5 10 mi
0 5 10 km
> 7000 feet
5000 feet
3000 feet
1000 feet
Province borders
Trail & main stops

Our packing finished, we sat in the midst of our baggage and watched as the women of each tent tossed their remaining belongings into gunny sacks, rounded up the chickens, and tried to keep animals from trampling valuables (Figure 9.2). Soon Taji sent a tray with bread, yoghurt, and a pot of hot tea for breakfast. It took nearly three hours for the men to load all the animals. We did not actually leave the camp until nine o'clock.

We leave Chin-i Zal

The herders had long since gone, though the cattle remained at camp with Safarali. As a result, he and Mohammad Ali did nearly all of the loading of baggage onto animals. The more I watched, the more I appreciated the art of packing a donkey or a mule so that the load is secure and balanced.

The two men rolled bulky goods such as tents, carpets, and reed screens like a scroll and then hoisted them onto a pack animal so that half hung down on either side of the animal (see Figure 8.1). Smaller baggage was then piled on top. Each load was finally secured by a single cinch, which is tied to a hook-shaped block of wood. The cord was passed first over the back of the donkey and then pulled up around its belly to join the hook. When the cord had been looped through the hook and drawn tight, it was pulled around the back of the animal, passing just below the tail, and finally it was looped around the first encircling cord and pulled tight again. Mohammad Ali worked the remaining cord back and forth, across and around the donkey, pulling it tight at each turn, until no more cord remained. He tied the end and the load was ready.

We finally began to move, led by Morad Khan on his fine brown mare with its colt trotting sprightly alongside (Figure 9.3). Next came five women precariously mounted high atop the swaying family bedding, with their legs spread out straight ahead of them (Figure 9.4). Next in line were the mules and donkeys carrying tents and other baggage, followed by Mohammad Ali on foot. His job was to keep the animals in line and moving. Following all were Safarali and the diminutive cattle. Sekandar rode alongside on his borrowed gray, while I brought up the end on my reluctant brown mare.

We had migrated no more than a hundred yards (100 m) when a load fell off an obstinate mule, causing us to stop for a quarter of an hour while the load was retied. I began to wonder whether the people were simply out of

Figure 9.2. After the tents have been taken down, the baggage is packed in sacks that can be loaded on the pack animals. The women are packing their baggage inside the low stone walls that shielded their tent from the winter wind.

Figure 9.3. Morad Khan on the trail, following behind a loaded donkey.

practice as loads continually slipped, forcing Mohammad Ali to run back and forth heaving sagging baggage into balance (Figure 9.5). But it was not only a matter of practice. The whole procession was in disarray. When Mohammad Ali was not securing loads, he was chasing mules that had strayed from the trail and exhorting the beasts to greater efforts.

It was apparent even to an unpracticed observer that more manpower would have been useful. I didn't see how Mohammad Ali could last the day pushing himself that way. Making due allowance for those who had gone by truck, including Morad Khan's eldest son, a rapid mental head count suggested that at least one male was missing. When Sekandar inquired about

Figure 9.4. With the loaded donkeys and mules, the camp starts the migration. The women, riding horses, sit atop the bedding.

this, Mohammad Ali told him that the sheep and goats had been split into two herds, thus wasting a man who was badly needed on the trail. Normally one of the older boys took the entire flock, but in this instance a second boy had taken charge of part of the herd. The boy, who had a fifth-grade education, announced in the morning that he was not going to do someone else's work. He said the animals did not all belong to his family and he was not going to give free labor to the others. With resigned exasperation, Mohammad Ali said the youth hated nomad life and, what was more, with the liberated views he had learned in the tent school from Mukhtar, he treated his family like animals.

Figure 9.5. On the rocky trail heading toward Kialon Kuh, Mohammad Ali had to chase straying pack animals. On rough trails it is normal for the people to walk and lead the animals.

Although Sekandar's patience was wearing thin, his sense of adventure was growing. He decided to show off some of his American education by playing cowboy on his spirited mount. The horse was willing enough—wheeling, charging, nudging, and driving—but the refractory pack animals hardly knew how to respond. They were used to receiving commands delivered via a stout stick from a man on foot. Sekandar raised a lot of dust to no avail and after a few hours he was nearly exhausted himself. As he grew more weary, his anger and frustration rose, and at the first opportunity in the evening he told the reluctant young herder in no uncertain terms that he was to take charge of the entire flock, like it or not. Watching this diatribe from a distance, I could see that the Baharvand still had some sanctions over the *homsa*.

We proceeded west out of Chin-i Zal at a pace that the slowest laggard could easily maintain on foot. In fact, the entire movement was such a comedy of errors that I began to doubt the reputed ability of nomads to move quickly over long distances and to vanish with evasive rapidity from pursuers. Legend has a way of making things larger than life, but to me this was absurd.

My miserable mount was no help. With apparently solicitous charity, Morad Khan had given me a spindly brown mare that was said to be absolutely dependable on the trail: it had never been known to fall or throw a rider. What distinguished this beast from the others was its intense dislike of being followed. No matter where I began in the column, the horse rapidly worked its way to the rear. Despite my attempts at Luri commands and the heavy use of a switch, the wretched animal refused to alter its pace. With Safarali's cattle pushing at my horse's flanks, we moved resolutely, if stolidly, ahead. I resigned myself to being caboose to the caravan. I would arrive home with many pictures of the backsides of nomads.

The first day we passed a tent camp that had not yet been dismantled. The residents said they were getting ready to leave, but I soon understood why they had delayed. The arable parts of Chin-i Zal were tall with ripening wheat that we carefully avoided trampling, even though the animals were clearly interested in eating. Nevertheless, not more than a mile from the remaining camp, Morad Khan allowed our animals to enjoy the lush green in fields planted by nomads who had already moved on (Figure 9.6). Had the fields belonged to another tribe, I would not have been surprised, but our pack animals were eating Baharvand fields. We dismounted for a rest while the animals munched down their midmorning snack. In Morad Khan's philosophy, "God will provide." Indeed He will, if you are the last ones through. It was no wonder there was general mistrust and the flaring up of hostilities among different camps of pastoralists.

As our trail took us west toward the highway that runs from Khuzistan to Khorramabad, we began to hear in the distance the noise of diesel trucks slowly climbing into the mountains. At about the same time, we turned north to proceed along the base of the mountains. Our trail took us past the ruins of the archaeological site built of boulders that we had seen on our way into Chin-i Zal. The site must once have spread nearly a mile along the banks of the stream, but as before I saw few artifacts to indicate its age. Mohammad Ali took the time to tell us that our trail was following an old caravan route

Figure 9.6. Morad Khan, on his horse at right, watches as the pack animals walk through a wheat field, munching along the way.

that had gone out of use when the highway was built during the Second World War.

For millennia pastoralists have migrated along routes that afford relatively easy crossing of the many steep mountain ridges. A few of these old trails were improved for caravan traffic through the building of retaining walls and bridges and—in the late nineteenth century—by blasting through obstacles. However, to my eye, there was little evidence of any appreciable trail maintenance. It is hard for me to imagine how goods could have been conveyed in any large volume along those narrow, twisting, steep, and often treacherous trails. The problem of crossing the mountains with commercial goods was first overcome in the 1930s, when German engineers built a railroad to link sea traffic in the Persian Gulf with markets in Tehran. Later, in order to move war material quickly from the Gulf up into Russia, American army engineers built a motorable road. It was still in use when we were there, but in deplorable condition.

Morad Khan told us that we would have only a short trip that day—just far enough to place us as close as possible to Kialon Kuh, a sheer mountain that we would cross the next day (Figure 9.7). Drawing closer to its base, we saw nomads converging from all directions. Soon the trail was clogged with animals and people stretching for miles into the distance. Kialon Kuh, which must be crossed by all nomads who spend the winter near the northwestern edge of the Khuzistan plain, has only one narrow, arduous pass. Kialon is a bottleneck into which people stream and out of which they disperse just as rapidly on the other side.

By noon we had left all traces of cultivation and proceeded along boulder-strewn lanes that twisted through natural openings in the rock formations. Occasional seeps of water that had collected in depressions in the white gypsum formations gave our dogs a chance to plunge in, drink, and soak their shaggy coats. My dry palate would have welcomed a fresh drink, but not from those brackish pools, however inviting they might have looked from horseback.

Riding at the head of the caravan, Morad Khan scanned the hillsides for a suitable campsite close to the base of the mountains. He wanted to leave early the next morning so that we would not be caught in a crush of traffic when we climbed toward Kialon's pass. We passed campsite after campsite, to either side of the trail, all occupied to overflowing. I began to despair that we would find a place, but we pushed ahead. As we passed the camps we were greeted more often than not only by snarling dogs who warned us away, and by the baleful stares of nomads from other tribes who were no more eager than the dogs to have visitors. Few words were exchanged between campers and passersby. With whole tribes on the move, the hospitality that would be accorded to a solitary stranger was eschewed.

Our trail eventually took us across a boulder-strewn dry streambed and then to a rapidly flowing stream. We turned to follow its right bank. Oak trees were beginning to appear on the hills in this heavily dissected rolling country, testimony to the greater rainfall at this altitude. Soon the remains of a ruin, reportedly an old caravan stop, came into view. A hundred yards above, Morad Khan pointed to a suitable campsite. We dismounted on the

Figure 9.7. The sheer face of Kialon Kuh rises above the tree line. Hundreds of tribes and thousands of livestock must cross the pass each spring and autumn.

slope of one of the hills, among a grove of oaks, and unpacked the animals. The women set up screens, gathered firewood from nearby oak trees, and got out the teapots (Figure 9.8). For a quick overnight stay, tents were left rolled and each family gathered within its screens. This part of travel was well rehearsed.

Beringe Kar

Sekandar and I looked over the site to find a place to bed down. After much thought and discussion we settled on a site at the edge of the camp, where we thought we would have less chance of being trampled by animals in the night.

Figure 9.8. On our first night, camp was close to the pass over Kialon Kuh. Only reed screens were set up to delimit each family's site, as an early departure the next morning was expected.

However, Morad Khan, who had been watching us silently, did not like the site we had picked out. He wanted us situated next to his camp in the front of the group. Mohammad Ali and Safarali concurred. They said our position was too exposed to thieves. Stubbornly I resisted and laid out the bedding where I wanted it. That evening we were told that in the future we must camp according to custom and the orders of Morad Khan.

Khawar, Mohammad Ali's wife, found a couple of eggs in the wicker basket in which her chickens had been riding and served them to us for lunch. She served them fried in sheep fat along with bread that she had baked in the morning. On migration chickens ride in elongate baskets that look like fat sausages. Several chickens can be put in a basket, which is hung on the side of a pack animal for the journey. Along the way some of them lay eggs.

Since we had gone no more than five or six miles and stopped about 1:30 in the afternoon, our slow, disorganized departure from Chin-i Zal had caused no problem. At the same time I had the lingering impression that our camp was a bit rusty in the mechanics of moving after their long winter's sedentism. We were camped at a place called Beringe Kar, after the fact that rice (*beringe*) had formerly been grown there in small, irrigated fields. The ruins belonged to a *caravanserai* (a sort of motel for caravans) that had been sustained by the limited agriculture nearby and through payments made by caravans when they stayed the night before crossing Kialon Kuh.

Sometime later I learned that Beringe Kar held special meaning for Sekandar, whose mother had given birth to him at that very spot while the family was on migration.

We were following the route that had been taken fifty years earlier by the British consular official, C. J. Edmonds, who had wanted to take a firsthand look at the tribal people who were preventing caravans from moving safely through (Edmonds 1922). That was a time when the British had secured a lease to oil land in Bakhtiari tribal territory and had built a road reaching southern Iran. A more direct route to Tehran ran through Luri territory, but the tribes there resisted outsiders. Taking advantage of their ability to disrupt trade, the tribes had taken over the transporting of goods and thereby secured the profit entirely for themselves. For British commercial interests, this anarchy made the route dangerous and unprofitable. Edmonds attempted a diplomatic approach. However, in view of the latent danger, he took hostages, one from each tribe that he would encounter, and held them in Dezful. Accompanied by leaders of two of the principal tribes, he hoped that his mission would establish secure trade routes through the various tribal territories. It did not (Edmonds 1922).

After lunch I decided to explore the ruins of the late nineteenth-century *caravanserai*. The mud walls were still intact, but the roof was missing, probably because the beams had been taken for use elsewhere. More interesting to me than the *caravanserai*, however, were the remains of a very extensive winter campsite of nomads. In itself this was not particularly noteworthy, but in this instance the camp was unlike anything in Chin-i Zal. Later, when we had a chance to quiz Morad Khan, he told us that

Figure 9.9. At our camp, there were facilities left by a previous tribe whose tents had floors of packed mud. In the back wall was a "chicken coop."

the Kurdalivand subsection of the Baharvand owned Beringe Kar, but the Turkashvand, a Laki-speaking tribe from the vicinity of Hamadan in the mountains, leased the land. Until the late 1950s, the Turkashvand had made their winter migration to the Salehabad area well to the northwest, near the border of Luristan and Kurdistan. Sekandar bitterly claimed that Morad Khan permitted the Turkashvand to use land that traditionally belonged to his tribe. Sekandar and many other nomads, like Khodarahm, thought that Morad Khan took money for his part in the deal. Once again, his loyalty to his people was called into question, but not his right as a Baharvand to make deals.

The Turkashvand campsite was well established, with the tents forming the perimeter of a large corral whose edges were defined by brush. Each of the tents had covered a level packed mud floor that provided a clean, smooth living surface (Figure 9.9). The Baharvand had nothing like this in Chin-i Zal: instead they lived on the earth, which they covered with carpets, if at all. As well as packed mud floors, each of these tents had one or more chicken "coops"—hen-sized hollows cut into the back walls. Approximately one half

Figure 9.10. In the early spring, the kids and lambs are kept next to the tent on a surface prepared with rocks and straw. This allows the urine to run off in channels and keep the pen dry.

of each tent area consisted of a stone pavement separated from the living area by a low stone or mud wall. When brush was laid over the stones, they served as stalls for the young animals in early spring (Figure 9.10). Under the stone pavements were drains that allowed urine to flow outside the tent, where it was washed away after rains by water flowing down the ditches around the tents.

Like all nomad tent sites, these had a low stone platform (*chul*) alongside the back wall, where the people piled their bedding during the day (Figure 9.11). A centrally located fireplace, usually lined with stones, completed the permanent fixtures inside the tents. In front of the tents were some mud ovens with open tops and bell-shaped interiors of a type (*tanures*) used by many tribes in Southwest Asia for baking bread. The people who camped here apparently did not use the round, convex iron bread pan over an open fire as most Lurs did.

Figure 9.11. The tents here are enclosed with low stone walls. Inside is a rectangular bed (*chul*) of rocks, on which baggage is set during the day. A stone-lined fireplace is in the center.

I was surprised at the investment in permanent facilities, as it was much more than among any of the pastoral tribes we had visited in Pish-i Kuh. This was probably due to the climate in the area from which the people came. Their home near Hamadan was at an altitude of around six thousand feet and was much colder than Baharvand territory. Indeed, since the Beringe Kar camp was also at a higher and colder elevation than the Baharvand used for their winter sites, the people there needed more protection from the weather. Strangely, however, in spite of the fine floors, the tents were not outlined by high stone walls, as they were among the Lurs we were traveling with.

I spent most of the afternoon mapping and taking pictures of the tent sites. Upon returning to our camp I was accosted, as usual, by fierce guard dogs, which were driven back by their owners as I approached. These dogs were about the size of German shepherds, but they were usually white or white with black or brown patches. Although I had not had any real trouble with the dogs, they were a latent danger, especially at night. They had become accustomed to seeing me come and go in Chin-i Zal, but in the new locale they were more nervous and excitable and consequently more dangerous. Accordingly I decided, for my own peace of mind, to make friends with them. The Lurs, like most Iranians, do not handle or pet dogs. Dogs are not pets in our sense. They are tolerated because they serve as guards. As pups they are often tortured and as adults they are treated with contempt and controlled by throwing rocks at them. Even the owners of dogs are not always safe. I constantly marveled at the way Safarali's dogs would assail him when he came back to his tent at night. No harm was ever done, but still the dogs were always roused to vicious display, and if he had not reacted with threats it looked as if they would cheerfully have chewed him up. Only small children seemed to be exempt from attack. When the children grow old enough to taunt the dogs, the latter turn on the former with no apparent compunction. Bites occur frequently.

My own strategy was simple. I began to bribe the dogs with bread, a trick I had heard about when people told me how thieves managed to get into houses or tents without raising an alarm. Sitting on my bedroll late in the afternoon, I began secretly to toss bits of bread left over from lunch to the dogs that were relaxing in the immediate area. They eagerly gobbled it up and even wagged their tails. I then resolved to include the dogs routinely in my share of meals, a practice that, after a few days, led to my being the only one in camp who was never bothered by them.

Late that afternoon, Taji received a visitor at Morad Khan's tent. By his dress and behavior it was obvious that he was not a Baharvand. Sekandar went down to find out what was going on. The visitor claimed to represent the shrine of Shah Ahmad, a mountain peak dedicated to a holy man. The peak, referred to as Morra Dahanda (the giver of wishes), was visible from much of Baharvand territory. Each year hundreds of pilgrims walked up its steep slopes to make prayers and offerings to the saint. The shrine was said to have great powers. Women who were barren, people who were sick, and even children who wanted to pass their examinations made the trip with the faith that they would succeed in their wishes. Sekandar explained that parents sometimes dedicated their children to the shrine, believing that the child would then be protected from harm. Such a dedication required annual contributions to the shrine. If the child was female, half her bride price went to her holy guardian when she married.

There were numerous such shrines throughout the Zagros Mountains, but only a few had the reputed powers of Shah Ahmad. The faithful often made offerings, whether they could actually make the trip to the mountain or not. We had passed such an offering site on the trail that morning. It consisted quite simply of hundreds of piles of stones set up like small pyramids. Believers passing such a point picked up a stone from the trail and set it on one of the growing pyramids, while offering at the same time a prayer that their wishes would be granted. Mohammad Ali's wife, Khawar, never failed to make such an offering, in the hope that her barrenness would end.

Our visitor was one of the caretakers of the little shrine at the foot of the mountain where pilgrims began their journey. There, before they began their ascent, it was customary for each pilgrim to give some money to the caretakers. The money was supposed to be used for the maintenance of the shrine and for the keep of the caretakers. With characteristic insensitivity to local belief, the government had begun taxing such establishments on the grounds that there was profit involved. The purpose of that day's visit was to take up a collection among the nomads who would pass within sight of the shrine but not actually visit it. In view of the hazardous journey ahead, the nomads usually deemed it prudent to make such an offering.

By this time I was beginning to realize that the pastoralists were distinctly anxious about crossing Kialon Kuh. I had heard them discuss the difficulty while we were still in Chin-i Zal, but I was not prepared for the tensions that increased with each passing hour while we waited to cross the awesome mountain. Sekandar told me then that it was customary to sacrifice an animal to Shah Ahmad before making the crossing as protection from the dangers of the mountain. The sacrifice was not to God (Khoda), but to Shah Ahmad. The practice probably began in antiquity—back when humans and animals started to migrate annually between mountains and lowland plains.

As dusk fell over the peak itself and began to envelop the camp, the pitch of conversation grew more intense. What would the weather be like? Would thieves strike the camp? Which group would get across first? Who should provide the animal for the sacrifice? At a time like that, the pastoralists could hardly afford to be niggardly, yet animals were expensive. There was understandable hesitation among the families in our camp to step forward with a sacrificial lamb. Debate took the place of action, and with debate came further anxiety.

Sekandar expected Morad Khan, as leader, to slaughter one of his herd. Traditionally this would have been his contribution to the welfare of the group. He gave no indication that he was going to carry out his obligation, however. Finally the pressure became intolerable to one of the *homsa*, who brought forth a lamb.

Without further discussion, the animal was given a drink of water, laid on its side facing Mecca, and killed with a cut across the jugular vein. Quickly the meat was cut up and passed out among the families, who retreated to their own tent sites to do the cooking. The obligation to Shah Ahmad had been met, and each person would get some protein just when he needed it the most. Unfortunately, because of my insistence that we place our camp away from Morad Khan's, we did not actually see the distribution of meat or hear the discussion that preceded it. In fact, we were studiously ignored. Under a partly overcast sky with a damp chill beginning to settle, we sat impatiently on our bedrolls for a long time waiting for a share of the meat or even a piece of bread. Finally, long after dark, Taji brought us a tray of rice and some small chunks of boiled meat. It struck me as a skimpy offering for such a momentous occasion, but that small lamb had to feed many mouths.

We finished our dinner in silence, watching the clouds play hide and seek with the stars while we contemplated the climb over Kialon, whose angular silhouette was chiseled into the evening sky. Around us in all directions, campfires flickered in the dark. Nomads in other camps were consuming their sacrificial meals and waiting for their herds to settle down. As bedtime approached, the men became more and more tense, straining their ears and eyes into the enveloping darkness, certain that each cracking twig and strange cry signaled an imminent raid by one of the many tribes that surrounded us. The fires were stoked higher to provide light against the dark and the terrors it concealed. As if nature were conspiring with the thieves, the sky grew more overcast with each advancing hour and the moon, although near full, was already in a descending arc.

Periodically, comments about our exposed position were directed toward us from the other tents, but the overt fear of the nomads only made me more determined to stay where we were. Nevertheless, with reproach ringing in our ears, we secured our belongings as close to our bodies as possible and piled our baggage around our heads to screen off the chill wind. I fell asleep to the continued murmur of conversation among the tents.

Crossing Kialon Kuh

At two in the morning Sekandar shook me awake, proclaiming that everyone was up and getting ready to leave. The idea of leaving at such an hour was so preposterous that I could only assume Sekandar had succumbed to the communal hysteria. I told him so as I turned over and went back to sleep. He shook me again and handed me a cup of tea that he had brewed over our small fire. As I focused my eyes, I caught the sound of a woman churning milk over the fire in the next tent. By three o'clock, even I was convinced that we were indeed getting ready to leave, although the moon was rapidly disappearing and we could scarcely see beyond the perimeter of our bedding. Sekandar handed me a piece of bread, which I used to spoon yoghurt into my mouth while I stared in silence.

Sekandar had not slept at all. No sooner had he bedded down than his mind had filled with scorpions, snakes, and thieves. Like the nomads, he too had strained his ears for telltale sounds. Like the nomads, he had gotten up and spent the few hours of rest hunching over the fire. It was not surprising that we were packing long before dawn. By 3:30 a.m., I could hear Safarali urging the cattle forward. The sheep and goats in charge of one herder left at 4 a.m. The rest of us, who had to load animals in the dark, left by 5 a.m., picking our uncertain way in the dark across the loose rocky slopes.

Back on the trail, we turned toward Kialon. When the dawning light expanded our horizons, I could see other groups forming on the trail behind us. The morning air was full of cries and calls of intense urgency as we pressed up the trail, straining man and beast to the limit. The psychological importance of the crossing grew more and more evident as the morning proceeded. Thousands of herds and people were pushing forward to gain position on the narrow trail up and across the mountain.

The trail began as a wide track that had been improved for vehicular traffic when a power line was installed across the pass a few years before. The high wires now carried electricity from the hydroelectric generating plant at the dam above Dezful, on the Khuzistan plain, to Khorramabad, just beyond our destination in the summer pasture. Like the nomads, the power line was following the easiest route across the mountain, but its straight track leapt gorges and scaled rock faces that would have been impossibly difficult for migration. For the most part we followed the timeworn foot trail.

The first hour was a relatively easy climb up a gently sloping trail, but the remainder of the trip was a torturing scramble over scree-covered slopes along a narrow switchback trail. The view on a clear day would have been magnificent, extending down as far as the town of Dezful, but overcast skies spoiled the scene that day. Dezful lay masked by low-lying clouds and dust carried aloft from the baking plain of Khuzistan.

When we reached the steep part of the trail, the nomads' pent-up anticipation was released in strident exhortations to their animals and the use of brute force to keep them moving. Quicker parties would pass us if we slowed. With each step the trail got steeper and the switchbacks sharper. We all dismounted to lead our horses and mules, for fear they would stumble and deposit us at the top of a long roll down Kialon. The difficulty of the terrain and the need to keep moving made it hard to appreciate the beauty of the oak forest and the scenery that lay before and behind us. I could not stop even to take pictures; if I had, the following groups would simply have passed me by. With cameras slung around my neck, I was forced to improvise shots, usually while I was moving and leading my horse at the tail end of our procession.

The higher we climbed, the narrower and more congested the trail became. Soon I began to see drops of blood on the rocks beneath my feet, blood shed by unfortunate pack animals ahead whose bindings had chafed or who had tripped against the sharp rocks. At times the trail was so steep that we had to wait while groups ahead of us beat, pulled, and shoved animals along particularly difficult stretches. Soon we began to see the animals that had failed, lying pitiably alongside the trail where they had been dragged and abandoned by their owners, sacrificed to the urgent need to cross this damnable and frightening mountain. Had it rained, there would have been horrendous carnage. The pastoralists told me the trail was almost impossible to cross in wet weather. Anxious glances at the cloudy skies affirmed their fear.

Kialon Kuh is a long sheer cliff jutting straight up to 4700 feet from its surrounding scree slopes (see Figure 9.7). We gained the top near eight o'clock that morning and worked our way along the face of a cliff that rose vertically hundreds of feet above us. The pass, a cleft perhaps half a mile across, separates Kialon's peak from the remainder of the ridge to the east. Below us, standing tall over the trees, were the pylons of the power line, which marched straight across the valley below and disappeared into the haze beyond.

During the climb up to the top of the talus, we were only dimly aware of the rising winds and increasing cold. But at the top, when the trail leveled out to follow the base of the cliff, the winds began to buffet us and the overcast skies screened out the sun's warmth. Suddenly it felt very cold. I started to remount when one of the women, who was carrying her baby in a sling, asked me for the flowered cloth that was tied over my saddle. I handed it to her and watched while she carefully shaped it around the baby, who was whimpering with the cold. Then I remounted and, hunched over against the wind, with hands shoved deep into my pockets, allowed my horse to plod along at its own pace in the long line of nomads and animals. Far below I could just make out Beringe Kar, almost hidden by the trees. The air was punctuated with the sounds of nomads urging their animals up the trail.

Within fifteen minutes we reached a level pasture surrounded by trees, where the travelers dismounted briefly to retie slipping loads, count their herds, and wolf down a few bites of cold bread (Figures 9.12, 9.13). Here and there, squatting under trees, mothers pulled babies from beneath layers of covers to let them nurse for a few minutes before we started the trip down.

Group after group appeared at this pasture, while others who had rested slipped away along one of the trails that descended from this spot. All trails from lowland pastures converge on the Kialon pass, but once across they diverge again, as each tribe heads toward its summer pastures along its traditional path. The route a tribe takes depends somewhat on the state of the

Figure 9.12. Atop the Kialon Pass the herds are rested, loads are retied, and the animals can forage for some grass. A newborn lamb is tied atop the load.

pastures, but for practical and political considerations the people of different tribes try to stay away from each other. Although there is no formal meeting of leaders to decide who will follow what route, the camps of each tribe stick together and, except at passes, avoid other tribes.

After we had rested, all of the animals were rounded up into a tight group for our descent. At the edge of the pass, overlooking the valleys and ridges to the north that we would cross in our migration, are little pyramids, left stone by stone by those thankful to have gained the summit (Figure 9.14)—they are offerings to Shah Ahmad, the granter of wishes. As I looked over the edge, the north side of Kialon looked as steep as the trail up, but I noticed the people were smiling. The tension of the morning's climb had dissipated.

I was struck with awe as we descended into a virgin forest of tall oaks, pistachios, maples, and other trees (Figure 9.15). Never before in my travels

Figure 9.13. Frank Hole stands with his horse during the rest stop on Kialon Kuh. Photo by Sekandar Amanolahi-Baharvand.

through Iran had I seen such wilderness, although I had read of such forests with disbelief in the accounts of eighteenth- and nineteenth-century travelers. Close to villages and towns, the trees are cut for fuel or shelter and as forage for goats, making such forests exceedingly rare. But high on Kialon, there were no villages and only a few overnight campsites. For the first time I began to appreciate the amount of wild food that may once have been available. I had heard many times that Luri nomads in times past had made bread of acorn flour and once had subsisted almost exclusively on this staple. In the midst of this forest I understood how that could be true, given the acorn riches that now passed before my eyes.

The trail took us down the north side of Kialon Kuh toward Takhte Chou. As we descended through the forest we could look out over the valley we were about to enter. On the far side were bare sheets of limestone sloping

Figure 9.14 (above). At the pass over Kialon we could see successive ranges of hills and ridges that we would cross in ensuing days. To signify a successful crossing, the people often add a stone to a pile or drive in stakes. Figure 9.15 (below). The trail down from Kialon Kuh is a slippery, scree-covered trail that descends through a forest.

toward the center of the valley, cut by steep-sided deep gorges that channeled tributaries into the Sar-i-Gol River, which eventually finds its way to the Saimarreh (Figure 9.16). A less hospitable vista could scarcely be imagined. The bedrock was sparsely marked by vegetation and the deep canyons would make lateral movement difficult. It was no wonder that wilderness forest existed on the slopes of Kialon, I thought, for there appeared to be no way to farm or even do much grazing.

Traditionally the valley belonged to the Mir tribe of Lurs, who were on relatively good terms with the Baharvand, but the trails that passed through were used by all tribes. As we descended farther, the land on the south side of the valley flattened out somewhat, allowing small patches of cultivation. After about an hour and a half of steady walking, we had worked our way down to the river, which flowed some fifty feet below, between steep-sided banks. A grove of pomegranates, which had once been part of a more extensive garden, testified to a permanent settlement nearby. Small fields alongside the river were carefully protected from passing caravans by fences of stone and brush. We did not encroach upon them.

We arrived at the river at about eleven in the morning, intent on finding a campsite. Morad Khan asked a man, apparently a Mir, where he could find good camping. The man took us to a lovely spot down in the valley alongside a small tributary of the Sar-i-Gol. Here, he said, we would have clear running water, shade trees, and level places to sleep. For some reason Morad Khan did not like the site. With haughty disdain he said we would find something better. Abruptly he wheeled his horse away and the rest of us followed as smartly as our mounts would allow, in a display of force and discipline that was designed to impress our Mir guide. We went back to the river and halted momentarily, while a discussion ensued concerning the best place to cross. Morad Khan favored a narrow crossing a few hundred yards away, but Sekandar pressed him to cross the shallow water right where we were. Morad Khan said he always took the other route.

"This one is slippery," he said.

Sekandar said he would go across anyway, but before he could act upon his words, Morad Khan began to lead our party across. Morad Khan, sitting smartly, was every inch the leader. The women followed, sitting high above their baggage, and finally came the pack mules and donkeys, all stepping gingerly on the rocks that lay a foot or so beneath the water's surface.

Figure 9.16. Takhte Chou is a deeply dissected limestone valley with sparse vegetation. A trail wends along the bottom next to the Sar-i-Gol River.

Suddenly and without warning, one of the mules slipped down, followed by the women's horses, which pitched riders and baggage into the water. In a moment every animal was thrashing around on its knees, and men, women, and children were floundering in the water. I had deliberately stayed behind to film the picturesque crossing, and so I caught this unexpected action quite by chance. The men quickly converged on separate animals to help them rise to their feet, but the skittish beasts seemed incapable of taking more than a step or two without falling again. In despair, some animals just lay in the water, despite urgings and beatings by the nomads. When the pack animals refused to budge, they had to be unpacked, and the men struggled ashore with the baggage. In the meantime, the women deposited their babies on shore and waded out to try to salvage what they could from the water. The whole episode lasted some fifteen minutes and turned our haughty rejection of the campsite into an ignominious debacle.

My horse stayed ashore, much to my relief. When all the animals and baggage had been dragged to dry land, I took the traditional route across without incident. The rest of the party repacked the animals, lamenting the damage that had been done, the extent of which would not become apparent until everything was completely unpacked later at the campsite.

Our crossing had been made near an old *caravanserai* and guard post. On several of the hills above the crossing we could see ruined stone forts that had protected the caravans. Otherwise there were no signs in the immediate vicinity of any substantial settlements, modern or ancient. The keeper of the pomegranates apparently lived in relative solitude.

Rather than camp next to the stream, Morad Khan decided on the sloping sheet of bedrock on the north side of the river, and it was to that destination that we headed. The animals had some difficulty negotiating the sloping slippery rock leading up from the river, but there was so little else in Baharvand territory that they were quite used to it. About three-fourths of a mile from the river crossing we found a campsite near the edge of the canyon above the river (Figure 9.17). In my opinion it was not a choice spot—certainly not nearly so good as the spot we had so recently vacated. Nevertheless we stopped where Morad Khan indicated, and the women went for water, collected firewood, spread out their baggage to dry, and put up the reed screens.

Everyone in camp was exhausted from the long day of exertion. The release of pent-up enthusiasm and excitement over crossing Kialon Kuh and the ardors of the trip had sapped everyone's energy. With welcome relief, when the carpets were spread on the rock surface, the men stretched out for a refreshing glass of tea and some lunch. Our personal baggage, which was under the care of Safarali, did not arrive for half an hour or so, until the cattle were driven into camp. When we started to unpack we realized that, although the donkey with our bedding was present, the mule with our other things was nowhere to be seen.

Everyone's worst expectations of the crossing of Kialon were realized in that agonizing moment of discovery. Cameras, notes, clothing, and other personal items were all missing, along with a valuable mule. A quick conference was held to determine where the animal had last been seen. All agreed it had been at the pasture atop the Kialon pass. There were three possibilities as to its

Figure 9.17. After the baggage had gotten wet during a river crossing, it was laid out to dry.

whereabouts: 1) it had been stolen and hidden somewhere in the forest, 2) it had fallen over a cliff, or 3) it had wandered off with another camp. Everyone knew what had to be done, but no one moved. The carpets held exhausted bodies as if by the force of gravity.

Avoiding action, we continued to drink hot tea heavily laced with sugar. Then Sayid Reza, a man well known to the members of our camp, came up to greet us. His group had arrived the day before. When he was apprised of the missing mule, he volunteered to take a horse and inquire of camps to the west of us whether they had seen the animal. At the same time it was decided that Mohammad Ali and Morad Khan would head back to the pasture on Kialon and search the forest along the trail.

The men stood up wearily, searching the horizons in the vain hope that a confused mule would be wandering aimlessly within sight. Morad Khan unstaked his horse, mounted, and with Mohammad Ali on foot, set out to retrace our route, first by searching near the river crossing. By the time they had finished this, Sayid Reza had returned with negative results, so the three headed back toward Kialon.

Sekandar and I would have been useless in this hunt, as we did not know the country and would have had a hard time recognizing our animal if it had been stripped of its load. Moreover, we might have gotten lost in the dark in unfamiliar territory. We just waited, fearing the worst. The notes that I had so laboriously accumulated over the past three months were my chief concern. Our hope was that anyone who had found the animal would immediately recognize that the baggage was not Luri. We hoped they would believe that should anything be taken, gendarmes would soon enter this nomad sanctuary to hunt down the thieves. More realistically, we knew that word of our presence was widespread, as was the knowledge that we were under the care and protection of Morad Khan, whose retribution was more to be feared than that of mere police.

While we were waiting for word of the mule, Taji sought to allay our fears by divining (*fal graftan*) its location, using a technique called *fal e dasti* (divination by hand). Seated with us on the carpet in Morad Khan's tent, she asked the question, "Where is the mule?" Then, using her right arm as a divining device, she proceeded to determine what had happened to it. With her right arm outstretched, elbow toward the ground, she placed the little finger of her left hand on the forefinger of her right, and extended her thumb over the heel of the right hand. Taji then drew the thumb and little finger of her left hand together on the forearm of her right hand. After this she asked a series of questions: had the mule been stolen? had it fallen from a cliff? in which direction did it go? had it accidentally wandered off with another group of nomads? At each question her fingers spread out as if by their own will toward the heel of her right hand. If her fingers spread widely the answer to the question was "yes." If the fingers remained close together, the answer was negative. In our case the last question induced the widest stretch of the fingers. Taji announced that the animal would be found. It had not been stolen. It had strayed and joined another group.

I was in a mood to be cheered by any ray of hope, but the emerging consensus among other members of the camp was that the animal had been stolen. There was talk of how a more substantial sacrifice should have been made the night before and various rationalizations of why it had not been. We kept our eyes turned toward the trail that the three searchers had taken.

In the meantime, the women explored the damage that had been done in the dousing. Some families had lost all their tea, rice, and sugar, which is usually kept in cloth bags. I asked why they did not use plastic containers that are on sale cheaply in all of the towns. They said they did not know about them. I remembered then that Baharvand women did not go to town. We continued to wait, the prospect of losing our belongings weighing on our minds.

Finally, at about four o'clock, we caught sight of Morad Khan through the trees on the other side of the valley. Two men were mounted and yes, there was a third animal. We could hardly wait for them to get back to tell where they had found the mule. They reached our camp half an hour later, Sayid Reza now doing the walking. The second rider was Mohammad Ali, whose strength had finally given out. They plodded slowly into camp, both heading for Morad Khan's tent, where they sank wearily into the carpet and quietly sipped hot cups of tea. Morad Khan told the story very simply. He said the mule had strayed from our group just before we descended Kialon and had joined another group, which took a trail in the direction Taji had predicted. The animal had fallen in with the Naziravand Lurs, a tribe closely allied with the Baharvand. The men in that tribe, recognizing that the baggage was not Luri, had assumed quite rightly that it belonged to the two "engineers" (as all foreigners and most Iranians who work in the countryside are called) who were traveling with Morad Khan. The people said they had recognized the baggage and did not touch the belongings but simply waited for the inevitable visit of Morad Khan. My relief was profound, but it did not deter me from checking to see whether the loose change I had put into a zipper pocket on the outside of a bag was still there. It was not.

The men in our camp rested after the exertion of the trip, but there was no rest for the women, who had to gather firewood and water and then make tea. No food had been prepared since the early hours of the morning, but while the search party was out, Ghamartaj fixed us some fried eggs, bread, and tea. She spent the rest of the afternoon making butter in the skin churn, going after water twice more, and making dough for the evening's bread. She and the other women were busy the entire afternoon.

After the men had rested, they decided it would be prudent to set up the tents. We had passed through intermittent showers on the descent into Takhte Chou, and the overcast sky warned of rain in the evening. The nomads prefer not to set up tents because they have to be dismantled again in the morning and repacked on the animals. In fine weather it is quite agreeable to sleep without a roof, and even light rain was not much of a problem to Sekandar and me, for we had some plastic sheets that we could throw over us. We caused quite a stir when we pulled these out of a bag. The people had never seen such stuff before. They were eager for the day we would depart and leave the plastic behind for them.

Chapter 10

Daily Life on the Trail

According to Morad Khan, Takhte Chou lacked permanent settlements, except for one small village of former pastoral nomads a few miles to the east. As I looked around, I saw that the valley had far better grazing than I had appreciated from my distant vantage on Kialon Kuh. Even the apparently barren limestone on which we were camped had a fair amount of short grass.

We learned that some families of the Dadabad, Dirkavand, and Mir tribes spent the winter there, in relatively permanent quarters, which we had not yet seen. Although they did some cultivation, the valley was formerly considered to be just grazing land. In greater antiquity than memory serves, however, there had been substantial villages in the valley—we could see the ruins from our campsite. Many of the hillsides had terraces where irrigation water was channeled onto fields, just as we saw in Chin-i Zal. Morad Khan, almost as an afterthought, told us about a very large ruin of this type near the trail that we took into the valley. My interest was piqued at this bit of news, and he said that Sekandar and I could go there in the morning and catch up with the group at the next night's stopping place.

The main caravan route, which some of the other tribes took, ran to the west of our camp, where there was reported to be a major *caravanserai* of Safavid age (fifteenth to eighteenth centuries AD). Still, it was apparent that some traffic passed over the slippery Sar-i-Gol River, or there would be no ruins of guard towers or the small *caravanserai* that once had room for fifty mules. As we found when we examined them, those structures sat upon yet more ancient sites. Glazed sherds in the sides of the hills indicated a Sasanian or Islamic age, somewhere between a thousand and fifteen hundred years ago.

Since we were not following trails that showed up on any of the maps I carried with me, I repeatedly took compass sightings of landmarks and made sketch maps of our camps and the surrounding areas. This aroused the curiosity and the anxiety of the nomads, particularly as much of the former Luri winter grazing land in Khuzistan had by that time been taken over for industrial agricultural development, even to the extent of displacing the villagers who settled there a generation earlier in accord with governmental policy. Typically the first manifestation of impending change was the appearance of foreign engineers with maps and compasses, who were soon followed by bulldozers and eviction notices. The same was true of mountain pastures in the watershed of the Dez River, which fed silt into the Pahlavi Dam at a distressing rate. As a result, the Department of Natural Resources had promulgated land conservation policies that prevented nomads from grazing flocks and villagers from planting crops. As one man put it, "They told us we couldn't do anything except raise chickens."

The power line cutting through the wilderness was only a beginning that the nomads feared would bring roads, agricultural enterprises, a further reduction of their mobility, and an increase of governmental control over tribes and lands. As it was, nomads were already prevented officially from cutting trees. But people whose bread must be cooked over open fires have little choice.

That evening I had a rather heated discussion with Sekandar, stimulated in part by his telling Morad Khan that my compass was an instrument that sees into mountains. I had told him that since there was no adequate map of the migration route, I took compass bearings on various landmarks and sketched topographic features so that I would later be able to reconstruct where we had been. My actions attracted quite a bit of attention, particularly as Americans were well known to be involved in exploiting Iran's mineral wealth. It was clear to the nomads, in spite of my disclaimers, that I was interested in something of great monetary value. Treasure, as everyone knows, lies inside mountains. Thus, Sekandar was only agreeing with prevailing opinion when he assented to the preposterous notion that I was conducting a mineral survey by peering inside mountains.

In exasperation, I said, "Sekandar, it's wrong to tell things like that."

He replied, "If I told them what we are really doing, they would think it is childish."

The problem was not as simple as that little exchange might suggest. The problem was that Sekandar was in an untenable position. As a Lur and Baharvand he had certain beliefs and expectations, based in large part on heroic stories told by his father. Many of his expectations were unrealistic because of changes that had taken place during his long absence from Iran. As an anthropologist, he wanted to understand his tribe and its history. As a student and host, he wanted to make a good impression on his professor. As an educated man, he wanted to bridge the gap between himself and his people.

I saw travel as adventure, a series of experiences that told me something about the country and the people I met. I saw physical discomfort as only momentary unpleasantness and quite unimportant to either the purpose or success of a trip. I had started the trip willingly and I would see it through enthusiastically. I was excited by the new sights and situations. As far as I was concerned, the migration had been a great success to this point. But for Sekandar it had been close to his vision of hell, both for the physical discomfort and for his embarrassment at our treatment.

Although he felt antipathy toward Morad Khan, whom he regarded as a deceitful old man, he could forgive him, because Morad Khan was an excellent informant. What really rankled Sekandar, I finally came to realize, was the lack of respect. By tribal standards, Sekandar was a big man, as important in his own way as Morad Khan. Yet Morad Khan lived in squalor and so, of necessity, did we. Moreover, Morad Khan had, it seemed to Sekandar, done as little as possible to ease this problem.

The realities of nomadic life came as a great shock to Sekandar—not nomadic life in general, but life in his own tribe. When we visited camp after camp of other tribes in the same situation, he took it gracefully and hinted that things would be better with the Baharvand. When things were not, it was difficult to swallow. As heir to a long succession of strong tribal leaders, Sekandar was accustomed to being served. He was used to deferential respect. In his dreams he may have imagined the leader's tent laid with beautiful carpets, surrounded by hundreds of *homsa* tending the thousands of sheep that grazed the succulent spring pastures. The old leaders agreed, as they sat in the dark around their campfires, that that was how it used to be. That was the romance of pastoralism.

The truth was that nomads experience long hours, unpredictable harsh weather, soaking rains, searing suns, diseases of the flocks, injuries, endless monotony, and only intermittent sleep. For a leader with abundant servants, life could have been a paradise of idle luxury, punctuated by occasional raids or hunts, and kept lively by incessant undercurrents of political intrigue. There was little of this for Morad Khan, or for Sekandar and the rest of the men.

Had it not been for me, Sekandar said, he would never have made the trip or stayed with Morad Khan. In his opinion, the old man ought to have retired from pastoralism.

"Why does he keep it up?" he asked rhetorically. "He could settle in a village, get plenty of land to farm, and be free from the onerous drudgery of migratory life."

I had heard the same thing from Morad Khan's son Mukhtar, who repeatedly complained that he could not get the old man to settle down. He and Sekandar thought Morad Khan was just obstinate, living in the past, unable to deal effectively with the present.

I was a bit irritated by Sekandar's attitude and told him so. But my own homily extolling the good things about pastoral life must have seemed as hollow to Sekandar as his diatribe did to me. We did agree that the life was hard for all, but he only grudgingly admitted that life had probably always been hard for the *homsa*. Our discussion helped relieve the tension that had been building between the two of us. I began to understand his unhappiness and he began to see that there was more to tribal life than the ruling families had chosen to admit.

Morad Khan's problems centered on lack of manpower. All agreed that nomadism was a good way of life only when a man had many sons who could help with the labor and eventually provide for their father. We saw several instances of old men, scarcely able to keep up on the migration trail, who had become dependent members of one of the son's tents. This was the traditional form of social and economic security, but it was not the case for Morad Khan: in his advancing age, he had to fend for himself.

Since, in the popular view, nomads preferred their way of life, it struck me that Morad Khan must like it, too. But judging such a thing was not easy. In talking with him and other nomads, I had come to the conclusion that they did not see the hardships as a burden; they were merely part of life. To move to a village would be to replace one set of problems with another set: problems that would be unfamiliar and not obviously better. Further, during his seventy years, Morad Khan had seen his and others' fortunes wax and wane as inexorably as the seasons passed. In every turn of events there was always optimism for the future. Even in hardship, the belief in divine causality sustained their spirits.

On the other hand, Morad Khan had once remarked that he would settle down if only he had enough farmland, and others among his tribe had expressed the same view. In Morad Khan's case, this may have been an empty excuse, because he had considerable land holdings. Most of the *homsa* did not. In my view, Morad Khan continued to migrate not because settling down was impractical, but because he preferred the intangible attributes of nomadic life and wanted to keep political fences mended through widespread peregrinations.

Much has been made of the idea that nomads look down upon farmers, but I found this was not necessarily the case. Virtually all of the Baharvand farmed, even though many of them were also transhumant pastoralists. But there is a great difference between farming pastures around tents and farming in a village. The former affords the opportunity of choice through mobility. With mobility, one can take advantage of favorable circumstances for farming on land where each plot is not already owned. The villager, on the other hand, is much more restricted in his fixed and densely settled locale, and he has fewer options to help him overcome bad years.

Equally important to the nomads is the sense of freedom. To be able to pick up and move away from one's neighbors or the law, and to be able to enjoy the beauty of the mountains and changes of scenery, is infinitely better to many than settling in the monotonous, disease-ridden squalor of a mud-walled village. In the village, one loses the clean air, bright skies, wide vistas, and open companionship of the campfires, settling instead for a closed compound that insulates the farmer psychologically and physically from his fellows and the larger world around him. Where the nomad confronts the world, the villager retreats from it.

There should be no mistake. Many nomads, especially of the younger generation, wanted to give up tent life. But their eyes were not on village life; they were attracted to wage labor in the towns and cities. The village was not the preferred alternative for many nomads. On the other hand, much of the nomad's dislike of village life stemmed from overcrowding. Nomads often asserted that they would settle down if they could make as good a living in the village. In spite of the rigors of their life, the nomads enjoyed a higher standard of living than did farmers, a fact that was generally true throughout western Iran.

Only a light rain fell that evening, and our sleep was undisturbed until 5:30 a.m., when we were awakened by a call. Although the weather looked threatening, Morad Khan announced that it would not rain anymore. The camp prepared to move on. Following our usual light breakfast of bread, yoghurt, and tea, Sekandar and I saddled our horses to take a side trip to the large ruins that Morad Khan had told us lay nearby. We would catch up with the camp when we were finished.

We recrossed the slippery river and made our way along its left bank for about two miles, when we unexpectedly came upon the remains of a fort built of mud bricks in the midst of a very extensive ancient site of vaulted stone buildings and agricultural terraces. Without adequate time to work, or aerial photos to aid our search, we could gain only a preliminary impression of the size of the settlement. The area was sloping bedrock descending from the flanks of Kialon, covered with an open forest of oaks that had grown up among the ruins, sometimes penetrating through the vaults of the semi-subterranean buildings.

As we wandered through the site, we came upon a mud-walled enclosure, inside of which were a series of heavily constructed mud-walled stables and stone foundations for nomad tents. While we were looking at this, Amir—an old man dressed in black and wearing a white felted skullcap, who tended the pomegranate garden near the old *caravanserai*—came up to greet us. According to Amir, the modern camp belonged to the Delfan, a tribe from Nurabad, some of whom had joined the Dirkavand, a tribe that was closely related to the Baharvand. These people passed the winter in Sar-i-Gol and then moved to summer pasture in a valley toward which our own group was heading.

Amir called the ancient site Shahr Mehdar. He said it was the only one of its kind in the valley, and that it must be very old, because there were no legends concerning it. It was far older, he said, than the *caravanserai* at the river crossing, which was used until about forty-five years ago. To me the ruins looked to be the same age as those in Chin-i Zal. The accumulating evidence was that the entire Baharvand area, which was now used almost exclusively for pasture by migratory tribes, once held a large, settled, and agriculturally advanced population. The enormous labor invested in the terraces, houses, and irrigation systems bespoke vastly different political conditions in the area than had been recorded in more than a thousand years.

I resolved to return to the site after the migration, when I would have ample time and equipment to map it. We then turned back along the river to catch up with our party. As we followed along the edge of the canyon, we took a closer look at the river itself, and observed three sets of water mills in ruins and several sets of terraced fields long since abandoned. In the cliffs on the right bank were several natural shelters, some of which, like those in Chin-i Zal, had been used as animal pens. I made a note to investigate these later for traces of ancient habitation or use.

We had been given only very general instructions about the route our camp would take, but we expected to pass other camps or shepherds along the way who would be able to give us explicit instructions. Instead we rode mile after tortured mile up the sloping sheets of limestone, which were covered with loose, slippery rock scree. Our faint trail ran alongside a deep canyon whose small stream flowed into the Sar-i-Gol. The only sign of other people was at a camp near ours of the night before, where children were swinging from ropes hung in the trees.

As the sun rose higher in the sky and a good two hours had passed without a sign of other humans, we began to wonder if we had taken the right route. It was eerie to travel so far without human contact, in a land where there had always seemed to be someone nearby. That day there was only solitude, and the faint trail rarely ran alongside any traces of human activity. Once or twice we saw where nomads had camped, but Sekandar said that part of the territory had so little water that people only stopped when rain collected in natural pools.

Figure 10.1. Throughout parts of Luristan there are tombs that once held bronze horse trappings and other artifacts used by an unnamed horse-riding people. Most of the tombs have been looted.

Around noon we caught sight of a lone person on the trail ahead. It was Mohammad Ali. He had come back to find us, assuming correctly that we would get lost. We were relieved to see him and dismounted to share a piece of bread he had with him. For dessert, I fished a supply of hard candy out of my saddlebag. We must have walked another hour before we reached the summit of the long slope, where we found the stone remains of another village with agricultural terraces. Mohammad Ali told us there were graves in the hills nearby, so we went to investigate them. A number of them had been looted recently, exposing the characteristic peaked vaulting of "Luristan" tombs (Figure 10.1). Since the 1920s, bronze objects—chiefly horse trappings and weapons—from these tombs had been eagerly acquired by museums and collectors the world over. The easily accessible ones had long since been taken. The best guess is that these date to between 1000 and 500 BC (Haerinck 2012; Muscarella 1989). Dealers send teams of diggers into ever more remote and formerly hostile areas in search of these artifacts.

Unfortunately for archaeologists, the looters rarely dig with care, so very little is known about the people who made these artistic bronzes. At that time, I thought it would not be many years before the tombs were all desecrated, given the rate of looting in the parts of Luristan through which we traveled.

The Luristan cemeteries were often discovered when erosion exposed the long rectangular stones used for their roofs. Once the location of a graveyard was known, it was a simple matter to find other graves by probing into the ground with a stick or steel rod that would hit other roofs not yet exposed at ground surface. Thus, in very short order, an entire cemetery could be looted by a few men with picks and shovels. Islamic graves in the same cemeteries were easily recognized and not disturbed. It was not for religious reasons; they contained nothing the looters considered valuable.

At the summit, we looked back on the entire Sar-i-Gol Valley, watched over by towering Kialon Kuh. The canyon that had been on our immediate right disappeared, and we followed some of its tributary drainages through gently rolling country with heavy stands of oaks. Among the trees high up on some of the hills were campsites occupied by nomads who had apparently settled in for the summer.

Duze Ab

About two in the afternoon we rode into view of a camp that Mohammad Ali said belonged to Khodarahm, the man who earlier had invited us to join his group. We entered, dismounting some distance from the tents so that the dogs would not spook the horses. A young man immediately ran up and led the horses away to graze. Khodarahm's camp was alongside a small permanent stream. Two similar camps were within view in this broad, tree-covered valley. While we were eating our lunch of fried eggs, bread, and *dugh*, Dust Ali told us that this was the best campsite in the area. He said Morad Khan should have stopped there. The site was summer pasture for people who had a village only about half a mile away. According to Dust Ali, heavy snows accumulated there on the flat land in the winter, so the permanent village was on a south-facing hill.

After lunch we rode across the valley, following a trail that passed mostly through open forest. We finally reached Morad Khan's camp about four. As there were few well-defined trails in the area, we almost missed the beautiful

Figure 10.2. A typical overnight camp in a forest of budding oaks.

little oak grove in a hollow some forty-five feet below the level of the plateau over which we were riding, where Morad Khan was camped (Figure 10.2).

The high pasture was called Duze Ab, and the oaks there were scarcely out of bud, whereas along Sar-i-Gol they were fully developed and growing acorns. Spring had just begun there, at about six thousand feet elevation. The tree line was only a few hundred feet higher. The pasture was protected from winds by the surrounding hills, and the imposing Daliche and Khargushan mountain ranges to the south and north were scarcely visible from its depth.

The rest of the camp had long since settled in, and they were engaged in the usual domestic chores or just relaxing. As the pasture had not been used previously that season, there was plenty of grass for all the animals near the campground (Figure 10.3). A small spring flowed only a quarter of a mile away. The open parkland of trees supplied abundant wood for fuel. A more ideal campsite could hardly be imagined, and I wondered at how little it was

Figure 10.3. Each household sets up its site. Once the screens are up, it is time for the women to collect water from a spring, heat water for tea, and start baking bread. The bedding is stacked against the back screen.

apparently used. Unlike most other places where we stopped, there were no visible traces of former campsites, yet it was a place where Morad Khan had camped in years past.

As we relaxed over tea, Morad Khan told us about the territory we had passed over. From the *caravanserai* at the river near where we had camped the night before, we had followed an old caravan route to the summit leaving the Sar-i-Gol Valley. At the summit, where we had found the graves, the trail branched: the caravan route headed left across Khargushan Kuh, and our trail went to the right, toward the higher mountains.

I had been impressed by the sizes and condition of the trees along the trail. Many of them were three feet in diameter and apparently had not been cut in generations (Figure 10.4). On the other hand, there were many trees that recently had been cut down. Large branches had been sawed off and were lying on the ground. Morad Khan said that nomads cut branches to provide forage for their herds where the pastures are thin. Goats will climb trees to get at the leaves, but sheep cannot. Although both sheep and goats eat leaves

Figure 10.4. Luristan once was renowned for its forests, of which only vestiges are left. This giant oak, with Mohammad Ali as scale, reminds us what has been lost.

Figure 10.5. Acorns are ground on boulders with heavy stones that are rocked back and forth over the acorns.

and acorns, the goats eat more and do better on this food. After the leaves are gone, the limbs are converted to charcoal: an illegal business that could not be stopped.

While we were riding into camp, we had passed a number of rectangular stone structures that looked like the remains of small houses. They were about six by nine feet in area and had walls standing some three to six feet high. Mohammad Ali said the nomads used to roast acorns in them. Nearby there were usually grinding stones that were used to pulverize the roasted nuts. Those stones were often far too large to move and were sometimes simply bedrock itself with a smoothed and slightly depressed surface. Lying atop many of those we saw heavy stones that were rocked back and forth over the acorns to mash them into flour (Figure 10.5). In an area with few other traces of human activity, those seemed to be ubiquitous where there were heavy stands of oaks. However, with the advent of farming, they were no longer used, except in dire emergency or under threat of famine.

Figure 10.6. Morad Khan prepares kabobs of a sheep that he has just butchered, while Frank watches. Photo by Sekandar Amanolahi-Baharvand.

The unsullied freshness and affluence of the area seemed to affect the nomads. There was none of the first day's grim determination in their relaxed conviviality. In celebration of the abundance of fuel, huge bonfires were built before every tent site, warming the chill evening air and providing welcome tongues of light.

In the early evening, a man appeared in our camp and went immediately to Morad Khan's tent. The nature of his business was uncertain, but his visit resulted in the killing of a goat. Morad Khan personally slaughtered the animal about fifty feet from his tent and butchered it nearby, using my pocketknife, which he had borrowed for the purpose (Figure 10.6). I was always surprised when the nomads asked for my knife, especially when I was assured that the nomads had plenty of knives of their own. Usually I was told that their knives had been misplaced somewhere in the baggage.

The fire in front of Morad Khan's tent was stoked to make a hot bed of coals, and the men sat on logs around the fire. With slow deliberation, Morad

Khan cut up the meat and skewered it for cooking. Mohammad Ali sawed off and discarded the horns, so that the head could be boiled the next day. I had long since learned that there is virtually no part of the animal that is not eaten. Only the gallbladder, spleen, and contents of the stomach and intestine were discarded. The dogs took care of these. First to be made into kabobs was the liver, the choicest part of the animal. This was cut into chunks roughly an inch and a half square, slipped onto a metal skewer or stick, and roasted over the hot coals. As soon as it was cooked, the liver was passed around among the men, who ate it with some fresh bread. The women and children seemed never to get any of the liver.

After we each had a few chunks of the steaming meat, Morad Khan took the next hour to carefully wrap the entrails, which looked like thin spaghetti, around the skewers. They eventually came to resemble untidy balls of kite string. When these were cooked they made a crisp, bland appetizer that the men sitting around the fire also ate. While the meat was cooking, the rest of the animal was cut apart for distribution among the members of the camp. Although Morad Khan had killed and butchered the goat, he did not cook for the entire camp. He laboriously made preliminary divisions of the meat, which was laid out on trays next to the fire for the women of the other tents to prepare for their families. Taji helped with this, discussing with her husband the quantities and qualities of the various cuts of meat and who should get what. By the time we had finished the liver and entrail kabobs, the portions were ready for distribution. After that, we settled down to the main course of rib kabobs.

Depending on circumstances, one or more of the men of the camp might be invited to eat with Morad Khan. On that night, Mohammad Ali shared the meal, and thus received rather more meat than he would have, had he taken only the share that went to his tent.

With dinner out of the way, we sat around the fire talking. Someone mentioned the wooden pigeons at Kamuteran, approximately at the place where we found the looted graves. There, in a field, were a number of pigeons carved out of wood. This naturally piqued my curiosity, and I was not a little irritated at having heard nothing of this while we were passing by. The trend of the conversation suggested that formerly there had been a great many pigeons in the field, but since they were rotting and some had been taken, there were not many left. No one had the slightest idea who had made the

Figure 10.7. In the evening Sekandar (left) often sat by a fire with Mohammad Ali (center) and Mohammad's brother Panjali.

birds or why they were there, but our visitor said he would procure one of the birds and send it on for me. I was particularly interested since woodcarving is not a common craft among Lurs, and because I had expected to find evidence of pre-Islamic shrines on some of the remote hilltops. I was very curious to see the area, as well as the birds, but Morad Khan said it was out of the question, since we had to leave early in the morning for the next day's long journey.

We slept that night next to Morad Khan's tent, enclosed by a reed screen on three sides. Just as we were bedding down, Sekandar turned on a transistor radio and received a loud, clear signal from Kuwait: rock and roll music announced by a woman who spoke English. Nothing could have been more incongruous, and I implored Sekandar to turn it off so that we could enjoy the sounds of our own camp and the peace of the starlit night (Figure 10.7).

We awoke around five o'clock under a cloudy, overcast sky with a cool breeze blowing. Contrary to the assertion last night, there was no apparent haste in leaving, so we enjoyed a leisurely breakfast of bread, yoghurt, fried

Figure 10.8. Crossing a small stream where the animals could rest and take a drink.

eggs, and several glasses of tea. The packing of animals did not begin until six, and it was around eight before we finally hit the trail. There was no sense of urgency in either the pace or the attitudes, although the trail was neither comfortable nor easy.

When we crossed a small stream, we halted while the pack animals drank and the women foraged for greens (Figures 10.8, 10.9).

Our trail climbed gradually through thinning trees and then changed abruptly to a very steep rock slope, where the going was slow and difficult. As we climbed, we passed light purple flowering almonds (Figure 10.10). The oaks had just budded out. We crossed the pass at 10 o'clock and were treated to a vista of mountains ranging far to the north and south.

At the top of the pass, Mohammad Ali's wife, Khawar, pounded a stick into the ground as another offering to Shah Ahmad. When she made these

Figure 10.9. During the rest stop, a woman, baby on her back, gleans from local vegetation.

offerings, they were always accompanied by a prayer that she might give birth to a son. At the same place were perhaps a hundred or more similar sticks, piles of rocks, and even rags tied to the branches of trees. These offerings were made by other nomads in gratitude for having reached the pass successfully and in supplication for personal favors.

The trail down the north side was a long, hard series of switchbacks along a steep rocky anticline. We slipped and slid down this trail for some three hours before we finally reached the forested green of the Anuro Valley. One settlement could be seen far to the east, but I was told there were few other villages.

Mohammad Ali said that twice when he had made the same crossing, it started raining after he had reached the top. He said it was nearly impossible to descend the wet trail safely. As I led my horse over difficult spots and watched animals slipping on dry rocks, I found that easy to believe.

Figure 10.10. Sekandar stands next to a flowering almond, one of the first trees to bud out.

Men and animals alike suffered from the trail. Many of the donkeys developed open sores where their bindings rubbed, leaving blood on the trail in mute testimony to their pain. My horse developed a painful sore on its shoulder, which I tried to alleviate with extra padding. Sekandar turned an ankle when he dismounted near the summit, and I jammed my right thumb painfully when the horse bolted as I was mounting. As only disabling accidents were worthy of note among the nomads, neither Sekandar nor I complained.

Darsafa

Only a few kilometers from the edge of the valley, we could see several groups of tents. Sekandar, who had not been feeling well, suggested that we stop at one for lunch, employing the time-honored practice of dropping uninvited into a strange camp. Having made up our minds to do this, we left our party. They continued on their way to a suitable campground. Meanwhile, we took a trail directly past one of the settled camps: all the tents were up, apparently because the people were planning to stay for some time. Sekandar was looking for the largest tent, that of the leader, and after inquiring of some herders, we made our way to his household. After dismounting a prudent distance away, we waited until a man came up to greet us. He led us to the leader's tent and had our horses taken to pasture. Sekandar quickly established his credentials with the headman, whose wife was already preparing the fire for tea. We declined the customary offer of a lamb and asked instead for an omelet. This was quickly produced while we sat and talked.

I asked why there were no villages in such a lush-looking valley. The obvious answer, the headman replied, was that there was little surface water, although there was adequate rain for crops. To my mind, that was also sufficient explanation for the lack of any ancient stone villages with agricultural terraces. The valley was used principally as a summer pasture, since it was very cold in the winter. Tribes that camped there passed the winter south of the Daliche range and used the Anoru Valley only in the summer. The summer camps were well established, with the tents up and brush outlining the reed walls to keep the animals outside. Neat piles of firewood stood in front of the tents and all of the baggage was unpacked and put in place for daily use, even though the people had arrived only a few days earlier. I was impressed with the orderly arrangement in this camp as compared with ours.

After lunch we traveled a little more than an hour before catching up with Morad Khan at Darsafa, our campsite for the evening. This place, called "four roads," was just alongside one of two main trails that crossed near the camp. The campground was about the same elevation as Duze Ab, to judge from the development of the trees. We camped in a forest that was relatively dense, except where the trees had been cut to make fields for agriculture. Again, in contrast with most campsites, this one showed little sign of previous occupation; it looked rather like an oak grove in an English countryside. The lack of use was evident in the heavy cover of dead leaves and quantities of dry wood for fuel.

When we arrived, Morad Khan was eating lunch with Taji. The animals were close by and most of the other nomads were also relaxing in their sites over lunch. Since the camp had not been set up, Sekandar asked Morad Khan where we should put our beds. He said they should always go in the same place, to his right. He repeated, "It is the custom in all camps for the tents to be placed in the same location."

Since wood was abundant, many of the men began to make new stakes to support the reed screens around their camps. They had simply abandoned the stakes they had made the night before. To me this seemed an unnecessary duplication of effort, but it was apparently customary when wood was available. Indeed, when one arrives at a camp that has been used recently, he often finds quantities of these stakes lying about. They are eagerly seized by the women for firewood, while their husbands go out and cut new stakes to support the screens. Later in the evening, I watched Morad Khan hardening stakes in the fire. Since the wood was green, it did not burn when he put the points into the charcoal for some three to four minutes. Thus hardened, the stakes drive readily into rocky soil without breaking.

While the camp was being set up, I watched one of the women carrying a small wooden trough (*talas*) by means of two sticks, taking obvious care not to touch the trough itself. Sekandar explained the trough was for the dogs' water. Because dogs touch it, it is considered unclean. Dogs are unclean because they are scavengers. Never in Iran have I seen a tribal person or a villager willingly touch an adult dog or show the slightest affection toward one. Ordinarily the dogs are fed only scraps of bread, but in season they may also be given the leftover *dugh*, the watery buttermilk that remains after churning.

Later in the afternoon, a Sayid, identified by his green turban, appeared in camp with three horses that he tied to a tree. Without greeting anyone, he went immediately to Morad Khan's tent, where he was offered, and smoked, a water pipe. I had no idea what they discussed while they smoked. When he was finished, the Sayid remounted his horse and disappeared. Sekandar said he thought the man was looking for a handout. As descendants of the Prophet, the Sayids are entitled to the tribe's support. A few Sayids were affiliated with every tribe, although none was in residence in Morad Khan's camp when I was there.

After smoking, the Sayid rode to a field near our camp, where about twenty horses were grazing in a field of wheat. He yelled at the horses, drove them out of the field with his own mount, and soon disappeared at a gallop across the valley back to his own camp. I thought to myself that when raiding of fields occurs today, during a time of relative law and order, it is no wonder that it was not the custom to plant crops in Morad Khan's younger days, when all nomads were armed and aggressively hostile.

As the afternoon passed, Morad Khan took a nap. Taji, sitting next to him and apparently oblivious to his slumber, kept up a steady stream of chatter. When a woman from another camp walked up, Taji got up to greet her. The woman carried with her a joint of beef from a cow that had been killed because it was dying. Taji immediately began cutting the meat apart and distributing it. While I watched, she made kabobs with some of the meat. Then I too succumbed to sleep and did not see who ate it. Beef was not considered fit for guests, so I would not have been served anyway. When I woke again, near dusk, I saw one of the women in our camp carrying a rib cage from last night's feast to another tent, thus extending the sharing of meat still further.

As dusk settled, I began to notice a number of strangers in the various tent sites. They were women from other camps who had come to visit friends and relatives. During migration, when all of the camps of the tribe are close together, there is a great deal of socializing. The women, who are normally confined to their own widely scattered camps, make the most of these semiannual gatherings. When a woman comes to visit another, she expects to receive a small gift of money, tea, sugar, meat, or some other valuable item. In due course these gifts are reciprocated, so that through visiting there is a small flow of petty cash and goods throughout the tribe.

At this time most of the men were out gathering wood. I noticed that Safarali had piled brush and limbs between his camp and ours. Other men were doing the same, and soon the entire interior of the camp area was ringed with a wall, inside of which they would corral the animals for the night. Although cheered by this unusual foresight, I was dismayed to see that the screen around our camp served as part of the corral. That meant animals would spend the night pushing against it.

Sekandar had turned an ankle earlier in the day, when he had dismounted on a particularly rocky part of the trail so that he could lead his horse. After resting for some hours, his ankle still pained him considerably when he tried to walk. He mentioned this to Safarali, who unexpectedly brightened at this news. It turned out that he was the local chiropractor. He immediately began to massage Sekandar's ankle with warm water. When he had done this for some minutes, he braced himself, facing Sekandar, and gave the ankle a prodigious pull. He kept this up for some time, to Sekandar's evident displeasure, and then abruptly stopped, saying that he had heard the ankle snap. Now, he assured us, it would be all right. After watching Sekandar's pain, I decided to keep quiet about my thumb.

Following these ministrations, Safarali turned once again to the trees, and almost at once had several of them ablaze, just outside the perimeter of our camp. This struck me as both unsafe and wasteful, and I asked why he was doing it.

"To keep the wolves and thieves away," he replied.

Soon he and the other men had the entire camp ringed with flames. The animals, in the meantime, had not been driven into the corral; they were grazing in a field of wheat a short distance from the camp.

When the nomads have an abundance of fuel, they joyfully build huge bonfires. In fact, although sometimes the supply of wood appears inexhaustible, the nomads have seen the progressive denudation of forests in their summer pastures. Their passive resignation to the eventual total demise of the forests, because of just these same kinds of acts, was hard for me to understand.

Well after dark, when the fires had been reduced to glowing embers, the animals were finally rounded up to be put into the corral. It was only at this time that the men noticed some of the cows were missing. Guilty speculation immediately centered on the possibility that the owners of the fields in which the animals had been grazing had stolen the cattle. It would not have surprised me. In any case, the men set forth on their nightly search for lost animals. The hillsides surrounding our camp were also ablaze with light from other camps, showing the common fear of thieves or their love of fire. Cries into the night from one camp to another announced the missing animals and it was determined that they were not in a nomad camp.

Looking for a dark-colored cow in a dark forest on a dark night over unfamiliar terrain is not easy. Morad Khan had not failed to notice that I had a flashlight and he requested it. I gave it to him, and he and the others went off into the night. In my opinion, it was to be a fruitless search. I heartily subscribed to the theory that the Dirkavand who owned the wheat had probably taken the cows. Nevertheless, along with men from Khodarahm's camp, Morad Khan's party fanned out into the woods. Three quarters of an hour later, much to my surprise, they were back with the cows, which had been wandering around where their grazing had taken them.

Dinner was delayed because of the search, but around nine Taji set herself to the task and eventually produced some kabobs that were left over from the evening before. As usual, she was in a talkative mood, so I elicited information about the nomads' diet before agricultural products were always available. She eagerly poured forth her knowledge of the subject, describing a whole series of dishes that were totally new to me. In fact, as they were dishes usually eaten during the winter, we had not had any of them on migration.

Winter dishes with wheat, barley, vegetables, and acorns

Wheat was prepared in three basic ways. To make *gondum bereshta*, or "fried" wheat, women soaked whole grain in milk overnight. In the morning, after it was dried on a bread pan over the fire, the grain was mixed with raisins and some small seeds that grew in bunches on *kolang* trees. The dry mixture was eaten like the crunchy snack called granola in the U.S.

Kashgeena was a mixture of rough ground or smashed wheat and thick *dugh* (a drink made from thin yoghurt) that was several days old. When the grain had soaked up the dugh, it was dried and stored for use in the winter. Before it could be eaten, it had to be soaked in water. Often boiled lentils or other seeds were added, along with oil or onions, to make a kind of porridge.

There were four varieties of *horrosh* (porridge). The first, called *partela*, consisted of whole wheat that was half-boiled and then smashed in a mortar to remove the husks. The grain was then added to boiled vetch, one of the local pulses. *Halim* was whole wheat boiled and smashed in the same way, then put in a basket to drain, then cooked in a pot with oil. *Halim* was also made in towns and sold as a stringy, glutinous, hot breakfast cereal, reminiscent of oatmeal. *Paleela* started with very dry granular bread dough to which boiled vetch or lentils and dugh were added. Sometimes some of the wild mountain vegetables and onions fried in oil were also included. When cooked, this was also a porridge. The fourth kind of *horrosh* was called *reshta*. Thin pieces of bread dough were dried in the sun, rolled, cut into small pieces, and added to boiled lentils. To this mixture was added *kashk*, the dried *dugh*, which had been stored for this purpose, along with fried onions and oil.

Barley was sometimes mixed with wheat to make bread when there were food shortages, but the nomads did not like the mixture very well. Barley could also be boiled in salted water and dried in a heated frying pan, after which it could be eaten. Or it may be boiled and then mashed and cooked with oil and sugar. In this form it was called *ghoweet*. In places where the nomads grow corn, they may fry it, roast the ears, or pop it.

Nomads often ate soups or thin stews. These usually included, singly or in combination, vetch, lentils, onions, oil, and sometimes sour lemons or pomegranates. Some of the vegetables that grew locally, such as *tula*, a clover-like plant, were eaten after boiling, but many were consumed raw.

Of more interest to me than these preparations of cereal grain, however, were the methods used to prepare acorns. Taji said that in years past the nomads harvested acorns, but that even though forests were more extensive than today, acorns were not always available. Heavy mast years (years when there were more acorns than normal) occurred irregularly, between two and five years apart. Typically, all the trees in a grove had heavy masts at the same time. Their growth was apparently affected by rain and temperature—the same things that determined the success of wheat. With enough searching, Taji said, it was usually possible to find groves that were laden with acorns, and it was there that collecting took place.

The nomads collected acorns in the fall by beating the trees with poles. Then they skinned the acorns and fried them in pans or roasted them in large stone ovens (we had passed some of these). The latter were obviously more suitable for large harvests. Next, they dried the roasted acorns thoroughly in the sun and removed the inside skin, leaving only the white acorn meat. The meat was then mashed on the large grinding stones that we had seen along the trails. The resulting coarse white flour was washed twice with boiling water to get rid of the tannic acid. Following this, they soaked the pulp in a skin bag for a day or so, until it became soft enough to squeeze between the fingers. Finally they put the mixture into a basket with leaves sealing the top and bottom. In the closed basket, natural fermentation took place, making the whole mass hot. The pulp was then put into running water overnight and was ready to use.

Kazka was made by grinding the paste once again, forming it in a cloth so that it held together, and flipping it out onto the metal bread pan. This resulted in sheets of acorn "bread." *Kalk* was a variation of thin bread made with the addition of some wheat flour, and *kalk varumadee* was a thicker flap of bread made with proportionately more wheat flour.

The local acorns, *balut*, are about 1½ inches long. They were also roasted and eaten directly from the tree. In my experience acorns prepared this way were reasonably tasty. The technique is to break the skin of the acorns before setting them in hot coals, so that the acids can escape as steam.

Another method is to fry skinned acorns and put them immediately into bags tied down in a stream for one week. After this time, they can be milled into flour and converted directly to bread in the proportion of one part acorns to two parts wheat.

Although acorn flour is not highly prized, it was once the principal "grain" in the diets of many herding people of western Iran, including the Boir Ahmad, another Lur tribe. It remains a staple in times of famine, and is sometimes used to cure diarrhea in a form called *tulya mast*, a paste of acorn and yoghurt.

My line of questioning elicited the inevitable "How do you fix acorns in America?" from Taji. I explained as best I could remember how the Indians of California prepared the nuts, and we both agreed that it was essentially the same process. By this time we were both weary and headed for our beds. In the moment or two before sleep overtook me, I was vaguely conscious of the animals milling about in the corral next to my head. When rain began to fall, I simply reached around in the dark and pulled the plastic over my head.

When I awoke at dawn, at the first sounds of activity, I was surprised to see that both Mohammad Ali and Morad Khan had their tents up. Although I had slept through it, Sekandar had paid attention to what was going on. According to him, when rain began and no one in camp had stirred to put up the tents, Morad Khan had called out in a loud voice, "I don't care if the water washes me away, I'm going to sleep." At this, the other men got up and pitched Safarali's tent over Morad Khan. While they were up, they erected Mohammad Ali's tent to shelter the rest of the camp. The method used by Morad Khan was the simple one of shaming. By speaking loudly of his plight to no one directly, he had embarrassed the *homsa* into assuming their traditional, albeit reluctant, role of servants to the Baharvand.

Well before dawn, Ghamartaj had been up churning the milk. Often in the early hours of morning, I heard the gentle slosh, slosh of the churns as they were being worked over the embers of the campfire to keep the milk warm. When the nomads are migrating, they cannot do the milking in the early afternoon, so necessary chores such as making butter are often left until after the rest of the camp has gone to sleep (see Figure 6.10). In Morad Khan's tent, the two wives took turns with most of the chores, although Ghamartaj, the younger and stronger of the two, invariably carried water from the spring.

Well before 6 a.m., our herds were gone, and by 6:30 a.m., animals from other camps were streaming by, heading for the next pass. We were delayed because a man from another camp wanted Sekandar's stallion to service his mare. The gray stallion was tied in a grove of trees and restrained while the mare was brought up. When the act was consummated, to the obvious pleasure of Sekandar's horse, the mare was unceremoniously driven away and our own camp made ready to move.

During the loading, a woman from another passing camp brought a joint of beef to Morad Khan's tent. This presented something of a problem to Taji, who was not sure how she would pack it for the day's trip. Seeing her problem, I provided her with a large plastic bag from the supply I kept to protect our things and to collect pottery from archaeological sites. Taji was quite impressed and said she would get some bags the next time she was in town.

While we were loading, two men showed up to help with the chores. Somewhat surprised at this, Sekandar asked who they were. They said they farmed the land on which we were camped.

Sekandar asked, "Who is your leader?"

"Morad Khan," they shot back.

I was more than a little taken aback by this news, as our animals had helped themselves to their grain. In a turn of events that demonstrated the depth of tribal cohesion, the men who had every right to be aggrieved had turned up to pay their respects and to help with the work. As Morad Khan would say, "God provides."

Chapter 11

Settlers in Bala Griveh

We finally got going about 8:30 a.m. We traveled west along the trail until we reached the crossroads, where we turned north through some relatively low hills. After reaching a low, easy pass by nine o'clock, we continued further in a generally northeast direction through more hilly country. The streams flowed close to the surface between grassy banks, unlike those in deeply cut stream beds in the territory we had passed through before. This land was rich with good grass and soil cover.

Many trees were still in bud—the same situation we had found the past two nights—but wild pear and almond were in bloom as we crossed a second easy pass around 9:45 a.m. Sekandar pointed out wild cherry trees on our descent. I remarked that the trees were more severely cut than previously. Morad Khan agreed.

"There are lots of nomads in here during the summer," he said.

We had departed late that morning because we were not going to travel very far. By midmorning we began to see camps strung out at intervals for more than a mile along a small stream. Even high on the steep hillsides among the trees we could see camps. Clearly this was a major stopping place, but it was not until we had settled into our camp that I found the reason for the short trip. It was quite simple. We were going to pass through some valleys that were fully settled, where no campsites would be available. I interpreted this to mean that the nomads were not strong enough to take the land for the night. It also meant that our next march would be relatively long.

As late arrivers, I thought we would find ourselves in a very inopportune position for camping. I was even more convinced of this when we reached the spot Morad Khan had picked for us. Our camp was on a rocky hillside without any level land, among a grove of oaks spaced in clusters some fifty feet apart. After I examined the situation, however, it seemed more favorable than I had first imagined. For one thing, the spring was nearly at our feet. Women from other camps had to walk much farther with their heavy water bags. Second, as we had fewer animals, we did not require as much space as some of the camps. Finally, we were in position to be the first to leave the following day. It looked as if this camp might have been reserved for Morad Khan by mutual consent, although neither Sekandar nor I ever heard any discussion to that effect.

We were surrounded by Baharvand, a comfortable feeling for nomads who were crossing through alien territory. Everyone was very relaxed. Our trip was finished long before noon, the herds were milked at their usual time instead of late in the evening, and we were among friends. Mohammad Ali, who told us he had never before worked so hard on migration, lay down and slept peacefully for an hour or two at his campsite. He was exhausted. Even Morad Khan spent several hours reclining on a carpet, sometimes playing with his baby daughter.

Sekandar spent some time talking with Morad Khan about Baharvand history until the hot part of the day was over. Late in the afternoon we climbed to the top of the ridge overlooking our camp. We looked down on the Tayi Valley, through which we would travel the next day (Figure 11.1). The valley was relatively narrow but contained a good stream of water for irrigation. I was surprised to see fields outlined with neat, well-built walls of stones picked up from the fields. The entire valley was a picture of agricultural

Figure 11.1. The Tayi Valley is occupied by farmers whose fields are outlined with stones. Our group avoided the fields and walked in the streambed.

competence and compulsive neatness. In my experience it was quite out of character with the usually primitive farming methods used in Luristan. It was now obvious why we could not expect to find a campground in that valley.

Sekandar said that the people who live in Tayi were closely related to the Baharvand and on excellent terms with them. In fact, he said, there were friends there whom he would like to visit as we passed through. When he had visited relatives in Tayi as a young boy, he had seen some archaeological sites, and he knew I would be interested in them. It occurred to me then that the present settlers were probably using vestiges of the ancient terrace and irrigation system, a conjecture that proved correct when we took a closer look the next day.

On top of the ridge we walked around and enjoyed the scenery as the sun gradually set. The ground was churned up in a number of places, as if someone had been digging. Sekandar said that wild pigs had been digging for truffles. Although it looked as if a great many of them had been at work, we never saw one in all our travels. Of course, Muslims find pigs even more contemptible than dogs. Among most tribal Iranians, there is intense curiosity concerning the eating of pig by foreigners, a topic that Sekandar skillfully fended off on my behalf. Only foreigners and the much-despised outcast Lutis are said to eat pig. However, according to our informants, neither has been caught in the act by any Baharvand.

When we got back to camp we found a number of women visiting Morad Khan's wives. In keeping with custom, Taji and Ghamartaj had to give them money, tea, sugar, or some other gift. On another day, gifts would flow the other direction—back to Morad Khan's tent. Taji, in particular, was an inveterate visitor, and she was soon to leave us for several days while she made her own rounds, collecting gossip and gifts.

I saw a man from another camp approach Morad Khan's tent. With the deference of a *homsa* asking a favor, he invited Morad Khan to dinner. According to Sekandar, who was watching, our old leader refused. He told the man there was no one to do his work, that he had been invited too late, and that he would not want the man to kill an animal in his honor. The visitor left in obvious dejection. Sekandar interpreted for me. He said the man was hurt because he thought that Morad Khan believed it was beneath his dignity to eat with him. However, the man had satisfied his obligation by extending the invitation, and Morad Khan saved him an animal. Whether there was any residual social or psychological damage to either, I was unable to tell.

Sekandar's stallion had been tied to a tree above our camp most of the afternoon. Suddenly it got into a fight with another stallion, which had wandered over while grazing. Virtually the entire camp rushed over to try to prevent our horse from breaking loose and either horse from doing damage to the other. After the animals were separated and Sekandar's stallion had calmed down, the mare that had been bred in the morning was brought back for another try. The stallion was more than up to the task and consummated the relationship a second time. Then, for the first time in the day, he began to graze.

During the lazy afternoon, many of the fires had died out. When it was time to make tea, the women scurried around borrowing coals to start their own fires. This seemed to happen at every camp. As soon as someone got a fire started, the other women borrowed coals or burning brands to start their own. I don't recall ever seeing matches in the camp, but someone must have had them, as the old iron and flint strike-a-lights were no longer used.

Late in the afternoon, the cows were brought in for milking. For cows, which give more milk than sheep or goats, five-gallon tin cans are often used as milk buckets. What was done to each cow after it had given milk, however, interested me. To help wean the calves, the women scooped up hands full of wet, freshly laid manure, which they then smeared over the cow's teats, thus rendering them offensive to the calves. I must admit this practice was as offensive to me, and I watched next time to see whether they were cleaned before milking the next day. They were.

Just before preparations for dinner got underway, a woman came to see Morad Khan with a problem that she asked him to solve. As she told the story, she had married a man from another tribe who did not treat her well. After enduring his abuse for some time she left him, and he immediately took her property as well as the children from her previous marriage. Although she did not want the man, she did want her children and her property. Morad Khan advised her to see the gendarmes. He said this was a problem that can be handled through legal channels. In the past, he would have dealt with the problem personally, but no longer.

In many instances, however, Morad Khan still exercised his role as troubleshooter and traditional leader. In fact, much of the conversation among the men who visited our camp concerned disputes of one kind or another. In these cases, Morad Khan acted as a sounding board, sometimes giving advice and sometimes agreeing to talk with the party who had allegedly given offense. Since he was literate, Morad Khan often laboriously wrote letters, which appeared to be treated with great respect. As there were few in the tribe who could write, literacy conferred considerable prestige.

In the incident mentioned earlier, Morad Khan had lost a mule in Chin-i Zal, and he thought he knew who might have it. Rather than travel to see this particular man, he sent a letter via a convenient courier. The reply came back that the man did not have the mule. This did not entirely convince Morad Khan, however, and he said that when he returned to Chin-i Zal in the spring, he would go out looking for his mule himself.

As usual, the men gathered around the campfires in the evening. Sekandar had a tape recorder with him, on which he had recorded Luri music. That night he was asked again to play all the old favorites. He had heard, however, that one of the herd boys had an excellent voice, and Sekandar said he would not play the tapes unless the boy would sing (Figure 11.2). The boy was reluctant to sing in public, but finally was prevailed upon with the promise that he too would be recorded. The boy did have a fine voice and contributed several variations on Luri music that have become a part of Sekandar's collections of this rare art form. Although the songs were highly stereotyped, each person could vary their contents with sexual allusions, rough joking, and reference to recent events. Some of the songs were not considered fit for public entertainment; hence, part of the boy's reluctance to sing.

We did not turn in until nearly midnight. To judge from the fires in other camps, most of the Baharvand were up late. When we finally did decide it was time to sleep, there were so many overnight guests that there was not enough room in the tent sites for all of them. Morad Khan had to sleep with us, but he had given up most of his bedding to a guest of Taji's. The next morning he complained that he had nearly frozen and had not slept a wink. In fact, that was the coldest night on the migration. All through the night a stiff breeze swept our exposed hillside, chilling everyone, so that sleep was fitful at best.

Most everyone was awake early because of the cold, and we huddled around our fires drinking hot tea. We had no sooner gotten up when Safarali, anxious to leave with the cattle, snatched our bedding to load on the donkey. The cows, which he drove, always arrived last in camp, and with a long day's march ahead he wanted to have a good start. While we ate breakfast we watched thousands of sheep and goats, driven by young boys and sometimes girls, filing along the trail that led into Tayi. These animals were from the dozens of allied camps, all following the same trail. Driving animals was interesting to watch, because the Baharvand used unusual techniques. In other countries, dogs help herd the sheep and goats, but in Iran, to my knowledge, dogs are never used in this way. Among some tribes, dogs accompany the herders and act as guards against wolves, but it is not customary among the Lurs; rather, the dogs stay around the camp. People drive the animals with constant verbal encouragement, the throwing of stones, and the waving of arms. The technique consists of throwing a stone to the side of the animals

Figure 11.2. In the evening, Mohammad Ali, Panjali, and Ghasamali (left to right) socialize.

where the herder wishes to redirect their course. The herder does not try to hit the animals; rather, the sound of the stone hitting the rocks tends to make them veer away. If stones are thrown directly in front of the herd, they can turn or stop the animals. Ordinarily, if the animals are not far away, the stones are thrown by hand, but when the herds are scattered across a hillside or across a ravine, the herder may use a sling. I watched boys use this device to hurl rocks with great force and accuracy to the distance of a couple of hundred yards; they succeeded in turning the herd and avoided the great effort of rounding them up on foot.

The most common method used with all animals was to raise and wave an arm with a kind of feeble-looking gesture in the direction that the herder did not want the animal to go. Since this was almost invariably done while the shepherd was behind the herd and out of sight of most of the animals, it seemed futile, and the vigor with which it was done suggested to me that the shepherds were no more impressed with it. Above all it looked like a gesture made in resigned desperation. But it appeared to be moderately effective when accompanied with vocal calls.

Driving pack animals called for sterner measures, such as constant vocal encouragement, using a different command for each species, and prodding with a stick. Sometimes a man would beat an animal that had fallen or was lying down, or pick it up and shove it on its way. Although animals were not treated well, they did respond and plod along, as good pack animals are supposed to do. It was clear that most of them were bred for service rather than for spirit.

While I was watching the animals, I also chanced to see a more intimate domestic scene. As most people are aware, Muslims usually eat with their right hands because they perform sanitary functions with the left. The degree to which this practice affects how one eats is somewhat variable, but the principle is the same. The reason behind this is that toilet paper is never used and running water is seldom available. Nevertheless, after defecation, it is considered proper to wash with water. For this purpose, people employed the *aftabe*, a tall spouted pot with a handle on the side opposite the spout. Such a pot was kept filled at the entrance to the tent. Periodically people picked it up and departed for the nearest tree or rock. The problem with this method was that it left the person wet, and on a cold morning it could be quite annoying. On that cold morning, I observed Morad Khan returning with *aftabe* in hand—he straddled the fireplace while flapping the seat of his baggy pants a few times in the warm air.

Tayi

Sekandar and I left camp early so that we could examine some of the sites in Tayi before the other members of the camp passed through. As we descended the pass into the valley, we could see far below many camps of nomads who had left early in the morning and were crossing the shallow river. They traveled in single file beneath a high cone-shaped hill, on which the ruined foundation of a fort—built to guard this pass—could be seen. While I was filming the nomadic procession, a man walked up and started talking with Sekandar. Among other things, he told him that there was pottery in the fields near a village that we could see in the valley below, about a mile and a half away. This sounded archaeologically promising, so when I had finished taking pictures, we left the trail and headed toward the villages. The hamlet consisted of about a dozen mud-brick, flat-roofed houses, typical of rural settlements in Iran. Sekandar asked a man who was sitting in a gateway where the site was. The man, who was probably taken aback by the unexpected query, professed ignorance of any site. Taking matters into our own hands, we went to the closest field and immediately saw some bits of pottery. Archaeologists know that newly plowed fields are likely places to look, as pottery sherds may be turned up by the plow and will not be obscured by vegetation.

No sooner had we bent to pick up these sherds than the sower of the field came out to greet us. He acted surprised at our finding the pottery, but in the ensuing conversation, which was carried out by Sekandar while I searched the field, he suddenly warmed up and pointed out where the pottery came from and told us what he had found in the past. While he was talking, a small knot of children gathered at a respectful distance. Presently the man directed one of them to bring some things from his house for my inspection. I was a little surprised at this turn of events, but soon learned from Sekandar that the man had known his father. With those credentials established, there was no difficulty in getting the man to talk about the site. As he explained what he knew about the site—combined with what we knew of similar sites—it was clear that it had been occupied by ancient people who had terraced and irrigated the valley. But for reasons not yet explained, the village and valley had been abandoned. For more than a thousand years after that, nomads had grazed their stock in the valley. Finally, after the recent settlement of the pastoralists, the valley had once again felt the scar of the plow. The new farmers had simply renovated and extended the old system. Near where we stood, the farmer had left the remains of one of the characteristic vaulted stone houses neatly fenced off in a field that had not yet been leveled for irrigation.

While we were inspecting this ruin, a young man, dressed in light shirt and dark slacks, walked out from the hamlet into the field and greeted Sekandar warmly. The two spoke with animation for some minutes before Sekandar introduced him as an old friend. This man was teaching in a village school like Sekandar had been when we first met near Khorramabad eight years before. The teacher immediately invited us to his house and we quickly accepted his invitation to eat some of the local truffles.

I put a small collection of pottery sherds from the site into my saddlebags and then followed Sekandar and the teacher to his house. It was a typical village house, a low rectangular mud-walled building with a wall surrounding its yard. We dismounted in the yard, leaving our horses in charge of a schoolboy. As I followed the teacher and Sekandar into the house, my head made heavy contact with the wooden lintel of his doorway. Ruefully I remembered that I was taller than most Iranians. Like most village houses, his consisted of two rooms: the first was a "living room" for entertaining guests, with a carpet on the floor but little else, and the second was a room for more domestic activities.

We sat on the carpet around a charcoal brazier that he fanned to make coals for cooking lunch. It seemed only moments before another boy brought in the teapot. While I sipped several glasses of tea, Sekandar and the teacher kept up a torrent of conversation and the teacher prepared lunch. First he poured oil into a frying pan on the brazier. When it was hot, he dropped in onions and large slices of brown truffles, which popped at first and then simmered, releasing a mouthwatering aroma.

Truffles grew under the oaks in the mountains above the valley. Our host told us that the one we were about to eat had weighed in at nearly six kilos. This may have been an exaggeration, but the truffles were excellent. Our snack finished, we excused ourselves, because we wanted to go to the far end of the valley, where Sekandar had previously seen other sites. On leaving, I again cracked my skull on the lintel, much to the amusement of the schoolboys who had gathered in the courtyard to look at the American.

When we mounted our horses, the teacher advised us that if we wanted to camp with Morad Khan that evening, we would have to forego our planned trip. He suggested another route, which would take us more quickly back into the line of migration. Thanking him for his gracious hospitality and good food, we took the route he had suggested, which led toward another small valley called Kowgan. We rode through some small hills and over a pass, from which the trail descended into the Kowgan Valley. As usual, it was a long, steep slope, covered with loose gravel and rocks, and our descent was painful and slow. We dismounted and led our horses most of the way down the slippery switchbacks, before eventually coming out into another picturesque valley. The stone fences and irrigated fields were like those we had seen in Tayi.

As the migration grew close to Khorramabad, the proportion of people Sekandar knew increased. He said he had some very old family friends in the small village at the end of the valley, alongside which ran a rapidly flowing, clear stream. There was also a second reason for going there, which interested me much more than the promise of a good lunch with Sekandar's friends. Morad Khan had told us that there was a veritable palace cut entirely into the side of a steep cliff. In anticipation, and with some impatience, we urged our horses toward the town.

When we rode into the village, Sekandar asked for directions to the house of his friend. We dismounted in front of a two-story house, and a boy came to take our horses. Soon we were greeted effusively by a man of about seventy years, with a magnificent white beard, and his nearsighted wife, who insisted on kissing me too. The man, Pirmorad, was head of the Kabkani tribe and was an old friend of Sekandar's father and grandfather. Unlike most village houses, this one had two stories, also built of mud brick. We entered the courtyard and then went to his second-story guest room, where we were surprised to find two young men dressed in a strange conglomeration of hiking gear. They claimed to be students from Isfahan Tech out for a weekend of mountain climbing and cave exploration. The two were fitted out with packs, sleeping bags, hiking knickers, boots, and yellow hard hats. They had arrived the night before, sought out the leader's house, and then proceeded to enjoy dinner and spend the night in the guest room. Having only recently finished breakfast when we came in, they began to put on their socks and shoes. They said their "camping trip" had consisted of a short hike to the cave we wanted to visit; otherwise they had not ventured outside the kindly headman's house. Soon they left, planning to catch the Jeep—part taxi, part supply van, which carried people and goods into and out of the valley once a day—for a ride back into town.

In their stead, we settled down onto the carpet and drank the usual three cups of tea, while the women of the ménage fixed lunch in the room below. Soon we were served a large tray of fried chicken, bread, *dugh*, and hot sugared milk, a meal we thoroughly enjoyed. While we ate, we plied the headman with questions about the site.

After lunch, trailing behind a dozen young men and boys, we hiked a short distance above the village to a knife-edged ridge that ended abruptly at the cleft through which the river ran. This ridge, we were told, was the site.

Stone walls—some of them obviously remains of houses and others that may have been defensive barriers—stood along the entire top of the ridge. The people were eager to show us one of the least evident but most impressive features—a hole in the ground that led down the side of the hill and terminated in a well. According to their description, it was a tunnel through which people could walk to secure water without being seen.

I looked into the inauspicious hole. Its upper end terminated just below the ruins on top of the ridge. I imagined that it had once led to a more substantial opening inside the fortress. Deciding it would be worth a look inside the tunnel, we sent for some lanterns and then slid inside on our bellies, our backs touching the ceiling and our heads sloping downward at an uncomfortable angle. As we wriggled farther, the tunnel got higher. Before long we were able to stand, albeit somewhat bent over. As my eyes grew accustomed to the light of the lantern, I realized that it was a real tunnel cut into bedrock. Its vaulted ceiling and some of the interior had been solidly plastered with the characteristic rock-hard cement that is found in the ancient stone buildings throughout Luristan. This, I thought, made the trip worthwhile, even if the site did not contain the fantastic rock-carved rooms that had also been described. Quickly we walked to the terminus of the tunnel, where we found a circular well about three feet in diameter. It was cut straight down to the water level, which was nearly one hundred feet below, judging from the sound of dropped pebbles.

Awed at the amount of labor implied by the well, we crawled back out of the tunnel and once again climbed to the top of the ridge. The view commanded the entire Kowgan Valley and the narrow valley to the north of the gorge, where the river made a sharp turn to the east. As we peered over the north edge, we looked down a nearly vertical sheet of rock some one hundred feet to the river below. The ridge was a limestone anticline, whose layers stood almost vertically. From a distance, we could see rock-cut rooms in the sheer face of the cliff above us.

We scrambled down a slope some three hundred feet or so from the cliff and hastily walked along it until we could see several large window-like rectangular openings cut into the rock face. While everyone watched intently, one of the boys from the village began to inch his way across the vertical rock face toward the lowest opening, feeling with each step for a toehold while pressing his body flat against the rock. We all watched with some apprehension as he reached for the opening and pulled himself in. Several more young men followed, and finally Sekandar and I also inched our way across and in.

Inside, once my eyes had become accustomed to the dim light, it looked as if the rooms had been intended as tombs. They look like the Sasanian age tombs (ca. AD 224–641) that tourists see at Naqsh-i-Rustam near Persepolis, where there is also a frieze showing Shapur I humiliating the Roman general Valerian. Here too, the rooms contained bin-shaped chambers that had been cut into the rock. There were traces of covering slabs, but no remains of any actual burials. The site was not particularly spectacular, except for the effort that had gone into creating it. The tombs had been cut into the rock at great cost, but there were none of the elaborate carvings on the walls that distinguished the better-known Sasanian tombs.

As we investigated further, we found the rooms to be joined by a corridor along a kind of lower story. Each room had its own burial chamber cut into the rock floor. Although there was a corridor, movement inside was not easy, for each of the rooms was at a different level. Evidently they were built independently of one another and only joined by the corridor at some later time. The village boys, who were used to scaling slippery heights after livestock, were amused at my conservative methods of scrambling and jumping from one level to another. But as I told Sekandar, "Better to be laughed at than break an ankle or arm."

In one large room we found traces of cement plaster that had once coated the interior to form the vault of the ceilings. But most curious was a Persian-style latrine on the lower story, which had been cut into the rock floor adjacent to the sheer rock face. It allowed a person to face inside, some forty-five feet above the ground below, while poking his posterior out over the edge. The rough finishing of the latrine and its exterior opening suggested that it too was a later addition.

When we were told that the second story was even more interesting, we elected to try to reach it. I recommend that future travelers take ladders, but we had come a long way and I was determined to try to reach the upper rooms. With the use of ropes and with a great deal of pushing, shoving, and pulling, we all managed to gain the top of a smooth rock face some twelve feet high, which led to the upper rooms. I shrugged off my bleeding hands when I saw that the rooms were in a much better state of preservation than those below, and they clearly showed the sequence of construction. The initial cutting had carved out rectangular rooms, probably separate tombs, which were then—most likely several hundred years later—coated with plaster and installed with vaulted ceilings. The main room was outfitted with a sunken pool and water reservoir and a "picture window" overlooking the stream and valley to the north. It was a veritable villa set deep inside a mountain fortress. In addition to the reception room, there were several side rooms. These were also plastered in the shape of long vaults, and there was another lavatory in the same design as the one below. Now the drop was probably close to sixty feet.

Whoever lived there had resided in style and security. This was the only ruin we found where such obvious defensive measures had been taken, and that fact suggested something special about the site. The valley was too small to support a large population, but it did lie, we were told, on an important migration route. A small group living in isolation on a major route of tribal migration may have felt the need for security. But there might be another reason for such an unusual site: simply that there were already rock-cut tombs that could be enlarged and converted into quite elegant living quarters for a person wealthy enough to command enough labor. That suggested a leader of at least regional importance had built the structure.

Little is known of local history, but one reference in Sasanian records is to Kozad Ravand, a contemporary of Hormuz I, who ruled for only one year (AD 270–271), but during that year founded the city of Ahwaz in Khuzistan. Legend says that Hormuz sent Kozad gifts to prevent him from closing the travel route. The description fits, but the site must be investigated thoroughly before we know for certain. It is also possible that the site was used by an unknown ruler or tribal chief who was accustomed to traveling seasonally through his realm, like the Achaemenian kings who had capitals at Susa, Hamadan, and Persepolis.

According to Sekandar, there is a local myth suggesting that Kahzad, a provincial leader during the Parthian dynasty (247 BC–AD 224) may have built the site. To me it seems unlikely that the local populations had remained stable long enough for such an oral tradition to have persisted.

In Luri the cave is called *askafte Kowgo* (Kowg Cave), and in Farsi it is called *Ghare Kabkan* (Kabkan Cave). In Luri, *kowg* means patridge. There is a spring and gathering ground where partridges "sing," so it is known as Partridge Cave.

Naturally, the site had been known and used by local nomads for as long as they had been in the area, but it had never been accurately mapped and described by archaeologists. Although it certainly merited such attention, I could not undertake the task without proper mapping instruments and ladders. Our venerable host at lunch told us that Sekandar's grandfather had lived there for some years when he was hiding from the law. That was during one of the clashes between nomads and the government at the time when nomads were first ordered to settle down. Today the site is regarded as only a curiosity, although there is evidence of recent digging in the structures on top of the ridge, presumably by persons looking for antiquities. As I heard later, I apparently missed one feature—a tunnel from the top of the ridge down to the village, built just like the water tunnel. Like the other ancient abandoned sites we passed—some of which were large towns, if not cities—the ridge-top retreat must remain a mystery for the time being.

Reluctantly we left the site, scrambling back down the way we had come in. Prudence again outweighed bravado. I let the local boys show off and shamed myself in their eyes by using ropes rather than leaping off into space. They were quite unprepared, in consequence, when I stepped out of the lower entrance and moved without hesitation across the narrow series of toeholds to the security of terra firma. The looks on their faces as I negotiated this stretch without faltering was worth the rope burns I had incurred earlier.

As we started down the very steep and loose talus, gingerly feeling our way to the river and our horses, I was nearly bowled over by obstreperous youths, who took one last chance to show off by catapulting themselves down the slope without regard for either their lives or ours. In spite of being bombarded by rolling rocks, we reached the bottom safely. Then we remounted, taking one last look at the towering sheer cliff with its strange openings. We headed east along the narrow cultivated valley whose southern edge was delimited by the anticline that we had just explored.

Evidence of modern agriculture and of ancient terraces continued as far ahead as we could see along the gently meandering, rippling brook, which was lined with willows. On a sunny and cloudless day, I could hardly have wished for a more pleasant countryside to ride through. Several times we passed ruins of old water-powered mills. One of them had recently been converted

Figure 11.3. An old grist mill, recently converted into a small hut. Water from a small canal dropped down the tower and powered a wooden wheel that turned the grist stone. Taking advantage of the disused mill, a herder built a small house.

into a house with the addition of a roof of branches and leaves, although it was unoccupied (Figure 11.3). Our goal was a place called Sedaron (Three Rivers), where Morad Khan was camped. A ride of an hour or so brought us to the confluence of two small rivers, and another sharp turn to the north through a narrow gorge revealed our camp, which was set among small oaks on the flanks of a hill just above the narrow river.

Sedaron

The entire area above the line of cultivation was occupied by Baharvand tents. We were to stay at that traditional camping ground for several days,

Figure 11.4. The Sedaron Valley. A small canal in the center carried water to the grist mill.

chiefly so Morad Khan could take care of political business, but also to enjoy the beautiful scenery and abundant pasture (Figure 11.4). The area was permanently occupied by a group of Mirs, another of the Luri-speaking tribes whose political interests had not always been in accord with those of the Baharvand. Basically friendly, but often at odds, they coexisted in the uncertain truce that characterized all tribal relations in that part of Iran. Across the river and high on the opposite sloping hill, the Mir leaders lived in mud-brick houses that they had recently built as their permanent settlement (Figure 11.5). It was with those leaders that Morad Khan had to discuss problems of mutual interest. It was not without significance that the Baharvand camps of Morad Khan entirely surrounded the Mirs' houses.

Figure 11.5. Across from Morad Khan's camp in Sedaron were the mud-brick houses of the Mirs.

Traditionally, the Mir leaders visited Morad Khan's tent the day he arrived, to invite him to dinner. By custom he reciprocated the following evening. However, as the afternoon wore on, Morad Khan mentioned to Sekandar that the Mirs had not made their customary appearance. He began to wonder at the significance of this oversight. He was clearly concerned and seemed to sense that something bad had happened. He speculated that someone had spread lies about what he had said about the Mirs, and he went to bed that night still wondering but not feeling that he ought to break the ice by visiting the Mirs first.

During the afternoon, while this apparent snub was still developing, the Dirkavand leaders with whom we had had lunch came by to greet Morad Khan. They rode up to the edge of the spring, where Safarali took their horses. As the men exchanged greetings with other members of the camp, Morad Khan had carpets spread on the ground about halfway between his tent and ours. Morad Khan sat cross-legged at one end of the carpet, his back to the stream, wearing his usual black baggy pants, brown suit jacket, and brown fedora. The gray-bearded Dirkavand and three younger men sat along the two sides of the carpet. The older Dirkavand man began a long series of plaudits to Morad Khan for his aid with their causes in the past. Our leader sat impassively through this formality, waiting to learn the latest problems. Eventually, when they got around to the point of their visit, Morad Khan joined in the conversation, speaking softly and gesturing with his hands. After a while, he called out to Sekandar for a piece of paper and pen. Sekandar took a page from his notebook and handed it to Morad Khan, and then he retreated to our tent. We continued to watch, although we were unable to hear the nature of the business. Laboriously Morad Khan wrote out a letter, carefully folded it, and handed it to the elder Dirkavand. Evidently satisfied, the four men rose, followed by Morad Khan. They returned to their horses and rode off the way they had come. Whatever the business had been, Morad Khan did not share it with us or the other members of the camp.

We were camped close to the snow line, where it was expected to be cold at night. Recognizing this, the men talked of setting up the tents, but before they could act upon this idea, some men from another Baharvand camp came by to help. Soon three of our tents were erected, and Morad Khan could entertain in fair weather or foul (Figure 11.6). We could see similar activity across the valley at other camps. Those who had sent their tents by truck would have to face the cold behind reed screens.

As the camp took on a more permanent appearance, everyone seemed relaxed, enjoying the freedom from travel and the new scenery (Figure 11.7). For the first time since I had been with the group, I was able to film some of their domestic activities. Previously, in Chin-i Zal, I had not yet become familiar enough with the women, or they with me, to feel comfortable about taking close-up pictures of their work. On migration most of the daily chores were done at dawn or at night, when filming was impossible. Now, in Sedaron, the conditions were favorable, and I spent several hours filming

Figure 11.6. Morad Khan's camp. His black goat-hair tent and our white canvas tent are side by side.

Figure 11.7. Relaxing in the Sedaron camp, Sekandar talks with a friend, while the woman on the left chops sugar and the woman on the right heats milk for yoghurt. A pan with bread dough, covered with a tray, is on the left.

women churning milk and making bread. As the camp was settled, a woman churned butter in daylight in front of her tent, under flapping laundry (Figure 11.8). Although the women were somewhat amused by my interest in these mundane matters, they took my filming in good cheer and even showed off. When Mohammad Ali's wife tore the sheet of bread she was making, she insisted that I film a good sheet too. While I was taking a movie of another woman churning, other women made a point of coming into camera view with their babies to talk with the churner. Even Safarali found it necessary to enter the picture. He came over, said a few words to one of the women, picked up a twig and went back to his own tent to sit contentedly with his water pipe.

The herders had their flocks up on the hills around us, but Safarali had put the cattle and donkeys to pasture just across the stream, where he could watch them without leaving his tent. Mohammad Ali was also able to relax, since he had no animals to watch. With time on his hands, he gathered up some straight sticks, which he made into tent stakes with an adze. One of the boys had a cup of tea before he returned to his flocks. Sekandar relaxed on carpets spread at one of the open campsites. The daily task of heating milk to make yoghurt continued unabated. Left alone, sitting on the ground, Iraj watched. Everyone except Morad Khan, who was worried about the Mirs, was at ease.

The night was so cold that even in our tent we felt it. The animals were restless too; a goat took shelter in our tent, trampling Sekandar and me, until we shooed it out. We then tied the door more securely and crawled back under chilled blankets to wait for dawn, but long before daylight we felt the tent shaking and woke to find a mule rubbing against the guy ropes. We debated whether the animal would knock down the tent, and whether we should go out and refasten the ropes. We chose to stay warm and did not emerge from the tent until the sun was up. Then we found out why the mule had been tugging at the ropes so persistently. He had chewed up a towel that Sekandar had hung on a guy rope to dry.

Although the herders left camp around dawn, as usual, the rest of the people sat around drinking tea and having a leisurely breakfast. Morad Khan and Sekandar got into a lengthy discussion about the history of the Baharvand tribe, while I wrote notes and reloaded my cameras. Finally, when the sun had risen high enough to take the chill out of the valley, we decided to explore the area.

Figure 11.8. Ghamartaj churns butter under flapping laundry in front of Morad Khan's tent.

Figure 11.9. Small streams, lying just a few hundred feet below the snow line, flow from meltwater.

We had heard that there was a grove of walnut trees a mile and a half or so upstream, so we saddled our horses and rode off in that direction, following a narrow trail that crossed and re-crossed the stream several times (Figure 11.9). It was easy to see why this was a favored camping ground. At intervals, clear, cold springs entered the stream, and bright orange fritillaria (*Fritillaria persica*) were growing in patches beneath the trees (Figure 11.10) On the ridges above there were still fields of snow, whose melting waters soaked the land below and gave rise to luxuriant spring growth. Among the trees and flowers, children (some of them scarcely taller than the blooming plants) tended herds of sheep and goats.

As we rode along, we asked some herders where to find the walnuts. Eventually we saw them growing in a dense stand on steep slopes where the

Figure 11.10. Bursting out of the snow-free ground, fritillaria provided splashes of color.

valley narrowed as it reached higher toward the snow. The trees, which had not yet budded out, were thought to have been planted by ancient peoples. This idea was supported by evidence of old irrigation canals, which were still used to feed fields farther downstream, where there was sufficient land to farm. In the grove with the walnuts were apple and cherry trees, which bore good fruit in the fall, just when the tribes returned through this area on their way back to Chin-i Zal.

About midmorning, as the trail was nearing its terminus only a hundred feet below the snow line, we stopped at a tent camp where Sekandar thought he knew a man. We dismounted and approached a woman who was working in her tent. Sekandar greeted her and asked for his friend. The woman replied that he was away. Since Sekandar and the woman were not acquainted, the conversation was a bit awkward until he convinced her that he was a Baharvand. Once he began to recite his kinship to people she knew, she warmed up and graciously invited us into her tent, where she spread a carpet and insisted on preparing us some food.

While she was doing this, other members of her camp dropped in and picked up the conversation. They told us that the camp was on a spot owned by a man who was reputed to be the oldest member of the Dirkavand tribe. In fact, they said, he was the oldest man anyone had ever heard of. Probably 120 years old, they insisted. The old man and his family were due any day, so the current occupants planned to leave the next morning for their own summer campsite. The men told us that during wet years, snow would still be on the ground, even down in Sedaron, where we were camped. Snow often lasted there until two months after Nowruz (March 21), or about the end of May, they said.

In a few minutes the woman served us some delicious fresh bread and butter, which we ate with gusto. She apologized, saying that at first she thought we were government officials because of our dress. This was understandable and completely justified her initial reticence. Also, as we well knew, it was not customary for women to offer hospitality to strangers if the men of the camp were not around.

Takasu

After we had thanked the woman for the snack, we continued up the trail as far as we could walk our horses through the dense vegetation. After tying them to a tree, we climbed on foot up to the snow and fields of fritillaria that were springing out of the soggy ground. Looking back toward our camp, which was not visible because of the trees, we could see that we had climbed several hundred feet. Beautiful though it was, it was not prime agricultural land. However, the irrigation canals that ran down from the source of the stream indicated that the land was once intensively cultivated wherever small terraces could be built.

When we returned down the trail, we stopped at the junction of the two streams, where there were some huge trees growing with their roots in the water. The place, called Takasu (where the *su* tree grows), was an ancient site on top of the hill adjacent to the trees. As usual, we saw ruined stone foundations, as well as the typical parallel lines of stone-edged terraces on the opposite hill. It was to those fields that the irrigation canals, which we had seen from far above, led. While we were taking a drink from the stream, a man suddenly appeared from a camp that had sprung up on the hill while we were exploring the trail above. He invited us to tea.

The man was a Dirkavand, whose tribe owned the land. The people had just arrived for the summer and planned to farm some of the old terraces that were irrigated by the canals. Since their tents were not yet set up, they spread several carpets for us to sit on while tea was prepared. We talked a bit about the area and then took a tour of the ancient site, where I picked up sherds while Sekandar discussed intertribal relations. One of the men told us that the old man who had been described by the people higher up the trail was named Atawak. His tent was about a mile and a half below our camp. It seemed worthwhile to pay him a visit, so we excused ourselves and headed back.

Along the way I noticed a large leafy plant with succulent stems, which Sekandar said was *shir shira*. Its white juice, mixed with milk, was a cure for diarrhea.

Chapter 12

Atawak's Memories: How it Was

We were both anxious to talk with Atawak, particularly about tribal nomadism as it had been before the government imposed changes on the nomads' lives and practices, which occurred during his lifetime. Our only concern was whether he would be able to recall his youth with accuracy. The day before, when we had been riding to camp from Kowgan, we had passed a very old man on the trail who was walking with obvious difficulty. He said he was too old to ride and his camp had moved on without him, leaving him to catch up as best he could. Normally, he said, he could do it well before dark. Although the man was not very lucid, he assured us that there was another man, Atawak, who was far older than he. It was with some misgivings, then, that we rode over to Atawak's camp.

As we approached the camp in late afternoon, a man with a long white beard, wearing a white turban, rode up to a tent site and dismounted. It was

Atawak, who had just been out for a ride. Seeing him apparently in good health heartened us, and we hastened to his tent. The old man had seated himself on a carpet near an equally aged woman within a screened area. Remaining seated, they greeted us warmly and invited us to sit with them. Sekandar took a seat next to Atawak, his back to the reed screen. The campfire in front was tended by a woman who was heating milk to make yoghurt. Judging from the number of younger men around, it was apparent that Atawak was not suffering from a manpower shortage. His wife had evidently borne him enough sons so that he would pass his last years in comfort.

The contrast between Atawak's camp and ours was obvious from the time we arrived. He had five men waiting to take our horses and to look after any errands or chores. According to those who spoke up, Atawak was anywhere from 100 to 125 years old, but his riding of the horse belied this estimate. It was important to establish his true age, however, so after reciting his genealogical credentials, Sekandar tried to figure out how old the man really was. His technique, used on many occasions with other elderly informants, was to ask the man whether he remembered certain significant events in Luri history, some of which can be dated in our calendar. Since the Lurs do not use a calendar, it is rare for any of the tribal people to have accurate knowledge of their age. Time is measured by events. Great famines, heavy snows, the Second World War, when the road to Khorramabad was built, notable battles between tribes, and similar events are widely known and used as points of departure for estimating age. By this means, Sekandar calculated that Atawak was about 85 years old. He had grown up before oil was discovered and Western commercial interests began to impinge on tribal territory and fortunes. Sekandar could not have successfully elicited information from Atawak if he had not been steeped in Luri history from his parents and grandparents. Because of this background and his education, he knew what questions to ask and what calendar dates to assign to the events.

Atawak's wife was a cackling, weather-beaten woman who entered into the conversation with nods, gestures, and giggles. She rocked back and forth, puffing on her water pipe, while the tea was simmering. More men continued to arrive, each greeting Sekandar as they introduced themselves. They all knew who Sekandar was, even though he had met few of them before. They had grown up hearing of his father's and Morad Khan's exploits when the tribe did more fighting than farming.

With the formalities out of the way, Sekandar began to ask Atawak about days past. As a boy, Atawak had never been south of Dezful or north of Khorramabad, the two cities at the extremes of Baharvand migration routes. When he was a boy, people seldom visited town and, for that matter, the old man added, he saw no reason to go to town now, or for the remainder of his life. He gave the distinct impression that town was for city folks and the mountains were for the nomads, and that no particular good had ever come from juxtaposing the people and places.

When Atawak was young, the only things nomads purchased in town were cloth and metal. In fact, he said, most people did not wear clothing made of machine-woven cloth. Instead, garments were woven by the women out of the same heavy fabric that we saw used for animal blankets, or people simply covered themselves with carpets. Such machine-made cloth as they did purchase had to be sewed into clothes in camp, since there were no tailors in town; only bolts of black cloth were sold. The documentary film *Grass*, which was filmed when Atawak was a young man, shows this clothing very well. Atawak specifically said, in response to my question, that his people had never used animal skins for clothing.

He also asserted, with considerable emphasis, that when he was young, people seldom wore shoes of any kind. He said a family of seven might share a single pair of *givas*, a crocheted slipper with a cloth or leather sole. As the shops in town did not make or stock many shoes, it was customary to place an order and come back six months later to pick them up, when the tribe returned to the area. The lack of shoes seemed remarkable to me, because the terrain over which we traveled was extremely rough. It had shredded the pair of shoes Sekandar bought in Khorramabad only a month before. Perhaps in the absence of good, cheap shoes, bare, heavily calloused feet were better. It seemed so when I excavated the site in Khorramabad, where I had met Sekandar. There, the workers went barefoot, seemingly oblivious to sharp rocks and thorns. The film *Grass* showed remarkable scenes of the nomads plodding barefoot through deep snow. Often I had heard the nomads remark that shoes should be lightweight, and I had seen their astonishment when they hefted my low-cut boots. They were not particularly heavy by hiking standards, but the nomads said they could never walk in them. In truth, the rough terrain of Luristan is better negotiated with firm, supple, lightweight shoes, or barefoot.

Although Atawak was quite positive in his remarks about clothing and shoes, his testimony was only partly supported by other informants or by accounts written by travelers in Luristan in the late nineteenth century. It was not clear whether Atawak had come from an unusually poor family or that he had exaggerated his story for our benefit. On other matters, however, his recollections were, so far as we were able to tell, quite accurate.

I asked about diet. Atawak said in the past it was much less varied. The nomads had no tea, and sugar was used only once a year to make halva for the Feast of the Dead before Nowruz, the spring equinox—a major holiday in Iran. Apart from that, sugar was not used at all. For beverages, they had only water and milk products. In the 1970s, life in rural Iran, whether among nomads or villagers, was scarcely conceivable without liberal use of tea and sugar, which supplied much of the energy they needed and refreshed them even on the hottest of days. Of course, both had to be purchased at markets, with cash earned from selling sheep and wool.

On the other hand, the pastoralists formerly ate much more meat, for they seldom sold their animals. Their practice was to kill the males and keep the females for breeding. When we were there, the price of meat was so high that the nomads could not afford to eat it. Also, in times past there were lots of wild animals. Atawak remembered shooting seven wild sheep one day for a feast, and he said if there were still any around he would have done the same for us. His story was confirmed by the diary of a Bakhtiari leader, Husain Quli Khan, from the late 1870s. He reported that his hunting parties killed game at will: "Thanks to God, the time passed very happily. At Asmari we killed 200 head of game" (Garthwaite [1983] 2009:149). Unfortunately, no one remembered having seen any wild sheep or goats in Luristan for the past several years.

Atawak made the point that it had "not been the custom" of the nomads to farm. He implied that farming was not natural for nomads. Instead, they made their bread from acorns. In his youth, the little farming they did was chiefly of barley, which was used for animal fodder. As noted earlier, travelers in the nineteenth and early twentieth centuries reported the same thing: some tribes subsisted on acorns.

Atawak also recalled that the forests were once much denser. In fact, he said, it was difficult to walk because there were so many trees. But as people settled, there was a great deal of cutting and burning to make charcoal and to open land for agriculture. I tried to find out how long people had been settled in the area, but received only evasive answers from the assembly of men. As land ownership was disputed, this was a sensitive issue (see the discussion of the history of land ownership in Chapter 17). I got the impression that irrigation was resumed about fifteen years previously. That seemed to be a fairly consistent story, because most of the areas we passed through had been settled for two decades at most, and the agricultural land was still being expanded. The mills along the trail, turned by force of water, were clearly more than fifteen years old, but I was unable to find out from the men just when they had been built. They were not much used because people preferred to take the grain to town, where it could be ground by machine. I doubted that the area where we camped saw permanent settlement from the time the ancient sites were abandoned until around 1950. If the forests were as thick as reported, the amount of grazing land would have been much less and the territory would have been more suitable for hunting and collecting acorns than for grazing.

I was quite interested in the extent to which the people had depended on markets for some of the products they required, and I asked Atawak about metal. He said the only metal they used was in copper or brass *aftabes*, large pots for making yoghurt and for cooking, and iron bread pans. All metal objects were made in the cities, but as they were durable it was not necessary to go to town even annually to obtain them. After the introduction of sugar, wooden bowls, made by Lutis, on which the sugar loaves are chopped, were ubiquitous. It had been apparent to me for some time that there was no smoking of cigarettes among these people, in sharp contrast to most of Iran, where men smoke either factory-made or hand-rolled cigarettes. As far as I could tell, none of the Baharvand ever smoked cigarettes. Atawak said that for as long as he could remember, they had had water pipes, and that was still the only smoking device his people used. It was the same in our camp, which had one water pipe.

Asked about general conditions in the past, Atawak expressed a view we had heard many times before: there were many fewer people in the old days, and the herds were larger. He also volunteered that there used to be more rain and snow.

"Each year it decreases," he asserted.

In effect, he was saying that it was drier in the 1970s. Possibly this was a consequence of more intensive grazing and cutting of the forests; it might also have been the result of a warming climate.

When I asked whether his people had ever tried to domesticate wild sheep or goats, he replied that they did capture wild sheep and raise them with their flocks, but they did not reproduce well in captivity. From what he said it seems that they kept the females with their herds and ate the males. In combination with the killing of domestic stock, this gave them enough meat to eat on a daily basis.

Atawak had no plans to settle into a village. He said he preferred the nomadic life because it was his habit. Others in his camp expressed the same view, showing no inclination to settle down; they preferred, as they put it, "to roam." The difference between Atawak's camp and ours was the availability of manpower, a factor that made nomadic life more attractive.

With a note of sadness in his voice, Atawak spoke harshly of modern times. According to him, people were much less cooperative than formerly because there were more goods available, and in order to accumulate the capital to buy the goods, people had to be greedy. Before, he said, people were happy just to have enough meat and an occasional dinner with rice. Apart from the general increase in goods, which had made migration harder, Atawak was convinced that nomadic life was much like it always had been. The animals were handled in the same way and the people followed the same migration routes. It was only the gradual drawing of the people into a market economy that had changed.

Atawak confirmed what we had learned from other old men in camps across Luristan. Pastoralists traditionally had little contact with towns and little need for agricultural products. Their economy was, in fact, considerably more self-sufficient than among nomads generally. One index to the extent of their contact with markets and outsiders was the time tea was introduced. Most of the tribes of Luristan began to use tea within the memory of the oldest living persons, and it did not become common until perhaps fifty years ago. Other indices are the use of cigarettes and, still more recently, of plastic. On both counts, the Baharvand pastoralists lag considerably behind those whose routes of migration take them closer to established towns and villages. But remoteness has its advantages, too. The Baharvand and Dirkavand live in a territory that has far richer wild resources than most, permitting a more self-sufficient nonagricultural diet and consequently less dependence on village agriculture. Because of their greater isolation than most tribes, these people probably more nearly represent a situation that obtained over much of

Luristan and Kurdistan for a thousand years or more, up to very recent times. After talking with Atawak, as we were about to leave, we were surprised to see Taji sitting in one of the tents talking with some women. It was then I learned that her brother was a member of Atawak's camp. She had come over to visit. It was no wonder we had been warmly received. Moreover, her visit would allow her to provide Morad Khan with a complete and accurate report of everything we had discussed.

Back in our camp, Ghamartaj immediately served us tea on the carpet where Morad Khan had held counsel with the Dirkavand men the day before. While we were drinking, we caught sight of several men approaching the river. As they crossed on a rough pole bridge, Sekandar told me that two of them were the Mir leaders who had been expected the night before. Since Morad Khan was away on a visit of his own, the men joined us for tea and invited us to dinner that evening. We accepted, wondering what Morad Khan's reaction would be.

While we talked, one of the men mentioned that there was a kind of dirt nearby that burned. He said it was black and flamed up when put into a fire. That sounded interesting, so we took a hike with him to obtain some of the material. The source was only about a quarter of a mile upstream from our camp and consisted of an outcrop of rock at the edge of the trail. It looked like an old seep of oil into a bed of limestone, probably an oil shale. Inasmuch as there was a great deal of oil in western Iran, this was not surprising, but I was curious to see whether there was an actual seep. The Mirs, on their part, wanted to find out whether or not it had commercial possibilities, but I had to tell them that I did not know. That evening we burned some of the rock in a fire, but it proved to have little flammable material in it, igniting only when placed on glowing coals. After the Mirs left, Morad Khan came back and was surprised to hear about the burning rock. He too was eager to see it burn, so we repeated the experiment. He was unimpressed. He was, however, interested to find out that the Mirs had extended a dinner invitation to Sekandar and me.

Around seven, as the sun was setting, the Mirs appeared again to take us to dinner. Seeing Morad Khan present, they quickly invited him as well. The invitation was just as quickly accepted and we all set out on foot across the river, toward the Mirs' house, past a number of Baharvand camps. On the way Morad Khan made a point of stopping at each camp and inviting some of the men to accompany him at dinner. Included in the group was Morad Khan's son-in-law, who was elegantly dressed in a flowered Luri coat with a bandolier of cartridges strapped over his torso, his shotgun in hand.

Sekandar and I both thought it a little strange that Morad Khan should invite all his friends to dinner, but we said nothing. It was apparently his custom to do this, and certainly the Mirs did not seem the least perturbed by either the extra guests or the armed man.

When we got to the houses we found that they had been carefully made of mud brick with stone bases. There were only two houses with outbuildings belonging to each of the two Mir brothers. It was not a typical village. The houses were set apart from one another and each had ample flat land around. The settlement seemed more like a nomad campsite than a farming village, which, of course, it had been, until recently.

Outside in the courtyard, women were stoking fires and making preparations for dinner. On the front porch were a number of large trays, water jugs, and samovars. We were ushered inside to take our places Luri-style on the carpet around the walls. Like a typical village house, the single room was perhaps fifteen feet across and twenty-five feet long. As it turned out, Morad Khan's men comprised only half the group. Morad Khan was seated opposite the entrance, while we were placed some ten feet down the back wall from him. The rest of the men, according to rank, filled in the remaining spaces until nearly the entire circumference of the room was occupied. As a gesture of respect, Morad Khan was given some free space on either side, and so were we; otherwise the men were sitting closely packed, side by side.

Customarily there would have been one guest of honor, Morad Khan, but tonight we were accorded the same respect. Sekandar wondered how this would be handled, since the guest of honor is supposed to be served first by the host, and one can't serve two people simultaneously.

The elder Mir inquired whether everyone was comfortable. Several men complained of a cold wind that was blowing in the door, so it was closed, and a fire was laid in the center of the room in a small iron brazier. The elder Mir then kneeled with his back to the door, facing Morad Khan, who, like most of the men, was sitting cross-legged. The Mir launched into a very long speech in which he told Morad Khan that he had not invited him to dinner the night before because he had been away arranging the loan of some money. He needed to do this, he said, so that he could hire a tractor to plow some of his land. The explanation, delivered in typical Luri fashion, with flowery references to the fame and benevolence of the guest and to the Mirs' undying friendship to the Baharvand, took about half an hour. Morad Khan responded in kind and kept the exchange going for nearly two hours. The rest of us just sat and listened, moving only enough to maintain the circulation in our legs.

Finally it was time for dinner. First came tea. We had surmised that this might be a crisis, since there was a shortage of serving utensils in most nomad camps, and both we and Morad Khan had to be served in the first round. The problem was solved when two servants entered, each bearing a pot of tea and glasses on little silver platters. One went to Morad Khan and the other to us. When we had finished the customary three glasses of tea, the glasses were washed and filled for the next person. In this way, eventually all the men were served.

Then it was time to wash hands. Two servants entered the room, each bearing an *aftabe* so that both sets of guests could wash their hands. We did this using elegant silver-plated *aftabes*, pitchers with matching covered bowls into which the water is drained. This done, the *aftabe* was presented to each of the other men. In the meantime, Morad Khan, who had washed his feet as well as his hands, commenced his evening prayers. Islamic worship (*namaz*) consists of standing, facing Mecca, praising God and reciting verses from the Koran. A man then bows, reciting further phrases to God, and then kneels with forehead and nose touching the ground, again uttering praise to God. A few other men followed him in this practice, but regular prayer was the exception rather than the rule among these pastoralists.

The hand washing and prayers were followed by the dinner itself, again delivered on large trays. The first two trays were brought as before and then several additional trays were set before the remaining men, who adjusted their positions to sit cross-legged in small circles around them, stuffing food into their mouths with their right hands. Dinner consisted of boiled lamb under rice with steamed chicken on top, fresh bread, yoghurt, and *dugh*. We all ate quickly and then pulled back from the trays. The servants removed the remains for distribution to the women and other members of the camp, who were waiting outside. Once again the *aftabes* were brought, this time with hot water and a bar of soap to clean our hands of the grease. At that point, dinner was finished.

Since I was tired of the interminable speeches, which promised to drag on for several more hours, Sekandar and I excused ourselves and returned to camp, where we found that one of Morad Khan's daughters had arrived, along with her child. She said she planned to stay for about a month. From the way she greeted Sekandar, it was apparent that they knew one another. As he later told me, she was married to his brother. Unfortunately she did not get along well with her husband and there had been talk of divorce, although nothing had been settled. In the meantime, the woman decided to return to her father's camp for a prolonged visit. Ordinarily such a long visit would not be tolerated by the husband, but in that case he had another wife to take care of things at home. Since he was not getting along with her anyway, the separation may have been welcomed by both parties. Whatever the case, Morad Khan would be happy to see his daughter again.

The next morning, Morad Khan said we would not move on for a few days because he was now obligated to give a return dinner to the Mirs and he had a number of political calls to make. In midmorning he headed toward Kowgan to visit the Dirkavand men with whom we had had lunch two days before. I did some more filming and explored the area around camp for a while before it occurred to me that it would be refreshing to take a bath.

When Taji, who had returned from her visit to Atawak's camp, heard of my desires, she carried a large copper pot down to the stream and built a fire under it so that I or anyone could bathe or wash clothes. The day was overcast and not too cold, but the meltwater in the stream was frigid. The hot water made the prospect of taking a bath bearable. I took my clothes off behind a tree and mixed hot water from the pot with cold water from the stream in an *aftabe* and poured it over myself. The constant cool breeze made this a refreshing but chilly bath.

Afterwards I gave Taji some clothes to wash and retired to the tent to take a nap, but some persistent little goats kept coming in and nuzzling me, so I resumed my observation of life in the camp.

Mohammad Ali was in camp most of the day, so I asked him how many animals each person had and how many pack animals were needed for migration. I had also asked these questions of many of the people we had visited, so I had an idea what the nomads consider necessary to maintain their way of life in reasonable comfort. Such questions touch on sensitive issues of property, wealth, and prestige, so one cannot always expect to get accurate answers. By this time, however, Mohammad Ali was no longer reticent with us and gave informative responses.

Earlier, Morad Khan had said that the ideal tent has six males and two or three females, six cows, fifteen mules and/or donkeys, and a hundred and fifty to two hundred sheep and goats. By today's standards this would be a very wealthy tent indeed, as the figures Mohammad Ali gave us attest. According to his count, our entire camp had eight adult men (not counting Mukhtar), seven adult married women, five children, and only fourteen mules, three horses, five donkeys, ten cows, four steers, fifty-four sheep, and one hundred and seventeen goats. Thus our camp had approximately the resources that Morad Khan thought were necessary to support one large family. It was apparent from our observations elsewhere that few families approached the ideal.

As Atawak pointed out, problems had increased in recent years with the addition of new kinds of baggage. Such things as the ubiquitous pillow bolsters were not previously used, and they take up a great deal of room on a pack animal. We used seventeen pack animals when we were migrating and would have needed twenty-two more if most of the heavy baggage had not been sent by truck. Morad Khan's tent alone would have taken three mules; a small tent, two mules. Clearly, it would have been impossible to move everything at one time with the available pack animals. This was a problem faced by most pastoralists. It was not uncommon in our travels to see caches of baggage left by people who had gone ahead with part of the load.

Sekandar was anxious to try his luck hunting partridges, so he and Mohammad Ali went off into the hills. I made a trip to one of the ancient sites in the area to collect pottery and record features that were visible from the surface. I heard a few shots in the distance and hoped that they had bagged our dinner. When I got back to camp, I found that they had hit a nice fat bird.

That night it was Morad Khan's duty to host the Mirs for dinner, and some men from other camps discussed this with him in his tent. Apparently, they prevailed on him to allow them to host the dinner in one of their tents, a gesture made out of respect to him. With that agreed, the men all left for the other camp, sending word to the Mirs where to meet them. Sekandar and I declined the invitation and remained in our camp. As the sun set and the cold of the night enveloped our narrow valley, we feasted on partridge and rice and then sat for a long time listening to Mohammad Ali playing Luri songs on Sekandar's tape recorder.

Around nine o'clock, Morad Khan returned, saying that dinner had been cut short because of the cold. Because there were no tents in the other camp, they had eaten outside and had been uncomfortably cold. This struck me as a particularly insensitive way to have reciprocated for the evening before, and I was happy we had declined the invitation to join them. Several hours of sitting on the ground in near-freezing weather, listening to men praise one another in the Luri language, did not appeal to me.

Morad Khan's return stimulated us to talk about him with Mohammad Ali. Sekandar was convinced Morad Khan was senile, but Mohammad Ali only agreed that he had changed a lot over the years he had been with him.

For example, he said, "He no longer cares what he wears … he now wears rags."

In fact, Morad Khan's dress was something of a scandal. But Morad Khan's stock retort was that, since everyone knew him, it did not matter what he wore. But even though nomads were not especially well dressed, the fact that Morad Khan, their leader, wore torn clothing was a little disgraceful. Mohammad Ali said that a leader like Morad Khan would usually give his clothes away when they were torn.

Iranians generally place great emphasis on dress. I remember how people we employed as servants on archaeological projects asked us for new clothes so that their dress would signify our prestige and importance. For a tribal leader to go about dressed as shabbily as Morad Khan was an obvious sign of his economic straits. But it was a sign we had seen among other leaders too. Clothes were very expensive.

I think in this instance Sekandar was wrong. Morad Khan was not senile or incapable of maintaining his social presence. He was quite right that people knew him irrespective of his clothes. But Morad Khan faced a nearly irreconcilable dilemma. As a tribal leader, he had to be generous—but he had little to be generous with. His *homsa* had deserted him. His son openly denigrated his style and traditions. His herds were too small. What was there for him to do but keep his spirit while his world gradually decayed before his eyes? He could not stem the rot with new clothes. His reward would come in the afterlife, when his mortal remains would lie alongside a trail somewhere in his beloved mountain pastures.

As we were talking, Morad Khan came to our tent to borrow the flashlight again. He needed to tie his animals. While he puttered around, more or less aimlessly, he left the light burning for more than an hour. I was a little unhappy with his profligate use of the batteries, and pointed out to Sekandar that Taji still had not returned his pocketknife either. As soon as I said that, I remembered that she had borrowed my knife to cut up the partridge we had eaten for dinner. God had provided once again, but His providence reminded me as well of Atawak's observation that people don't share now because they have gotten into the habit of acquiring things for themselves. Like the others, I was tied to my possessions.

Although I was annoyed by his casual borrowing of the flashlight, it eventually occurred to me that Morad Khan and Taji were subtly incorporating us into their social family. When we had tried to help with any of the labor, we were always told that finding firewood, helping with the packing, and so on was not our work. Our status was too high for such menial tasks. But we could contribute our knives and flashlights, and Sekandar could amuse the group by playing tapes of Luri music. In our own way we were contributing to the welfare of the camp and inadvertently showing people things they had not seen before, like jackknives, cameras, plastic, and other things.

Upon rising the next morning, we could see nomads from other camps beginning to pack for the last stage of migration. However, we were in no rush and enjoyed a leisurely breakfast in Morad Khan's tent. When we had finished our last glass of tea, Taji, without comment, handed us the flashlight and Sekandar's knife, which she had had for two weeks. Perhaps she had learned of our earlier discussion, or overheard what was said.

That morning, like almost every other morning, a mule had wandered away from camp during the roundup and had to be retrieved. A mule that wants to be caught will simply come when called, but mules have earned their reputation for unpredictability and stubbornness and rarely follow commands unless backed by a show of force. If you get behind a mule it may give a nasty and dangerous kick, as I learned the hard way when a hoof just grazed my chest. It is difficult to apply force to a loose mule, so other means have been perfected. Safarali was the camp master at running them down. Since the mule belonged to Morad Khan, Safarali borrowed an aluminum bowl with some salt in it from Taji and then went out to "bribe" the animal, as Sekandar put it.

While walking out toward the animal, making coaxing sounds, Safarali held the bowl of salt in front of him, where the mule could see and smell it. As he approached, the mule was alternately nervous and curious. He finally succumbed to the latter urge when Safarali set the bowl on the ground in front of him. Safarali remained bent low to the ground, near the mule's front legs but out of the mule's sight. He waited for the animal to bend its neck toward the salt. Then, with a quick grab, he put both hands around the mule's leg. There ensued a comic scene: Safarali, mule's leg in hand, began to dance around in circles while the mule kicked out its hind legs. If he held on long enough, it might be possible to put a rope on the mule. Sometimes the strategy worked and sometimes the mule broke away. That morning a rope was secured, and the mule was brought back to camp.

Once I watched a mule being chased by nearly all the members of the camp. At first Safarali caught the mule, but it broke loose from his grasp and started to run. Its escape in one direction was closed by a line of waving, shouting people, so it turned back, ran some fifty yards and found the other exit closed. Back and forth it wheeled, five or six times, before some of the men found a long rope and stretched it across the track where the mule was running. The animal crashed headlong into the rope, sending men sprawling, and it was only after fifteen more minutes of chasing that someone was able to throw a rope around its neck. Among the innovations I would add to the nomads' equipment is a lariat, a device they never use.

The spring

After watching the mule capture, Sekandar and I saddled up our horses and headed out to survey some of the archaeological sites nearby, leaving the camp to pack and take their own trail. We arranged to meet on top of the last ridge into Dareh Nasab, the summer pasture. As we headed up the rapidly flowing stream, we met one of the Mirs, who happened to arrive just as we were leaving. The Mir was anxious to show us where he had seen bituminous water seeping from the bank of the stream. While we rode, he loped along the trail on foot, expertly skipping across the tops of rocks where we forded the stream at the many crossings.

The alleged bitumen spring turned out to be nothing other than a ruse so that he could accompany us. When we reached the so-called bitumen spring, where we had taken the burning rock the other day, he said we should go to the Takasu spring. It seemed that the spring's location had recently shifted, much to the detriment of irrigation. We decided to have a look, so we walked on to the big trees of Takasu, where I picked up more sherds from the ancient site and terraces.

According to the Mir, the spring had ceased to flow after a heavy rain some two years ago had filled it with dirt. The Mirs' solution to this was to arrange a meeting at the big trees with government officials to see whether they would provide financial assistance for the digging out and rebuilding of the spring. For the occasion, he told us in elaborate detail, leaders of all the people who used the water for irrigation brought food and slaughtered a sheep for a feast in honor of the government officials. With unmistakable irritation, the Mir pointed out the precise spot where they had eaten and sat in consultation. After the feast, during which the officials are alleged to have promised some 10,000 *tomans* to aid in reconstruction, the entire party went to see the spring. Needless to say, the government money had not been delivered.

We retraced their route as we worked our way up the streambed. The country did not look to me as if it were very favorable for irrigation, and I said so.

"This is not the place," the Mir said. "The water did not flow along this natural stream."

Because of a diversion dam at the spring, the water flowed into Dadabad, a nearby valley. He asserted that a thousand people depended on the irrigation water. I regarded the population figure skeptically, but the fact that the water had been diverted became apparent as we neared the spring itself.

Situated on the south side of a steep narrow valley, it consisted of an opening in the ground about twenty feet across, where there had once been a pool that overflowed into a canal. From there the water followed a circuitous route alongside the opposite slope of the valley and out of sight beyond. It was clear that excessive erosion had indeed filled the pool, for the gaping hole was filled with rock and dirt from the slopes above. Since water flows by gravity, it can only irrigate land that is lower than the spring. Now, with its outlet blocked, the water issued about twenty feet below its former level. This was below the canal that had been used for irrigation, so most of the land could not be irrigated.

To my eye it seemed that a small crew of laborers could have easily shoveled out the dirt and shored up the banks to prevent a similar collapse in the future. I wondered aloud why the people who were affected by the disaster did not clean it out themselves instead of waiting for the government to do it. If it really had curtailed all irrigation for a thousand families, or even a few hundred, it would have been the logical course, it seemed, for the interested parties to take a week or two to rebuild the system.

I put the question to the Mir, who replied that the tribal people have no effective leadership anymore.

"No one can make anyone work anymore," he said. "Who is the man who will work for anyone else's possible gain?"

Thus immobilized, for two years the people had waited for the government to act while they lamented that the officials had eaten their food and had given promises but no cash. In the meantime, they could not grow crops.

The basic problem appeared to be one of organization. The government had stripped tribal leaders of their traditional authority, but it had not filled the void with persons who could act on a local level. In consequence, each family was essentially on its own, and each was reluctant to commit its resources to a project that would benefit others as much as themselves. In my naiveté, I had assumed that people would, if pressed hard enough, take steps to ensure their own livelihood, at least in regard to essentials such as food. The problem with the spring, however, was larger than one man could handle, and it was precisely because of their inability to cooperate that every man, and consequently all men, became powerless.

I was reminded of an incident during a trip to the Saimarreh Valley about two months before. There we had found a beautiful rushing mountain brook spilling down a steep rock gorge lined with trees and wildflowers. As the stream approached a small village, some of its water was diverted through a pipe into a concrete tank. From there it was conveyed into the village by means of an underground pipe, which supplied taps where women could draw their drinking water. Such systems are found in many villages in Iran, having been installed by the government to help the people obtain dependable supplies of pure water for drinking. In this instance, heavy rains had caused flooding in the river and the tank had become choked with sand and gravel, thus shutting off the flow into the village. When this happened, the women reverted to the time-honored practice of trudging to the river itself with their water bags. During springtime, this was acceptable and afforded good water, but later in the year, when the stream was reduced to a trickle, it was likely to be contaminated by animals coming for a drink.

When I asked why they did not clean out the tank, the villagers said they were not allowed to do so.

"The tank was built by the government and the government must clean it out," was their response.

I could see the point that the government might be responsible, but the job seemed so easy I could hardly imagine that an official from town would punish the villagers for scooping sand out of a tank. The people agreed that they might not be punished but pointed out that they did not know how to do the job. Of course "how" in this case was as much a matter of organizing a work force as of technique. Here too, the people felt powerless, both because they were awed by the government's authority and because they felt impotent to deal with technology that was not of their making.

When Luri farmers, at best a generation removed from a strictly nomadic pattern of animal husbandry, tried to confront the expanded horizons of farming, irrigation, and water supply, they were hampered by indecisive leaders profoundly ignorant of even simple technology. Government officials, at least on the level that reached the nomads and farmers, were no better equipped to deal with the practical problems and could offer only promises of money—which, if forthcoming, had to be used to hire "experts" to direct and execute the projects. The problem was not that the people were lazy or stupid, or even too quarrelsome to cooperate. A nomad can scarcely be accused of being lazy, and the stupid would not last long in a world where common sense is essential. What is more, the nomads had demonstrated again and again their ability to cooperate, to the extent of building and maintaining large and viable tribes. But there were no technically skilled nomads, and no sanctions that would enable any such person to lead. Indeed, the essence of government policy had been to emasculate tribal authority in order to eliminate all vestiges of possible opposition to the royal regime, thus leaving the people like a ship without a captain, safe in calm weather but imperiled in a storm.

After listening to the Mirs' story, we took our leave. We turned our horses along the defunct canal toward the Dadabad plateau, where we were to meet Morad Khan and the members of our camp. As we topped the divide and looked down onto the plateau, we could make out the line of pastoralists working their way toward us. The plateau was treeless, lying very close to the tree line, but we could see numerous fields under the plow where farmers, in the absence of irrigation water, were attempting to raise a crop through rainfall alone. In a dry year like that one, the chances appeared slim.

Chapter 13

The Promised Land

Migration takes a toll on people, their herds, and—through grazing and cutting—on the landscape itself. Nevertheless, migration sustains a tribe's traditions, secures its rights, and, most importantly, ensures the success of their livelihoods.

Spring is the time of rejuvenation. Warm, sunny days help soothe tired bodies and portend the growth of herds and crops. After sheep shearing and sales, it is a time for replenishing supplies. It is also a time for fun—visiting relatives, gathering at weddings, and holding circumcision ceremonies. The fresh surroundings are a promised land to be enjoyed for some months until the trek back down to secure, but confined, winter quarters.

Dareh Nasab

When the group reached us, we headed toward the last pass across Hashtad Pahlu, the highest range we had to cross. This mountain is a long series of snow-covered peaks that stand as a barrier to the summer pastures and the Khorramabad Valley below. It had been visible from several passes previously, marked by its serrated series of peaks and wide fields of snow. In wetter years we would have been traversing snowfields, but it was our good fortune to be able to ride along a dry and relatively safe scree-covered trail. Flowering almond bushes appeared along the trail, and they grew into small trees in a sheltered slope higher up the pass.

The pass itself was fairly easy. We had begun the day at a high altitude, so we had only a few hundred feet to climb across generally barren rock with patches of snow. Since our group was moving slowly, Sekandar and I went on ahead to take pictures and enjoy the view. Behind us, in silhouette, were all the passes we had crossed since we left. Ahead we could see the Khorramabad Valley (Figure 13.1). Once, when I dismounted to take a picture, my horse, caught up in the spirit of reaching summer camp, headed along the trail by itself, stopping only when it had caught up with Sekandar, half a mile ahead.

Everyone was in high spirits in anticipation of reaching their summer campgrounds in the beautiful Dareh Nasab Valley, which lay along the northern base of Hashtad Pahlu. It was the end of a long trip and a homecoming: they looked forward to seeing familiar places and people. Once they reached the pasture, the daily packing and unpacking would cease. Ahead was a summer of lush grass, tall trees, flowers, running water, and clear, cool air.

We slowly descended the trail, little more than a track, along the north side of Hashtad Pahlu. The snow had left much of the trail soggy and slippery from innumerable rivulets. Leading his horse down the slippery path, Mohammad Ali wore his Luri tunic and bandolier and carried a rifle (Figure 13.2). He and Sekandar stopped to examine a little patch of snow. Parallel tracks made by grazing sheep and goats were grooved into the hillside (Figure 13.3). Soon we were in dense forest again, damp from the melting snow, and the trail became difficult to follow because of the underbrush and low-hanging branches. Fritillaria bloomed in the boggy soil below the snow, sometimes in fields of an acre or more (see Figure 11.10). In other fields were yellow narcissus (*Narcissus* sp). These broad-leafed plants had a pleasant garlic smell. Most had not yet bloomed. Mohammad Ali said the dried pods of this plant were added to *dugh* for flavoring.

Figure 13.1. The Khorramabad Valley, home of the settled Baharvand, is visible from Hashtad Pahlu.

Arriving at the summer camp

Our group had started late that morning; other camps had arrived sometime before. Below we could see herds grazing in the patches of vegetation and an occasional wisp of smoke from a tent hidden in the trees. At one such camp, down a steep side trail, two men were leading pack animals to a trickle of water. Sekandar recognized Latif, Khodarahm's son. When we hailed him, he invited us to his tent for lunch, an offer we gladly accepted, as we had been riding for six hours and were in no great rush to rejoin our own camp.

Figure 13.2. Mohammad Ali crosses Hashtad Pahlu, the last barrier to the summer pastures, wearing a traditional Luri tunic and carrying a rifle and bandolier.

Figure 13.3. Sekandar and Mohammad Ali inspect a snow patch on Hashtad Pahlu. The horizontal lines of the slope in the background are grooves left by generations of foraging sheep and goats.

Khodarahm's tent was set by itself under a broadly spreading tree next to a field of narcissus several acres in extent. It looked as lush and verdant as one could want, but there was very little grass and, except for the snow-fed trickle, no water. This was only a temporary camp; later, Khodarahm would move down close to the arable land, where he would plant a field. He received us warmly for tea, and before long, his wife set before us a fine lunch of chicken, yoghurt, and bread.

After lunch he told us how to reach Morad Khan's camp, and we set out across the country, departing from the little trail so as to save time. Trails

Figure 13.4. Overview of Dareh Nasab, summer pasture for the tribe.

in that part of Dareh Nasab were very poorly defined anyway, so we just worked in the general direction, avoiding the densest vegetation and heading downhill (Figure 13.4). Eventually we found Morad Khan's tent, which had been set up, along with ten or more other Baharvand tents, at the upper margin of the forest. Only a few hundred feet above lay a massive snowfield. Before electricity and icemakers were installed in Khorramabad, nomads used to carry snow to town in the summer on donkey back, a day's trip each way, for the small amount of cash it provided.

By the time we arrived, all the tents had been set up in sites that were used year after year, and only the final unpacking remained. There was no question that the weather would be cold, so shelter was the first consideration. The expanded camp was a scene of conviviality and subdued bustle as the women set up their households. Donkeys, released from their burdens, raced around braying. I went off to take pictures of the camp and its surroundings, glad to be walking again, while Sekandar and Morad Khan sat talking on a carpet spread in front of the tent.

By the time I returned from exploring the valley, the pastoralists had unpacked nearly all their baggage. Each tent was set up just as if it had been there for weeks. The animals were out in green pasture, some of the men were drinking tea, the babies were crawling around in front of the tents, and little wisps of smoke curled from the fires where the women were getting ready for an evening meal. The camp had sprung up almost instantaneously, like the spring plants at the edge of the melting snow.

Hasty departure

The new camp was a picture of relaxation. Taji sat on a carpet playing with two babies, and Safarali sucked contemplatively on his water pipe. The air was growing colder as the sun began to dip behind Hashtad Pahlu, and I began to think of laying out the bedding and getting our own fire stoked. I was tired from the long day's ride and wanted to sit quietly with my cup of tea and reflect on the day's activities. Heavily, with a sigh of relief, I sat down on the carpet where Sekandar and Morad Khan were still talking and gratefully accepted the tea and piece of bread. My thoughts were not at all on the conversation as I savored the sweet, strong brew that trickled down my throat. I lay back full length with my head resting on the camera case. In another minute I would have been sound asleep.

My reverie was jolted when Sekandar announced that we were about to leave. My mind recoiled while my body sank deeper into the carpet. We had already endured nine hours in the saddle. We had finally attained our objective.

"Why leave now?" I asked. "Why not tomorrow?"

Sekandar said he was anxious to return to Darayi and his family. Moreover, Morad Khan wanted to get the baggage that had been sent there by truck. Until the tents had been brought up from town, some people would be without shelter. Plans had already been made. Mohammad Ali and Safarali were to accompany us to town with some pack animals, onto which they would load the baggage and return to Dareh Nasab the following morning.

"But Mohammad Ali and Safarali are tired," I protested.

They are homsa, came the answer. They do as they are told.

"It's not a hard trip," Sekandar said.

"But how about the animals?" I knew that my wretched mount was as tired as I, and most of the pack animals were bleeding and bruised from the exertions of the past two weeks.

"They won't be loaded," Sekandar said, "and they'll be OK. Morad Khan is going to give us mules to ride instead of the tired horses."

That topped it all. Mules are enormously strong animals, far stronger and more sure-footed than horses, but they can be unpredictable. Luri legend is replete with stories of mules that have thrown their riders. They seem to have a penchant for kicking while ambling down a trail, or shying and bolting at the sight of a pebble. I was less than eager to mount one of these beasts for our final descent, but even as I protested, I could see Mohammad Ali and Safarali putting our saddles on two of the mules.

Suddenly I realized that we really were going to leave, despite my protestations. What had I forgotten to do? Had I taken all the pictures I wanted? Where was our baggage? Where were all the people I wanted to thank and say goodbye to? My immediate concern was to make sure all our baggage was loaded onto the donkeys. By the time I had made a cursory check of the little piles of things that lay around the tent, the packing was finished. Mohammad Ali said it was time to go. The descent would take about three hours and we wanted to get down before dark.

We stood there next to our new mounts and made a few perfunctory and, to my view, unsatisfactory goodbyes to Morad Khan's immediate family. The other members of the camp were scattered, either with their herds or in their tents. They took only a passing interest in what was going on. They fully expected that we would be back again, as did I. While we were standing there, Sekandar presented Morad Khan with a fine pair of binoculars. The old man, who had enjoyed using them on the trip and obviously prized them, refused to take them. It was a customary refusal. He did not want to appear to want them, let alone seem to need them. Sekandar implored him again to take the glasses and again Morad Khan refused. Finally, Sekandar laid them on the carpet, mounted his mule, and off we went.

Morad Khan, riding bareback on Sekandar's horse, went with us a mile or so to show us an ancient ruin in the bottom of the valley. It lay at the

Figure 13.5. The small hill in the center, next to the stream, is a prehistoric site. Wheat fields, planted in the fall, are beginning to grow.

confluence of two streams, which flowed off high ranges to the north and south. There, in the sloping fields, were the same kind of stone foundations and terraces that we had seen throughout our trip. Part of the ancient site had been given over to recent burials but otherwise looked undisturbed, except for some recent plowing and robbing of stones. Since we planned to return in a week or so for a thorough survey of Dareh Nasab, I gave the site only cursory inspection. As we were about to leave, Morad Khan said he knew of another site. He pointed a short distance away, toward a small high mound just at the junction of the two streams (Figure 13.5). When I climbed on top of this site, I was surprised to find, for the first time in our travels, sherds of early prehistoric age. Unfortunately, recent graves in the top and the possible foundations of a building obscured the nature of the site, but it looked as if it might have been a small camp. I made a hasty collection of pottery and then, with the sun falling too low to allow delay, suggested that we had better be going.

We followed the stream east along a well-worn trail, leaving Morad Khan behind. Soon we joined Mohammad Ali and Safarali, who had gone ahead and were resting with their animals in a grassy field. Dareh Nasab was divided down the middle by an anticlinal ridge, along whose north side the river runs. The sides of the valley were generally steep, leaving little room for agriculture, although here and there were patches of cultivation and an occasional tent site. We could see some mud houses of recent construction, built by nomads who were now settled in this high, cold pasture land, apparently for the first time since people had lived in the ancient stone-walled houses.

When we began, Safarali was still on foot, driving the pack animals. But the mules, being without burden, ran wild, taking advantage of every growing field and running far from the trail at every opportunity. He and Mohammad Ali, who was riding bareback on a mule, dashed back and forth time and again trying to keep the animals in line. Finally they tried leading the animals by their halters, but the ropes broke and the beasts dashed off again. Both men were weary after a hard day, and in no mood to spend the rest of the afternoon chasing fruitlessly after the mules. Eventually Safarali combined our baggage with some things the camp was sending into town on one animal so he could also ride. Then he tied the loose animals to his own mount. This proved more effective, though not entirely successful, as we continued down the trail.

After riding in this manner for several miles, we came upon an old tomb, a small white building with a domed roof built in the characteristic Islamic fashion. This shrine, Jamalkal, was particularly sacred to the Baharvand, who attributed various miracles to it. But within the year, to the great despair of the people, it had been excavated and robbed. It was hard to imagine why anyone would want to rob an Islamic shrine like that one, because there was typically nothing of value buried with a Muslim. The body, facing Mecca, with toes tied, and wrapped in a clean sheet, is simply interred in the ground without any grave goods. I speculated that the tomb may have been dug into a prehistoric graveyard where bronze might be found. I was glad to stop there for a quick look, as the gait of the mule was decidedly choppy and uncomfortable, and my back ached.

We entered the square tomb through its door and descended a sloping ramp into its lower chamber. There, under the dome, the coffin lay asunder and various religious articles were strewn about. Bits of green cloth, brass hands of Ali, and signs in Arabic script, all accoutrements of thriving shrines, lay in unbroken disarray among the dirt and rocks removed from the burial. Nothing of evident value was left and there was no trace whatsoever of prehistoric material. I was numbed by the senseless vandalism, as were my long-faced, mute companions.

This was not an isolated incident. Many such holy places had been desecrated. Morad Khan had talked about this. He said it had shaken the faith of his people. In the past, people respected the holy places so much that they feared divine punishment even for cutting a branch from a tree growing nearby. But by the 1970s, apparently, shrines were being wrecked with impunity. The people said, "If the shrines were still powerful, the people responsible for these outrages would have been killed instantly." As there was no evidence that anyone had suffered the consequences, it was apparent that the power of the shrines and, by implication, the power of their religion, was seriously waning.

We discussed who might have dug up the tombs. No one could offer an explanation. It was generally conceded that "outsiders" must have been responsible, since the Baharvand and other tribal people would have been afraid to carry out the dastardly deed.

"But," I said, "I have seen looted shrines next to villages. Surely the people know who did that."

It was almost unthinkable that no one had seen the digging, and in a tribal area, where a stranger would be spotted instantly, the news would spread quickly from camp to camp. I could only conclude that there had been complicity in the desecration by "insiders."

Reluctantly, we remounted and moved forward again at a quickened pace, soon sighting another fifteen men and mules ahead of us. Khodarahm and his men were also heading into town to pick up their belongings, so we joined them. This unexpected meeting was an occasion for exuberant displays of horsemanship—or mulesmanship, as the case dictated. There was no holding back the men or animals. With excited cries signifying release from the burdens of migration, the men spurred their mounts into wild dashes and long gallops, glorying in speed and freedom. No longer were the straying animals an onerous burden. With reckless abandon they were run down and put back on the trail while men whipped their steeds and shouted to one another like boys let out of school. Although I was in some pain from the constant riding, and most of the men had been dog tired before they began, it was clear that this was real sport to be enjoyed, even by me, at whatever the cost.

Soon the river turned away from our trail, and we reached a pass where we paused long enough to survey the scene. Behind us, towering overhead, were the snowcapped slopes of Hashtad Pahlu. Below us, like a miniature city at the neck of a broad valley, lay Khorramabad. Somewhere in the valley below, a speck obscured by haze and the deepening shadows, was Darayi, the village where the baggage had been stored. We began our long descent at 5:15 p.m.

As I think back on it, that was the longest, hardest ride I have ever had. The trail was not particularly difficult, but the unrelenting downslope caused the mules to walk with care, jolting along with a spine-cracking gait. The effect on me was worsened by the fact that, in order to ride vertically on the animal, I had to lean backwards over its rump to keep from falling off. On we plodded, my shoulders and back aching.

The inevitable jolting motion was relieved only once, when we came to a spot that all the men knew for a famous event that had taken place some forty years before. It seemed that one man, on the trail we were following, fired his rifle and hit a man in a camp across the steep gorge (there was a camp in the same spot on our trip). I estimated the distance to be around five hundred yards, which was no mean shot, even with a modern rifle and telescopic sights. The feat was regarded as the finest example of marksmanship in Luri history, and was commemorated by a small cairn of stones where the man stood as he fired.

Our trail was now broad—evidence of its extensive use. Across the ravines and gorges we could see small camps of pastoralists, who were on their migration to valleys north of Khorramabad. It was striking and sad to see how many trees had been cut. The closer we got to town, the more severe was the cutting. The lower we descended, the scrubbier the vegetation became, until, near the bottom of the slope, the trees were only bushes.

Although cutting of trees had been prohibited for some years, it had continued, especially close to towns; as settlement expands, it takes its toll on trees that are used primarily for fuel. Older nomads remember forests where there are now only clearings or bushes. The need for charcoal, used mainly in the villages and towns, was the chief reason for cutting, but each pastoral family also needed wood for its fires, and timbers were still cut for roof beams. It would take active prevention measures to stop the cutting, but they would have to be accompanied with an alternative to supply needs of the people for fuel and building materials. I wondered as I looked at the denuded slopes whether the same scene had been played out centuries before, when people had lived in vaulted houses throughout this pastoral territory.

This was my first trip into the Khorramabad Valley for several years and my first from a vantage high above. I first entered the valley in 1961, while on archaeological survey. At that time Khorramabad was a small town with a single bridge across the river, and horse-drawn troikas still plied the streets.

It was apparent that a great deal had changed. Cutting across the plain was the power line that we had followed as we climbed Kialon Kuh, and several roads leading to military installations and a pipeline were also new. Otherwise the valley looked much as I had remembered it. Scattered across its bottom were small villages of mud-brick houses amidst fields of wheat. As we came closer to the valley, I could see that the limits of cultivation had greatly expanded. Steep, rocky hillsides were being plowed. Indeed, it looked as if every patch of land that might conceivably give a crop was under cultivation. Most of it was dry farming, watered only by rain, and most of it would fail that year because of the drought. It was no wonder that people were pushing once again into Dareh Nasab and other high, remote valleys. As the population continued to increase and the nomads settled, there would be less and less land available to farm or to graze.

As dusk enveloped us, around nine o'clock, we finally reached the valley floor, about three miles from the village. There were about twenty-five pack animals and eight riders in our party as we plodded wearily along. About a mile from the village, we could see figures on rooftops. The animals sniffed the air expectantly. We broke into a trot and then into a gallop. Even the mules that had been going all day strained forward with fresh vitality. All of us were exhausted, but we derived fresh vigor from the racing finish. Each of the men began yelling and whipping his mount. Many of them carried sticks, which they brandished like sabers, making military maneuvers as if we were a band of nomads attacking a defenseless settlement. In those fleeting moments I too became an attacker and reveled in the terror we would wreak on the hapless village. There was no staying our assault as we raced along the trail, clouds of dust magnifying our power.

From the rooftops, the villagers had seen us coming from a long distance, and a number of them had strung out along the road to greet us. We were still galloping when a deep canal with flowing water suddenly appeared, stretching across the road. In an agonizing flash I thought my mule would balk and throw me headlong into the chocolate-colored stream. With all the strength I could muster I pulled on the reins, but the mule seemed unstoppable. As we approached the brink, he suddenly veered off to the right and pulled up in a muddy field, panting and pawing at the canal bank. One mule had gone across, but the rest had followed mine, and we stood in indecision. Finally one of the village boys showed us the way to an easy crossing. With much coaxing we got our animals across and walked up to the village. There we dismounted, and eager young boys took our animals. Sekandar and I followed a dusty lane between anonymous walled compounds. We reached a double door that opened into the courtyard of Iskandar, Sekandar's brother, who taught school in one of the neighboring villages.

Iskandar escorted us into his guest room, which was carpeted but without furniture. We sagged onto the floor, surrounded by pillows to ease our weary bones. I was too tired to enjoy the tea, and after twelve hours in the saddle I merely toyed with my dinner of chicken on rice. I was in no mood even to talk. That evening we slept in a room on a carpet. I slept fitfully, waking often because of the unnatural silence. It takes a while to become accustomed to enclosure and comfort.

As usual, I was awake by five. Commotion in the courtyard told me that the household was already up. When I opened the door, Mohammad Ali and Safarali were squatting near a fire, having their breakfast. As soon as they finished, they rounded up the pack animals. Amid a great crowd of villagers, they loaded the animals with the tents and other gear that had been sent from Chin-i Zal by truck. I watched this for a few minutes and then said goodbye to the two men, as they led their animals back toward the trail to Dareh Nasab and their homes among the hills.

The episode had ended too quickly. The departures had been too abrupt. There was no closure. I was left with a feeling of dissatisfaction, of unfulfilled expectation. I would have preferred to return to Dareh Nasab, where I could collect my thoughts, fill out my notes, and observe the pastoralists' summer activities in their beautiful, cool pastures. But it was not to be. Sekandar and I had to return to Dezful to make arrangements to dig an archaeological site. It would be some weeks before we would return to Dareh Nasab. Knowing that we would return, however, made the prospect of heading into the suffocating heat of Khuzistan somewhat bearable.

Chapter 14

An Ancient Pastoral Camp

After the migration, Sekandar and I returned to Khuzistan to excavate a site that we thought was about 8000 years old (Figure 14.1). This had come about somewhat accidentally when, a few months before, Professor Henry Wright of the University of Michigan found a site he thought might interest me.

The winter before the migration, when I was in town between trips to pastoral camps, I had stayed in Henry's house in Dezful. Henry was not especially looking for early villages. He found the site while he was inspecting an irrigation canal dating back 2000 years in a section of Khuzistan that was marked for land leveling prior to installing new irrigation canals. In dirt that had been banked up next to one of the ancient canals, he found some early pieces of pottery. When he showed me the sherds, I immediately recognized their similarity to pottery I had excavated in Deh Luran, so I made a brief trip to the site with him at dusk one evening to collect more pottery and flint tools. During this visit, we both thought the site had been a small village, now nearly buried. Only a small, low mound, topped by a *konar* tree (*Ziziphus spina-*

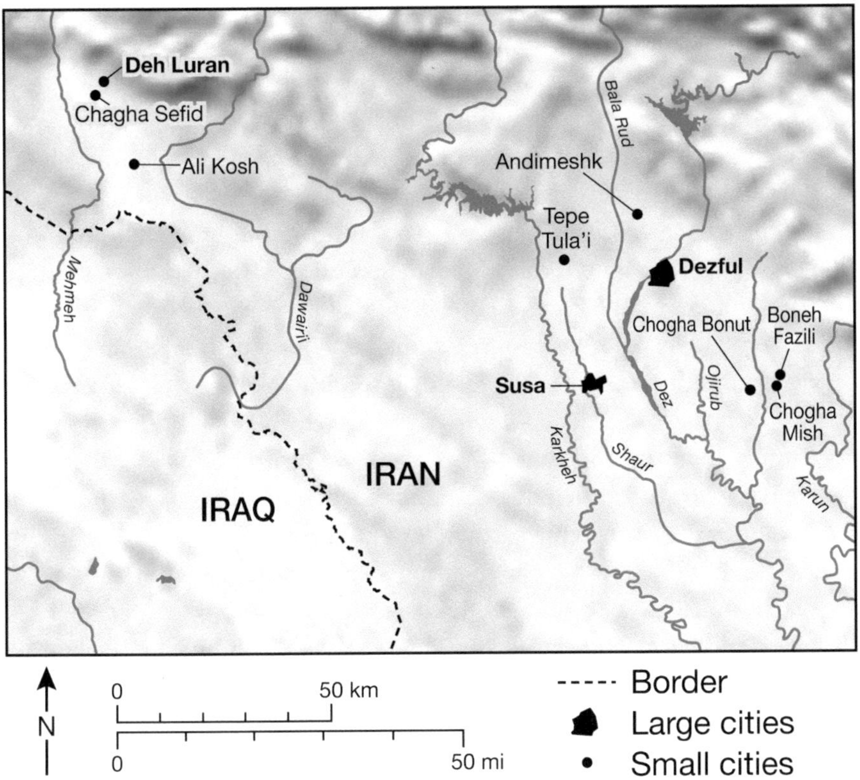

Figure 14.1. Tula'i, which is near the Karkheh River in upper Khuzistan, is some 60 km from Chogha Bonut and Boneh Fazili, village sites of about the same age.

christi), marked the probable existence of this village. The same Sasanians whose canals and vaulted buildings are in the valleys of Luristan had dug one of their canals through part of the site and thus brought the 8000-year-old artifacts to the surface, where we found them.

The land on which the site sat was part of a tract of some 20,000 hectares that had been leased by the Iranian government to a company, Iran California, for an agribusiness. Indeed, all of the most fertile parts of the Khuzistan plain had been set aside for similar developments, largely by foreign companies. These projects were sponsored by the government, Khuzistan Water and Power Authority, which retained 51 percent interest while private enterprise supplied the financing and technical and managerial skills. To irrigate this huge plain, a dam had been built on the Dez River some years before and another was under construction on the Karun River. Together the two rivers would provide irrigation water for most of Khuzistan.

One problem with Khuzistan as an agricultural plain was that it contained a tangle of old and new canals running across the surface; many mounds of ancient archaeological sites; low, natural hills; and hundreds of modern villages, as well as camps of transhumant herders. In short, Khuzistan suffered from millennia of planned and unplanned development, and the traces of it were everywhere. The government's solution—one of the grandiose plans developed under the aegis of the Shah's White Revolution—was to efface all existing canals, mounds, and villages and start over again. The key to the new system was the irrigation canals that, since 1960, had been under the design and construction supervision of American experts—the same experts who had built the American Tennessee Valley Authority system.

The final phase of development, which was to level the land, was underway in 1973. The process, in its simplest form, consisted of lining up huge grading machines side by side at the upper end of the plain and driving them downslope. In the process, everything that was higher than the predetermined grade was removed and the excess dirt was dumped into hollows. Since irrigation water moves by gravity and the natural land was already essentially flat, only a very slight slope was needed. The effect was to make Khuzistan appear as level as a billiard table, the flatness relieved only by the banks of the new irrigation canals, which stood as much as 10 to 15 feet above the plain.

The scope of this work was unprecedented in Khuzistan. It was done at the expense of the villagers and nomads who had used the plain previously. Only recently freed from their absentee landlords by the Shah's much publicized land redistribution plan, these same people were now being forcibly ejected from their villages and offered the opportunity to resettle in geometric, brick and cement block towns that were built near work sites to house the laborers and their families. That is, in the name of progress, nearly all of the original villages across Khuzistan were demolished to make way for agricultural development (Goodell 1975). According to the government's plan, the entire rural population of Iran would one day reside in little workers' communities, of which these were the prototypes and models. They would have electricity, and they would get water from spigots set up at intervals along streets. Those villagers who still occupied their homemade native mud houses were understandably concerned. Although most would have welcomed electricity in their homes, they were apprehensive about losing the ability to practice subsistence agriculture, to keep livestock, and raise vegetables, for these activities were specifically prohibited in the pristine, showy labor villages. If this were not sufficiently demoralizing, the people also had to give up the independence of individual activity for wage labor, if it could be obtained. The large farms were predicated on mechanization, which would need few laborers, so that there was no work at all in agriculture for most of the displaced people, in spite of government claims to the contrary. Those who had neither work nor claims to a house in a new town migrated to Arab countries on the Gulf, where they could find work in massive development projects, or they went to Tehran and other large cities to add to the mass of unemployed squatters. The little town of Shush—the location of biblical Susa—supported only a handful of people in 1960. The last time I saw it, in 1978, it was bursting with a reported 30,000 persons, most of whom were living in the most temporary of structures on land that had not been reclaimed for an agribusiness.

The social situation in Khuzistan thus was bleak. Add to this the sporadic fighting along the border with Iraq, and the situation was somewhat jittery. It had been this way for several years because the predominantly Arab population in the southern parts of Khuzistan resented the exportation of oil wealth from Khuzistan, which left few benefits for the native population of the region. Early in the 1960s, one goal of the development that had culminated in the leveling of Khuzistan had been to return some of the profits from oil to the region. Unfortunately, things went the way such things usually go—the principal beneficiaries were Iranian officials and foreign companies rather than the indigenous populace.

Just before we went on the migration, the land where the ancient site stood was leveled. Henry Wright informed me and suggested that I have a look to see if the site was still there. I went, fearing that the site had been totally obliterated. I wondered whether I would even be able to find it again in the absence of landmarks. I recalled that the site, a low mound with a small tree on top, was just north of one of the new irrigation canals and only a few hundred yards from one of its gates. I drove along the canal, silently ticking off the few landmarks I remembered. First the high mound of Tepe Sinjar, a mile or so to the north, then across the dusty, flat, scraped land to the brick building at the canal gate. Just beyond that, I stopped. I spotted the little mound with the tree. Just a few acres of land remained as an island in the midst of a scraped surface that extended as far as the dust and glare allowed one to see. Apparently the little hill had been left because it would have been more trouble to remove than it was worth. As probable spoil from the old Sasanian canal, it was thick with gravel that would not have been desirable farmland anyway.

It is hard to describe how barren Khuzistan looks after winter's rains have ceased and the grass has turned brown. Still harder to describe is the utterly desolate appearance of the landscape scraped clean of all vegetation. Around me stretching to the horizon were tire tracks in the dust left by the giant graders and scraping machines. The flourlike dust swirled in devils or hung suspended in a permanent haze. There was no relief from the sun. No clouds and no shade: just the glare screaming back into my eyes off the light brown earth.

Tula'i, as the place is known locally, is a hill about 150 feet (50 m) in diameter, its center about 4 feet (1.5 m) above the surrounding plain. It gave the appearance of a tell or *tepe*, hills that represent the debris from ancient mud-brick settlements. Since ancient sites are usually partially buried, I could not estimate how extensive or how deep the site may have been below the surface. Sites in this part of Khuzistan are buried naturally when waters carrying dirt from the mountains wash over them. During the course of thousands of years, as much as 10 to 15 feet (3 to 4.5 m) of dirt may accumulate over the land that people once lived on. I suspected that the part of Tula'i I could see was just the tip of a much larger mound.

I eagerly surveyed the isolated island of pristine earth, focusing quickly on the little mound. The site clearly had promise, for its sherds were nearly identical to those I had excavated in Chagha Sefid, a village near Deh Luran some 60 miles to the west (Hole 1977). They were also similar to those from Chogha Mish (Alizadeh 1996, 2003; Kantor 1976), and Chogha Bonut (Alizadeh 2003), excavated by American archaeologists from the University of Chicago and UCLA. These were some of the oldest villages with pottery that had yet been found in this region. I was excited to find such a site because it offered hope of learning more about the way agriculture developed. Oddly, there were no permanent villages in the immediate vicinity of this site, unlike many parts of Khuzistan. Usually we find early archaeological villages in the same places where people live today. The difference here was the lack of a stream or spring to provide water. On the other hand, the region looked to be good for herders, who might walk some miles to the river for water or use natural ponds that fill after rains. But it was not as suitable for rain-fed agriculture as many parts of the plain are.

During that visit I did no digging, but I scraped at the surface with a trowel in several places and discovered that the area in which there were artifacts was more extensive than just the little mound. The next day, Dr. Firouz Bagherzadeh, then director of the National Center for Art and Archaeology in Tehran (an organization within the Ministry of Culture, through which archaeologists receive permission to work), visited Khuzistan. I decided to ask for permission to test the site—that is, to do just enough digging to determine its importance. Dr. Bagherzadeh was interested in preserving sites that were significant in Iran's heritage, and he would take steps to protect the site if it was deemed to be significant. He was in Khuzistan to visit several excavations and talk with Iranian and foreign archaeologists who were in the area. During lunch at Henry Wright's house in Dezful, we discussed my work with the nomads and the possibility of testing Tula'i. He agreed that immediate testing was necessary before agricultural development caused further disturbance. He said he would obtain a two-week permit for me as soon as he returned to Tehran. This fit nicely with my schedule, as I was then about to leave on migration. I warned him, however, that it was important to expedite permission so I could begin work immediately on returning from migration, before the weather in Khuzistan, already uncomfortably warm, became unbearable.

Preparing for the excavation

After the migration, when I returned to Dezful, my written permission had not arrived, but I soon learned from Henry Wright that my permit had been granted verbally and that a man from the Tehran Center was to be assigned to work with me. Since the permit was not in hand, I decided to take the train to Tehran to get it personally from Dr. Bagherzadeh. The trip was timely because I also had to renew my visa.

Dr. Bagherzadeh received me the day after we arrived. Our permit, he said, was good for fifteen days. In our conversation I discovered that he had granted permission to dig three days after he left Dezful, but, of course, word had not reached me in the mountains of Luristan. He had written to officials in Khorramabad, who also were unable to reach us. No matter, I said—we had to come to Tehran to renew our visas anyway.

The Center was in the process of making up new rules about the division of artifacts between Iran and foreign archaeologists, but Dr. Bagherzadeh said there was no problem with seeds, radiocarbon samples, and "study collections." He said he would write to all the necessary officials in the area explaining our purpose and the nature of our permit to dig. But there was one small problem. He had not yet assigned a man to travel with us. It is the law that an Iranian from the Center must be present wherever there is an excavation. These men are sometimes students of archaeology who are expected to participate in the work as part of their training, and they contact local officials to expedite the work. Often they are very helpful in these matters, but sometimes they choose not to become closely involved in the actual excavation. Traveling to Khuzistan at this time of year to work on an American project was not an opportunity that every Tehrani would jump at.

We also discussed the looting of sites that I had seen in my travels. I told him that many Bronze Age tombs and even saints' tombs had been looted recently. He seemed surprised at the extent of the activity and said he should send instructions for guards to be placed. Part of his plan for an effective national organization was to have a network of trained guards protecting the nation's significant sites. Heading this organization was Mr. Mohammad Khorramabadi. Years before, during the summer when we first met Sekandar, this man had served as our representative from the government.

Sekandar was particularly upset at the defilement of the saints' tombs and holy places. He suggested that Dr. Bagherzadeh request local gendarmes to keep an eye on sites in their region. I was surprised when Dr. Bagherzadeh replied that he did not trust the gendarmes. He explained that at one of the famous sites he had visited in Khuzistan, he found the gendarmes had been selling inscribed bricks. The men were summarily dismissed but, as Dr. Bagherzadeh recognized, the problem could not be solved so easily. Sekandar then suggested that local people—headmen in the tribal areas—be given authority to guard sites. Dr. Bagherzadeh was also against this because it would give certain people leverage over others and would call attention to the sites. He preferred no publicity. Silently I wondered whether any information that we passed on would result in protection. In particular I had the feeling that holy shrines were not high on the list of sites to protect.

We returned to Khuzistan with permission in hand but without our representative. Before we could dig, I had to go to Deh Luran to pick up tools that Henry Wright and I had used over the years, which we had stowed in a room owned by an old worker of ours. After collecting the tools, we returned to Dezful, taking advantage of proximity to pass in the vicinity of Tula'i. Sekandar and I stopped at the closest village to ask whether there were any laborers available. We had already been told in Deh Luran by some of our former workers that labor was very scarce and farmers would be harvesting their fields at this time of year. We were not surprised then to be told that there were no men available in the village. Our driver, Reza, volunteered that we could hire men off the street in Dezful, a solution that I did not favor for several reasons. In the first place, Dezfulis are not respected by the tribal villagers and might have caused strife at the site. Moreover, we would have had to transport them to the site every day, and their wages might have been very high. All things considered, I preferred to work with locals, if possible.

Sekandar thought it might be prudent to visit the leader of the tribe whose people had occupied the land prior to leveling and who were still in some of the villages that had not yet been destroyed. Tula'i is within the traditional territory of Sagvand Lurs, who formerly used the region seasonally for grazing. Part of this land had, however, been appropriated for use in agribusiness. The Sagvand leader, Nazem, who lived in Andimeshk, a town about ten miles west of Dezful, asked Sekandar to bring me with him the next day to discuss workers.

His brick house was built around a large courtyard in which there were little garden plots containing tomatoes, cucumbers, flowers, and prickly pear cactuses. I was surprised to see the cactuses, because they are native to America. He was surprised but unimpressed in turn when I said they grow red fruits that are used as food and that even the leaves, peeled of their spines, can be eaten.

Nazem said he could produce twenty workers plus a guard from the ranks of several tribal villages in the vicinity. He told us it was good that we were planning only to work until early afternoon, because the men had their own work, too. According to him, Iran America, the company that had leased the land, hired workers for twelve to fourteen hours a day at 11 *tomans* (then equivalent to $7.40), but many laborers were only getting 6 *tomans* a day. At that time of year there was a lot of work, particularly in setting out irrigated fields, but for much of the year there was little work for the farmers who had been displaced from their land.

It should be apparent that we were preparing for the excavation—or rather, for a brief "sondage," or testing of the site to determine its significance—under conditions that were far from ideal. As an archaeologist, I was ready and eager to begin. Sekandar, the ethnologist, had no previous archaeological experience, and he would have preferred to begin his own research. He was not happy to be working in the heat of Khuzistan with reluctant workers but he, as always, was game. To augment our slim staff we had recruited Farhan, a dependable Kurd from Deh Luran who had worked for us in previous years. He was responsible for keeping the household in order, washing the artifacts, running errands, dealing with local tradespeople, and so on. Dr. Bagherzadeh was also to send Mohammad Jaffar Nikha, a young man who had experience in Khuzistan with another archaeological project but little formal training in archaeology. The final member of the staff was Mindy Zeder, a student at the University of Michigan who was in Dezful working on a project in archaeozoology. She was studying the effect on their bones of raising sheep under different conditions of stabling, pasturing, migration, and feed. For several months she had been helping with an archaeological survey and collecting skeletons of animals. She had not yet had excavation experience in Iran, but she volunteered to lend a hand.

With this staff I reckoned we could hire as many as twenty workers and keep them busy and under careful watch. The uncertainty was the workers. Would we be able to hire enough men? Would they learn the routine quickly? Would we have problems over wages or working conditions? I pushed those problems to the back of my mind, hoping that Sekandar's tribal connections and his own considerable skills would enable him to meet and overcome any labor problems.

The excavation

Since we had a permit for only fifteen days' work, we needed to find out quickly what the site held. I decided to focus our effort on digging a single pit into the mound, attempting to hit the bottom. We would also dig around the edges of the site, where we had seen pieces of pottery. The main pit was to be about 13 by 16 feet (4 by 4.8 meters). Previously I had also observed artifacts and ashy earth on the edge of the leveled land, where the bulldozers, which had scraped down about three feet, had cut into the old canal banks. I decided to explore this too, by scraping and brushing a room-sized area clean to see whether there were remains of walls, posts, fireplaces, or other indications of buildings. At that time, I still thought Tula'i probably had been a village of mud-walled houses.

We had four objectives in digging: (1) to obtain a set of artifacts that would help us compare this site with others and determine the periods when it was occupied; (2) to recover animal bones and seeds that would expand our knowledge of early agricultural practices; (3) to take advantage of the land leveling to expose large areas of architecture; and (4) to obtain charcoal suitable for radiocarbon dating.

With these plans made, it became imperative to hire workers and purchase the remaining supplies. My first concern was to have a shelter at the site where we could get some relief from the sun and leave our tools overnight. For this purpose we bought a supply of poplar poles and straw mats in Dezful and had them hauled to the site in a small pickup truck.

Apart from Sekandar and me, on the first day our crew consisted of Farhan and our driver Reza. Building a shelter was a simple matter of setting the poles in holes and then nailing a framework to them that would support the reed mats. We finished the roof about noon. Hot and tired from the exertion in the stifling dry heat, we immediately went inside our shelter for lunch. My field notes record precisely what the four of us ate: four kilograms of cucumbers, a dozen oranges, a cantaloupe and a melon, and three large round flaps of native bread. Farhan brewed the hot tea. We finished the building in the afternoon, and Nazem sent a couple of men who wanted work. We told them to return early the next morning. The next day I was up at 4:30 a.m., because first I had to go to Andimeshk to meet the train that our Tehran official, Nikha, was supposed to be on. He failed to appear, so we returned to the site without him, arriving at 6:30 a.m., well after sunup. Our workers were there, so we began to clean up the site preparatory to digging. About 9:30 a.m., Nazem arrived in a taxi to ask how things were going and to invite us to dinner on the following night. Sekandar then went in our Jeep to Haft Tepe, a train station farther down the line, to see whether Nikha had disembarked there. Apparently he had done so and then gone to Dezful to find us.

The important thing to me was that we were finally working. Now we would find out what secrets Tula'i held.

The men who turned up for work on the first day were a mixed lot. Most were young and unmarried; a few were old enough to be fathers of the younger men. None of them was particularly enthusiastic about working. I had feared this problem, but for other reasons. Unlike many potential workers, these men were not accustomed to agricultural labor, so we were not competing with other employers for their services. These men professed to be gamblers. As they put it, since enforced settlement, the mainstay of village economy had been gambling. Their village, situated near the highway, attracted a steady set of players from among the truck drivers, an especially individualistic and rugged group of modern transhumants who moved goods from the Gulf to Tehran. My workers' attitudes toward gainful employment were more like those of a streetwise hustler in an American city than they were of the typical Iranian village agriculturalists. Nazem had guaranteed workers, and he had delivered, but it would be up to us to get them to work.

I organized the workers into three-man teams. Each team consisted of a pickman, who loosened the earth; a carrier, who removed the dirt; and a sieveman, who passed the dirt through a set of screens and picked out the small objects that had been missed by the pickman. In sites of this age, the greater quantity of material—consisting of small pieces of pottery, flint tools, clay figurines, and animal bones—is usually found in the screens. With the work organized this way, I was able to keep track of the pickmen, teaching them how to dig along predetermined levels or to follow features in the soil, and help when difficult problems arose.

Mindy and Jaffar Nikha (who had finally arrived at the site), with other workers, cleaned off the large scraped areas where I had seen artifacts. Our first problem, as on any site, was to determine what we were digging through. Was it a trash heap, remains of a house, an open courtyard, or what? Secondly, we had to recognize and interpret the layers as we dug further into the site (and hence back in time). Layer by layer we would peel off the debris that remained from the multitude of activities that had been carried out many millennia earlier.

The upper levels of the site contained a mixture of crude, soft, early prehistoric pottery sherds; coarse, hard-fired Sasanian sherds; large numbers of flint knives; hammerstones; and fragments of lightly fired clay figurines.

The layers also contained a lot of gravel, indicating that they had been disturbed during the digging of the Sasanian canal. It was only after we had dug down some 50 centimeters that we found only early prehistoric artifacts. Whatever the site was, I knew its age was within a few centuries of 6000 BC. The problem was to discover what kind of site it was, for we were unable to find traces of mud buildings or other architectural forms; mostly it looked like jumbled layers of trash. Close examination of the sides of our pit revealed large animal burrows and other evidence of substantial disturbance and overturning of layers.

The following evening we went to Nazem's house for dinner. Although he was nominally the leader of the Sagvand, he said there really wasn't much to lead anymore. His uncle, Gholam Khan, the last of the big leaders of the Sagvand (who allegedly had been poisoned a decade earlier), had been a distinguished military leader. Sekandar's father and grandfather had fought alongside him in disputes with Arabs in Khuzistan, when the Baharvand allied themselves with the Sagvand. Nazem was an employee of Iran California, reportedly at a pay of 900 *tomans* a month. His job as "troubleshooter" was to keep the tribespeople under control. The tribespeople widely believed him to have sold them out but, displaying traditional respect for his leadership, avoided actions that would have discredited his position. The actions and reactions were disconcertingly similar to those we had observed in Morad Khan's camps. Once again we saw how traditional deference ostensibly led to social impotence. However, to the tribespeoples' way of thinking, Nazem's position afforded them a vital entrée to the company and hence to jobs. If Nazem lost his job, the workers might lose theirs too.

Dinner that evening was a curious affair, typical in its way yet quite foreign to American custom. Westernized Iranians usually entertain Americans much the way we do, except that we usually offer something other than tea as the first hospitable beverage. The tribal Lurs, however, who have had no occasion to host Americans, treat their guests as they would an honored member of their own culture. If they perceive a great difference in status, as Nazem apparently did that evening, they serve the guests separately from themselves. So it was that Nazem welcomed us into one of his reception rooms—a room with a large TV in the corner. After hot tea, he set various cold drinks and a bowl of excellent Iranian pistachios on the floor in front of us before withdrawing, leaving Mindy, Sekandar, and me to entertain ourselves. After the very hot day, we were tired and thirsty. The evaporative air conditioner in a window hummed forth its cooling breeze. We thirstily downed our drinks and relaxed on the soft carpets.

After perhaps half an hour Nazem reappeared with kabobs of chicken and lamb served on a tray lined with a flap of bread, which we eagerly attacked. Although we three were alone, we found the evening vastly entertaining, as we told one another stories of our various experiences. After the platters of food were removed, one of our host's sons came in and turned on the TV to a station that featured loud American rock music. After listening to that for a short while, fatigue overcame us, and we took our leave. Nazem, the perfect host, had his driver take us home.

Following our good start the first day, I looked forward to the second. It also started out reasonably well. I assigned men to various jobs and let them work. Sekandar moved from team to team, reinforcing my instructions and conversing with the men. He was fluent in the dialect and sensitive to the potential problems, and he tried to build the men's spirits up and keep them moving. But like young men with better things on their minds, the workers carried on loud conversations, joking and taunting one another. At one point, when the joking between two men began to get rough, Jaffar became alarmed and unwisely attempted to intercede. One of the men raised his pick as if to strike Jaffar. Sekandar, who was fortuitously nearby, stepped forward and calmed the situation. After first easing Jaffar out of harm's way, Sekandar spoke with the men, who told him that Jaffar had no business butting into their affairs and the next time they would carry through with their threat to hit him. All of the men seemed stirred up by the episode and even I felt the tenseness of the situation.

We were all uncomfortable due to the heat and the devilish winds, which kept our eyes and mouths filled with dust. That evening I bought a thermometer so that I could see how hot it was. Inside the shade of our shelter in midmorning the temperature was in the high 90s, and by quitting time, at 2 p.m., it was close to 110°F. The men continued to be a bit boisterous and hard to manage for the next couple of days, but no serious problems erupted. In retrospect, we may have been lucky to get through the first five days—and payday. The men showed real enthusiasm for the first time when they had money in their pockets.

The following morning I recorded 80°F at 4:30 a.m. In the low humidity, I had been cold sleeping at that temperature. When we arrived at the site, the men were ready to work, but they wanted a raise in pay to 11 *tomans*. I figured as long as they were at the site they probably would not leave if I turned down their request. We had, after all, agreed on a price just five days before. I was wrong. They left, at the instigation of a bearded, middle-aged gambler by the name of Sabz Ali. I still thought it was a bluff and that they would soon return.

In the meantime, we had work to do in cleaning up parts of the site for photographs. Farhan and Reza helped. We discussed what to do about the workers. Sekandar argued that we should send for the men but not offer them more money. Jaffar was fearful that we had created a difficult incident, and he wanted to go himself to convince the men to return for more pay. After the affair of the previous day I feared for Jaffar's safety and told him to stay put. One of our guards had stayed behind, although he was not helping us, and we decided to send him with our driver, Reza, to ask the men to return. Shortly the two returned, saying that the men would come back to work at the same pay.

Not long after work had resumed, Nazem came by. He had not been to the site earlier, he said, because of a death in his family. He talked with the men and told them they were free to quit but they must give a day's notice if they planned to do so. His presence seemed to quiet things down. Maybe it was just the enervating heat. We worked relatively quietly the rest of the day.

Most of the time the men kept up a running, joking conversation among themselves that I could not understand. Sometimes Sekandar told me some of what was going on. That day there was a heated discussion between some of the young men and Sayid Ali, the oldest of the workers. It was clear to me that Sayid Ali disapproved of something that was going on. I asked Sekandar what it was all about. He said the older man was chastising the young men for taking their earnings into Dezful and spending it on prostitutes. One of the young men had caustically retorted, "In your day you had sheep."

I asked them what else they did in Dezful. The major activity, they said, was watching TV in a teahouse. Much of thc conversation concerned what they had seen on TV. As there was no electricity in their village, they had to go into town to watch. They were clearly men who were intent on exercising their free choices and minimizing their regimentation. Idleness passed in the pleasure of convivial society was their goal. They would work for me no longer than necessary.

Tent sites

Archaeologists will tell you that some of the most interesting and important finds turn up on the last day. It wasn't quite the last day when I made the important discovery, but the way things were going it looked as if we wouldn't have very many more days of willing workers.

While we were digging on the mound, I would often take a walk around the site to see what might catch my eye. For a couple of days I had noticed what looked to be rocks out in the leveled land about 200 feet away from the mound. Since the soil was extremely fine grained, billowing up in dust with every passing breeze, I was intrigued by the presence of rocks, so when I had time I went to have a look.

As I walked across the scraped surface toward the rocks, raising dust with each step, the sun glared off numerous other scattered rocks, and then I noticed below my feet ashy patches that stood out against the light tan dirt. Ash means fires, and those patches looked like remains of fireplaces. But why were they so scattered? When I got to the rocks, I found that some of them were in lines and others were in clusters. Many of them had been hit and moved by the blades of the graders, but others had only barely been exposed. There were far more rocks just visible at the surface than I had seen earlier. This was exciting, because it was unlike anything that I had seen archaeologically before. It looked like the remains of a nomad encampment. I immediately called Mindy, Sekandar, and Jaffar to have a look, and I told them to take some workers and clean off some of the lines of rocks, so we could see what they looked like (Figure 14.2).

For years, when I had been out looking for sites, I had come across remains of tent camps left by nomads. There were usually rows of stones and a fireplace, along with pieces of teacups, old *giva* soles, bits of rope, and other similar discarded material. I had never seen a campsite that I thought might be very old. Indeed, the reason I was studying nomads was to try to learn whether the pastoral way of life was very old at all. At Tula'i I had to find conclusive proof of the camp's age. If I found modern pottery mixed in among the stones, even if I also found prehistoric artifacts, I could not be sure that the camp was old. Modern nomads could have just happened to camp on an area that had prehistoric artifacts.

Because the surface of the land had been removed by the graders to a depth of anywhere from a few inches to three feet, I thought the alignments

Figure 14.2. Grading machines leveled the plains in this section of Khuzistan to prepare the land for irrigation. The grading obliterated homes, villages, archaeological sites, and vegetation. It also exposed some sites, such as this roughly 8000-year-old ancient tent camp. Sekandar observes as the workers uncover stones.

of stone were probably old. That belief was reinforced when I looked at some of the stones and found that they included broken querns or stone slabs for grinding grain; mortars; and what may have been small stone lamps (Figure 14.3). All of those artifacts could have been 8000 years old, but they could equally have been much more recent. The stones alone were not sufficient. Mindy's crew turned to the task of clearing the stones, most of which were unaltered and were shaped just as they had come from the riverbed, some four miles away. They had been deliberately brought to the spot. I could see them in all directions. The camping area extended more than half a mile. This implied that people had used the same general area for many years, returning seasonally, probably in the winter, to put up their tents.

I could hardly wait to see what would turn up among the rocks. Would there be bottle glass, pieces of rope, or shoe soles? Would there be Sasanian pottery, like we had found on the upper part of the mound? As one group of rocks after another was cleaned, the answer became clear and unequivocal: There were only early prehistoric artifacts. We found pottery, flint and obsidian knives, clay figurines, fragments of grinding stones, little mortars, spindle whorls, and other objects that were typical of the earliest villages of the region. We had a very early site—a pastoral camp!

The workmen knew this.

"Why, it's nothing but a tent camp," they said. They could not understand my enthusiasm. "We used to camp here ourselves … This was our traditional camping ground until we were forced to settle and live in villages."

"What was it like when you camped here?" I asked.

"The land was grassy with low hills and depressions where water would accumulate after rains. Most of the time we stayed here in the winter and moved into the mountains in the summer, but some of the people lived here all year. We made our camp out of poles and branches that we carried from the river."

The men were describing the *kula*, a shelter made of poles, covered with leafy branches, laid out in exactly the same way as a tent, and traditionally used by Luri tribes during warmer weather.

I interrogated one of the older men, Sayid Ali, who remembered the days before the tribe was settled and who had been very cooperative and hardworking. He said the rectangular groups of stones were the *chul*, the platform on which bedding is placed inside the tent. This is always next to the rear or side wall of the woman's section of the tent or *kula*. Sayid Ali observed that if the tents were occupied in the winter, they faced toward the south, whereas in the summer, they opened toward the north. During spring and fall, when weather was mild, they might face either direction. The change of openings was to take advantage of prevailing winds in the summer and to provide shelter from them in the winter. He said his tribe had lived in tents made of woven goat hair in the winter and in *kulas* during the summer. Incidentally, the use of *kulas* among the still migratory tribespeople had been prohibited for some years as a means of preventing destruction

Figure 14.3. The ancient tent site. At right is the stone platform (*chul*) on which bedding was stored during the day (see also Figure 9.11).

of the remaining forests. Nevertheless, one still sees an occasional *kula* in remote places.

During the winter, he said, the cooking fires were inside, but in summer they were usually outside, where the heat would dissipate more quickly. Outside the tents are places where people dumped their ash. Those were the ashy areas that I had seen as I walked across the leveled land. Since Sayid Ali was so sure of himself, I decided to put his knowledge to the test. We were then digging a rectangle of stones about three by six feet in extent that he had identified as a *chul* (Figure 14.3). I asked him where the fireplace was. He looked around, lining himself up with an imaginary tent, took two quick paces to his right and said, "here."

"Dig," I said.

He did and quickly revealed the ashy pit in which the fire had been kept. I then asked him where the ash had been thrown when the fireplace was emptied. Again he oriented himself and strode out the imaginary front entrance, angled off the left, and said, "here."

Again he dug and again he found the ash. This was a remarkable example of the persistence of spatial tradition. Modern tribal pastoralists organize their lives in space very much as their ancestors did 8000 years ago.

I then raised the question of food. Did the Sagvand ever use grinding stones and mortars? Sayid Ali replied that herders formerly ate little grain. They obtained most of the flour from acorns that they harvested in the mountains during the fall and stored for use in the winter. The acorns or cereal grain would have been ground on stones similar to those we found at the site; the mortars were for smashing spices and salt. Like all the pastoralists we had talked with, these said they used to eat meat regularly. Sayid Ali claimed that in the good days pastoralists had killed a goat each week. Now, at best, they ate bread, yoghurt, occasionally chicken, and rarely goat or lamb.

Who had lived in these tent sites? Were there any differences between tents? It was not a fair question because we had only a few fragmentary remains, but Sayid Ali rose to the occasion. He walked around the various groups of stones, discussed the situation with some of his friends, and then said that one of the tents belonged to a headman.

"Why?" I inquired.

"Because it is larger than the others," he answered.

That would have been a good idea to test, because a headman's tent should have had two fireplaces rather than just one, but at that point we ran out of time. The men would work no longer, and we had to fill in the holes we had made.

We had done what we intended: we knew the age of the site to be between 6200 and 5900 BC, based on comparisons with our work in Deh Luran. We had a large quantity of artifacts that showed changes during this span of occupation. We had demonstrated the existence of a pastoral camp far older than any that had been discovered before. And we could recommend that the site be protected so that we could return another time to carry out full-scale excavations.

I did not decide which would be the final day. The final day came when it became obvious that we would not have workers for another day. We ended our testing of the site after ten days of work—five days less than I would have liked, but all in all a very successful project. The last day we attended to necessary tasks, such as cleaning rocks for photographs and mapping and filling in the holes we had dug. The workmen showed some spirit at the prospect of finishing, and we were ready to go by noon. I paid the men and gave our little hut to Sayid Ali, who could then distribute the materials in it according to tribal custom. Within a few hours all traces of our activity had been removed. Tula'i was once again just a scorched, dusty hillock in the midst of endless scraped fields, awaiting the next episode in its long history.

A few years later, when I took some archaeological colleagues to see the site, we found the old tent sites covered with maize growing under irrigation.

Chapter 15

A Last Look at the Nomads

The excavation had briefly interrupted my main objective, which was to participate in a migration and learn how the nomads carried out their daily activities. I had learned a great deal about how they moved over the landscape and what their camps looked like. I had also gathered much information that I hoped to apply to the question of how archaeologists could uncover the history of pastoral nomadism. Owing to the necessity to keep moving and not to interfere with the nomads' needs, I had not been able to carry out serious archaeological exploration, but I expected to do so when I could work independently of the nomads. I wanted to explore the many sites of ancient agriculturalists that we had passed along the way, as well as the villa built into the side of the cliff in Kowgan. Most importantly, I wanted to see whether I could find and date old campsites in Bala Griveh. First, I wanted to have a look at the summer campgrounds that we had so precipitously left two weeks before.

Return to Dareh Nasab/Baveh

The morning we left to return to the mountains, the villagers crowded around as we loaded up. A big strong mule was saddled for me and, before the expectant crowd of onlookers, I heaved myself onto his back. Suddenly the mule reared up, pawing the air, while I pulled back hard on the halter to control him. The harder I pulled the higher the mule reared, and it started to bolt away. Only quick thinking by one of the villagers, who grabbed the mule's head, prevented him from throwing me. Laughing at my narrow escape, they told me that I should not pull so hard on the halter; it would make the mule rear up. Accordingly, I left the halter slack and the mule stood there calmly. This left me with no visible means of control, but I admit to knowing very little about mule psychology and was willing to follow advice.

When the mule and I had calmed down, we set off. Sekandar led the way through the village on his mule, down a path that led to a small wooden bridge over a canal that cut through one edge of the village. Sekandar's mule turned smartly and trotted across the bridge. Mine did not. Instead it started to run along the bank of the canal. Following instructions to the letter, I continued to leave the halter slack. The mule quickened its pace, much to the horror of all who were watching, and to mine, the one still on his back. Suddenly the mule made an abrupt left turn down one of the narrow lanes while I hung on desperately. Clearly the mule had its own ideas about where it was going, and I was only going to be a spectator—as long as I stayed on the animal. It ran down the lanes like a rat in a maze. Suddenly and without warning a small boy stepped out of a doorway, and the mule slid to a quivering stop inches from the lad. I held on, grabbing the mule's neck as I slid forward.

The boy sized up the situation immediately and seized the halter, while I tried to recompose myself. Behind us I heard the shouts of a troop of people running toward us along the lane. Half the village, with Sekandar in their midst on his mule, were galloping up to see the carnage. When they saw that I was unharmed, smiles and laughter began to replace their distraught expressions. The whole thing became a huge joke.

Sekandar was visibly shaken by the experience and told me that when mules run away with their riders, they sometimes run through low gates to knock them off. He said some of the Lurs have been killed in this way, and I should count myself very lucky.

"Why didn't you pull up on the halter?" he asked.

"But," I protested, "you just told me not to."

"Oh," he replied, "that was different."

By the time we returned from that trip, my handling of mules had improved considerably, but I must confess that I still mistrust them.

Our progress back up the mountain was uneventful and considerably more comfortable than the descent. We stopped often to take pictures and to enjoy the warm sun, clear air, and the fresh smell of new vegetation. This time we investigated some of the side valleys, which we had missed on the first trip. Our route followed little trails that I could see on aerial photographs. We followed them to spots where I thought we might find archaeological sites. It was a relaxed, easy trip. We stopped at springs to drink or brew tea, Sekandar found friends with whom to talk, and I plotted sites on my maps.

Well after noon we entered the Dareh Nasab Valley and followed the little stream back toward the prehistoric site that I wanted to investigate more thoroughly (see Figure 13.5). Far ahead, alongside the stream, Sekandar spotted two men with a herd of pack animals and cattle. He thought it might be Morad Khan and Safarali. As we drew closer, we could make out Morad Khan's battered fedora. When we reached them, we dismounted. Mukhtar was with the two older men, apparently having rejoined the camp in our absence. Morad Khan took Sekandar aside and started a serious conversation, so I decided to go ahead and explore the archaeological site. My mule was enjoying the pasture, however, and refused to budge. I was in no great rush, so I didn't press the issue.

Soon Morad Khan and Sekandar came over to where I was sitting, and the older man invited us to stay the night with him. His camp was several miles away and not at all convenient for our purposes. However, it was obvious that we had to stay somewhere, so I was inclined to accept, partly for the opportunity to see what had happened in camp since we left. Sekandar, however, was less than enchanted with spending another night in his tent, so we declined the invitation. We told Morad Khan that we had much work to do and that all of it was centered a good distance from his camp. The tribal leader was visibly dismayed by this decision. He considered it an affront to his honor, even though our rationale could be defended. I told him that our time was limited and that I had to survey the site this afternoon, so we moved on up the trail, leaving the two old men to watch their animals.

Mukhtar, dressed in a clean white shirt, tagged along. He wanted to talk with Sekandar, partly about his impending marriage. Since we had been away, Morad Khan had arranged a marriage for his son. It was to take place during the summer, and Mukhtar was anxious to have both of us attend. While I went to the site, Sekandar and Mukhtar sat alongside the river and talked. From the top of the site, the two looked like a couple of college students out for a weekend stroll. Although they were both raised in the tribe, they were no longer a part of it. Sekandar was in Dareh Nasab by choice; he would never live there again. Mukhtar was there by necessity; he would never have chosen to remain. Mukhtar's white shirt stood out among the nomads. He had lived in a white canvas tent alongside his father's. When he had helped take down the tent, he had worn gloves to protect his hands. Now he was exclaiming to Sekandar about how he was trapped in a system from which he could not escape. Marriage and his lack of education and experience would only draw him deeper into a life he found intolerable. Unless he found a way to complete his high school degree, the best he could hope for would be a minor teaching position in a village, and perhaps later in a small town.

After an hour or so at the site, I rejoined the two, and we headed back downstream to where Morad Khan and Safarali were still tending their animals. Again they asked us to stay the night, but this time we made our decision firm. Since we had planned to leave Dareh Nasab early in the morning and had a long trip planned, we would have to stay close to the trail we were going to take. We would look for a closer camp.

Morad Khan asked us if we had found his camp satisfactory and if he had treated us well. I could honestly answer that I had found the trip all I could have expected, and I thanked him warmly for his hospitality. Then we left with the empty feeling of not knowing exactly where to go. Behind us the two darkly clad old men and Mukhtar stood watching until we had disappeared in the distance.

Our departure came with regrets, for I had wanted to see more of our camp and what people did in the summer. Most of all, I felt that I was leaving behind a way of life, epitomized by Morad Khan. His life history, from "riches" to rags, paralleled the decline of the tribes. He stood at the junction between tradition and the modern world, unable to live comfortably in either. As Sekandar describes in Chapter 17, we were witnessing a final transformation of the type of nomadic pastoralism that had begun in the remote past, but that would change in unpredictable ways in the future. Mukhtar exemplified one avenue of change, but he too was trapped in unhappy uncertainty, about to be married to a tribal woman.

A number of camps dotted the hillsides around us, but we had been told as we rode into Dareh Nasab that Mohammad Ali had a camp somewhere along the trail. We both wanted to stay with him if that were possible. Aside from its convenience to our plans, our relations with his family were much easier and less strained than with Morad Khan. But if we could not find his camp, it mattered little, for there were others that would serve for a night's stay. It was for sentimental reasons that we both wanted to find Mohammad Ali.

During the summer the nomads may shift around, so that there are different families in the camps. This has to do with pasturage, friendships, and the location of fields. When the pasturage is lush, some of the camps may have ten to fifteen tents, but as the grass grows thin, the large camps break up again. Some of the people go out in isolation for a few weeks and then reconvene when it suits them. Summer is a time for people to visit friends and relatives, and most of the important social activities take place then. Mukhtar's marriage was scheduled to take advantage of this.

The mood in the summer is buoyant, the pace of life relatively relaxed, and money is available for cash purchases after the young animals have been sold and the older ones sheared.

Presently we spotted a camp on the left bank of the stream, just at the base of a landslide. This is where we had been told that Mohammad Ali was camped, but there was no one in sight that we recognized. We headed our mules down to the stream, dismounted and waded across. Mohammad Ali was not at the camp, but two old women greeted us and offered to make tea. Sekandar was not at all sure that we should stay as long as Mohammad Ali was not present, but we decided at least to have tea. Presently, both Khawar, Mohammad Ali's wife, and Sadighah, Hirdali's wife, came to the tent and struck up conversation. Sekandar grew more and more uncomfortable. It did not really look right for us to be entertained by women. Moreover, he was somewhat concerned about what Morad Khan would think of our having decided to stay with one of the *homsa*. In a few minutes, however, the tension was relieved when Mohammad Ali arrived back from town. He had heard from nomads along the trail that we were in the area and he had hurried so that he would have a chance to see us. With the man of the camp there it was settled that we should stay the night, and the customary offers to kill a lamb were extended. We declined as usual and suggested a chicken instead.

Mohammad Ali was visibly happy to see us again. He said that he knew we would be back, and it gave him great honor to have us as his guests for the night. Aside from any personal feelings he may have had for us, his prestige among the members of his camp was measurably increased. And Khawar, the faithful and gracious wife, relished the role she could play in making our stay comfortable.

Mohammad Ali told us that he had already been back to Chin-i Zal to cut the grain. He and some of the other men had made it in only two long days of riding. The harvest had not been good. Chin-i Zal by this time was extremely hot. In some years, Mohammad Ali told us, men working in the fields cutting the wheat by hand had died from dehydration.

He also told us that more of the tombs that we had seen along the way had been looted. The ubiquitous "men from Kermanshah" were reportedly responsible. Somehow they had managed to get a four-wheel drive vehicle into the area. I asked about the wooden pigeons and he said that he had not seen any. Maybe they had all been taken too. Or possibly they had been destroyed by pious nomads who regarded them as the work of infidels.

As we talked, Mohammad Ali sometimes put his hand to his ear, as if something were bothering him. Sekandar asked him what was wrong. Mohammad Ali said that his ear hurt. He thought that an insect had gotten inside, because he could feel something moving. He said he could hardly hear. He had gone to see one of the traveling doctors that are sent by the government into tribal areas and was told that he should go to town to be treated in the doctor's office. Sekandar thought that the doctor was trying to make some money on the case, because he was not allowed to charge the people on his trips into tribal territory. He then gave Mohammad Ali 200 *rials* to help pay the cost of the office visit, and to ensure that he would go.

As we had ridden into Mohammad Ali's camp, I had noticed a nearby landslide (Figure 15.1). Curious, I excused myself and went out to look at the landslide. The camp was just at its base, alongside the wash of gravel and boulders that had slipped down from the ridge, leaving a deep notch some one hundred yards across in its top. The ridge was one of the anticlines that run throughout western Iran. From above they look like accordion pleats. In one of these ridges, just outside Baharvand territory, is the world's largest

Figure 15.1. A small version of the Kabir Kuh landslide is in Dareh Nasab. In both cases, water undercut the anticline, allowing a large chunk of soil and rock to slide.

landslide, a cleft some nine miles long marking the spot where layers of rock up to one thousand feet thick slipped off the Kabir Kuh and spread out over sixty-four square miles of the valley below (Figure 15.2). In miniature, the slide in Dareh Nasab was identical. In both cases, the river undercut the beds of rock until they gave way in a slurry of rocks and gravel, which sent boulders bounding across the valley and dammed up the rivers to form lakes.

Small though it was, the landslide in Dareh Nasab was a symbol of the irrepressible forces of nature, which work on even the seeming impregnable majesty of the mountains. That such forces were still at work could also be seen directly across the stream, where a small Luri hamlet sat on one

Figure 15.2. The Kabir Kuh landslide, nine miles wide, filled the Saimarreh Valley and dammed up its river. The land between the mountain and the figure on the hill consists of debris from the landslide.

flank of a hilly gully. The original settlement, which had been founded only about fifteen years previously, had long since dissolved into a heap of mud. Unusually high rains had carried houses and artifacts down the slope, along with much of the hill itself (Figures 15.3,15.4).

Picking my way through the debris and clambering over the fallen rocks, I wondered how long ago this land had slipped and whether it had trapped any people. Even a small landslide like this would have obliterated any traces of a camp like our host's.

About dusk I returned to the tent to find dinner ready. Already the air was chilled by winds rushing down into the valley bottom from the snowfields. The rustling of the leaves portended a cold night. Sitting around a tray of

Figure 15.3. The remains of a small hamlet in the unstable landscape that was buried by a landslide.

chello morgh (chicken on rice), we edged closer to the fire while we greedily fingered chicken and rice into our mouths.

Dinner was followed with more tea and conversation, as men from other tents gathered around. One by one the men drifted off, and we prepared for bed. There was little spare room, but we all stretched out our bedding under the tent. Extra blankets were passed out in anticipation of a really cold night, and finally we crawled beneath the covers. Only the wind and the rush of water over the rocks below competed with the soft sounds of animals. The quiet quickly induced sleep for most, but my mind refused slumber. This was to be my last night in a black tent.

Figure 15.4. When people settle and farm on slopes in the high pastures, erosion ensues.

I lay awake for a considerable time, thinking about the migration and other adventures, trying to pull together in my mind threads of continuity in what I had observed. I had begun my study as an archaeologist, looking for archaeological information. I had hardly realized in the course of the work how my attention had been diverted toward the human problems of nomadism. The feeling that this was as important as my original intent became acute, for after that evening I would be left only with impressions. There was no time or light by which to write as my mind raced ahead, seeking meaning in trivial incidents, and finally came to rest on the problems that plague nomads today and that leave their future uncertain.

Departure

I was not conscious of finally drifting off to sleep, only of waking in the morning to the commotion of Sekandar rolling up his bedding. It was cold. The sun's rays had not yet crossed the mountain ridge. It was a quarter to five. Khawar was heating water for our tea so that we might leave early for our long trip back to Darayi. I went down to the stream and slapped cold water on my face and immediately felt my hands cracking in the wind. Then we crowded close to the fire for bread and tea while our animals were being loaded. We were on our way by 5:30 a.m. Mohammad Ali and Khawar wished us God's protection, and we said we would be back another time.

Our trail out of Dareh Nasab led directly up the other side of the valley, a steep slope, which forced us to meander back and forth through the forest. Only occasionally could we glimpse the camp through the trees. By six, we had reached the summit, and the sun was finally casting its first rays on the ridge above Mohammad Ali's camp. As we watched, the curtain of light illuminated the landslide. We dismounted and watched the sun gradually fill the valley. Far away, in the morning haze, I thought I could make out the white school tent in Morad Khan's camp.

I was struck by thoughts of the fragility of man and by the precarious Luri intrusion into Dareh Nasab. When would the next sodden hamlet slip into oblivion, its demise hastened by the erosive effects of farming? When would God conspire to snuff out a camp under a landslide or sweep it away with a flood? Was Khawar's barrenness a symbol of the future of Luri nomadism? Was it a sign that Mohammad Ali's life too would slip away unnoticed, its thread of kinship broken? Would these people, like the ancients who had once occupied their slopes, eventually disappear without trace into the muddy waters that course toward the desert wastes far beyond and below?

Once again we had departed too suddenly, leaving a hollow sensation of having missed a satisfactory closure. Still, I thought that I would be back another time to carry out my long-range plans. I knew that if I did return, it would not be in the company of a camp of nomadic pastoralists. My companions, if any, would be fellow archaeologists, hoping to build on what I had learned.

We remounted without another look back into the shadows of Dareh Nasab and started our descent down the other side, along a slope that was already warm with the heat of the sun.

Chapter 16

The Situation of the Nomads in the Twentieth Century

That last night in Dareh Nasab, I ruminated on my experiences and impressions and what I had learned about the nomads from my visits to many camps and from the migration. The next day, when we stopped in Darayi, I wrote down my reflections, which were purely personal observations about the lives of pastoral nomads.

As Iran developed its transportation, communication, education, and industry, creating new jobs and opportunities for higher standards of living, nomadic life suffered a corresponding decline. Partly by design and partly as an unforeseen consequence of national development, this decline directly affected nearly a tenth of the country's population. To the pastoral population we could add a similar number of settled tribal people, whose traditional subsistence farming was likewise imperiled during the transition toward a progressive industrial economy. Clearly industrial progress was in the long-range interests of the country, but in Iran, as in all countries, there were human problems that attended rapid development.

Major changes took place in the twentieth century. First, the nomads were brought under government control through the use of force, intrigue, and the confiscation of arms. The effect of this was to usher in an era of peace for a people who had been in constant conflict with neighboring tribes and other intruders into tribal territory. But peace was not an unequivocal blessing, nor was the settlement that attended it. Both led quickly to a rise in population: young men were no longer killed in numbers, and camps could remain securely settled seasonally. As new lands were put to the plow, people could raise sufficient food to feed the young and store their crops against want. In both the mountain camps and in the villages, populations began to grow. At first the tribal people considered this welcome, because large families provided security and labor.

Equally important were the new roads through Luristan and the government's ability to secure them from nomadic depredations. This made markets accessible to the nomads, who soon discovered more and more products to buy for cash. The nomads accordingly began to sell more of their flocks. In time they came to value the cash income more than they did the animals, so they largely gave up eating their own stock. With a corresponding rapid decimation of wild game, the nomads were left to rely upon poultry to satisfy their taste for meat.

Although the nomads had to give up eating lamb except on special occasions, peace among the tribes of Luristan afforded them the opportunity to farm and thus to do away with acorn bread, except in times of famine. They were able to buy tea and sugar, which they rarely had in the old days. Thus, over the last hundred years, nomadic diets changed dramatically. The nomads agreed that there was more variety in their diet, although by Western standards it was still unrelentingly bland and boring. Whether the changes resulted in better nutrition is a matter that needs study.

During my visit, in 1973, the Lurs spoke little of these changes. What concerned them was their effects: a lack of manpower—paradoxically, because of overpopulation—and a reduction in the available land. These factors struck at the very foundation of viable pastoral nomadism. Among nomads there was more manpower when the populations were smaller. When the people were few, the herds of each family could be larger, and there was more wild game and arable land. Under those conditions, extra manpower could be used to good advantage in herding, farming, and fighting. As long as there were large herds and plentiful wild resources, extra people were useful and desirable. However, with overpopulation there was a chronic shortage of manpower because the family herds were too small to support persons who did not contribute directly and consistently to subsistence and the daily routine tasks. Young men, therefore, departed for the city. The situation worsened when game and other wild resources were depleted through overharvesting. And finally, large populations were subject to greater hazards during drought, disease, and blizzards, because on the crowded ranges there was less chance to escape local conditions through mobility.

Rising populations, therefore, were at the crux of many problems, but equally important were changes outside the immediate sphere of the nomads. Most important were the rapidly developing markets, which offered a range of goods to tempt even the most traditional nomad. To buy these goods, nomads sold their animals (and hence some of their food); and they bought more than they could carry. When numerous bulky commodities are introduced into a nomadic camp, they considerably reduce its ability to move. It was a cruel paradox. As the nomads acquired goods that eased their way of life and provided them with both comfort and some luxury, they found they could not afford either the animals or the manpower to transport the goods. Not only were pack animals expensive to buy, they were expensive to keep: they had to be fed grain seasonally, and the rest of the year they competed with the herds for grass. The same was true for the extra people a camp would have to maintain in order to handle the chores on the trail: their keep would be expensive.

Perhaps those problems would have been accommodated internally, if it were not for three other factors: the availability of employment for the *homsa*, education, and military conscription. It became common for tribesmen on hard times to take wage labor in towns and cities, and many of those men never returned to the camps. But it was education that was draining off the young manpower. Once the boys had been through elementary school, they eschewed nomadic life for the promise of a sinecure in a government office. The schools taught, not the arts of animal husbandry, but the values of modern Persian society, and with them, the means of escaping nomadism. Military service removed many young men from their tribal lands and exposed them to the world beyond.

If we looked beyond nomadism to the village sector of tribal life, we would find similar processes at work. With increasing population, land reform villagers were cultivating plots farther and farther from their villages, and they were actually founding new villages in former pastures like Dareh Nasab. Thus the available grazing land was further reduced, and there was increased pressure on wild resources, especially oaks, which could provide emergency rations. Moreover, plowing loosened the soil on fragile hillsides, leading to erosion and landslides.

The crowning blow was the government policy of appropriating favorable land for large-scale agribusinesses. That policy removed the tribal populations, whether they were farmers or nomads, and replaced them with plantations and wage laborers. In addition, there were measures to conserve forests and soil in pure pastureland, and to mitigate silting of the new reservoirs—those measures also resulted in the expulsion of tribal peoples from their lands.

Nomads and outsiders

As I reflected that night on nomadism and on tribal life, those changes seemed to me to be at the root of the nomads' plight. None of the problems was of the nomads' conscious making; most were imposed directly or indirectly by the government. The nomads' reactions to the changes, however, were a direct outcome of their traditional training and style of life. Traditional training had shaped their modes of thought and behavior toward people outside the tribal system. The nomads ordinarily came into contact with two well-defined groups of outsiders: merchants or shopkeepers in local towns, and government officials.

When Sekandar and I were traveling by Jeep, we had a driver, Reza, who was from Dezful. Among the nomads who wintered on the Khuzistan plain, where Dezful was the principal market town, there was a profound dislike of Dezfulis. When we visited tents and camps of nomads, Reza was always the butt of jokes, which he accepted either in silence or with good-natured resignation. He did not himself speak Luri, although he understood a fair amount. The joking emphasized that the nomads thought Dezfulis were cowardly and untrustworthy. The nomads said that, during the heyday of nomadism, tribesmen would stride through Dezful, taking what they wanted at gunpoint—and this proved that the city folk were cowardly. The nomads also felt that they were certain to be cheated when they dealt with a Dezfuli merchant, and they would travel long distances to trade elsewhere. In fact, merchants from Kermanshah, which is in Kurdi territory, had a much higher reputation for honesty than the Dezfulis. We found this to be true in camps of Arabs, Kurds, and Lurs, all of whom had learned through painful experience and the fanning of legend over campfires. In addition, Dezful has long had a reputation as a bastion of fanatical religious conservatism. Feelings of similar intensity were not expressed about any of the other cities that nomads visit.

Although the tribal people mistrusted outsiders—especially those from the city, whom they regard as effete, dishonest, and rapacious—still they relished visits to the cities. In Dezful, Khorramabad, Shiraz, and Isfahan, the streets were full of nomads in season. They eagerly crowded the bazaars in search of cloth, jewelry, harness equipment, and utensils. They walked in twos or threes, erect and proud in tribal dress, observing with awe and interest the things for sale and the goings on, like country boys walking through Manhattan. But the nomads always left. Their homes were their tents, their thoroughfares were mountain trails, their city of lights was a cluster of campfires, and their wages were in the animals they tended.

The second group of outsiders that nomads came into contact with—directly or indirectly—was government officials. The officials were not tribesmen, but to the point that it suited their purposes, they learned the art of tribal politics. For as long as history records, officials had played on the nomads' sense of honor in order to cheat them out of their holdings and lure them into ambush.

I repeatedly heard stories of how, two generations ago, when the Lurs still had military pretensions and the government was trying to break their power, tribal leaders were brought to council to reach agreements that were sealed with an oath on the Koran. Tribal leaders considered these oaths sacred and obeyed them. The officials saw them only as a tool of policy and broke them at will. With much bitterness, I was told how time after time tribal leaders had been brought to the city on promise of safe passage to conclude agreements between the tribes and the government, and I heard how these leaders, lured by the sacred oaths, were summarily hanged or sent to prison in the most remote parts of the country. Similar ruses were still being employed in the 1970s to separate the nomads from their land.

Among government officials, there was a subgroup that nomads were particularly concerned with: the secret police (SAVAK). Most nomads had never come in contact with the secret police, but they were aware of them. As we traveled through western Iran, we often questioned people about modern and past conditions of herds, farming, health, changes in population, and the like. Sometimes responses to our questions were made in guarded language because, it was universally said, conditions had gotten worse—but to admit this was to imply criticism of the government.

One time, when a man said that health had declined because the people were using vegetable oils in cooking, others around the fire quickly hushed the speaker. Having broached the subject, however, the man was determined to speak his mind. To the great and obvious discomfort of all, the man let us know that it was the Shah himself who had promulgated the importation of vegetable oil to take the place of animal fat. (This was like the difference between refined lard and vegetable shortening.) The men around the fire were concerned because the man had accused the government of contributing to the problems of the people. They were certain that this indiscretion would become known—perhaps even via a secret informer in their small group.

As far as I know, nothing happened to this forthright man, whom we saw again after some months, but government officials of any kind alarmed the nomads. They had no sense of what to expect of officials except what was based on rumor, and they had no effective means of countering arbitrary abuse. This was largely because there were no structural links between the tribal people and the government. Each poor nomad or farmer saw himself as an isolated individual, without rights or recourse, before the full weight of the government. The people might ridicule officials in coarse joking among trusted friends and relatives, but not to their faces.

Their reflexive mistrust of outsiders was partly due to the nomads' isolation and lack of experience. In part, however, it was because tribal life, in its emasculated form, had no way to aid its people in dealing with others. The tribes had no power nor any leaders who could help them negotiate the difficult transition from traditional tribal isolation to modern commercial and political integration into the mainstream of Iranian society.

An outsider's perspective on the nomadic life

It might seem fair to ask, "Why are nomads conservative and traditional?" "Why don't they adapt to changing conditions?" and "Why don't they help themselves?" There are many facile answers to such questions, but they come only from an outsider's point of view. The question is not why nomads don't do something else, but rather, what do the Lurs prize in life? And, what are their expectations as Lurs?

Nomads are at the same time highly disciplined and notably disorganized; they work hard, yet their work is sloppy; they depend on animals, yet they treat them roughly; they live a hard, active life, but prize above all inactivity and comfort; they suffer from the misfortunes brought by nature, yet they stoically accept these as the hand of God: when misfortune is caused by man they suffer passionately from the injustice. Paradoxes like these pervade nomadic life, but they hardly seem incongruous to a nomad. When I perceive paradoxes, I link events, activities, and attitudes in a way that would never occur to a nomad. I judge them in my terms, not theirs, and in so doing perhaps make them much less than they are.

Nomadic discipline stems from the series of necessary tasks that must be carried out each day. The herds must go to the pastures, food must be prepared, firewood gathered and water drawn from a spring, animals must be guided through the fields and returned safely to camp, the tents must be made secure each evening, and so on. To meet the elementary needs of animals and people, the nomads must discipline themselves.

People raised in an urban industrial setting often do not appreciate the demands animals put on the people who keep them. From afar it might look as if the farmer or herder can do just about whatever he wants to when he wants to. A farmer is not under any such illusions. According to an old joke, someone once asked a dairy farmer, "What is the difference between dairying and being in jail?" The farmer replied, "In jail you don't have to milk the damn cows."

The work is unrelenting, but it need not be carried out with either dispatch or notable efficiency. A shepherd can be sloppy, taking naps when he should be watching; the animals can be rounded up and counted only after nightfall makes it difficult to find any stragglers or strays; mules can be caught at great risk to life and limb by tricking them into sniffing salt; the tents can have baggage strewn about them; and there can be daily indecision about where to pack particular things during migration. None of these things makes any particular difference in the outcome of life. Each person can be an individual, he can procrastinate when he wishes, and he can avoid tasks until the last moment so long as he eventually gets his jobs done. Freedom from routine is in just these personal peccadillos. And a lot of recreation comes in the crisis of having to recapture what was lost during pleasant hours of procrastination. To solve daily crises and to savor the sensations of fear that accompany them takes the place of vicarious enjoyment through TV or film and engages the mind and body in a brief but satisfying resolution of disorder.

It is hardly necessary to remark that nomads depend on their animals. In a strict sense they are the central component in their economic success, both for the food and goods they provide and for the transport they afford. It is probably only paradoxical to a city person, therefore, that animals are not treated with sympathy. Among the nomads, animals are a resource very much like trees are to a nurseryman. They are to be consciously propagated, kept safe from predators, and then harvested and sold. They are recognized individually, but they are part of a forest of similar things whose only rationale for being is to serve humans. The animals are useful only when they do what their owners want them to do. They will be beaten if they fail to keep up on the trail or if they stumble and lie down.

In their daily work, the nomads are physically active. Members of both sexes are accustomed to carrying heavy loads, walking long distances over difficult terrain, being exposed to the weather, coping with lack of sleep, and so on. They do these things because they are necessary, not because they are ennobling. A man may take pride in his endurance, but he is not likely to want to test it.

Routine occupations in most nomadic camps proceed in spite of the vicissitudes of nature. Searing, scorching heat and drought are expected. So are blizzards and gale-force winds. So are fine days and nights and pastures overfilled with grass. So are bumper crops of lambs and kids. And so are devastating diseases. The nomads' lives fluctuate between prosperity and catastrophe under forces over which they have no control. These swings of the pendulum are expectable, if not precisely predictable, and they are accepted. God may be implored to make things better, and nomads may question their own fallibility when things are worse, but they accept God's wrath along with his blessing. These are not things that one can control. But nomads worry about what other men can and might do to them. Will there be a raid? Why is so-and–so marrying his daughter to so-and–so? Is it to create an alliance against us? Why did Morad Khan lease our land to a camp from another tribe? What can we do when a girl from our camp is beaten by her husband in another camp? These kinds of questions are continually being asked and discussions of their possible answers occupy much of the conversation over the campfire. It is the social world that is of immediate and compelling interest. God's ways are inscrutable and immutable, but man is prejudged to be dishonest and can and must be counteracted. The loss of a flock in a blizzard is an act of God, but the loss of a pasture through political intrigue is the act of a devious personality—a man who can be reached by bullet if not through political intrigue and social pressure. Talk of violence runs close to the surface when men are being discussed, and this talk is reinforced by action often enough to be taken seriously.

In nomad life, there are demands on young and old of both sexes for constant activity. It seemed that no one was ever completely relaxed. They were always either doing or anticipating. In fact, in nomad life there is little leisure as we understand its meaning, nor are there many formal activities for relaxation, such as games and parties. Somewhat surprisingly, of all the peoples on earth, hunters and gatherers seem to have the greatest amount of pure leisure—time which is theirs to spend as they see fit with no pressures to do anything in particular. They may spend only a few hours a day in the food quest. Uneducated nomads whom I employed on the excavation of Tula'i after the migration were quite positive about the inhuman demands of steady employment. With a job to which they were supposed to report at a given hour, followed by eight hours of labor—and then, in the midst of work, to quit at the appointed time—the nomads found themselves psychologically hemmed in. Work at a steady job was certainly no salvation, even though it did provide needed wages.

Although nomads worked long hours every day, they scheduled their own activities and they were not constrained to associate with or to work for people for any motive other than respect, convenience, or friendship. If they did not like a situation, often they left it. But more importantly, as nomads, they were trained to expect such a life. No nomad was trained from childhood to be a laborer or to work under a nontribal boss, separated from the kinship and security of the tribe and family.

As discussed, the hard work in nomadism is not entirely unrelenting. Nomads are also accustomed to long periods of relative inactivity when they are herding animals, which require observation but not much attention. Perhaps it is for this reason that nomads who go into town for wage labor frequently take on tasks, which, aside from requiring little skill, make few demands for a particular schedule. For many years, nomads of both Luri and Kurdi origin have been employed as porters (*hamals*) in cities and towns where goods are still moved by human carriers.

In years past, being a nomad was one's birthright and future. Men married, hoped for many sons, and prayed for increase of the flocks. When his home was threatened, a man defended it. When a life was taken, a nomad sought revenge or blood money in recompense. It was a self-contained and self-sustaining system where the values of life were clear. Prestige went to the successful sire, provider, and protector. A man could hope for no more than to build a strong family foundation for his sons to enlarge. It was the custom for sons to carry on and to provide and care for the father, so that he might enjoy his later years as a respected elder.

It is paradoxical that this is still the ideal. It is paradoxical because today a man cannot provide an inheritance for many sons: the flocks are too small and the land too crowded. It is paradoxical because the youth no longer see the nomadic life as one of opportunity. It is paradoxical because the elders no longer receive the respect due them, and their later years are often filled with bitterness and privation.

Nomadism is no longer either self-contained or self-sufficient. There are government taxes, censuses, military draft, usurpation of land, and school. And there are appointed officials to adjudicate disputes and to make decisions. By the late twentieth century, tribal nomadism had become a relict preserved in its remoteness, carrying out a fossil form of society governed by an archaic set of values, respected and lived by an ever-dwindling number of migratory pastoralists.

Several years ago, Fred Gearing wrote an essay in which he took a deep look at another tribal people, the Fox Indians who live near Tama, Iowa, in the United States. In a poignant tale of how he learned to understand the Fox, Gearing wrote of Fox traditional life in the modern context.

> I came to be persuaded that a satisfying life in any small and semi-autonomous community requires the systematic arrangements of tasks carried out by men in a coherent system of social positions. A human lifetime in such a society is a movement through these positions, a performance in sequence of these tasks. The meaning of each task is made evident by its coherent place in the large design. Traditionally, being a hunter was meaningful because one's wife

> and children were not hunters, and because one was once a boy who could not hunt and would become an old man who would not need to hunt.

The shape of the nomadic environment

The environment and its resources lie at the heart of adaptation. The ranges of Bala Griveh rise from the plain of Khuzistan in stair-step fashion to the central plateau. Elevations range from 200 meters to over 2500 meters. There is relatively little flat land, while steep slopes and rocky soils are typical. Water emanates from a few springs and rivers, some of which are seasonal. Trails across the ridges follow natural passes, which can be tortuous to traverse.

There are sufficient natural resources to enable human survival within a range that can be walked in a matter of days: various grasses and vegetables; trees and shrubs; stone for construction; acorns, pistachios, walnuts, cherries, and almonds in season, as well as vegetables, truffles, medicinal plants, pitch, aromatic gums, and reeds for baskets and mats; rare flint for stone tools; and meat, hides, and hair from domestic and wild animals. In short, with even a low level of technology, the basics of sustaining life are available.

If we look closely at the natural sources, we find that they are pliable and irregular in shape and form. The trunks and branches of trees and plants; stems and stalks of grass and reed; the curl and wave of hair and wool; the natural enclosure and conformability of hide or skin; the many shapes of stone; the texture and moisture of soil and gravel; the abrasive flow of water and wind; the four-legged mobility of the stock; the leafy nourishment of vegetables and herbs; the acorns and seeds of grain; the honey and sap. There is no rigidity in any of these in form, local distribution, quality, or use. These things are where they are and are used as needed. They are not stockpiled or propagated. God has provided them for use.

The people are likewise supple in their adaptability: they are lithe, lean, and agile. They delight in leisure and comfort but are undismayed by hard work and discomfort. When they plan, they know their plans are likely to change to accommodate the unexpected. They tend to the vicissitudes even as they bend to the irregularities of the land and the burdens they bear.

The same is true of the objects they craft. The tents are woven of goat hair and supported by stout poles, which are carefully joined in sections so that they conform to the sharply turning trails and the animals that will bear them. The reed screens are modules to enable packing and balancing them on animal backs. A tent lashed securely on a donkey is a shifting, creaking, stretching, compressing, organic mantle, which reacts to the movements of the beast.

The rigid containers of metal compete with the curves of muscle and the fluidity of motion; they gouge the flesh and cut the bands. They are foreign to this environment. On the trail, attention to detail is quietly obliterated: the landscape tears, jolts, punctures, and rips all that passes through it. Rain turns gear sodden and sun bleaches what cannot be covered. Compulsive care in these circumstances is not a luxury; it is not even thinkable.

In these circumstances, people must make their own trappings and be responsible for moving them when herds need fresh pastures. Their clothes are minimal, durable, and adaptable to quickly changing conditions. The felted cloaks protect against the sun, wind, rain, and cold; they can be used as a bag and serve as ground cloth or blanket. Trousers are basically of one design: loose-fitting, baggy, and capable of being rolled at the waist to shorten or lengthen them. Loose-fitting shirts and felt skullcaps complete men's garb. Women's skirts become dresses over their baggy trousers, and their heads are covered with loose-fitting turbans. Both sexes often go without shoes, allowing their calluses to absorb the punishment of the terrain.

Women carry their infants in cloth slings on their backs as they go about their household chores. Large bags of loose netting enclose metal pots and pans on the backs of animals, and they are used to carry straw from the fields. Chickens are transported in elongate wicker baskets, which are tied atop donkey loads of household goods. Thus ensconced, the birds can breathe, while the baskets yield to the strain of rocking, pitching sideways, and the constant abrasion of the shifting cords.

Coarse carpets and carrying bags for salt, flour, and grain are woven at crude vertical looms, while tent covers are woven on narrow horizontal looms staked out on the ground. When tents are erected, the meter-wide strips are joined together with wooden pegs to form the tent cover. Inside the tents, women make the cords of goat hair and horsehair that tie the animals, bind loads, and hold down tents.

The nomads bend to the land, the climate, and the peculiarities of their resources in a kind of benign opportunism. It is accepted that fussiness and precision are incompatible with need and opportunity. We see the same attitude in political relations. In the power plays between tribes there is a strong element of drama, which is acted out in lieu of destructive action and serves to defuse acquiescence on the part of the subservient. A momentary loss is perceived as a chance happenstance, which will be rectified with the next toss of the political dice. Ethical rigidity rather than practical principle would be destructive. Bending but not breaking, yielding without suffering heavy loss, remaining pragmatic rather than standing uselessly defiant: These are qualities of tribal people, and they seem consistent with their lives, the nature they suffer, and the materials they employ.

Rough is the texture of nomad life. The earth itself, modified by mass wasting, which converts mountains to slopes of scree, bears the scars of landslips, the folding and contorting of sedimentary basins, the pitting and eroding of exposed rock, the tough stubble that grows in meager soil, the scraggly bush with its grabbing thorns, the crooked oaks and bushy almonds. The eye searches in vain for a smooth rock, ankles deflect the ripping thorn and scuffing rock. A nomad's skin knows not the softening effect of warm water, soap, and oils. The wind and the open fire are drying towels. Rough too, is the texture of a nomad.

These are cracked and callused hands that tug on the bindings and tie the ropes, that gather the firewood, that herd the animals. The sprains, the bruises, the cramps, and the aches are ignored. Fatigue is a hardship to which one grows inured, as one defies the cold north wind, the freezing slush on bare feet, the steady pelting of icy rain. The enervating heat, the crackling thirst, and the swarms of flies pass with the day and relief of night is sufficient rejuvenation. Famine, disease, and accidents are expected and lamented, but serve only as reminders that people are not mortal and by God's grace alone will survive.

We may liken nomads and their society to the cords that shape and restrain their material lives. Like a rope, a nomad is supple, capable of stretching and rarely breaking. The families in a camp are bound together in mutual support reinforced by a network of marriages and alliances. The tribes too are much like the shifting load on a donkey—a house of cloth whose bindings require constant attention lest the load shift and split apart.

The nomad builds his house on the firm foundation of heredity and reinforces it through marriage. The nomad's house is built not on lines of stone, but on lines of kinship. A nomad without heredity is a nomad without a home. Without family, friends, and allies there is no life.

Chapter 17

A History of the Baharvand

by

Sekandar Amanolahi-Baharvand

and Frank Hole

In Chapter 3, we gave a brief overview of what is known historically about Luristan. In this chapter we focus specifically on the history of the Baharvand tribe, based on interviews and documents compiled by Sekandar Amanolahi-Baharvand. In 1972 and 1973, Sekandar traveled widely in Luristan for his dissertation research. Using published accounts, records, and manuscripts that he obtained, and dozens of interviews with elder members of his and related tribes, he has compiled an authoritative history of the Baharvand (Amanolahi-Baharvand 1975). Tribal history centers on individuals and land, for there is no tribe without genealogical continuity or territory.

The migration in 1973 was a mere two weeks out of a centuries-long continuum of pastoral nomadic life in Luristan. While the essence of pastoralism—moving seasonally with herds of livestock—has not changed, the lives of the pastoralists have changed, and dramatically. Although Luristan is a rugged landscape and relatively isolated geographically from more prosperous areas, it has also been affected by elements outside the control of the nomads. The processes of consolidation and fluctuation of political and military power, as well as the forces of economics and the global economy, have all penetrated Luristan, as they have virtually all parts of the world. Morad Khan's tents are a physical manifestation of ancient ways, which belie the transformation of the lives of their inhabitants. While pastoral nomadism may be as old as the initial domestication of sheep and goats, over the millennia there may have been little biological continuity in the herders. Thus the Lurs, Bakhtiari, Kurds, and others may be latecomers to a succession of herding people in the modern territories. What has not changed is the immutable demand of herds for pasture, regardless of who is controlling them.

The history of nomadism in Iran has been exhaustively researched and documented by Daniel Potts, who believes that the modern practice of seasonal transhumance has a relatively short history and is dependent on horses and agriculture. "That a nomadic element was present throughout much of continental Iran by the mid- to late first millennium B. C., however, seems clear" (Potts 2014:119). His account is based on historical texts and his belief that, given the lack of horses and agriculture (which he sees as essential to the nomadic way of life), seasonal transhumance could not have obtained in the remote past. This is a questionable basis for asserting the impossibility of alternative ways of life. Moreover, it does not take into account the vast changes in the landscape itself. What we see today is only a vestige of what may have obtained in the remote past, both environmentally and socially.

Whether or not Potts is correct, it is equally true that there are no written records of nomadic life that extend into the deep past, because most nomads were illiterate. This is not to say that all tribesmen were illiterate, but we have no records of any writing by them. Tribes are mentioned at least to the time of Herodotus (about 450 BC), but it is only in the nineteenth century that we find any direct mention of the tribes of Luristan, and these accounts are more in the nature of military assessments or anecdotal observations of Western travelers and surveyors (see Chapter 3). Still, over the centuries, the people of Luristan have been caught up in the pulses of conflict between regional and international entities, whose hegemony involved tribute, military conscription, agro-irrigation settlement, land reform, development of infrastructure, opening of the economy, education, and more.

There are clues that things have not always been the same in Luristan. During the migration we passed a number of ruins. Some were recent, such as the *caravanserais* and gendarme posts that were to guard the commercial caravan route across the mountains. They were accompanied by small settlements for the guards. After the construction of a highway, they were no longer needed. More important for the question of the origins of nomadism, and in particular of the Baharvand, are the ancient sites. Some of these are quite extensive, including the one in Chin-i Zal, where vaulted rooms still stand and canals and agricultural terraces are obvious. Throughout our trek we encountered other examples of similar structures and traces of canals. Our informants had no knowledge of or interest in them. Nevertheless, they signify a time—perhaps centuries long—when there was intensive agriculture and possibly year-round settlements in Luristan.

One cannot help being struck by the expertise and labor required to build these irrigation systems. There is stark contrast with the reluctance or ineptitude of the nomads when faced with merely cleaning out a spring. Clearly the ancient builders had skills not possessed by the current occupants of the land. Where did they acquire these skills? Contemporaneously, large-scale irrigation systems were built under "imperial" direction in Deh Luran and Khuzistan, potential sources of skill and labor (Adams 1962, 2006; Neely 1974; Wenke 1976). The circumstances that allowed expenditure on the relatively small-scale potential of Luristan is not known. The size of the systems we saw implies "niche construction," undertaken, not at imperial direction, but locally (Wilkinson et al. 2012). These systems resemble the small-scale ones on the Deh Luran plain rather than the massive structures seen in Khuzistan and Mesopotamia. Perhaps such rural extensions could have tapped the potential of the region for rearing livestock, to provide animal products for consumption both in the mountains and in the settlements of the lower plains (Panahipour 2019). Whatever the case, the expected payoff was agricultural products. Who built them?

Another mystery is, what happened to the settlements? As far as Luristan is concerned, this is a Dark Age. Since Potts' book focuses on the history of nomads in Iran and is an exhaustive review of all available literature, one might expect Luristan to be mentioned for the centuries following the demise of the Sasanian Empire. It is not. What seems clear is that the land and people of Iran were impacted repeatedly by incursions from the north, as well as the needs of local governors and kings. However, most of this concerns the northern parts of Iran or Fars in the south. Grazing and agricultural lands were prized, while the mountain fastness of much of the Zagros received little attention. As a result, herders of various ethnicities occupied the interstices, free to form their own alliances and forms of governance. It is likely that tribes themselves, as mutual protection organizations, developed most fully when the nomads were under duress. They were generally regarded as unstable, fragmented, and adaptive, but always seeking advantage; hence constant feuds and warfare among the tribes.

In the midst of what might be considered anarchy, as tribes and central governments vied to control the land and its products, the history of the Baharvand tribe comes into focus. The only written account of the Baharvand is Sekandar's dissertation (Amanolahi-Baharvand 1975), a synopsis of which follows. As we will see, Baharvand history, as well as that of other tribes, depends very much on individuals who gain advantage over others. Like the histories of competing regimes, rulers, and governors across Iran, the history of the Baharvand is a story, written on a small stage, of precisely the same behavior at the tribal level.

History of the Baharvand

In the following pages, we discuss the expansion of the Baharvand from a small lineage to a powerful tribe and its subsequent history. The name of the tribe is derived from a man named Bahar (spring) who lived some 360 years ago, contemporaneous with the Safavid Dynasty (AD 1499–1735).

The early period (AD 1550–1830)

According to Baharvand oral history, Bahar was the grandson of Sabzvar, who was a member of the Kalhor, a Kurdish tribe from Kermanshah. Due to a feud, Sabzvar left his tribe, migrated to Luristan, and settled in Robat Village, north of Khorramabad (Figure 17.1). Sabzvar's son was Karam, who was the father of Bahar. Bahar left Robat and went to Dirak, a powerful tribal chief of the Dirkavand tribe whose summer territory was in Dareh Nasab, south of Khorramabad. Because Bahar was a capable young man, Dirak married him to his daughter. After that he became Dirak's deputy and consultant regarding tribal events. The descendants of Bahar continued to spend the summer in Dareh Nasab. They used Varun Mahur in Korki, north of Chin-i Zal, for their winter territory. Toward the end of the Early Period (i.e. early 1800s), the descendants of Bahar ceased migrating to Dareh Nasab and remained in Varun

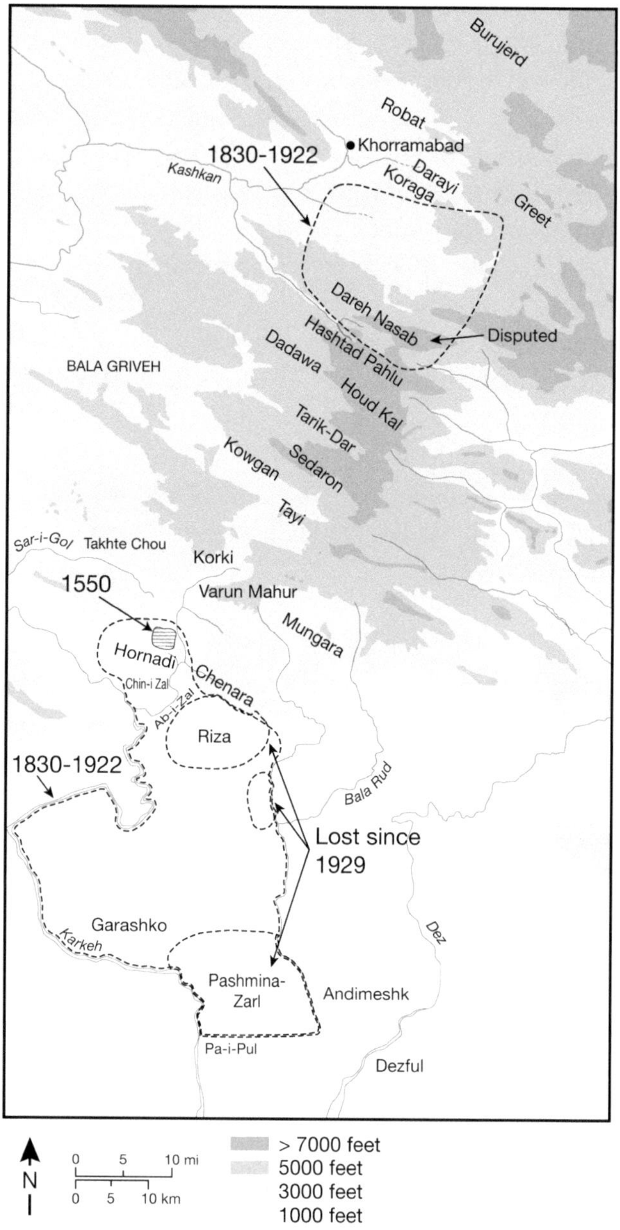

Figure 17.1. Territories held and lost by the Baharvand tribe in Bala Griveh since 1830. The place names are in the native dialect and refer to mountains and valleys that are important in tribal history.

Mahur the entire year. Their campsite, known as Zar Malga, was where their herding and agricultural activities remained year-round.

The descendants of Bahar remained in Varun Mahur until 1830, after which they divided into two small lineages: Maralivan (Moradalivand), the descendants of Moradali, and Kurdalivand, the descendants of Kurdali.

Dynasties: anarchy and insecurity

Prior to the Qajar Dynasty, the Lurs of Luristan established a local dynasty known as Atabakan. That was replaced in 1596 by the Safavid Dynasty, who installed the Wali Dynasty (1597–1929). The *wali* (governor) was in charge of Luristan and maintained peace and security. Unfortunately, anarchy and insecurity became prevalent during the Qajar Dynasty (1796–1925). However, once the Qajar took control of Iran, they divided the *wali*'s territory and limited his rule to Pusht-i Kuh (currently known as Ilam province), while Pish-i Kuh (now referred to as Luristan province) was ruled by the Qajar princes. Corruption and mismanagement by these princes caused tribal revolt and anarchy in Luristan, and in 1915 the central government lost control of the province. During this time, each tribe had to fight for its security, territorial integrity, and its overall survival. As the Luri say, "Might is right's brother" or "Might and right are brothers," which describes the political condition of Luristan at that time. The Luri refer to this period as *Dowray-i khadsar*, meaning "Do as you like."

Under the situation of anarchy, the survival, expansion, or the decline of a tribe depended not only on competent, judicious, and brave leadership, but also the availability of an able fighting force. The number of fighters increased through natural procreation as well as the incorporation of men from other tribes. Judicious leadership, along with the able fighting forces and the semi-democratic nature of the Baharvand tribe, led to territorial expansion, but also the conquest or absorption of members of the other tribes that joined willingly. While the descendants of Bahar formed the core of the tribe, and held leadership and the ownership of the tribal territory, the population of the non-Baharvand, who had become attached to the Baharvand, increased significantly. They formed the majority in some sections of the Baharvand. The non-Baharvand are known collectively as *homsa*, which literally means neighbor, but with the connotation that they are the "followers."

Survival and prosperity of the tribe depended on fair treatment and protection of the followers, who were necessary for tribal survival. Leaders who displayed benevolent behavior became popular and attracted more followers. On the contrary, those who treated the *homsa* badly would lose them. For instance, the son of one of the leaders, who wanted to have his own camp separately, asked his father to allow some of the *homsa* to join him. His father, who was aware of his son's irascibility and his mistreatment of the *homsa*, told him, "I will allow ten families to camp with you, but I doubt if they will remain with you for too long!" While in their summer territory, the son established his camp separately, with ten families around him. However, within eight months, nine families had fled and joined another tribe. When he migrated from the winter territory to the summer territory, he was accompanied by one family only!

I asked about the behavior of this man, who passed away a couple of decades ago. I was told that he was too arrogant and mistreated his followers. He treated them like a bunch of servants; his behavior was so intolerable that people avoided him.

Historical evidence from Luristan clearly shows that anarchy and insecurity resulted in political intensification among the tribes and tribal leaders. It was so because a tribe's integrity and survival were under constant threat. Under these circumstances, political alliances provided mutual support for common goals concerning offense and defense. Alliances took place within the sections of a tribe or between tribes, either through marriage ties, or under threat of a common enemy, or simply because of common interest. Nevertheless, political alliances between the tribes often shifted as circumstances changed. Thus, when tribes were threatened by the armed forces of the central government in 1915, they became united despite the enmity between some of them, and they wiped out the governmental forces. True to form, however, some tribes and tribal sections allied with the central government when it was to their advantage.

In order to indicate the significance of politics on tribal affairs, let us review the case of the Saki tribe. The Saki tribe, under the leadership of Husain Khan, had made an alliance with the governor of Luristan and the Baharvand, who had become the strongest tribe of the Bala Griveh. Husain Khan first made an alliance with the governor of Luristan and then with the Mir tribe. Thus, the Saki and Mir tribes managed the Zal Valley. However, later on, a dispute between the two tribes over land led to a conflict. Husain Khan, who was supported by the governor of Luristan and the Baharvand, forced the leaders of the Mir tribe to flee to Deh Luran in Pusht-i Kuh. However, in the meantime, Husain Khan committed an intolerable act—dishonoring Gowhar, the wife of the Mir's leader. Gowhar, who was from the Dirkavands, sent her *tara* (scarf tied around the head) to the Baharvand and other Dirkavands, which symbolically meant that if they did not take revenge on Husain Khan, they were women too. Thus, the Baharvand, Qalavand, and other Dirkavands became united against Husain Khan. Eventually Husain Khan was killed and the Saki tribe was dissolved and its members dispersed (Amanolahi 1975:46).

Gradually, from 1830, the Baharvand expanded their territory. They managed to expand their winter territory by taking Raza, Chin-i Zal, and Bidrowa from the Sagvand tribe, who had become weakened by the Saki tribe. Around 1850, the Baharvand territory consisted of Darki, Sar-i-Gol (in Takhcho), Varun Mahur, Hornadi, Chin-i Zal, Raza, and Bidrowa. At that time, the distance between their summer and winter territories was around twenty miles. They migrated around April 10 or 15 from Chin-i Zal to Beringe Kar in Kialon and thence to Sar-i-Gol, only two migration stages away. They remained there for nearly four months. They migrated back to Darki, north of Chin-i Zal, and later returned to the plain of Raza and Chin-i Zal, where they cultivated wheat and barley. The Baharvand expansion to the north began around 1898 (see Figure 17.1).

The period of expansion (1830–1922)

Baharvand political and territorial expansion began around 1830 and continued until 1922, when the armed forces of the central government managed to take control of Luristan. During this period, the Baharvand grew from two small patrilineages into two independent tribes: Moradalivand and Kurdalivand. After this, the term Baharvand became limited to the former. Some decades of expansion followed. According to Wilson (A. T. Wilson 1912:9), the Baharvand (Moradalivand) had become the strongest tribe of the Dirkavand. He estimated that the tribe consisted of one thousand families with a force of one thousand, of which five hundred were armed with rifles.

Socio-political organization

The traditional socio-political organization of the Baharvand was based on kinship—that is, consanguinity or affinity (through marriages). The

Baharvand consisted of unequal patrilineal groups in which the individual's identity, social status, rights, and obligations were determined by membership within his lineage.

The smallest social unit of the Baharvand was the family, consisting of nuclear, patrilineal, extended, joint or incomplete family. The level above the family was *bowa* or *dodomu* (sublineage), consisting of families with a common male ancestor. The next level, known as *tira* (patrilineage), was composed of several sublineages who shared a common male ancestor. The next level was *tayefah* (tribe), which was made up of a number of patrilineages, who were the descendants of Bahar and who formed the core of the tribe. In addition, there were various non-Baharvand patrilineages from other tribal groups who for various reasons had joined the Baharvand. They were known as *homsa*.

Lineages and leaders

During 1898, Baharvand consisted of two tribes: the Maralivand (Maradalivand), the descendants of Marali, and the Kurdalivand, the descendants of Kurdali. Maralivand consisted of five lineages (Figure 17.2). The Keyu lineage was the strongest and had assumed the leadership of the tribe. Keyu had attracted many non-Baharvand and consisted of five lineages known as Panj Boweh Keyu (five lineages of Keyu), which included Amanola (Amandah), Bowak (Babak), Vali, Yaghu (Jafar), and Ahmadvak (Ahmadbak known as Masay). Each of these lineages was a semi-independent unit with its territory and leadership. There was no single leader dominating the leaders of all lineages, and each lineage might have more than one leader. So the leadership within the Baharvand consisted of the total leaders of those lineages who were the descendants of Bahar and formed the core of the tribe. Any decision regarding the Baharvand's affairs had to be made in a gathering (assembly) in the home of the leader, who provided lunch for the guests. The assembly consisted of the leaders of the lineages, along with few members from each lineage. The case was discussed, the leaders expressed their views, and finally a decision was reached, based on a majority consensus.

There were a few leaders from the strongest lineages who were more influential, and they were recognized as the main leaders. For example, in 1898, the following leaders, all of them from the Keyu lineages, were the most influential leaders of the Baharvand:

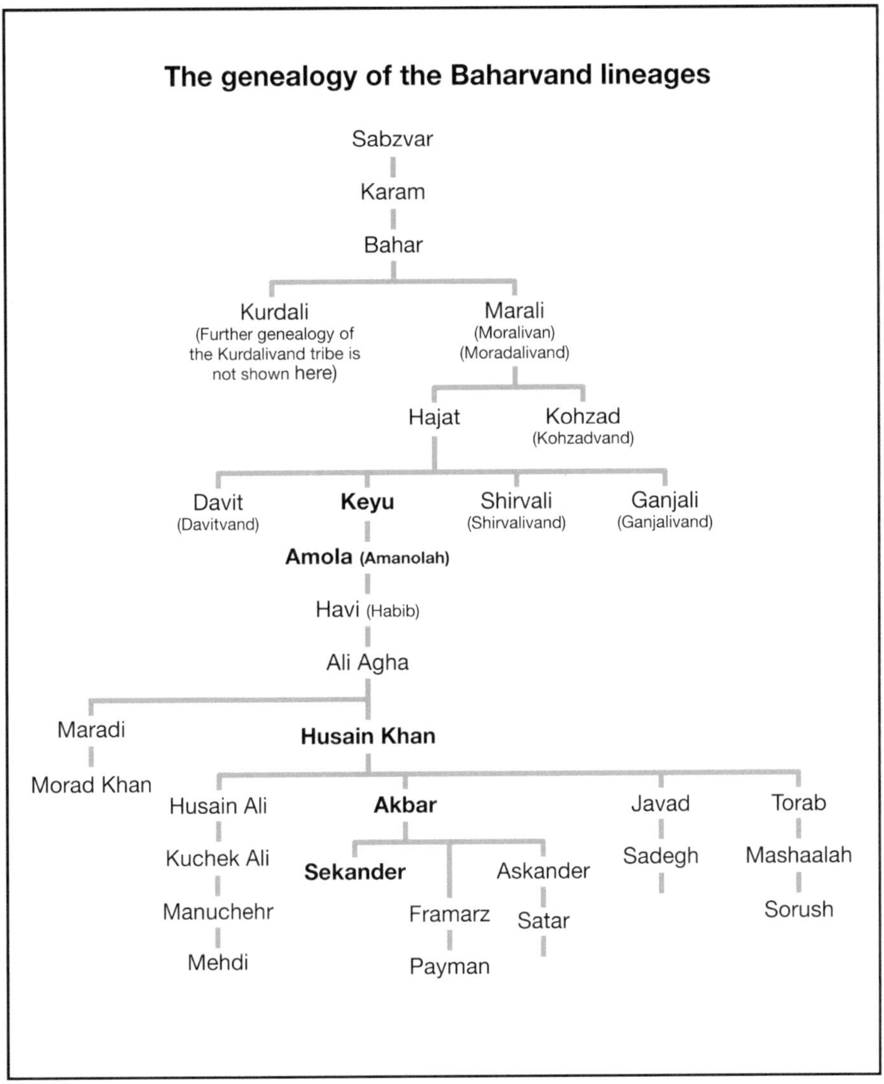

Figure 17.2. An abbreviated genealogy of the Baharvand tribe, which is also the lineage of author Sekandar Amanolahi-Baharvand.

Husain Khan (Amanola, Amandan) = Amola (Amanola)
Barani (Bowak=Babak lineage)
Jafar (Yaghu=Jafar lineage)
Padar (Vali lineage)

Husain Khan's alliances

Traditional tribal society of Luristan included bravery, fighting ability, horsemanship, marksmanship, honesty, tact in social relationships, hospitality, and political cleverness. That is, the ability to maintain political alliance, usually established through consanguinity or affinity ties within or outside of the tribe. Political alliance was for mutual support. The tribal leaders of the Bala Griveh region devoted a great deal of their time to *bai'at bazi*, which means seeking allegiance or making alliances. For instance, Husain Khan (my grandfather), was the leader of the Amola lineage of the Keyu. He was the most influential leader of the Baharvand from 1884 to 1929. He maintained an alliance with the leaders of the Baharvand and established alliances with the leaders of the tribes of the Bala Griveh region through marriages of his sons and daughters. Examples of Husain Khan's alliances follow.

Jadaki tribe. The daughter of the chief of the Agha Mirzayi section was married to Husain Khan's youngest son in settlement of a blood feud. Husain Khan's brother had been killed by the Jadakis.

Ghalavand. The daughter of the chief of the Bash Agha section was married to Husain Khan's son.

Papi. Husain Khan's daughter was married to the son of the chief of the Manasar section.

Sagvand. Husain Khan's daughter was married to the son of the chief of the Ali Khani section, while the daughter of the chief of Rahim Khani was married to Husain Khan's oldest son.

Mir. Husain Khan's daughter was married to the son of the chief of the Mohammad Khani section.

Kurdalivand. The daughter of the chief of the Mahammad Mirza lineage, who was famous for his hospitality, was married to Husain Khan's son (my father).

Husain Khan's daughter was engaged to the son of Mirza Rahim Khan Chagharvand from Khorramabad, who was the governor's deputy (Moein al-Saltaneh) of Luristan.

Territorial expansion in summer territory

The Baharvand movement toward the summer territory in Dareh Nasab took place under the leadership of Barani (Babak lineage) and Husain Khan (Amanolah lineage) around 1895. First, they moved to Tayi and they remained there for five years. Then they moved to Dareh Nasab, their traditional summer territory, which was occupied by the Papi tribe. The Papi tribe occupied Dareh Nasab after Karim Khan Zand, the founder of the Zand Dynasty (1749–1794) took some of the tribes of Luristan, including the Baharvand, with him to Shiraz, but they returned to Luristan after Karim Khan's death. The Baharvand returned to Dareh Nasab, and after heavy fighting, the Papi were forced to leave. After their settlement in Dareh Nasab, the Baharvand attacked the Papi in Taf and occupied that territory as well. Both Dareh Nasab and Taf were divided among the members of Panj Boweh Koyu (five lineages of Keyu). The Kurdalivand and Kahzadvand occupied Chanar Bagali and Baweh west of Dareh Nasab, while Shirvalivand and other smaller lineages (such as Ganjalivand, Haidarvand, and Davitvand) occupied HudKal, Sevtal, and Tarikdar, all located south of Dareh Nasab, behind the Hashtad Pahlu Mountain.

The occupation of Koragah Valley (Khorramabad Valley)

In 1914, the two sections of the Baharvand had become strong enough to become autonomous tribes. The term Baharvand became limited to Moradalivand, while Kurdalivand were referred to by their name. Although the two sections became two independent tribes, they gave support to each other in time of need.

In 1914, a rumor spread that the Bairanvand was expanding its territory and planned to capture Koragah Valley. If they did so, the Baharvand would have a hard time reaching Khorramabad, the main market center and the capital of Luristan. For this and other political and economic reasons, the Moradalivand and Kurdalivand made a preemptory occupation of the valley and divided it into two parts. This division was made at a canal known as Sha-joo or Shah Jooy (King's canal). Kurdalivand took Zir-i Joo, the western part, and the Moradalivand took Posht-i Joo, the eastern section. Moradalivand was divided among the members of Panj Boweh Keyu only: Amola (Amanola) and Vali received two shares (Darayi, Dinarvand, and Sora-Deh), Jafar received one share (Sali and Chu-Tash=Chub-Trash), and Babak received one share (Blailvand and Taluri). The rest of the Moradalivand remained in Dareh Nasab.

The Baharvand had expanded their summer territory in the north, and also they had added to their southern territory (winter territory). The newly won winter territory extended from Raza south to the Deh Luran Road at Pol-i Karkheh. Thus they were in control of a very large territory, bounded on the north by Keyalan, Hornadi, and Chenara Mountains, on the east by Bala-Rud, on the south by Deh Luran Road and Pol-i Kharkha, and on the west by the Saimarra and a boundary beyond Shah Ahmad Kuchic (Amanolahi -Baharvand 1975:43–50). This was the peak of expansion.

The period of forced settlement and detribalization (1922–1980)

The forced settlement and detribalization of the Baharvand and other nomadic pastoralist tribes in Iran resulted from modernization of the national army, a process begun toward the end of the Qajar Dynasty (1794–1925), which was fully developed during the Pahlavi Regime (1925–1978). The modernization of Iran took place under the impact of the scientifically and technologically advanced Western societies. One of the outcomes of this process was the establishment of a strong central government and modernization of the army. The forced settlement of the nomadic tribes took place mainly under the Reza Shah (1925–1941), the founder of the Pahlavi Dynasty (1925–1978). Reza Shah's main goals were to establish a modern centralized and unified state under his absolute rule. Richard Cottam stated, "Reza Shah had two overriding goals that were for him inseparable as to be one and the same thing. He wished to restore some of the greatness of Iran and to establish for himself an absolute power with the reconstructed nation. His pursuit of these goals was determined and ruthless. Any forces that stood in the way of his achievement were mercilessly attacked and, so far as possible, destroyed. Thus, the independence of the tribes, the strength of the landowners, the Qajar court and liberal, democratic ideas—all were subject to his attacks" (Amanolahi-Baharvand 2002:201).

Reza Khan's military campaigns against the tribes of Luristan began in 1922. The history of the seven years of fighting that established government control over all of Luristan is one of shifting alliances among the tribes, some of which resisted, while others embraced the army. A detailed description of this, which is too complex to relate here, is found in "Reza Shah and the Lurs:

the impact of the modern state on Luristan" (Amanolahi-Baharvand 2002). Since the tribes never achieved unity of purpose, the government was able to divide and conquer. While the fighting was sporadic and affected each tribe differently, the result was total domination of Luristan for the first time. This prolonged period of conflict was succeeded by draconian measures designed to emasculate tribal power and integrate the Lurs into the national society of Iran. These events occurred while Atawak and Morad Khan were young men and directly involved in the conflicts.

Policy measures enforced by the Army in 1929

Exile of some of the tribes

Some of the tribes, such as the Mir of the Saimarra region, a section of the Bairavand, the Agha Reza'i of the Sagvand Rahim Kahni, and most of the Sayid (the descendants of the prophet and Imam Ali), were exiled to Khorasan Province, northeast of Iran.

Execution of leaders (1925)

Moein al-Saltaneh (the governor's deputy from Khorramabad) and Shir Mohammad Khan Sagvand, who were closely allied with the government and had served as the governor's deputy and *pishkar* (the adviser to the governor and army, respectively), along with nine other tribal leaders, were executed in Borujerd in 1925. General Khaza'i, under the influence of General Amir Ahmadi—who is known as the Butcher of Luristan—had invited these leaders to Borujerd for negotiation, swearing on the Qu'ran that he guaranteed their safety. However, when they arrived, they were captured, jailed, and eventually executed. General Khaza'i acted according to the traditional Qajar treacheries and unjust executions. Their policies resulted in further bloodshed and the continuation of hostilities between the tribes and the army.

Disarmament of the tribes

Disarmament of the tribes of Luristan started in 1924. However, it actually took place from 1928 onwards, as the army gradually took full control. This was necessary for the state to control and establish peace and security. The state allowed only the *kadkhodas* (heads of the villages) to have guns for the protection of the villagers from intruders and thieves.

Replacement of the khans by military officers

As soon as the army gained power, the tribes came under the military government (Hokumat-e Nezami). Each tribe came under the supervision of a military officer, who resided among the tribe. The military governor replaced the tribal leaders, but the the heads of the sections (*kadkhodas*) were reestablished formally as the representatives of the state, albeit without any salary. The military governor maintained law and order with the assistance of the kadkhodas, while the khans, the most influential and powerful tribal leaders, acted as mediators between the governor and the members of the tribe. In short, the army had total power over the life and property of the peoples of Luristan. There are numerous cases in which the territory of one tribe or group was taken by force and given to another tribe, group, or individual.

Exile of the tribal leaders (khans)

Many of the tribal leaders—including Ali Mohammad Khan Ghazanfar from the Amra'i tribe of Kuhdasht, Alimorad Khan from Judak, and Husain Khan and his brother Moradi from the Baharvand, along with leaders of other tribes, including Bairanvand, Mir, Papi, Delfan, and others—were exiled to Tehran, where they remained in jail until Reza Shah's abdication in 1941.

General Ahmadi had betrayed some of the influential leaders, including Shir Mohammad Khan Savand, Moein al-Saltaneh (the governor's deputy from Khorramabad), and Husain Khan from the Baharvand, along with others who supported the army all the way. In 1929, he sent a letter to Husain Khan to meet him in Massur Castle, near Khorramabad, to discuss some important matters (personal files). Husain Khan was captured upon his arrival and imprisoned in Falako al-Arlak Castle. Shortly after that, he was exiled to Tehran and imprisoned in Qasr-i Qajar (Qajar's Palace). In the meantime, his brother Moradi was exiled to Mashhad City in Khorasan Province. Husain Khan remained in Qasr-i Qajar until 1935, when General Razmara, the commander of the army in Luristan, found out that Husain Khan, along with Ali Mohammad Khan Ghazanfari and Ali Morad Khan, from the Judaki tribe, were innocent. He wrote a letter to Reza Shah and pleaded for their release from jail (personal files).

Consequently, Husain Khan was moved from Qasr-i Qajar to Baharestan, a place in Tehran where Shaikh Khazal, the influential Arab leader from Khuzistan, was residing. In 1935, as Husain Khan was walking in Baharestan

Circle, he met Reza Shah by chance. Husain Khan had met Reza Shah in Luristan years previously, while he was a colonel and was taking a gift from Hashmat al-Dowleh, the Qajar prince, to Kholam Reza Khan, the *wali* of Pusht-i Kuh of Luristan. Reza Shah asked him whether he would like to marry and remain in Tehran or whether he would like to return to Luristan. He gladly chose the second suggestion. Reza Shah provided him with a note and sent him to one of his generals. He took the card to that general, who provided him with a military Jeep and an officer, who brought him to Luristan.

Forced settlement

During the Qajar Dynasty in the late nineteenth century, the state wanted to settle the tribes, but it was unable to achieve that task because the tribes were too powerful. As soon as the newly established regime gained power, the policy of forced settlement of the tribes, including those of Luristan, was implemented for the first time in the history of Iran. Reza Shah detested pastoral nomadism and viewed it as a savage way of life. Obviously, the motivation behind the settlement was political, because once the tribes lost their mobility, it was easier to keep them under tight control.

Unfortunately, the settlement took place without necessary planning and without considering the consequences. The economy and livelihood of the pastoralists depended on being able to move according to the seasons. When they had to remain settled, they could no longer sustain their flocks or establish self-sufficiency in agriculture. Although a few families from each section of the tribes were allowed to continue their migration in order to utilize the summer and winter pastures, most were forced to settle. To support settlement, the state constructed buildings in some places, but they were no substitute for mobility. Settlement in its early phase was economically devastating for the tribes.

In the view of the state, settlement of the tribes was necessary for the establishment of law and order. Furthermore, the settlement of the tribes was necessary for agricultural development and other developmental planning for the modernization of the country.

Imposed dress codes

In 1929, the National Assembly of Iran (the *Majles*), under the direct order of Reza Shah, outlawed the traditional clothes and obliged the adult males to wear Pahlavi caps (*Kolah-e Pahlavi*) and Western clothes. However, in Luristan, this law was never enforced fully. The Lurs refused to change their traditional clothes, and only an insignificant number of males, particularly those who were dealing with the government, adopted the Pahlavi cap. Gradually, however, the forces of modernization resulted in the adoption of Western clothes in Luristan and all over Iran.

The role of the modern state in the detribalization of the tribes

The establishment of the modern government offices in Luristan and the enforcement of the governmental modernization programs resulted in great changes in traditional society of Luristan, including detribalization of the tribes. The detribalization of the tribes of Iran was an unprecedented event in the long history of Iran. In the past, tribal exile, settlement, and the detribalization of a particular tribe took place for a variety of reasons. The detribalization of the tribes in general, as occurred in Luristan, was a new event. In addition to these events, the following factors played a significant role in the detribalization of the Baharvand and other tribes of Luristan and in Iran in general. In the following pages, I will indicate briefly the role of the modern state on the detribalization of the tribes.

Termination of tribal autonomy

Before Luristan was under state control, each tribe was an independent socio-political unit. Each tribe was like a mini-state—responsible for the security of its members and its territorial integrity. When the state took control, the tribes became part of the state and subject to state's laws. Consequently, tribal autonomy was terminated.

Establishment of governmental offices

As Luristan came under control of the modern centralized state, various governmental departments were established, such as the Justice Department, Army and Gendarmery, Police, Departments of Education, Registry, Health, Finance, the office of the governor of the province (*ostandar*), and the office of the governor of the county (*bakhshdar*). Khorramabad remained the capital of the province. The control of the state led to changes in traditional state-tribe relationships and also resulted in changes in various aspects of the traditional society of Luristan.

Land reform

Ownership of land and pasture was the source of power, income, and prestige under pastoral nomadism, all of which affected the individual and the groups' social status. Furthermore, the ownership of land and pasture has always been the main factor responsible for the tribal unity and its survival. The land reform laws of 1961 changed tribal communal ownership by registering land individually. Distribution of land between the members of the tribe led to the reduction of the individual's dependency on the tribe. Individual ownership of land, along with provision of security and peace by the government, affected the traditional pattern of the protection and well-being of the members of the tribe. In this way, land reform contributed significantly to the detribalization of the tribes and affected the lives of villagers as well.

Traditionally, members of the tribe had access to pastures, agricultural land, and water sources, and these resources were collectively owned by the tribe. In other words, the individuals as the members of the tribe utilized these resources. Consequently, the collective utilization of the tribal resources required collective protection of these resources, which required tribal unity. Land reform destroyed this system.

Modern education

One of the major policies implemented under Mohammad Reza Shah Pahlavi was the White Revolution (1962), which, among other things, worked toward universal literacy through the establishment of schools. Modern schooling was also a powerful factor in detribalization. It provided new knowledge, which contradicted traditional tribal knowledge but also prepared the individuals for different professions, enabling them to find employment outside the tribe. This resulted in financial independence and geographical mobility for the educated tribal members, who were no longer obliged to live within tribal territorial boundaries or to depend on tribal resources to earn their livelihood. Paradoxically, it was the *homsa*, who had little tribal allegiance, who were able to take advantage of this. Chapter 18 describes the ways members of Morad Khan's camp and other Lurs have adapted to the modern world.

Recently, some of the Baharvand have attended university and are engaged in occupations such as medicine, banking, and engineering. Some are high-ranking military officers, university professors, and shopkeepers. Furthermore, many Baharvand now live in major cities, including Tehran, Isfahan, Shiraz, and Mashhad. Tribal territory and affiliations are no longer necessary for individual success.

Rural-urban migration: The expansion of urbanization

The rapid expansion of urbanization in Luristan and Iran during the past several decades is unprecedented in Iranian history. In 1925, when the tribes were under military siege, the population of Iran was estimated at ten million. From 1975 to 2020 the population of Iran increased from thirty-four million to eighty million. In 1975, fifty-four percent were rural, and in 2020, twenty-four percent were rural; most of the population was concentrated in cities of greater than 500,000 residents (Doroudian 1976:170; Ganji and Milani 1976:Table 2; McMorris 1978; Worldpopulationreview.com/countries/iran-population).

Traditionally, in the past two centuries, there were two small towns in Luristan: Khorramabad and Borujerd. Currently, there are some eight urban centers in Luristan. The expansion of urbanization in Luristan and Iran has occurred because of a) the rapid growth of the population; b) the concentration of economic, educational, and governmental institutions in urban centers; c) the increased opportunity for employment, which is concentrated mainly in urban centers; and d) the migration from rural areas to urban centers in search of work, better quality of life, and access to modern educational institutions such as colleges and universities. Sixty percent of the population of Luristan now resides in urban areas.

Changes in traditional social status

Traditionally, the social status of individuals—identity, rights, and responsibilities among the pastoral nomadic tribes—was determined by their affiliation with paternal kin groups. Previously, social status among the pastoral nomadic tribes was ascribed by these affiliations; now social status is achieved according to choice of occupation outside of herding.

Conclusion

The forces of modernization have changed traditional Iranian society, including the relationship between its triple segments: villagers, pastoral nomads, and urbanites. Furthermore, each of the segments has changed drastically. Following the decline of pastoral nomadism and detribalization of the tribes, few families of the Baharvand continue the nomadic way of life. The physical expansion of Khorramabad has engulfed villages like Darayi. Nevertheless, detribalization does not mean that tribe's identity and tribal loyalty have disappeared. Rather, two factors—the concentration of the tribes mainly in Khorramabad and other urban centers and the modern means of communication (such as cell phones, computers, and TV)—have facilitated communication between the members of the tribe. Furthermore, the sense of tribalism is manifested during the elections for the public offices, such as the representative of the Majlis (parliament), the election of the mayors, and the members of various councils. Finally, despite integration into national society, there has been a revival of ethnic identity among the members of the tribes, as well as among urbanites. The newly urban Lurs have developed associations based on the tribes, and they support Luri candidates for election into civil offices.

Chapter 18

Postscript

Regrets

Before we joined the migration, Sekandar and I had traveled widely through Luristan, interviewing herders and studying recent, unoccupied camps to determine what we might expect to find archaeologically. I continued this practice during the migration, but as a guest of the tribe, I had to stay with them as they moved. Consequently, I was unable to conduct more than a cursory exploration of likely spots for camps. Nevertheless, I fully expected that I would be able to return as an archaeologist to carry out a study of the vaulted room settlements, as well as search for the slender traces of ancient campsites.

In the event, that did not happen, primarily for reasons of funding and official permits, which I would have needed to explore tribal territory. Within a few years, the Iranian Revolution took place, and all archaeological research, whether by foreigners or natives, came to a halt. The Iran-Iraq War, centered on western Iran, further rendered research off limits. It was not until the twenty-first century that a new generation of capable Iranian archaeologists resumed serious archaeological work.

During this hiatus in fieldwork I continued to write on aspects of pastoral nomadism and to compile photos and other records of campsites for use in lectures on ethnoarchaeology at Yale and Masaryk University in the Czech Republic, where I held a series of visiting professorships.

Following the migration, my research shifted geographic focus to Syria in 1984. As well as excavating sites, I embarked on a series of surveys designed to record evidence of modern pastoral camps and discover evidence of ancient nomad campsites (Hole 2019). I had my last season there in 2009, during a devastating drought and the eve of the Syrian uprising.

After a number of productive years there, my archaeological research was once again closed down by revolution and war. An opportunity to join an ongoing project in northern Mongolia in 2013 and 2018 allowed me to investigate migratory pastoralists in the northern steppe and forests. This vastly different environment required adaptations to seasonal changes (short growing seasons and extreme cold in winter). Still, the needs of the herds dictated the movements and activities of the herders, just as they had in Iran.

In 2011, I returned to Iran to give some lectures. With the help of Sekandar and his family, I was able to return to Chin-i Zal to see for myself what had transpired in the intervening years. Sekandar's brother's son, Satar, drove us on a new road from Darayi up the mountain, passing through forested land following an old caravan route. We stopped briefly at a *caravanserai* (Figures 18.1, 18.2) and shrine dedicated to Shoja al-Din Korshid, the leader of Atabakan Lur Kochek (AD 1184; 580 HQ). Sekandar's grandfather was buried in the little cemetery next to the shrine. Husain Khan's tomb bore a modern inscription (Figure 18.3). (See Figure 17.2 for an abbreviated outline of Sekandar's Baharvand genealogy.) Older stones in the cemetery were carved in traditional style, depicting symbols relating to male (Figure 18.4) and female (Figure 18.5) activities. Similar stones are depicted and described in Inga Mortensen's book, *Luristani Pictorial Tombstones* (Mortensen 2010).

In an hour or so, we were back in Chin-i Zal, where our two-week migration had begun. Changes were pervasive. On the site where Morad Khan's camp had stood, a new camp had been built, using the shelter of the same bluff. Instead of tents surrounded by roughly laid stone walls,

Figure 18.1 (above). A *caravanserai* on an old caravan trail high above the Khorramabad Valley.

Figure 18.2 (opposite). Near the *caravanserai*, which is no longer in use, is the shrine to Shoja al-Din Korshid, the leader of the Atabakan Lur Kochek (AD 1184; 580 HQ).

هو الباقی
سعدیا مرد نکونام نمیرد هرگز
مرده آنست که نامش به نکویی نبرند
آرامگاه شادروان
حسین خان امان الهی بهاروند
فرزند مرحوم علی آقا
از سران ایل بهاروند
که همواره با نام نیک زندگی کرد و در مردمداری
و دادرسی زبانزد بود
تاریخ وفات پاییز ۱۳۶۳ هـ قمری
برابر با ۱۳۲۱ هـ شمسی
یادش گرامی باد

Figure 18.3 (opposite). In the cemetery in front of the shrine is the tomb of Husain Khan, Sekandar's grandfather.

Figure 18.4 (above). A traditional headstone for a man, depicting a horse and weapons.

Figure 18.5. A woman's gravestone, engraved with her scissors and other utensils.

new, permanent structures had been built, partly of stone and partly of mud brick (Figure 18.6). About the same size as a tent, the new house was tightly covered with plastic under a black tent. Storage bins were also covered with plastic sheeting, and a stable was under construction. A water trailer stood outside the house, implying the use of a diesel pump to draw water from the river (Figure 18.7). A large volume of water would have been needed to fill the concrete-lined water troughs that were next to the new buildings (Figure 18.8). A stable was under construction, surrounded by stone walls and with a framework for a light peaked roof, perhaps a black tent (Figure 18.9). Clearly this was no longer just a temporary camp; it was built for year-round occupation. Because the camp's owner was absent, we did not linger except to explain who we were to the woman who lived there. She was naturally apprehensive and glad to see us leave.

Looking around the valley, I saw another similar camp where a large truck was parked (Figure 18.10). It appeared to be outfitted similarly to the one we had just visited. Facing north, a new four-lane asphalt highway emerged from a tunnel close to the Zal River (Figure 18.11), not far from the pass at Kialon Kuh.

Little did I realize in 1973 how rapidly things would change in Luristan, although there were many hints. I had noticed the degradation of pastures and the intrusion of farmers, which circumscribed migrations. I had guessed that the system of nomadic pastoralism would give way as children gained education and the land was put under private ownership.

What I did not anticipate was the Iranian Revolution or the prolonged Iran-Iraq War, which led to the development of a road system, military facilities, and standing militias. The abrupt change from an autocratic imperial government to one based on theocratic rule was like an earthquake in its impact on the citizenry. The profound social and economic effects of these changes were magnified and enhanced by the emergence of rapid communication through telephones and TV. Now no part of Luristan was without access to local and foreign news, or to the many consumer goods that had suddenly raised standards of comfort. The shift from a rural to an urban demography and the rise of economic opportunities, some engendered by the many new universities, had transformed the country.

A few sentences describing the events of the past forty years cannot do justice to the changes in Iran, and this is not the place to try. What is important

Figure 18.6 (opposite, top). In 2011, we visited a newly built house on the same site where Morad Khan had his camp in 1973. This is now a year-round occupation with solidly laid stone walls and a plastic cover beneath the black tent.

Figure 18.7 (opposite, bottom). In front of the new campsite is a water trailer and feed troughs.

Figure 18.8 (above). Concrete-lined water troughs indicate the need for the water trailer, probably filled via diesel pump from the river.

Figure 18.9 (opposite, top). A stable under construction next to the house will probably have either a plastic or black tent cover.

Figure 18.10 (opposite, bottom). Across the valley is another similar camp, with a large truck for transporting animals.

Figure 18.11 (above). Near the cleft in the mountain through which the Zal River flows are the tunnels of a four-lane divided highway that carries traffic from Khuzistan to Khorramabad and beyond.

in the context of this book is how the decades of changes have affected the people we traveled with.

The present

In Chapter 2 we saw how modernization impacted Sekandar's life. His transformation began some twenty years before our trek with the tribe, so he had a substantial head start over the people we traveled with, and an unquenchable ambition to succeed. None of the adults in camp, men or women, had had the benefit of schooling, apart from that given to all pastoralist youth in the camps. How would they adapt to life away from the tent camps? Fortunately, Sekandar was able to follow the lives of some of the people through personal observation and interviews. The most complete picture is of Mohammad Ali's family, which now extends to three generations. In a way, Mohammad Ali's transformation, and that of his family, was as remarkable as Sekandar's, for he had a much later start toward modernization.

The younger members of the camp, who had received elementary education, were able to move into the urban milieu in various occupations. The older generation, although removed from tent life, took the first steps toward economic self-sufficiency by taking jobs that required little formal training. Their children made the great leap to the modern world.

Sekandar acquired current information about the members of the camp, as well as recent photos of individuals and their families. We can compare these with photos taken in 1973. Thanks to Aazam, Mohammad Ali's daughter, Sekandar was able to borrow photos that are reproduced here and fill in details about the family. Naturally, they focus on Mohammad Ali's family. The photos are grouped into four figures (Figures 18.12, 18.13, 18.14, 18.15).

Morad Khan

Morad Khan had no formal education. He learned to read and write from a member of the tribe. His first wife bore him two sons, Mukhtar and Mohammad Khan, and three daughters. The second of these, Ozra, resided in Morad Khan's tent. She is now married. Taji, Morad Khan's second wife, who presided over his tent, was barren, but his third wife, Ghamartaj, gave him a daughter, Hava, who attended the University of Luristan and is now teaching in Khorramabad.

Mukhtar

Mukhtar, Morad Khan's oldest son, now retired from teaching, has three daughters and three sons. Two of his daughters have bachelor's degrees and the third finished high school; all of them are married. One of his sons completed his bachelor's degree, the second has completed two years of college and is married, and the third has finished high school. Unfortunately Mukhtar's wife passed away in 2016, and he now lives alone in Khorramabad.

Mohammad Khan

Mohammad Khan was employed by the Andimeshk municipality and is now retired.

Ozra

Morad Khan's second daughter, Ozra, is married.

Mohammad Ali

Khawar (Figure 18.12A) was his first wife. After moving to Khorramabad and opening a grocery, Mohammad Ali took a second wife, Hanifeh (Figure 18.12F), who bore him five sons and a daughter. His daughter, Aazam (Figures 18.12A, 18.12B), received a PhD and is married, but not working outside the home. His sons are Mohsen, Bahman (Figure 18.12C), Mortaza (with his daughter, Figure 18.13A), Mostafa (with his son, Husain, Figures 18.13E, 18.13F), and Hamza, who is a truck driver (Figure 18.13C). In Figure 18.13D, Hamza's daughter, Raheh, is dressed in Luri garb, reflecting the old tribal ways.

Ali

Mohammad Ali's brother, Ali, joined the army and retired as a colonel (Figures 18.12D, 18.15B). He now has a shop in Khorramabad selling furniture. In 1973 he was attending Mukhtar's tent school (see Figure 6.7) and he took care of the lambs in camp.

Hirdali

Mohammad Ali's brother Hirdali (Figures 18.14C, 18.15A) married Sadighah and had a son, Iraj (see Figures 6.8, 18.14D), who received a master's degree and currently is deputy of water and sewerage of Khorramabad.

Figure 18.12 A-C. Members of Mohammad Ali's family in recent photos. A: Khawar (Mohammad's first wife), Aazam (his daughter), and Mohammad Ali. B: Aazam. C: Mohammad Ali's sons Mohsen and Bahman.

Figure 18.12 D-F. Other members of Mohammad Ali's family in recent photos. D: his brother Ali. E: His brother Papi. F: His second wife, Hanifeh.

Figure 18.13 A. On the next three pages, three generations of Mohammad Ali's family. Here, Mohammad Ali's son Mortaza with his daughter.

Figure 18.13 B-D. Mohammad Ali (B) and his son Hamza (C) and Hamza's daughter Raheh (D). Raheh is dressed in tribal garb.

Papi Ali

Another of Mohammad Ali's brothers, Papi, was Hirdali's shepherd (Figures 18.12E, 18.15B).

Paina

Khawar's brother Paina (Figures 18.14A, B, 18.15A) had recently married when we were in camp. He moved to the city, became a welder, and took a

Figure 18.13 E-F. Mohammad Ali's son Mostafa (E) with Mostafa's son Husain (F).

second wife after the death of his first. He has four sons and four daughters, all married. Ahmad has a bachelor's degree in humanities and is employed by a private company. Masoud, who is a photographer, has a high school diploma (Figure 18.15A). Mohammad has a diploma in accounting and works for a private company. Sajad has a bachelor's degree in management and works for a private company. Kayhan has three years of high school. Fatemah has a high school diploma, as does Zahra. Zainab has a bachelor's degree in accounting. All of the women are housekeepers.

Figure 18.14 A-B. Some of the family in 1973. A. Paina (left) and Ghasamali (right) showing differences in sheep ears. B. Mohammad Ali, Panjali, and Ghasamali (see also Figure 11.2).

Figure 18.14 C-D. C. Hirdali, Mohammad Ali's brother. D. Hirdali's son Iraj in 1973 (see also Figure 6.8).

Figure 18.15 A. In this 2018 photo: Mohammad Ali's brother Hirdali, Masoud (Paina's son), Paina, and Ghasamali.

Figure 18.15 B. Mohammad Ali with his brothers Ali and Papi in front of a mosque.

Ghasamali

Ghasamali, a relative of Paina, was Paina's shepherd in 1973 (Figure 18.14A). He found work as a welder in Khorramabad (Figure 18.15A), and he has five daughters and a son. His son, Hamid Reza, has a master's degree in natural resources and is the deputy of the municipality of Nehevand. His youngest daughter, Sara, is a university student and single. Three daughters—Fatameh, Nargas (both married), and Freshteh—finished high school, and Zahra has a bachelor's degree.

Safarali

Safarali is now deceased. He had one son, Shirali, who was killed in a fight in Dehmosan. Shirali had three sons. Bartali, who is illiterate and works in a factory, has a son and three daughters. Moosa finished high school and is employed. He has a son and a daughter. Amin finished high school and sells pastry, and he also has a son and a daughter.

Figure 18.16. Satar (Sekandar's nephew), Sekandar, and Frank in Chin-i Zal in 2011.

Generational changes

As of 2020, it appears that the young men of the tribe have been successful in adapting to the modern world, and have been especially prolific in having children, a number of whom have received advanced education. This number of children would have made the older generation very happy. Take Mohammad Ali, for example. With five sons, he could have lived the life that Morad Khan could only dream about. There is no doubt that education provided the means for upward mobility, but it was also the case that under the conditions in 1973, herding was becoming less and less feasible or attractive to those who could find alternatives. With the growth of urbanism and the expansion of Khorramabad, opportunities for wage labor or modest entrepreneurial activities, available even to the illiterate, made it possible to move away from the mountains and tents.

The nomads in 1973 could not afford to eat their own sheep. It is ironic that today the price of lamb has risen so much that herders can become rich. As Sekandar put it, "The income of the pastoral nomads has increased tremendously because the price of one kilo of meat is *rials* 13,000,000. Prior to the revolution, one could buy a nice house with this money. Presently the income of a family of pastoral nomads is much higher than the income of the high-ranking government officials, including university professors." According to Sekandar, Dust Ali, whom we met on migration, is still illiterate, but earns more from the sale of his herds than the salary of a university professor.

The conversion rate of *rials* to dollars was 1,340,000 in early 2020, but the *rial* is continually losing value and the government has just announced that it will issue new currency. Rather than *rials*, the new currency will be the *toman* and three digits will be removed from the bills. Before the revolution, $1=60 *rials*. Given the economics, it is little wonder that raising livestock may be attractive again.

Let us be clear, however. Herding is not the same as it was. To be sure, the sheep and goats must move seasonally to find grass, but it is no longer necessary for the people to travel by foot or mule. Heavy gear can be moved by truck, and even the herds can be taken by road to pastures. Nevertheless, there are still some who migrate in the traditional way. In 1973, as Atawak attested, the nomads had much more baggage than in the past, thus requiring either more pack animals or vehicles to move them. With the newfound prosperity resulting from the prices of meat, it is inevitable that the nomads have acquired even more goods from the market than they had in 1973.

This is just a cursory view of the changes that have taken place, and it would take significant fieldwork and investigation to describe and understand their ramifications, a subject that has been at the heart of many of Sekandar's publications. An older analysis is Black-Michaud's *Sheep and Land*, which discusses the economic, political, and social impacts being felt by the Hasanvand Lurs at about the same time we were in the field (Black-Michaud

1986). In *Nomads in Postrevolutionary Iran* (Beck 2015), Lois Beck has written an excellent and detailed review of how changes have impacted another formerly migratory tribe, the Qashqa'i. Also contemporary with our migration, Grace Goodell's book, *The Elementary Structures of Political Life: Rural Development in Pahlavi Iran*, describes the series of draconian measures taken by the government in Khuzistan, to the pain of the former nomads and villagers like the ones we hired at Tula'i. After receiving land during land reform, they lost it to the agribusiness corporations (Doroudian 1976:159; Goodell 1986:26–27).

Dramatic political, economic, and demographic changes within the past one hundred years have affected all of the formerly migratory pastoral nomads of Iran, not to mention the villagers and urban dwellers. In this context, the story of the Baharvand is, like the migration itself, merely a moment in an ever-changing landscape. As such, it tells a story, albeit a small one, that reflects the larger world around it. But the story is important to the people who lived it and for whom it is a tangible witness to their heritage.

It is to the generations of Baharvand, whose story we have told, that this book is dedicated.

Five short documentary films on the migration and other aspects of nomadic pastoralist life in Luristan in 1973 are available on Fulcrum at https://doi.org/10.3998/mpub.12031336.

Bibliography

Adams, Robert McC.

1962 Agriculture and urban life in early Southwestern Iran. *Science* 136:109–122.

2006 Intensified large-scale irrigation as an aspect of imperial policy: Strategies of statecraft on the late Sasanian Mesopotamian plain. In *Agricultural Strategies*, edited by J. Marcus and C. Stanish. Cotsen Institute of Archaeology, UCLA, Los Angeles.

Alizadeh, Abbas (editor)

1996 *Chogha Mish, Volume 1: The First Five Seasons of Excavations, 1961–1971*. Oriental Institute Publications 101. The Oriental Institute of the University of Chicago, Chicago.

2003 *Excavations at the Prehistoric Mound of Chogha Bonut, Khuzestan, Iran: Seasons 1976/77, 1977/78, and 1996*. Oriental Institute Publications 120. The Oriental Institute of the University of Chicago, Chicago.

Amanolahi, Sekandar

1988 The Tribes of Iran, Vol. I: The Tribes of Luristan, Bakhtiari, Kuh Gilu and Mamasani. Human Relations Area Files, New Haven, CT.

2016 The Lurs of Iran. *Cultural Survival Quarterly Magazine* 9/1(Parks and People):1–8.

Amanolahi, Sekandar and Edward Norbeck

1975 The Luti, an outcast group of Iran. *Rice Institute Pamphlet: Rice University Studies* 61(2):1–12.

Amanolahi-Baharvand, Sekandar

1975 The Baharvand: Former Pastoralists of Iran. PhD dissertation, Department of Anthropology, Rice University, Houston.

2002 Reza Shah and the Lurs: the impact of the modern state on Luristan. *Iran and the Caucasus* 6(1/2):193–218.

2007 Supernaturalism among the pastoral societies of Iran. *Iran and the Caucasus* 11(1):45–55.

Amanolahi-Baharvand, Sekandar and W. M. Thackston

1986 *Tales From Luristan*. Harvard Iranian Series 4. Harvard University Press, Cambridge, MA.

Beck, Lois

1980 Herd Owners and Hired Shepherds: The Qashqa'i of Iran. *Ethnology* 19 (3): 327–351.

1986 *The Qashga'i of Iran*. Yale University Press, New Haven, CT.

1991 *Nomad: A Year in the Life of a Qashga'i Tribesman in Iran*. University of California Press, Berkeley.

2003 Qashqa'i nomadic pastoralists and their use of land. In *Yeki Bud, Yeki Nabud: Essays on the Archaeology of Iran in Honor of William M. Sumner*, edited by N. F. Miller and K. Abdi, pp. 289–304. Cotsen Institute of Archaeology, UCLA, Los Angeles.

2015 *Nomads in Postrevolutionary Iran: The Qashqa'i in an Era of Change*. Routledge, New York.

Black-Michaud, Jacob

1986 *Sheep and Land: The Economics of Power in a Tribal Society*. Cambridge University Press, Cambridge.

Cooper, Merian C.
1925 *Grass*. G.P. Putnam's Sons, New York.

Cribb, Roger.
2004 *Nomads in Archaeology*. New Studies in Archaeology, Cambridge University Press, Cambridge.

Curzon, George N.
(1892) 1966. *Persia and the Persian Question*, 2 vols. Barnes and Noble, New York.

DaBell, Bijan
2013 Iran minorities 2: ethnic diversity. In *The Iran Primer*, https://iranprimer.usip.org/blog/2013/sep/03/iran-minorities-2-ethnic-diversity. Accessed 2020.

De Bode, C. A. Baron
1845a *Travels in Luristan and Arabistan II*. J. Madden and Co., London.

1845b *Travels in Luristan and Arabistan I*. J. Madden and Co., London.

Digard, Jean-Pierre
1981 *Techniques Des Nomades Baxtyari d'Iran*. Cambridge University Press, Cambridge.

Doroudian, R.
1976 Comments and Discussion. In *Iran: Past, Present, and Future*, edited by Jane W. Jacqz, pp. 257–265. Aspen Institute for Humanistic Studies, New York.

Douglas, William O.
1951 *Strange Lands and Friendly People*. Harper & Brothers, New York.

Edmonds, C. J.
1917 (published Feb. 1922) *Notes on Luristan*. Anglo-Persian Oil Company Limited.

1922 Luristan: Pishi-Kuh and Bala Gariveh. *The Geographical Journal* 59(5):334–451.

Feilberg, Carl Gunnar.
1944. *La Tente Noire*. Nationalmuseets Skrifter series.
1952. *Les Papi*. Nationalmuseets Skrifter series.

Firoozi, Ferydoon
1970 Iranian censuses, 1956 and 1966: a comparative analysis. *Middle East Journal* 24(2):220–228.

Friedl, Erika

1989 *Women of Deh Koh: Lives in an Iranian Village*. Smithsonian Institution Press, Washington, DC.

1991 The dynamics of women's spheres of action in rural Iran. In W*omen in Middle Eastern History: Shifting Boundaries in Sex and Gender*, edited by N. R. Keddie and B. Baron, pp. 195–214. Yale University Press, New Haven, CT.

2007 *Folk Tales From a Persian Tribe: forty-five tales from Sisakht in Luri and English*. Verlag fur Orientkunde, Dortmund.

2014 *Folktales and storytellers of Iran: Culture, Ethos and Identity*. I. B. Tauris, New York.

2018 *Folksongs from the Mountains of Iran: Culture, Poetics and Everyday Philosophies*. I. B. Tauris, New York.

Friedl, Erika and Agnes Loeffler

1994 The ups and downs of dwellings in a village in west Iran. *Archiv für Völkerkunde* 48:1–44.

Ganji, Manoucher and Milani, Abbas

1976 Iran: developments during the last 50 years. In *Iran: Past, Present, and Future*, edited by Jane W. Jacqz, pp. 33–55. Aspen Institute for Humanistic Studies, New York.

Garthwaite, Gene R.

(1983) 2009 *Khans and Shahs: A History of the Bakhtiari Tribe in Iran*. Paperback edition. I. B. Tauris & Co. Ltd., London and New York.

Goodell, Grace

1975 Agricultural production in a traditional village of northern Khuzestan. *Marburger Geographiske Schriften* 64:245–289.

1986 *The Elementary Structures of Political Life: Rural Development in Pahlavi Iran.* Oxford University Press, New York.

Haerinck, Ernie

1986 The chronology of Luristan, Pusht-i Kuh in the late fourth and first half of the third millennium B.C. In *Préhistoire de la Mésopotamie,* edited by J.-L. Huot, pp. 55–72. Editions du Centre National de la Recherche Scientifique, Paris.

2012 The Early Bronze Age in Western Pusht-i Kuh (Ilam Province). Proceedings of the International Syrmposium on Iranian Archaeology: Western Region 8:67–79. Tehran.

Harrison, J. V.

1946 South-west Persia: a survey of Pish-i-Kuh in Luristan. *The Geographical Journal* 108:55–70.

Harrison, Marguerite

1935 *There's Always Tomorrow: The Story of a Checkered Life*. Farrar & Rinehart, New York.

Haynes, Simon J. and McQuillan, Henry

1974 Evolution of the Zagros Suture Zone, Southern Iran. *Geological Society of America Bulletin* 85:739–744.

Hole, Frank

1962 Archaeological survey and excavation in Iran, 1961. *Science* 137:524–526.

1966 The Palaeolithic culture sequence in western Iran. *Proceedings of the VII Congrès International des Sciences Préhistoriques et Protohistoriques* 1:286–292.

1977 *Studies in the Archaeological History of the Deh Luran Plain: The Excavation of Chagha Sefid*. Memoirs No. 9. Museum of Anthropology, University of Michigan, Ann Arbor, MI.

1978 Pastoral nomadism in western Iran. In *Explorations in Ethnoarchaeology*, edited by R. A. Gould, pp. 127–167. University of New Mexico Press, Albuquerque, NM.

1979 Rediscovering the past in the present: ethnoarchaeology in Luristan, Iran. In *Ethnoarchaeology: Implications of Ethnography for Archaeology*, edited by C. Kramer, pp. 192–218. Columbia University Press, New York.

1980 The prehistory of herding: some suggestions from ethnography. In *L'archéologie de l'Iraq du début de l'époque néolithique à 333 av. n/ère: perspectives et limits de l'interpretation anthropologique des documents*, edited by M. T. Barrelet, pp. 119–130. Colloque Internationale No. 580. Éditions du C.N.R.S., Paris.

1987 *The Archaeology of Western Iran*. (Translated into Farsi 2002). Smithsonian Institution, Washington, DC.

1987 Archaeology of the Village Period. In *The Archaeology of Western Iran*, edited by F. Hole, pp. 29–79. Smithsonian Institution Press, Washington, DC.

1996 The context of caprine domestication in the Zagros region. In *The Origins and Spread of Agriculture and Pastoralism in Eurasia*, edited by D. R. Harris, pp. 263–281. University College London Press, London.

2004 Campsites of the seasonally mobile in western Iran. In *From Handaxe to Khan: Essays Presented to Peder Mortensen on the Occasion of His 70th Birthday*, edited by K. von Folsach, H. Thrane, and I. Thuesen, pp. 67–85. Aarhus University Press, Aarhus.

2009 Pastoral mobility as an adaptation. In *Nomads, Tribes, and the State in the Ancient Near East: Cross-Disciplinary Perspectives*, edited by J. Szuchman, pp. 261–281. Oriental Institute Seminars, Vol. 5. The Oriental Institute of the University of Chicago, Chicago.

2017 The creative centuries: diversity and innovation in Iranian Neolithic ceramics. In *Neolithic Near Eastern Pottery in Context*, edited by A. Gomez and M. Molist, pp. 109–119. Serie Monografica del MAC`, Barcelona.

2019 Traces of nomadic pastoralism in the Jebel Abd al-Aziz region. In *Between Syria and the Highlands: Studies in Honor of Giorgio Buccellati and Marilyn Kelly-Buccellati*, edited by S. Valentini and G. Guarducci. Studies on the Ancient Near East and the Mediterranean (SANEM 3), Arbor Sapientiae Editore, Roma 2019.

2019 Tepe Tula'i and the question of nomadic pastoralism. Unpublished report.

Hole, Frank and Kent V. Flannery

1967 The prehistory of Southwestern Iran: a preliminary report. *Proceedings of the Prehistory Society* 33:147–206.

Hole, Frank, Kent. V. Flannery, and James A. Neely

1969 *Prehistory and Human Ecology of the Deh Luran Plain*. Memoirs No. 1. Museum of Anthropology. University of Michigan, Ann Arbor, MI.

Howarth, Anthony

1976 *People of the Wind*. 110 minutes. DVD ed. The Milestone Collection.

The Iran Primer: Power, Politics, and U.S. Policy.

2010 United States Institute of Peace. https://iranprimer.usip.org. Accessed 2020.

Jacqz, Jane W. (editor)
1976 *Iran: Past, Present And Future*. Aspen Institute, New York.

Kantor, Helene
1976 The excavations at Coqa Mis, 1974–1975. *Procedings of the 4th Annual Symposium on Archaelogical Research in Iran* 4:23–41.

Lattimore, Owen
(1940) 1962 *Inner Asian Frontiers of China*. Beacon Press, Boston.

Loeffler, Reinhold, Erika Friedl, and A. Janata
1974 Die materielle Kultur von Boir Ahmad, Sudiran. *Archiv für Volkerkunde* 28:61–142.

Loeffler, Reinhold and Erika Friedl
1967 Eine Ethnographische Sammlung von der Boir Ahmad, Sudiran. *Archiv für Volkerkunde* 21:95–207.

Macrotrends.net. www.macrotrends/IRN/Iran/population. Accessed 2020.

McMorris, David S.
1978 Demographic setting and education. In *Iran, A Country Study*, edited by Richard F. Nyrop, pp. 67–105. US Government Printing Office, Washington, DC: Foreign Area Studies, the American University.

Minorsky, V.
1936 Lur. In *Encyclopedia of Islam*, first edition, edited by Martijn Theodoor Houtsma. Brill.

Mortensen, Inge Demant
1983 Women after death: aspects of a study on Iranian nomadic cemeteries. In *Women in Islamic Societies*, edited by B. Utas, pp. 26–47. Curzon Press, London.

1991 From ritual action to symbolic communication. In *Sacred and Profane: Proceedings of a Conference on Archaeology, Ritual and Relition*, Oxford, 1989, edited by P. Garwood, D. Jennings, R. Skeates, and J. Toms, pp. 80–87. Monograph. vol. 32. Oxford University Committee for Archaeology, Oxford.

1993 *Nomads of Luristan: History, Material Culture, and Pastoralism in Western Iran* (The Carlsberg Foundation's Nomad Research Project). Thames and Hudson, New York.

2010 *Luristani Pictorial Tombstones: Studies in Nomadic Cemeteries from Northern Luristan, Iran*. Acta Iranica 47. Peeters, Leuven, Paris, Walpole, MA.

Muscarella, Oscar White
1989 Bronzes of Luristan. *Encyclopaedia Iranica* 4(5):478–483.

Nafici, Hamed
2006 Lured by the East: Ethnographic and Expedition films about nomadic tribes – The case of *Grass* (1924). In *Virtual Voyages: Cinema and Travel*, edited by J. Ruoff, pp. 117–138. Duke University Press, Durham and London.

Neely, James A.
1974 Sassanian and early Islamic water-control and irrigation systems on the Deh Luran Plain, Iran. In *Irrigation's Impact on Society*, edited by T. E. Downing and M. Gibson, pp. 21–42. Anthropological Papers, No. 25. University of Arizona Press, Tucson, AZ.

Neely, James A. and Henry T. Wright
1994 *Early Settlement and Irrigation on the Deh Luran Plain: Village and Early State Societies in Southwestern Iran*. Technical Report 26. Museum of Anthropology, University of Michigan, Ann Arbor, MI.

Nyrop, Richard F.
1978 (editor) *Iran: A Country Study*. US Government Printing Office, Washington, DC: Foreign Area Studies, the American University.

Oberlander, Theodore
1965 *The Zagros Streams: a new interpretation of transverse drainage in an orogenic zone*. Syracuse Geographical Series, No. 1. Syracuse University Press, Syracuse.

Panahipour, Mitra
2019 Land use and environment in a zone of uncertainty: a case of the Sasanian expansion in Eastern Iraq – Western Iran. *Iran: Journal of the British Institute of Persian Studies* 59(1):90–108.

Potts, Daniel T.
2014 *Nomadism in Iran*. Oxford University Press, Oxford.

Salzman, Philip C.
1971 National integration of the tribes in modern Iran. *The Middle East Journal* 25(3):325–336.

Stein, Mark Aurel
1940 *Old Routes of Western Iran*. Greenwood, New York.

Tapper, Richard
1997 *Frontier Nomads of Iran: A Political and Social History of the Shahsevan*. Cambridge University Press, New York.

Varahram, Farhad
1988 *Taraz*. An Iranian film about seasonal migration from Khuzistan to Bakhtiari. https://letterboxd.com/film/taraz-1988/

Watson, Patty Jo
1979 *Archaeological Ethnography in Western Iran*. Viking Fund Publications in Anthropology 57. University of Arizona Press, Tucson, AZ.

Wenke, Robert
1976 Imperial investments and agricultural developments in Parthian and Sasanian Khuzestan: 150 B. C. to A. D. 640. *Mesopotamia* 10:13–221.

Wilkinson, T., Remy Boucharlat, Maurits W. Ertsen, Gavin Gillmore, Derek Kennet, Peter Magee, Khodadad Rezakhani and Tijw DeSchacht
2012 From human niche construction to imperial power: long-term trends in ancient Iranian water systems. *Water History* 4:155–176.

Wilson, A. T.
1911 Military report on S. W. Persia: Luristan.

1912 *Luristan*. Simla.

1941 *SW Persia: A Political Officer's Diary 1907–1914*. Oxford University Press, London.

Worldometers.info/demographics/iran-demographics/#urb. Accessed 2020.

Worldpopulationreview.com/countries/iran-population. Accessed 2020.

Zeder, Melinda A. and Brian Hesse
2000 The initial domestication of goats (*Capra hircus*) in the Zagros Mountains 10,000 years ago. *Science* 287:2254–2257.